Foundations of Secure Computation

ACADEMIC PRESS RAPID MANUSCRIPT REPRODUCTION

Foundations of Secure Computation

Edited by

Richard A. DeMillo
Georgia Institute of Technology
Atlanta, Georgia

David P. Dobkin
University of Arizona
Tucson, Arizona

Anita K. Jones
Carnegie-Mellon University
Pittsburgh, Pennsylvania

Richard J. Lipton
Yale University
New Haven, Connecticut

ACADEMIC PRESS   NEW YORK   SAN FRANCISCO   LONDON   1978

A Subsidiary of Harcourt Brace Jovanovich, Publishers

ACADEMIC PRESS, INC.
111 Fifth Avenue, New York, New York 10003

United Kingdom Edition published by
ACADEMIC PRESS, INC. (LONDON) LTD.
24/28 Oval Road, London NW1 7DX

Library of Congress Cataloging in Publication Data
Main entry under title:

Foundations of secure computation.

Papers presented at a 3 day workshop held at
Georgia Institute of Technology, Atlanta, Oct.
1977.
Includes bibliographical references.
1. Computers—Access control—Congresses.
I. DeMillo, Richard A. II. Georgia. Institute
of Technology, Atlanta.
QA76.9.A25F66   001.6'4   78-15034
ISBN 0-12-210350-5

PRINTED IN THE UNITED STATES OF AMERICA

Contents

List of Participants

Timothy A. Budd, Department of Computer Science, Yale University, New Haven, Connecticut 06520

James E. Burns, School of Information & Computer Science, Georgia Institute of Technology, Atlanta, Georgia 30332

Ellis Cohen, Computing Lab, University of Newcastle upon Tyne, Newcastle upon Tyne, England NEI 7RU

George I. Davida, Department of Electrical Engineering & Computer Science, University of Wisconsin-Milwaukee, Milwaukee, Wisconsin 53201

Richard A. DeMillo, School of Information & Computer Science, Georgia Institute of Technology, Atlanta, Georgia 30332

Dorothy Denning, Computer Sciences Department, Purdue University, Lafayette, Indiana 47906

David P. Dobkin, Department of Computer Science, University of Arizona, Tucson, Arizona 85721

Robert S. Fabry, Electrical Engineering & Computer Science Department, University of California-Berkeley, Berkeley, California 94705

Frederick C. Furtek, Mitre Corporation, Bedford, Massachusets 01730

R. Stockton Gaines, The Rand Corporation, 1700 Main Street, Santa Monica, California 90406

Robert Grafton, ONR-New York, 715 Broadway, New York, New York 10003

Patricia P. Griffiths, IBM Research, San Jose, California 95193

Leonard Haines, Office of Naval Research, Arlington, Virginia 22217

Michael A. Harrison, Computer Science Division, University of California-Berkeley, Berkeley, California 94720

Anita K. Jones, Department of Computer Science, Carnegie-Mellon University, Pittsburgh, Pennsylvania 15213

John B. Kam, Department of Computer Science, Columbia University, New York, New York 10027

Charles S. Kline, Department of Computer Science, University of California-Los Angeles, Los Angeles, California 90024

Richard J. Lipton, Department of Computer Science, Yale University, New Haven, Connecticut 06520

Nancy A. Lynch, School of Information & Computer Science, Georgia Institute of Technology, Atlanta, Georgia 30332

Larry McNeil, Management Science America, Inc., 3445 Peachtree Road, N.E., Atlanta, Georgia 30326

Jonathan K. Millen, Mitre Corporation, Bedford, Massachusetts 01730

Naftaly Minsky, Rutgers State University, New Brunswick, New Jersey 08903

Michael O. Rabin, Department of Mathematics, The Hebrew University, Jerusalem, Israel

Steven P. Reiss, Department of Applied Mathematics, Brown University, Providence, Rhode Island 02912

Ronald Rivest, Laboratory for Computer Science, Massachusetts Institute of Technology, Cambridge, Massachusetts 02139

Walter L. Ruzzo, 1371 Shattuck Avenue, University of California-Berkeley, Berkeley, California 94709

Norman Z. Shapiro, The Rand Corporation, 1700 Main Street, Santa Monica, California 90406

Lawrence Snyder, Department of Computer Science, Yale University, New Haven, Connecticut 06520

Preface

The present book started as a four-way debate concerning the interaction of theory and design in computer security. To fix the discussion, let us note that many computational processes proceed on the assumption that a naïve or a malicious user may attempt to disrupt the process or to make undesirable inferences from observing aspects of the computation. Security is concerned with avoiding this sort of penetration. On one hand, we saw that, over several generations of systems, designers had addressed security issues with varying degrees of success and in the process a considerable body of folklore and genuine technology developed. On the other hand, we knew of theoretical work with models simple enough to permit rigorous analysis, and we wondered about the real-world implications of these theoretical results.

Fortunately, we found support among our colleagues. The papers collected herein all lie near the "crack" between theory and practice; they all address issues at the foundations of security.

The contributing authors met in October 1977 in Atlanta, Georgia, for a three-day workshop. During this time, most of the technical details of the contributions were reviewed and discussed in informal presentations. We also met for an extensive round-table discussion concerning the history, current state, and prospects of research in secure computation. Many of these discussions were taped and edited. They appear sprinkled throughout the volume.

The atmosphere of our meeting in Atlanta was charged by an external (and unexpected) sequence of events. In the summer of 1977 the national news media began to release a series of stories concerning aspects of security research—these developments concerned results in which the interaction between theory and practice figured prominently. Even at this writing, there are news reports concerning security research. Clearly, the ideas discussed in these pages will have public impact. In a fashion, this is a resolution of our debate: theory and practice do interact visibly.

A few words about the level of the 19 papers contained in the sequel may help the reader. We anticipated that a considerable body of new technical results would issue from our meeting. We were pleasantly surprised to find ample survey material scattered among the research papers. Therefore, in addition to being a timely collection of research contributions, we offer the current collection as a book suitable for collateral readings in a seminar or an advanced course in computer security.

This project was given generous support from a number of sources. The Office of Naval Research and the U.S. Army Office each provided grants to support travel to Atlanta and the assemblage of these papers.* Gordon Goldstein, Marvin Dennicoff, Robert Grafton, and Lenny Haynes of the Office of Naval Research, and Paul Boggs and Jimmy Suttle of the U.S. Army Research Office were particularly valuable in bringing about the meeting. Support was also provided by the Computer Science Departments of Carnegie-Mellon University and Yale University. In addition, the School of Information and Computer Science at the Georgia Institute of Technology cordially extended its considerable resources to us in holding the meeting and in providing the administrative support needed to assemble the papers into their final form.

Academic Press gave us valuable help in putting the volume together. Finally, Brandy Bryant deserves special thanks. She not only typed and retyped all of these papers, but she ran herd on the project. She made sure that we did not miss our deadlines by more than a month or two, and she insisted that we do things right.

*ONR grant no. N00014-76-G-0030, ARO grant no. DAAG29-77-M-0086.

THE FOUNDATIONS OF SECURE COMPUTATION*

Richard A. DeMillo

School of Information and Computer Science
Georgia Institute of Technology
Atlanta, Georgia

David Dobkin

Department of Computer Science
Yale University
New Haven, Connecticut

"How do you insure privacy?"

"By coding," I said. "A two-word signature is required to gain entry to a section of the memory bank. Each word is made up of fourteen bits, making a total of twenty-eight bits."

"Then the odds are about one hundred million to one against a chance guess" ... "What if I entered someone else's code by mistake?" ...

"Nothing would happen. A countersign is necessary which requires another fourteen bits ..."

Duckworth shook his head.

"I still don't like it," he said.

I was annoyed by his obstinancy and responded by behaving childishly.

"Here," I said. "I'll let you enter any two fourteen bit words..."

Duckworth seems startled at my suggestion, but he complied ... The Confirm register lit up.

"What does that mean?" asked Duckworth.

I bit my lip.**

---

* *The preparation of this paper was supported in part by the Office of Naval Research under Grant N00014-75-C-0450 and the National Science Foundation under Grant MCS 76-11460.*
** *L. Eisenberg, The Best Laid Schemes, MacMillan, 1971.*

I. INTRODUCTION

Professor Duckworth's canny guess retrieved information from
a fictitious Federal Investigation Bureau. In this case, fiction
is paler than life and therein lies a frightening fact. The
computer is often used (simultaneously) as an excuse for an
instrument of insensitive and destructive policy. Evidence is
the maintenance of information in machine-readable form with
only slight technical guarantees of security.

Computer security has been an important issue since the first
computer was developed. However, with the advent of faster and
more accessible machines used by many users and large quantities
of shared data, this issue has achieved far greater importance.
It is no longer sufficient to rely on a system of password
control through which a user is protected by having a 7-letter
code known only to himself, since while this may, in the best
case, prevent other users from directly accessing the users area,
it does little to prevent indirect access. The potential dangers
from such indirect access increase manyfold. In this survey,
we shall discuss protection in two forms. The first involves the
problems of unauthorized users gaining access to restricted data.
In this case, it is necessary to discuss access control mechanisms
that can be brought to bear in order to protect each users
security. A second and far more subtle method of compromising a
system is through what is called "statistical inferencing". Here,
the user obtains information that is available to him legally and
uses this information to infer information to which he has no
access privileges. As more secure access-control mechanisms are
proposed to guard from illegal access to protected data, it is
this problem which looms as the major important problem of data
security. And, this problem can never be totally solved since we
must grant to authorized users access to data of this type. As
an illustration of this problem, consider a problem faced by the
census bureau (or any other creator of administrative databases).
In such a database, sensitive information is collected about a
group of individuals while guaranteeing each individual that data
collected about him will not be made available to users at large.
However, in order to do research on large segments of the population, it is necessary for aggregated forms of this data to be
made available to certain users. Suppose that a sociologist
wishes to study correlations among a population with respect to
various characteristics. Then, it might be necessary to give
this sociologist access to the data. However, in order to
guarantee each individual's privacy, we will wish to do this in
a statistical manner. That is, we will refuse to answer questions
about an individual or small set of individuals, but will make
available information about larger segments of society in a manner
that does not give information about any individual. And the
problem arises as to how to insure that no malicious user can use

this information in order to determine the characteristics of a
single individual. A common method that has been proposed is to
refuse access to information about any set of individuals which
consists of too few people and in this manner restrict access to
individual data. When data is given about a set of individuals,
it will then be given in an aggregated form consisting of mean
or median characteristics or counts of the number of people
having a certain characteristic. However, as shown below, such a
limitation is often not sufficient to guarantee individual
privacy. Furthermore, refusing to answer a question often gives
as much information as an aggregated answer since one might be
able to infer information from the reason for a non-answer.
Another area where this problem is of great significance is in
the problem of medical record-keeping. Here, we may wish to
track a set of people having a certain ailment in their early
life (or people who have been exposed to certain phenomena) in
order to determine long range effects of medications or exposures.
In so doing, we want to make the data as helpful as possible to
medical researchers while guaranteeing individual privacy.
Because of the nature of such data, it is of great value to
malicious users.

In this survey, we shall study the recent developments in
these two areas, improved access-control mechanisms and guaranteeing statistical confidentiality. We begin with a study of
the former problem in the next section. The problem of statistical security, which seems to be a major problem in the area, will
be studied in detail in the third section. The goal of the
survey shall be to highlight issues and recent developments in
those areas. Because of our limited space, we cannot go into
any issues in any amount of detail. The interested reader is
referred to Hoffman's book [13] for an elementary survey of these
issues and remaining papers a [3] for details of the state of
the art on such problems. It will be clear in what follows that
the interplay of theoretical and practical research has led us to
question the *limitations* which we place in the notion of security
as well as to create "secure" systems.

II.   ACCESS CONTROL MECHANISMS

In operating systems, the most common forms of protection
access-control are the access control mechanisms first introduced
by Graham and Denning [11]. Access control mechanisms are capable of enforcing rules about who can perform what operation or
who can access an object containing certain information. For
example, users may be able to access objects via READ, WRITE,
SORT, DELETEFILE, or APPEND commands with different users allowed
restricted access to individual files. Access control may be
represented by a subject-object matrix through which a subject

i's privileges for object j are represented as element ij in the
matrix. Given such a system, one will wish to determine if it
defines a secure system: can a subject obtain access to
restricted objects by combining a set of privileges? In general,
the problem of determining security is undecidable by a result
of Harrison, Ruzzo, and Ullman [12]. While this result is of
theoretical interest, it does not address the problem in a
practical manner, since for particular access control mechanisms,
it may be possible for specialized algorithms to solve the
security problem. Thus, it may still be possible for the designer of a given system to determine the security of his system by
an efficient algorithm, even though no general procedure exists
for testing the security of arbitrary access control matrices.

   A basic question is whether it is possible to design a
protection mechanism of sufficient richness so as to be capable
of admitting a complex variety of sharing relationships, while
being of a sufficiently simple form to have an efficient algorithm for checking its integrity. One important step toward
answering this question has been made by Jones, Lipton and
Synder [15, 16, 26]. Under a restricted model called the Take-
Grant System, there is a linear time algorithm for testing
subject security [15,16] and hence the system can be regarded as
having a high degree of integrity. Furthermore, the rich
instances of this system demonstrated by Snyder [26] suggest that
this system will also be satisfactory in an environment where
complex sharing is desired.

   A Take-Grant model can be represented by a finite, directed,
edge-labelled state graph and a set of rewriting rules to allow
for state transitions. Vertices are labelled as either subjects
(represented as s_i), objects (represented as o_i) or unknown
(represented as u_i). A vertex u_i may be either a subject or an
object. Edges are labelled with rights consisting of either t
(for take), g (for grant) or t,g. We have four rewriting rules.
Rules allow for transitions by allowing subgraph a to be replaced
by subgraph b if a==>b is one of our rewriting rules. The rules
are then given as a take rule, a grant rule, a create rule and a
remove rule which serve to handle sharing and file handling in
the user environment.

Graphically, these rules are:

(1) Take: $s_1 \xrightarrow{t} u_2 \xrightarrow{a} u_3 \;==>\; s_1 \xrightarrow{t} u_2 \xrightarrow{a} u_3$ with $s_1 \xrightarrow{a} u_3$

allowing subject 1 to take the privilege of u_2 to u_3 since s_1 has take rights.

(2) Grant: $s_1 \xrightarrow{g} u_2 u_3 \;==>\; s_1 \xrightarrow{g} u_2 \xrightarrow{a} u_3$

allowing subject 1 to grant his privileges to u_3 to u_2 since s_1 has grant rights.

(3) Create: $s_1 \;==>\; s_1 \xrightarrow{a} u_2$

allowing s_1 to grant u_2 a subset a of his rights.

(4) Remove: $s_1 \xrightarrow{b} s_2 \;==>\; s_1 \xrightarrow{b-a} s_2$

allowing subject 1 to remove rights of a from u_2.

We then phrase the security question as a test of whether or not x can "a" y. This situation corresponds to being given an initial configuration and asking whether we apply a set of rewriting rules to obtain a graph containing an edge from x to y containing the label a. In contrast to the results of [12], a test is available under which security in this model can be determined in linear time [15,16]. Furthermore, Snyder [26] demonstrates implementations of this method in which sufficiently rich user sharing is available.

III. SECURITY OF STATISTICAL DATA BASES

While the methods mentioned above are important for securing operating systems, they are of limited value in considering the data base security problem. Here, we are dealing with an environment where most users have only READ access to the information in the data base. The problem is to determine whether users can manipulate this access to compromise the data base. It is no longer the case that we may determine whether a user may obtain rights which should not be available to him, since every user has the same rights and no rights can be taken or granted beyond these basic rights. The issues run deeper. Users are granted access to information regarding the population served by a database and we wish to guarantee that no user may use this information to *infer* data about protected individuals (or groups) served by the data base. We are, thus, dealing with nebulous inference mechanisms

rather than simple security violations. We must discern whether
a user can infer information about guarded individuals from the
information we have made available to him. With the additional
considerations of inferences, the problem becomes more complex.
We are still faced with the tradeoff between richness and
integrity: we wish to produce a system rich enough to supply
useful information to those using the database while assuring
the system's integrity in protecting those represented in the
database.

A simple example of the subtlty of such a problem was first
given by Hoffman and Miller [14] who showed that with sufficient
queries a dossier could be complied on an individual represented
in a database. Typically, one wishes to be able to ask questions
of a database of the form:

"How many people in the database satisfy properties
$P_1, P_2, \ldots, P_k$?"

"What is the mean (or median) value (of a parameter) of
people satisfying properties $P_1, P_2, \ldots, P_k$?"

Such a parameter might be "salary" or "number of times hospital-
ized with a certain disease." Typical properties might be "male",
"over 50", or "having an income greater than $10,000." Such
questions or *queries* are necessary in a variety of applications.
For example, suppose that one wishes to dtermine the incidence of
cancer among workers in plants using certain types of chemicals
[25], to track a population having a certain ailment in child-
hood to determine their adjustment to society [18], or to draw
correlations between salary and standard of living.

As an example of the ease with which such a database can be
compromised*, we consider the following example from [7] consisting of the characteristics of a number of persons who have
contributed to a political campaign.

---

* *We will say that a data base has been compromised (or cracked)
if a user may infer from the response to valid queries a
characteristic of a person served by the data base.*

Person	Business Area	Party	Favoritism Shown by Administration	Geographic Area
P1	Steel	D	High	Northeast
P2	Steel	R	Medium	West
P3	Steel	I	Low	South
P4	Sugar	D	Medium	Northeast
P5	Sugar	R	Low	Northeast
P6	Sugar	I	High	West
P7	Oil	D	Low	South
P8	Oil	R	High	South
P9	Oil	I	Medium	West

Suppose that in order to protect individual integrity, we are
only willing to make available to a user the average contribution
of people sharing a common attribute, e.g., contributions from
the steel industry consisting of the average of the contributions
of the first three people. In this manner, we might hope to
secure the database. Observe, however, that we may generate a
system of twelve equations in the variables $C_1,...,C_9$ with C_i
corresponding to the contribution of P_i (e.g., $C_1 + C_2 + C_3$ corresponds to the contribution from people in the steel industry) and
may then solve these equations to determine the individual values
of C_1, C_2, ... C_9. While this example provides only a simple view
of the problem in securing a database, it forebodes the difficulties that actually occur in large administrative databases.
This issue has been previously investigated by [2,9,10] from a
statistical point of view and [21,22] has considered the implications of such schemes from a medical point of view.

We are, therefore, led to consider the techniques that might
be applied to *enhance* the integrity of the database. The enhancements are basically of two types both dealing with restricting
data flow. We might either restrict the number and types of
queries which a user might be allowed or we might restrict the
form of the answer given to a query. In both of these instances,
we must take care to insure that the restrictions we place on
the model do not sacrifice its richness. Previous studies of this
problem have appeared in [1,6,4,7,8,19,20,23,24]. In [5], this
problem is shown to be basic to the study of combinatorial
inference and is related to a number of well-known combinatorial
problems including group testing and balance problems.

We turn now to exposition of the methods which have been
proposed to handle this problem. For each, we also describe the
known results concerning its efficiency.

Limiting Overlap Between Mean Queries

In this case, queries are allowed about the mean value of a characteristic corresponding to a group of people with the restriction that no two queries may overlap in more than r positions. To enhance system security, the further restriction that all queries involve at least p people may also be added. If we define $S(p,r)$ as the minimum number of queries needed to compromise the database, then

$$S(p,r) \leq \frac{2p}{r}$$

which is a small number of queries in a database designed to provide useful information to its nonmalicious users.

Only Allowing Median Queries and Not Allowing Mean Queries

As we have seen, mean queries are too powerful. What if they are not allowed and the user is given the median value of a characteristic corresponding to a group of p people? This seems promising since while the median does actually give the value corresponding to one person, it supplies no information about other members of the database other than their relationship (or about a given value). Indeed, this helps sine - in this model - it is not possible to determine certain values occurring at the tails of those considered in the sample (other than determining a lower bound on those values at the top end and an upper bound on those values at the bottom end). However, for values situated near the median of the original sample, compromise is easily arranged. In $O(\log^2 p)$ queries concerning the median value associated with a set of p people, a database can be cracked and someone's value may be determined exactly. Information regarding relative values associated with different people can generally be obtained more quickly and this is often sufficient to compromise the database.

Lying

If exact information is so dangerous, answers may be distorted slightly while maintaining the integrity of answers given. This distortion may be achieved by adding "noise" to all answers in a manner that does not vastly change their implications. However, if the noise is not of sufficient size to cause significant changes in answers given, then it is also not statistically sufficient in securing the database. Variant proposals involve giving only a "feel for the data". This might be achieved by returning the value corresponding to one individual involved in the query without either identifying the individual or his ranking (e.g., max, min, median ...) in the set encompassed by the query. In the most simple form of this type of lying, we allow only queries involving n individuals, restrict to 1 overlap among queries and return results at random. By appealing to results from matching theory, we can show that n^2-1 queries can be successfully answered without compromising the database. However, using a simple strategy based on finite geometric, n^2 well chosen queries generally suffice to compromise. While this number is possibly large enough to discourage all but the most malicious of users, it is obtained for a model more restrictive than is realistic; "real" systems will surely be more vulnerable.

Distorting the Data

In implementing this procedure, we must take care to guarantee that the data are distorted in such a manner as to make answers obtained from the database meaningful. One such method consists of having the census taker ask two questions at random with certain fixed probabilities in such a manner that the census taker does not know which question the person answering the question is answering. The questions are chosen so that their answers will have similar statistics. For example, if one wishes to determine the number of abortions that members of a population have had, he might have the subjects choose a card at random from a deck such that p% of the questions in the deck ask about abortions (e.g., number of births, or visits to a certain place. ...). In this manner, the system is supposed to be secure (assuming p$\neq$ 50) since even if cracked, we do not know which question the compromised individual answered. However, such claims of security may be questioned since in our world models, we often have sufficient information (or can obtain such information) to discern between which of the two questions an individual answered.

Although the procedures for compromising databases when any of the security precautions presented above are highly non-trivial, they must be taken quite seriously because often their benefits outweigh even large costs of their implementation. In 1972, a cadidate for Vice President of the United States was forced to resign from the campaign after disclosures that he had had electric shock treatment for nervous disorders. It would be worth significant probing for an opposition party to obtain such information about a leading candidate. The lengths to which politicians and their operatives are willing to go in securing information was graphically illustrated in the Watergate disclo-sures. Certainly, all of their administration's efforts were sufficiently greater and more dangerous than the efforts they would have needed through a scheme of the type mentioned here to compromise security in any of the measures we've given. Hence,

it is extremely important that database designers of the future
be aware of the results reported here and use them as a guideline
in designing their access control and limiting measures.

One question that arises in any consideration of data
security is the auditing question. Often if we cannot totally
secure a system, we at least wish to determine when and how it
was compromised. To date, most security violations have been
discovered by accident [17]. In one case, a successful criminal
told a friend who turned him in. Other computer criminals have
been caught when others noticed changes in their lifestyles
brought about by their increased wealth. However, it is very
dangerous to rely on flaws of human character to guarantee that
those who violate computer security will be apprehended. In a
consideration of auditing procedures for detecting security
violations under the models proposed above, we observe that in
the case of means, medians and arbitrary selections, procedures
do exist for checking on security violations. However, all of
these procedures are far more complex than the actual running of
the database system and would typically require that the machine
lie dormant for about two-thirds of every day while checking the
potential results of answers given during the rest of the day.
And, no such procedure has been proposed that can take into
account the possibilities of collusion among database interroga-
tors or of information obtained from other sources.

IV. CONCLUSIONS

Methods do now exist to greatly enhance the security of
operating systems and databases. While such methods may never be
unbreakable, significant progress has been made towards such a
goal. The "foundations" of security research is concerned with
the exact locations of these dividing lines. It is now the case
that theory exists sufficient to design a system for which
illegal access is so difficult or a database for which inferences
from legal data is so complex, that security violations will be
beyond the realm of all but the most dedicated and sophisticated
penetrators. And, the design of systems sufficiently secure with
respect to such penetrators will perhaps never be achieved. One
can only hope that the cost of compromise will increase to exceed
the possible benefits that could be derived from such a compromise.
In this paper, we have explored recent theoretical developments
on these problems which greatly increase the cost of compromise.

The major open problems remaining include implementing a security system based on the Take-Grant model and improving upon the methods for enhancing security of data in an administrative database. In the latter case, many problems of significant theoretical interest remain. A major open problem requires the construction of a method of collecting and disseminating information to authorized users without compromising the security of any individual represented by the database. The remaining papers in this volume [3] contain close relations of these problems, and address issues whose eventual resolution will help guide our policies for the use of computers in sensitive applications.

REFERENCES

[1] Budd, T., "Databases That Are Hard To Compromise", unpublished manuscript.

[2] Dalenius, T., "Privacy Transformations for Statistical Information Systems", *Journal of Statistical·Planning and Inference*, 1, (1977), pp. 73-86.

[3] DeMillo, R. A., Dobkin, D., Jones, A. K., and Lipton, R. J., this volume.

[4] DeMillo, R. A., Dobkin, D., and Lipton, R. J., "Even Data Bases That Lie Can Be Compromised", *IEEE Transactions on Software Engineering*.

[5] DeMillo, R. A., Dobkin, D., and Lipton, R. J., "Combinatorial Inference", this volume.

[6] Denning, D. E., "A Review of Research on Statistical Data Base Security", this volume.

[7] Dobkin, D., Jones, A. K., and Lipton, R. J., "Secure Data Bases: Protection Against User Inference", Research Report No. 65, Dept. of Comp. Sc., Yale Univ., April 1976, also *ACM Transactions on Data Base Systems* (to appear)

[8] Dobkin, D., Lipton, R. J., and Reiss, S. P., "Aspects of the Data Base Security Problem", pp. 262-274, *Proceedings of a Conference on Theoretical Computer Science*, Waterloo, Canada, 1977.

[9] Fellegi, I. P., "On the Question of Statistical Confidentiality," *Journal of American Stat. Assoc.*, 67, 337, March 1972, pp. 7-18.

[10] Fellegi, I. P., and Phillips, J. L., "Statistical Confidentiality: Some Theory and Applications to Data Dissemination", *Annals Econ. Soc'l Measurement*, 3, 2, (April 1972), pp. 399-409.

[11] Graham, G. S., and Denning, P. J., "Protection - Principles and Practice", *Proceedings 1972 SJCC*, 40, pp. 417-429, AFIPS Press, 1972.

[12] Harrison, M. A., Ruzzo, W. L., and Ullman, J. D., "Protection in Operating Systems", *CACM*, 19:8, (1976).

[13]   Hoffman, L., *Modern Methods for Computer Security and Privacy*, Prentice-Hall, Englewood Cliffs, New Jersey, 1977.

[14]   Hoffman, L. J., and Miller, W. F., "Getting a Personal Dossier From a Statistical Data Bank", *Datamation*, 16, 5, (May 1970), pp. 74-75.

[15]   Jones, A. K., Lipton, R. J., and Snyder, L., "A Linear Time Algorithm for Deciding Security", *Proceedings of the 17th FOCS*, Houston, Texas, October 1976.

[16]   Lipton, R. J., and Snyder, L., "A Linear Time Algorithm for Deciding Subject Security", *JACM*, 24:3, 1977.

[17]   Parker, D., *Crime By Computers*, Scribbners, New York, 1976.

[18]   Roughman, K., private communication, November 1977.

[19]   Reiss, S. P., "A Combinatorial Model of Data Base Security", Technical Report, Yale University, Dept. of Comp. Sci., 1976, also *JACM*, (to appear)

[20]   Reiss, S. P., "Medians and Data Base Security", this volume.

[21]   Schlorer, J., "Identification and Retrieval of Personal Records from a Statistical Data Bank", *Methods of Information in Medicine*, 14, 1, January 1975, pp. 7-13.

[22]   Schlorer, J., "Confidentiality of Statistical Records: A Threat Monitoring Scheme for On-Line Dialogue", *Methods of Information in Medicine*, 14, 1, (January 1976), pp. 36-42.

[23]   Schwartz, M. D., Denning, D. E., and Denning, P. J., "Securing Data Bases Under Linear Queries", *Proc. AFIPS 1977*, pp. 395-398.

[24]   Schwartz, M. D., Denning, D. E., and Denning, P. J., Compromising a Statistical Data Base", Dept. of Comp. Sci., Purdue Univ., 1977.

[25]   Science Magazine, October 28, 1977, pp. 382.

[26]   Snyder, L., "On the Synthesis and Analysis of Protection Systems", *Proc. 6th ACM Symposium on Operating Systems Principles*, November 1977, pp. 141-150.

SECTION I. DATA BASE SECURITY

A theme of the introductory article in this volume is that databases of personal information will continue to be constructed. In addition, this information will be communicated among several processing sites, and users at these sites will expect to be able to extract usable information. A significant task of researchers in database security is to point out "danger spots", i.e., sources of possible insecurity in the system before they are actually constructed.

The four papers in Section I address tradeoffs between usability and security. Dorothy Denning's survey of statistical database security reminds us how far we have come in realizing the limits of the notion of database security. The extant methods of compromising large statistical almost always involve transparent uses of information delivered in response to queries. The article by Richard DeMillo, David Dobkin and Richard Lipton discusses the more subtle kinds of combinatorial *inferences* which can be formed out of query responses. Compromise in the statistical sense is not the only security problem in database design. The pragmatic issues stemming from the authorization of access to database and data communication systems are outlined in the contribution by Don Chamberlin, Jim Gray, Patricia Griffiths, Moscheh Mresse, Irv Traiger, and Bradford Wade. The final paper of this section by Stephen Reiss returns to statistical compromise with a detailed technical study of the insecurity inherent in databases which allow a certain statistical query strategy.

A REVIEW OF RESEARCH ON
STATISTICAL DATA BASE SECURITY*

Dorothy E. Denning

Purdue University

I. INTRODUCTION

The objective of a statistical data base is providing statistical summaries about a population without releasing the specifics about any individual. But this objective often cannot be met. It is frequently possible to deduce private information by correlating summaries. If so, the data base is compromised.

This paper surveys recent research in the security of statistical data bases. We begin with a general model of a data base.

II. DATA BASE MODEL

Consider a statistical data base containing sensitive information about n individuals. Each individual is assigned to one or more *categories*, plus has numerical values in one or more *classes*. At least one individual belongs to each category, and no category comprises all individuals. The data base is static; i.e., insertions, updates, and deletions do not occur over the time period of interest. Summary statistics are requested from the data base with *queries*. Queries use classes as domains but apply only to particular individuals or individuals in specified categories.

* *Work reported herein was supported in part by NSF Grant MCS75-21100.*

Table 1 shows an automobile insurance data base of size n = 12. Each individual belongs to exactly one category in each of these sets:

    Sex = {M, F}
    Marital Status MS = {S, M, W}
    Age Group AG = {(16-25), (26-60), (61-100)}

TABLE I.   *Data Base for Automobile Insurance Company*

Keys		Categories			Classes		
Numeric	Symbolic	Sex	Marital Stat.	Age Group	Accidents	Violations	Premium
1	Adams	M	M	26-60	0	0	100
2	Boggs	M	S	26-60	0	1	112
3	Cook	F	M	16-25	1	0	135
4	Dodd	F	M	26-60	0	0	95
5	Hays	M	M	16-25	0	0	107
6	Jones	F	W	61-100	0	0	105
7	Lynn	M	M	26-60	0	2	130
8	Moore	M	M	26-60	2	0	150
9	Rose	F	M	26-60	0	0	95
10	Smith	M	S	16-25	2	1	185
11	Trip	F	S	16-25	0	1	125
12	Wood	M	M	26-60	0	0	100

Each individual has values for three classes: Accidents, Violations, and Premium. The possible values for each class may also be viewed as categories:

    Accidents A = {0, 1, 2}
    Violations V = {0, 1, 2}
    Premium P = {95, 100, ..., 185}

All examples will refer to this data base.

Compromise occurs whenever it is possible to deduce from the responses of one or more queries information not previously known about an individual. The compromise is *positive* if it reveals that the individual belongs to some category or has a particular

value in some class. The compromise is *negative* if it reveals
only that the individual does not belong to some category or have
a particular value in some class. For example, learning that
Lynn had 2 traffic violations is a positive compromise; learning
that he had at least 1 violation (i.e., "he did not have no
violations") is a negative compromise. *Partial compromise* occurs
when information about a subset of individuals in the data base
is deduced; *complete compromise* occurs when everything in the
data base is deduced. A data base is *strongly secure* if both
positive and negative compromise is impossible.

Researchers have studied two basic forms of queries:
characteristic-specified and key-specified. *Characteristic-
specified* queries request statistics about all individuals in the
data base who satisfy a given logical formula over the categories.
The set of individuals satisfying a characteristic (formula) C,
denoted X_C, is called the *query set*. The *query set size* is

denoted $|X_C|$. An example of a characteristic is

C = (Sex = M *and* AG = (26-60)). The query set for this
characteristic is X_C = {Adams, Boggs, Lynn, Moore, Wood}. An

example of a characteristic specified query is "How many
individuals satisfy C?"; that is, "How many are male and in the
age group (26-60)?" Another is, "What is the mean number of
traffic violations among males in the age group (26-60)?"

Key-specified queries request statistics for a set of m
individuals identified by a list of keys Z = $(z_1,...,z_m)$. The

keys may be the names of the individuals or, more likely, a set
of categories uniquely identifying the individuals. Examples of
key-specified queries are "How many traffic violations were in-
curred by Hays, Jones, and Moore?" and "What was the median
premium paid by Boggs, Moore, and Smith?"

We shall review separately the studies made of characteristic-
specified and key-specified queries.

III.   CHARACTERISTIC-SPECIFIED QUERIES

Research prior to 1976 concentrated on characteristic-specified
counting queries. Denoted *qcount*(C), a counting query returns
the number of individuals satisfying a characteristic C; that is
qcount(C) = $|X_C|$. For example, *qcount*(AG = (16-25) *or*

AG = (26-60)) = 11.

In one of the first published papers on the inference problem, Hoffman and Miller described a simple algorithm for compromising a data base responding to counting queries restricted to conjunctive characteristic formulae; only the logical operator *and* is allowed in a conjunctive formula [Hom 70]. Their algorithm is based on the principle of using queries which return small counts to isolate an individual. For example, consider these two queries and responses:

$$qcount(\text{Sex} = \text{F } and \text{ MS} = \text{S}) = 1$$
$$qcount(\text{Sex} = \text{F } and \text{ MS} = \text{S } and \text{ V} = 1) = 1$$

If it is known that Trip is female, single, and represented in the data base, then the second query reveals that she had 1 traffic violation. In general, if it is known that an individual belongs to categories $c_1, \ldots, c_k$ and if $qcount(c_1 \ and \ldots and \ c_k)$ = 1, then the query $qcount(c_1 \ and \ldots and \ c_k \ and \ c_{k+1})$ reveals whether or not the individual also belongs to category c_{k+1} (according to whether or not the response is 1 or 0).

Haq formalized these concepts [Haq 74,75]. He determined conditions (too complex to enumerate here) necessary and sufficient to achieve positive and negative compromise (which he called personal disclosure). His conditions take into account an intruder's supplementary knowledge about the individuals represented in the data base. Although his theorems provide a means to check if a data base is secure, it is not clear they can be applied in practice since the supplementary knowledge of the users is not likely to be known.

Schlorer investigated whether medical data bases could be secured under counting queries using general characteristic formulae [Sch 75]. He noted the danger of compromise when queries return small counts. Thus, he considered the security of a data base of size n whose queries do not respond unless the count is in the range [k, n-k], for some k > 0 (the upper bound n-k protects against finding the answer to $q(C)$ from n - q(*not* C)).

He showed that compromise may be possible even for large values of k. To illustrate his "tracker" technique, suppose k=4 for the automobile insurance company data base -- i.e., no responses are given to queries whose count falls outside the range [4, 8]. Suppose it is known that Trip is female and single. Consider these queries and responses:

$$qcount(\text{ Sex} = \text{F } and \text{ MS} \neq \text{S}) = 4$$
$$qcount((\text{Sex} = \text{F } and \text{ MS} \neq \text{S}) \ or \ (\text{Sex} = \text{F } and \text{ V} = 0)) = 4$$

Because the responses to both queries are the same, it can be concluded that no single female has no traffic violations; therefore, Trip must have had a violation. Palme suggested a similar technique for queries that compute means [Pal 74].

Chin studied data bases whose queries respond with a sum and a count of elements in the query set, provided $2 \leq |X_C| \leq n-2$.

Denoted $qsum(C; Y)$, a summing query returns the sum of the values in class Y for all individuals satisfying the characteristic C. For example, $qsum(\text{Sex} = M; \text{Violations}) = 4$. In general,

$$qcount(C) \quad = \quad \begin{cases} |X_C| \text{ if } k \leq |X_C| \leq n-k \\ \# \quad \text{otherwise} \end{cases}$$

$$qsum(C; Y) \quad = \quad \begin{cases} \Sigma Y_C \text{ if } k \leq |X_C| \leq n-k \\ \# \quad \text{otherwise} \end{cases}$$

where Y_C denotes the set of values in class Y for all individuals in X_C and "$\#$" signifies an unanswerable query. Chin's data bases also satisfied the property that no two individuals belong to the same categories (this assumption is violated by our sample data base -- e.g., Adams and Wood have identical characteristics).

Using "query graphs" to represent the state of a data base, Chin estiblished necessary and sufficient conditions for compromising. A query graph for a data base is an undirected graph whose vertices correspond to the individuals represented in the data base. If an individual i is identified by characteristic C_i and an individual j by characteristic C_j, there is an edge from vertex i to vertex j if and only if there is a characteristic C that isolates individuals i and j; that is $qsum(C; Y) = qsum(C_i; Y) + qsum(C_j; Y)$ for any value class Y. Chin proved that if the characteristic identifying some individual is known, then compromise is possible if and only if (a) the query graph has at least one odd cycle or (b) there exists a characteristic C such that $qcount(C)$ is odd and ≥ 3.

Schwartz, Denning, and Denning studied data bases which respond to queries for counts and sums for arbitrary k [SD2 77, Scw 77]. We found that even for large values of k, most data bases may be compromised by a "general tracker" technique related to Schlorer's tracker. A general tracker provides a means of obtaining the answers to queries with small (or large) counts. We found further that most data bases satisfy the conditions for compromise. Hence, methods much more powerful than simply restricting the range of allowable query responses are needed to prevent compromise.

Three other proposals for preventing compromise include modifying the answers to queries, providing answers based on random samples of the data base, and partitioning the data base. Several studies have been made of rounding schemes for modifying the answers to counting queries [Fep 74, Han 71, NaS 72, Pal 74, Ree 73, Sch 76]. One such approach is pseudo-random rounding. Truly random rounding is not secure since the correct answer to any query can always be determined by averaging a sufficient number of responses to the same query. With pseudo-random rounding, the same query always returns with the same response. A second approach is to always round the actual response down to the nearest multiple of some integer. Both rounding schemes can be reasonably effective against compromise. However, any kind of "stochastic error" added to responses is subject to removal by well known methods from communication theory.

The second approach to preventing compromise is apply queries only to a random subfile of the data base, but not the complete data base [Han 71]. Even if some element of the subfile is identified, it may not be possible to learn which individual in the data base was selected to be this element. For example, the Census Bureau in 1960 provided statistics based on a "1 in 1000" sample. This technique is effective only for very large data bases. It also breaks down if the use of multiple extracts is allowed.

The third approach to preventing compromise partitions the data base into groups. In the Yu and Chin scheme [YuC 77], queries must be for characteristics involving entire groups, making it impossible to isolate any particular individual. For example, the sample data base could be partitioned into 3 groups: G1 = "no accidents or violations", G2 = "violations but no accidents", and G3 = "accidents". The query "How many males had no accidents?" would be modified to "How many males *and females* had no accidents?" before a response would be given since the first characteristic is not satisfied by all members of groups G1 and G2. Yu and Chin show that the technique may be effective even if the data base is dynamically undergoing insertions, deletions, and updates.

Several studies have also been made of "threat-monitoring" techniques designed to detect the possible occurrences of compromise. Felligi showed that it is at least theoretically possible to determine whether the response to a query, then correlated with the responses to earlier queries, could result in compromise [Fel 72]. Unfortunately, the method is extremely cumbersome. Hoffman and Miller suggested that a log or audit trail of queries be kept and inspected for unusual bursts of activity or queries returning small counts [Hom 70]. Schlorer suggested that frequency counts of categories be used to determine whether or not a given query might lead to a compromise because of small counts [Sch 76]. Response is not made to any query involving categories $c_1,\ldots,c_k$ unless the product of the frequency counts $qcount(c_i)/n$ (for $i = 1,\ldots,k$) is above some threshold.

IV. KEY-SPECIFIED QUERIES

The security of key-specified queries was not investigated until 1976. In the first published paper addressing the problem, Dobkin, Jones, and Lipton considered summing queries over fixed-size subgroups of the data base. A key-specified summing query denoted $qsum(Z; Y)$, returns the sum of the values in class Y for the m individuals identified by the list of keys $Z = (z_1,\ldots,z_m)$.

For example, $qsum((Hays, Jones, Moore); Violations) = 0$. Since the query set size, m, is known, counting queries are of no interest. Dobkin et al. showed that, even if no two query sets can overlap by more than a given amount, compromise may be achievable in linear time (in m) without prior information, provided the data base is sufficiently large (roughly at least m^2 elements). Small data bases are secure. Davida et al. have also examined conditions under which compromise may be achieved when queries return sums and maximum values [Dav 76].

Dobkin, Jones, and Lipton also considered queries for the median value of fixed-size subgroups and conditions sufficient to compromise in this case. Subsequently, DeMillo, Dobkin, and Lipton showed that compromise may be possible even if the data base "lies" about the median value -- i.e., responds with some randomly chosen value from the set [DDL 76].

Schwartz, Denning, and Denning extended these results to weighted summing queries over fixed-size subgroups [SD1 77, Scw 77]. We were surprised to learn that if the weights were unknown, compromise is possible (in linear time) provided one value in the data base is initially known. But compromise is impossible without initial information -- even if overlap between queries is unrestricted. In contrast, as shown by Dobkin et al., compromise may be possible without prior information for ordinary summing queries (all weights = 1).

Kam and Ullman considered summing queries over subgroups of size 2^p for some p [KaU 76]. The reason for this unusualy choice of allowable query set sizes is their data base model, which

assumes that the data base comprises n = 2^t individuals, for some t. Each individual is identified by a key which is a bit string of length t. Exactly one individual corresponds to each possible bit string. Query sets are specified by fixing s of the t bits, so that the number of individuals in any query set is

2^{t-s}.

It is unclear whether this model is applicable in practice. For example, we could attempt to put our sample data base in this context. Each key would be a bit string $s_1 s_2 \ldots$ with s_1 = 1 if Sex = M, 0 if Sex = F, etc. The difficulty is that certain keys will not be represented in the data base (e.g., no individual is male, single, and in the age group (61-100)).

Chin commented on this severe limitation of this model. He proposed a similar model which allows for the possibility that certain keys are not represented in the data base [Chi 77]. In this case, the queries are characteristic-specified rather than key-specified since the query set size is determined by the number of individuals having the characteristic. Chin's results were discussed in the previous section.

The studies of key-specified queries are probably not of practical interest. Most, if not all, statistical data bases are queried with characteristics involving variable-size subgroups rather than fixed-size subgroups. However, the studies have theoretical interest in that they provide insight into the nature of compromise.

V.   CONCLUSIONS

Preventing compromise in statistical data bases is difficult; possibly impossible without severely restricting the free flow of information. The "obvious" techniques for reducing the threat of compromise -- e.g., limiting the range of allowable responses or restricting the amount of overlap between query sets -- are easily circumvented. The fruitful direction of research is in security measures that do not return "exact" answers from the original data base: rounding responses, modifying the data, extracting random samples of data, partitioning the data, and other threat monitoring schemes. Further research is needed in dynamic data bases; except for the work by Yu and Chin [YuC 77], little is known about safeguards for constantly changing data bases.

ACKNOWLEDGMENTS

It is especially a pleasure to thank Mayer Schwartz whose ideas and perceptions strongly influenced this paper. It is also a pleasure to thank Peter Denning for his suggestions on an earlier version of this paper.

REFERENCES

Chi77 Chin, F. Y., "Security in Statistical Data Bases for Queries with Small Counts", Dept. of Comp. Sci., University of Alberta, 1977.

Dav76 Davida, B. I. et al., "Data Base Security", TR-CS-76-14, Dept. of EE and Comp. Sci., University of Wisconsin, July 1976.

DDL76 DeMillo, R. A., Dobkin, D., and Lipton, R. J., "Even Data Bases That Lie Can Be Compromised", Research Report #67, Dept. of Comp. Sci., Yale University, May 1976.

DJL76 Dobkin, D., Jones, A. K., and Lipton, R. J., "Secure Data Bases: Protection Against User Inference", Research Report #65, Dept. of Comp. Sci., Yale Univ., April 1976.

Fel72 Fellegi, I. P., "On the Question of Statistical Confidentiality", *J. Amer. Stat. Assoc., 67*, 337 (Mar 1972), pp. 7-18.

FeP74 Fellegi, I. P. and Phillips, J. L., "Statistical Confidentiality: Some Theory and Applications To Data Dissemination", *Annals Econ. Soc'l Measurement, 3, 2*, (April 1974), pp. 399-409.

Han71 Hansen, M. H. "Insuring Confidentiality of Individual Records in Data Storage and Retrieval for Statistical Purposes", *Proc. AFIPS FJCC, 39*, (1971), pp. 579-585.

Haq74 Haq, M. I., "Security in a Statistical Data Base", *Proc. Amer. Soc. Info. Sci., 11*, (1974), pp. 33-39.

Haq75 Haq, M. I., "Insuring Individual's Privacy From Statistical Data Base Users", *Proc. AFIPS NCC, 44*, (1975), pp. 941-946.

HoM70 Hoffman, L. J. and Miller, W. F., "Getting a Personal Dossier From a Statistical Data Bank", *Datamation, 16, 5*, (May 1970), pp. 74-75.

KaU76 Kam, J. B. and Ullman, J. D., "A Model of Statistical Data Bases and Their Security", TR-207, Dept. of EECS, Princeton Univ., June 1976.

NaS72 Nargundkar, M. S. and Saveland, W., "Random-Rounding To Prevent Statistical Disclosure", *Proc. Amer. Stat. Ass., Soc. Stat. Sec.*, (1972), pp. 382-385.

Pal74 Palme, J., "Software Security", *Datamation, 20, 1* (Jan. 1974), pp. 51-55.

Ree74 Reed, I. S., "Information Theory and Privacy in Data Banks, *Proc. AFIPS, 42*, (1973), pp. 581-587.

Sch75 Schlorer, J., "Identification and Retrieval of Personal Records From a Statistical Data Bank", *Methods of Info. in Medicine, 14, 1*, (Jan 1975), pp. 7-13.

Sch76 Schlorer, J., "Confidentiality of Statistical Records: A Threat Monitoring Scheme For On-Line Dialogue", *Methods of Info. in Medicine, 15, 1*, (Jan 1976), pp. 36-42.

Scw77 Schwartz, M. D., "Inference From Statistical Data Bases", Ph.D. Thesis, Purdue University, August 1977.

SD177   Schwartz, M. D., Denning, D. E., and Denning, P. J.,
        "Securing Data Bases Under Linear Queries", *Proc. IFIPS 77*,
        (1977), pp. 395-398.
SD277   Denning, D. E., Denning, P. J., and Schwartz, M. D.,
        "The Tracker: A Threat to Statistical Data Base Security",
        Computer Science Dept., Purdue University, CSD-TR250, Oct.
        1977.
YuC77   Yu, C. T. and Chin, F. Y., "A Study on the Protection of
        Statistical Data Bases", Dept. of Computer Science, Univ. of
        Alberta, 1977.

DISCUSSION

Dobkin: When you say "weights", are those arbitrary weights -- or can you show for all weights that can't be done?

Denning: As long as they are not known. However, if you have one piece of information, you can solve for the weights, and once you have the weights, you can solve for everything else.

Harrison: The example with the weights is somewhat amusing. You can't do it if you don't know anything. You just add yourself to the database, that gives you the one point you need ... (laughter)

COMBINATORIAL INFERENCE*

Richard DeMillo

Georgia Institute of Technology
Atlanta, Georgia

David Dobkin
Richard Lipton

Yale University
New Haven, Connecticut

I. INTRODUCTION

We propose a new area of study in theoretical computer science: combinatorial inference. The basic problem is as follows.

> We have a finite set $X = x_1,\ldots,x_n$ and
> we wish to infer properties of elements
> of X on the basis of sets of "queries"
> regarding subsets of X.

There is an immediate and apparent distinction between combinatorial inferences and the more broadly construed kinds of *logical inferences* also studied in computer science. By restricting our attention to a sort of interactive dialog with a device which may deliver information concerning a finite set, we obtain problems which - *a fortiori* - concern *feasible inference*.

* *Supported in part by ONR Contract number N00014-75-C-0752,
and ARO Grant number DAAG29-76-G-0338.*

The forms of the allowable queries vary with the particular application being considered, but a great many problems in computer science, combinatorics, and optimization can be modelled in such a manner. In this paper we survey some applications of this general problem statement. We then illustrate some of the techniques available for dealing with combinatorial inference by solving some problems with particular relevance to current issues in theoretical computer science.

We begin by considering the following problems:

1. *Database Security Problem* [1,2,3]   A database is created to contain census information concerning some subset of the population of the United States.   The information is confidential and we wish to respect the privacy of individuals represented in the database.   However, as the census data also contains important aggregate information about subsets of the population, we must allow serious researchers to access the aggregate information so long as no individual's is compromised.

2. *Function Identification Problem* [4]   It is required to determine the structure of a computer program by observing selected parameters of its operation.   For example, we may be given fragments of the coding of a program which computes an unknown function and we wish to determine the value of the function at a given point.

3. *Group Testing Problem* [5]   A group of blood samples is to be processed as rapidly as possible to identify diseased persons.   This is accomplished by mixing samples to determine whether or not any members of a set of subjects is infected, so that he can be identified in future samples.   However, the disease is such taht sets of carriers of different strains can negate each other's effects in certain situations.

4. *Physical Search* [6]   A guessing game is played in which the answer can be verified if found, but in which answers to queries need not be truthful.

5. *Balance Problems* [8,9]   These are classical inference problems.   One has a number of objects of some standard weight β and two objects (identical in appearance) which are defective in the sense that one weighs slightly less than β while one weighs slightly more than β by an identical amount.   The defective objects are to be isolated by weighings on a three arm balance.

6. *Multidimensional Search* [10,11]   Given a set of X = $\{x_1, \ldots, x_n\}$ with geometric structure we wish to determine whether or not X "contains" (i.e., determines) a point y.

For instance, in the case of binary search, X is a set of points on a line and y must be determined to be equal to one of the points by simple comparisons. In higher dimensions, X may be a set of linear varieties, one of which may contain y.

7. *Coin-Weighing Problems* [12] X is chosen from $\{1,\ldots,k\}$ and the queries are of the form "what is $|S_i \cap X|$" where each $S_i \subseteq \{1,\ldots,k\}$, the problem being to insure that $S_1,S_2,\ldots,S_k$ determine X.

These problems may be studied by varying several parameters.

(α) *Choice of Primitives*. Solve the indicated problem by using only queries from a suitably restricted set.

(β) *Upper Bounds*. Determines a general strategy to insure that queries $Q_1,\ldots,Q_i$ always solve the problem, where k (measured as a function of problem size and other parameters) is small.

(γ) *Lower Bounds*. Determine minimal numbers of queries needed to infer the required properties.

(δ) *Auditing*. Prove upper and lower bounds in the complexity of determining whether or not a given sequence of queries allow inference of a given property.

(ε) *Enumeration*. Determine the number of "unsafe" problems for a given number of queries.

The references [1-12] consider for instance the problems (1α), (1β), (1γ), (2α), (2ε), (3β), (4β), (5ε), (6α), (6β), (6δ), (7β), (7γ), and (7ε). Each of these is easily seen to be an instance of a combinatorial inference problem. More important, each problem instance contributes its own special flavor to the general problem. These appealing aspects of the problem domains in turn contributes to our stock of technical tools for combinatorial inference problems.

In (1), for example, x_i represents the value of some attribute of the ith individual of the census population. A query might ask for the arithmetic mean of the attributes for a specified subpopulation. In general, the specification of a subpopulation may be rather inhomogeneous so that it may be possible to find, for instance, the average salary of the subpopulation composed of computer scientists who are either residents of a certain county of Idaho or tenured faculty at mid-western colleges. Clearly given the average salary of such a group is unlikely to compromise the privacy of any individual. Yet, it is not at all obvious that some clever sequence of such queries couldn't yield such informa-

tion. Thus if (1α), (1β) have feasible solutions, a solution to
(1δ) may be required to design an "enforcer" to restrict access
on questions that might compromise the salary of an individual.
There are many methods for dealing with such a situation in
practice. An enforcer could actually keep track of all previous
queries; alternatively such a mechanism may give out information
which differs *slightly* from that which is requested (e.g., a
value may be given which is only *near* the true mean). These last
two suggestions have been considered previously [1,2,3,13,14],
and shown to be relatively ineffective since the solution to (1)
allows compromise in less than the number of queries typically
used ty a researcher wishing to obtain legitimate information.
This leads naturally to consideration of (1δ).

To interpret problem 2, let x_i be the value of a function F
at point i; the problem is to infer from this value $F(y) \notin X$.
For instance, we might be allowed to calculate residues of
numbers modulo only certain primes and an allowable query might
then consist of asking whether or not such a value can be found.
Thus, for queries of the form "what is the value of n *mod* any
number in $\{M_1, \ldots, M_t\}$?" a (2β), (2γ) problem then might be how
many such moduli are required to allow the value to be found, if
it can be found at all.

The third problem emerges quite naturally in a number of
contexts. It may be modelled as the database security problem
was modelled with the *proviso* that is known that the result of
certain tests may be incorrect, but that these tests occur with
probability less than some p, or than these outcomes occur only a
bounded number of tests. Or perhaps, we can determine the
conditions under which the test fails and in those cases observe
that one of a small set of situations can exist. Alternatively,
we might be able to determine a proper set of linear combinations
of samples that guarantee success of the test. This might
correspond to allowing queries to be arbitrary functions of the
x_i in order to find faster schemes for determining whether an
individual has the given condition. Unfortunately, we can show
that being allowed to compute any separable function of sets of
data is no more valuable than being able to compute the mean to
the same sets.

II. A TYPICAL PROBLEM

All of the problems of the previous section are subsumed by the following. A set X is given as the underlying database of the problem; a problem is specified by a set of primitives F and a set of restrictions R on the allowed queries. The primitives of a problem determine the legal operations to be carried out in a query while the restrictions place restrictions on the form of queries.

Examples: (i)   In (1) let F consist of *median* $\{x_1, \ldots, x_m\}$

$x_k \epsilon X$, $m \geq t$ while R consists of the conditions that $g(X_1, \ldots, X_m)$ is $\leq q\%$ from the true median is p.

(ii)   In (3), let F consist of all weighted sums of subsets of X and let R consist of *failure conditions* for the tests.

This is perhaps a good place to point out an interesting interpretation of problem types (β) and (γ). The problem statements "what is the least number of queries necessary to determine which of a set of blood donors is infected?" and "in how few queries can this database be compromised?" point out that upper and lower bounds can be significant for different reasons. We are often interested in *worst* case upper bounds and *best* case lower bounds.

In [1,15,3] F consisted of median operations or averages, while arbitrary selections from X were treated in [2]. In each of these studies surprisingly small upper bounds were obtained, causing us to search for restrictions to make the problem more difficult. Some apparently reasonable restrictions have been to restrict the amount of information transferred between queries (i.e., "overlap") and to restrict the number of correct versus randomly generated answers to queries. By overlap, we mean that we control the number of objects that different queries can have in common. For the operations above under various restrictions the respective upper bounds are $0(\sqrt{N})$, $0(N)$, $0(N^2)$, where N is "query size". The second is optimal to within a constant factor for the indicated choices of primitives. One of the results of this paper is to present a nontrivial lower bound for median queries.

III.   MAIN RESULTS

We begin by considering the case in which F consists of an arbitrary selection function; i.e., for a given set of N elements from S, the F-queries select in some (unspecified) fasion one of these elements and return its value as the response to the query. More exactly, a query is defined by a set of integers $i_1, \ldots, i_n$ and a legal response is any x_j such that $j = i_m$ for some 1 m N. Note that the response does not identify "j". This type of scheme has been proposed as a practical method of ensuring database security [13]. The authors have shown [2] that if $|X| \geq N^2$, $O(N^2)$ queries are always sufficient to determine x_i for some i, even if R contains the restriction that queries overlap in at most one position. This proof depends on the existence of certain finite geometric. Now, we ask whether or not this number of queries is necessary, i.e., whether a database security enforcer can always require that a user ask this number of questions in order to make the correct inference. The following result answers this question in the affirmative.

Theorem.   If F consists of arbitrary selection operations on sets of $N > N_o$ indices and $|X| > N^2$ queries are required to associate i and x_{i_2} for some $i = 1, \ldots |X|$, and any set of N -1 queries can be answered in such a way that no such inference can be made.

The key argument in this result appeals to results from transveral theory [16].

Next, we turn to problems of type (δ), i.e., we want to audit the set of queries to determine what information may be inferred on the basis of the known queries. In a given combinatorial inference problem a set of queries may be given and the problem posed to determine the strongest valid inference which can be made based on the results of the queries. Such problems arise, for instance, in the blood sampling problem in which it may be desirable to determine if, after a certain set of tests are complete, the data thus obtained are sufficient to determine which of a set of donors is infected. If not, then further tests are required. Such procedures may also be used to guide the search for a good "next query".

We have been able to reduce inference problems of type
(δ) to certain problems in matching theory as follows. Construct
a bipartite graph with a vertex i for every $x_i \in X$, and a vertex

r_k for every Q that returns r_k as an answer. An edge is drawn
from each i to each r_k that is the result of a query containing
i. In this graph, an edge that belongs to all maximal matchings
[17] is said to be *critical*. Criticality turns out to be an
exact characterization of when a set of queries and results allows
an inference. Determining criticality is called the *offline audit*
problem.

Theorem. The offline audit problem for any $|X| = N$ can be
solved in time at most $O(N^{2.5})$.

The offline audit problem is only one of an entire class of
audit problems (δ) that can be formed by varying certain of the
conditions defining the problem; e.g., there is an *online* (i.e.,
adaptive) problem formed by allowing the results of queries to be
used in formulating new sets of queries.

For problems of type (α) there is quite a lot known about the
behavior of inference strategies with respect to varying choices
of primitives. One natural choice is to let F be composed of
median queries; i.e., a query on a set of indices returns the
median of the values of the indices. In work reported elsewhere,
it has been shown that there is an algorithm which, when
restricted to using queries of size N, can make a correct
inference using only a set of queries of size $O(\sqrt{N})$. The lower
bound (problem type γ) for this choice of F is not so obvious to
determine. Indeed, a nontrivial lower bound for median queries
carries with it a great deal of practical information for the
case of Problem 1, since it helps to characterize the difficulty
of securing a statistical database from unwarranted extraction
of information. The result which follows is established by an
information-theoretic argument.

Theorem. If X is a set of rationals and F computes medians
of sets of size N, then no inference problem (γ) can be solved in
less than $c\log_2 N$ queries, where c is a suitable constant,
independent of N.

The final category of problems considered here contains (7γ)
aspects which run in directions which are, in some sense,
orthogonal to those considered above. The Coin Weighing Problem
(7) considered in [12] is treated in several ways. First,
is solved by information-theoretic arguments. Then it is pointed
out that (7β) is really composed from two problems: the one in

which results of previous queries can be used to influence the
choice of next query and the one in which *all* queries must be
selected before results of queries are announced. Let us call
the first strategy *adaptive* and the second *nonadaptive*. The
bound (7γ) given in [12] holds for both adaptive and nonadaptive
strategies. We have already remarked on the applicability of
these concepts to the database security problems and audit
problems. We turn next to the closely related Balance Problem of
(5). The previously known results for this problem deal with
$\leq$ 6 objects.

Let us define $T_A(N)$, $T_B(N)$ to be the minimal number of
adaptive and non-adaptive queries needed to solve the balance
problem with $|X| = N$. We have the following results:

Theorem.   (1) $T_A(N) \leq 1.23 \log_2 N$

             (2) $T_B(N) \leq 2 \log_3 N$

             (3) $T_A(N) = \Omega(\log_2 N)$

             (4) $T_B(N) = \Omega(\log_2 N)$

The lower bounds are established by rate-of-growth arguments. It
is noteworthy that the optimal adaptive strategy cited in the
previous theorem is the only instance of which we are aware in
which an adaptive upper bound has been shown to asymptotically
improve a nonadaptive upper bound.

IV.   CONCLUSIONS

In this paper, we demonstrate a rather broad category of
problems which appear to have common formulations and which may
be susceptible to the same methods of attack. The specific
inferential problems which we consider give some evidence for
this. In addition, the results we obtain carry some independent
interest both as combinatorial results, and as results in the
indicated problem domains.

REFERENCES

[1]   Dobkin, D., Jones, A. and Lipton, R., (to appear in ACM TODS), "Protection Against User Inference".

[2]   DeMillo, R., Dobkin, D. and Lipton, R., "Even Data Bases That Lie Can Be Compromised", IEEE Transactions on Software Design, Jan. 1977, Vol. SE-4 (1): 73-75.

[3]   Reiss, S., (1976), "A Combinatorial Model of Data Base Security", Technical Report, Yale University, Department of Computer Science.

[4]   Feldman, J. A. and Shields, P. C., (April 1972), "Total Complexity and the Inference of Best Programs", Stanford AIM-159.

[5]   Pippenger, N., (1976), "Group Testing", IBM Watson Research Center Technical Report.

[6]   Ulam, S., (1976), *Adventures of a Mathematician,* Scribners.

[7]   Katona, G. O. H., (1973), "Combinatorial Search Problems", *A Survey of Combinatorial Theory,* (j.N. Srivastava, Ed.), North Holland, pp. 285-308.

[8]   "Shades of E 712", (November 1973), *American Mathematical Monthly,* Vol. 80, No. 9, pp. 1064-1065.

[9]   Vilenkin, N., (1972), *Combinatorial Mathematics,* MIR Publishers, Moscow.

[10]   Dobkin, D. and Lipton, R., (June 1976), "Multidimensional Searching Problems", *SIAM Computing,* Vol. 5, No. 2, pp. 181-186.

[11]   Knuth, D. E., (April 1977), "Algorithms", *Scientific American,* pp. 63-80.

[12]   Erdös, P. and Spencer, J., (1974), *Probabilistic Methods in Combinatorics,* Academic Press.

[13]   Conway, R. and Strip, D., (Oct. 1976), "Selective Partial Access to a Data Base", *Proceedings of the ACM 76 National Conference.*

[14]   Denning, D. and Denning, P., Private Communication.

[15]   Dobkin, D., Lipton, R and Reiss, S., "Aspects of the Data Base Security Problem", *proceedings of a conference on Theoretical Computer Science,* Waterloo, Canada, 1977.

[16]   Mirsky, L., (1971), *Transversal Theory,* Academic Press.

[17]   Hall, M., (1967), *Combinatorial Theory,* Ginn and Blaisdell.

DISCUSSION

Reiss: Does it effect things much to, rather than give an
exact answer, give a ball park "lie"?

Dobkin: That's something that's been suggested: answer and
perturb it randomly by some percentage less than one percent.
For that case, we don't have total insight into the problem yet.
That seems to be much more difficult. A lot of our results are
based on combinatorial lemmas and physical principles, and you
can't apply those results when you go to that sort of strategy.

Shapiro: It is easy to prove that very small "lies" can
result in very large changes in summary statistical information,
which could be disasterous to a statistical database user.

Dobkin: I hadn't realized that. That's good to know.

Denning: I have a question concerning the results about the
databases that lie. If you compromise the database, you have no
way of knowing whether or not the answer you got is a lie.

Dobkin: In the type of lying I'm talking about, you actually
do know that if I guessed Dorothy Denning's salary is so many
dollars, then it's actually Dorothy Denning's salary. In the
type of lying I was talking about before, where you go a certain
percent one way or the other, then you don't know the salary that
you have is the correct one.

Cohen: I'm concerned that there may be other kinds of
a priori information; for instance, relationships among elements
in the database, so that one could compromise without actually
having compromised in your sense. For instance, it may be more
important to know one's salary is more than somebody else's or
that you've compromised the database that with someone's exact

salary with a 90% limit of confidence.

   Dobkin: Yes. That just means that you have to be more rigorous about what it means to compromise the database. You can compromise down to the digit or you can compromise in some other sense.

DATA BASE SYSTEM AUTHORIZATION

D. D. Chamberlin
J. N. Gray
P. P. Griffiths
M. Mresse
I. L. Traiger
B. W. Wade

IBM Research Laboratory
San Jose, California

I. INTRODUCTION

This paper focuses on the rather specialized topic of authorization of access to a Data Base-Data Communication system (DB-DC system). Many DB-DC systems currently need little authorization beyond that provided by the operating system (e.g. in-house or one-person data bases). However, there is a growing class of large and sophisticated data management systems which require tight controls over the use and dissemination of data.

The next section discusses how large existing (commercially available) systems appear to do authorization. The remaining sections suggest improvements to these mechanisms.

II. A TYPICAL SYSTEM

A. User Roles

Large DB-DC systems typically have several *roles* for users.
The broad roles are:

- System Administrator: defines and installs the system.
  Makes policy decisions about the operation of the system.

- System Operator: handles the operation of the system,
  manages system startup-shutdown, responds to user requests,
  and manages physical plant.

- System Programmer: installs and maintains the DB-DC code,
  and the underlying operating system.

- Application Programmer: defines and implements new application programs to be used by end users, by the system
  administrator, and by the system operator.

- End User: uses the system to enter and retrieve data.

These roles are (typically) further refined into sub-categories
(e.g. end users include the roles: teller, loan officer, branch
manager, auditor,...). Over time, a particular user may perform
several of these roles, but usually a user is authorized to
perform only one role.

The concept of role serves the purpose of grouping users of
the system together, thereby decomposing authorization decisions
into the two questions:

- What should the authorization of a role be?
- Who should be authorized to use the role?

B. Authentication

Individuals sign onto the system in a particular role. The
individual's identity is validated by a combination of

- Personal identification (key, magnetic stripe,
  password...)

- Physical location of terminal (teller must be at
  own bank...)

- Physical security of terminal (it is in a bank...)

- Time of day (bank teller terminals only work at
  certain hours...)

This mechanism is usually specified as a decision table so that it is easy to understand. In the above instance, the decision table would be:

PERSON X PASSWORD X TERMINAL X TIME -> ROLES

C. Transactions

Once a person establishes a role, he is authorized to perform certain *transactions* on the system. There is great variety among the transactions available to different roles. Someone on the shipping dock will have a different set of transactions than a member of the purchasing department. So there is a further table which authorizes

ROLE -> TRANSACTION.

An installed transaction's definition carries a complete list of the objects it accesses (except for objects passed as parameters to the transaction such as input and output terminal or queue). The transaction is strictly limited to this domain when executed.

When the transaction is invoked, the data management system constructs a domain consisting of only these objects and operations. This domain is usually represented as a set of control blocks (one per object) in protected storage. Since these control blocks are in protected storage, they perform the functions of capabilities <3>. All operations by the transaction name one or more of these objects (control blocks). This limits what objects can be touched by the transaction. The control blocks further limit what operations may be performed on the object (e.g. a file may be read-only).

D. Authorization Aspects of Roles

We now discuss authorization as viewed by each generic role.

End users are usually limited to pushing buttons which cause forms to appear on the display screen. After filling in a form, another button causes the form to be validated, and if it passes the test, to be acted upon by the system.

The application programmer defines (implements) transactions. Depending on the degree of care exercised by the programmer, he may be able to prevent the users from doing terrible things to the data base. For example, the transaction might refuse to handle withdrawals of more than five hundred dollars without the branch manager's approval. In general, the application programmer seeks only to guard against end user abuses and mistakes.

The application programmer might be able to protect the privacy of his data from the system operator and from the data base administrator by encrypting it.   Communication over insecure lines is often unprotected.   Some systems do encryption/decryption in order to protect the security of communication data.   For example, some cash dispensing terminals encrypt customer passwords and transaction information when communicating with the central host.   However, the usefulness of *local* encryption of data residing within a host is doubtful at present because data appear in the clear while in main storage (accessible to almost anyone reading a dump), and because operational personnel usually have a back door to the authorization system.   Lastly, there are technical problems associated with constructing indices on encrypted data and keeping a system log that contains encrypted log records.   In summary, the application programmer must trust the system administrator, system operator, and system programmer.

The system administrator defines system objects and authorizes access to them.   The principal system objects are users, terminals, transactions, views, and physical files.

When installing a new transaction, the system administrator is careful to validate the program and to narrowly describe the subset of the data and terminals available to the transaction. Installing a transaction consists of entering its programs and descriptors into system catalogs and authorizing one or more roles to use the transaction.

In order to proscribe the domain of a transaction, the system administrator:

- Limits the transaction to access a particular set of files.

- Within each file, makes only certain record instances visible.

- Within a record instance, makes only certain fields visible.

- Makes only certain visible fields updatable.

Continuing the example above, a bank teller transaction might be allowed to see only those records from the central ledger which pertain to the local branch and be allowed to update only the balance field of the teller cash drawer records.

Aside from deciding which transactions and files will be stored and what access paths will be maintained on files (indices, hash chains, sibling pointers, etc), the system administrator also installs *exits* (data base procedures) which enforce the integrity of the system. Examples of exits are:

- Exit to encrypt-decrypt objects on secondary storage.

- Exit to validate the reasonableness of the contents of records being inserted into the data base.

- Exit to check the authorization of the caller to manipulate the objects named in the DB-DC operation.

These exits allow an installation to tailor the system to perform authorization appropriate to its application.

The system operator is limited to a very special set of commands which allow him to manage the physical resources of the system, to restart the network and the system, and to reconfigure the network and system. In point of fact, the system operator has the "keys to the kingdom" and can easily penetrate the system.

Similarly, the system programmer has a very limited set of commands. However, to ease debugging and maintenance, one or more of these commands opens almost any door in the system.

In general, users are not unhappy with the rather primitive access control mechanisms outlined above. In general, user level authorization is quite application dependent (e.g. only the military seems to understand or care about the star property <4>). Hence, there seems to be general agreement that this authorization should be imbedded in exits or in application code rather than being included in a general purpose DB-DC system.

III. PROBLEMS AND TRENDS

A. *Why We Expect Things to Change*

At present, most "real" systems are doing "operational" processing. They are very static applications which have automated the "back-office" of some large enterprise. Usually, human tasks were directly replaced or augmented with computers. These applications are often prescribed by law or accounting practice and are reasonably well understood.

Computers are moving into the "front office" and into smaller
operational units. At first, these systems will be small and
isolated (i.e., stand alone mini-computer). But eventually, these
systems will be integrated with the "back office" system and with
other front office systems. This implies that networks of
loosely coupled systems will appear.

When this happens, one should expect the system to be much
less static and expect control of the system to be much less
centralized.

B. *The Case Against a Central System Administrator*

The definition and control of objects (transactions, users,
queues, data bases, views, catalogs,...) has been a highly
centralized function residing with a single individual or group
of individuals (system administrator). Several trends encourage
the development of a less centralized administrator function.

- The foremost trend is that systems are becoming much
  more dynamic. A large system typically has several
  groups of users. Each group wants to share a central
  pool of data and perhaps share data with some other
  groups. But also it wants to be able to easily create
  and maintain private data and transactions. The
  requirement that all new definitions be funneled through
  a central system administrator is quite restrictive as
  well as inconvenient.

- The existence of a central system administrator also has
  the psychological drawback that the "owner" of the data
  does not control it. Rather, the system administrator
  controls it.

- Independent data management systems are being integrated
  in order to selectively share information among co-
  operating organizations. Even if the network is homo-
  geneous (similar machines and data management systems),
  each node of the network is an autonomous unit with its
  own management and procedures. This is because networks
  cross organizational lines and yet responsibility for the
  data at a node ultimately rests with the organization
  which maintains that node.

C. *Sketch of a Decentralized Administrator Function*

Our goal is a simple mechanism to dynamically create and share objects among users of a data management system. This simplicity is important for a community of individuals who control their own data, as well as for a more centrally controlled system where authorization is handled by a (human) data base administrator.

We have been able to draw on the experience and techniques used in operating systems for authorization to files. However, we have had to refine these facilities because more semantics are associated with the objects.

We have been trying to design a decentralized authorization mechanism which provides the following functions: The system administrator function is distributed among all application programmers and even to some end users. The central system administrator allocates physical resources (space and time) and grants some transactions to particular users thereby delegating his authority to others. These objects include views of system catalogs and transactions which install new users, new terminals, and new space.

Much as in a traditional operating system, the user has a *catalog* of named objects he can manipulate and use. Objects come in three general flavors:

   • Data objects: physical files and logical files (views).

   • Communication objects: logical ports and message queues.

   • Transaction objects: encapsulated (parameterized) programs which perform operations on data objects and communication objects.

Each object type has a set of operators defined on it and these operators are individually authorized.

A user with no transactions in his catalog can do nothing. The catalog of a minimally privileged user consists of a limited set of transactions which may be invoked. The catalog of an application programmer might contain transactions (commands) which allow him to define new objects and grant them to others. Each time a user defines a new object, an authorized entry for it is placed in his catalog.

The authors of the system implement transactions which allow the invoker to define system objects. These transactions include:

- DEFINE-USER: enrolls a new user in the system.

- DEFINE-TERMINAL: makes a new terminal known to the system.

- DEFINE-FILE: defines a new physical file.

- DEFINE-INDEX: defines an index on some file.

- DEFINE-LINK: defines a N-M mapping from records to records.

- DEFINE-VIEW: defines a new view in terms of existing files.

- DEFINE-TRANSACTION: defines a new transaction in terms of existing data objects.

Other transactions are available to MODIFY, DROP, GRANT and REVOKE objects.

Each of these transactions may be invoked from the terminal or from a program so long as the invoker is authorized to run the transaction. Other commands are available to MODIFY definitions and to DROP definitions and their associated objects. Currently, we propose that only the creator of an object can modify it and only the creator or the person who enrolled him in the system can drop an object.

By selectively granting these transactions to users, the system can delegate the function typically thought of as "system administrator" to autonomous individuals.

Once an object is defined, the creator may grant other users access to the object (subject to constraints explained below). A unique set of authorities is associated with each object type. Individual users are granted subsets of these authorities. Each authority has two possible modifiers.

- GRANT: the ability to grant another user this authority to this object (this is a property of a granted privilege to the object rather than being a property of the object itself).

- REVOKE: the ability to selectively revoke this authority. (only the grantor may revoke access so REVOKE implies GRANT).

For example, RUN authority for a transaction may be granted in the following modes:

- RUN & GRANT & REVOKE
- RUN & GRANT & REVOKE
- RUN & GRANT & REVOKE

It is not clear that one need distinguish GRANT and REVOKE in which case it might be called CONTROL. Chamberlin <2> and Griffiths <5> discuss these authorities in greater detail.

D. Authorization to Data

Authorization to data objects has traditionally consisted of making certain files, records and fields invisible (a subset of the database). Much finer control can be obtained if one can, in addition,

- Do *value dependent* authorization (i.e., only fetch or replace record instances whose field values satisfy certain criteria).
- Define *views* (virtual files) which are not physically stored but are synthesized from existing stored files.

Files and view objects have the additional authorities:

- READ: the ability to read records.
- INSERT: the ability to insert records.
- DELETE: the ability to delete records.

And for each field of the file or view:

- UPDATE: the ability to update values in this field.

The justification for providing update authorization on individual fields rather than on the entire view is that some fields within a record are more sensitive than others. For example, one might be allowed to read and update the QUANTITY-ON-HAND but only to read the UNIT-PRICE field. The view as a whole carries the authorizations for READ, INSERT, and DELETE. As explained in the preceding section, each of these authorities potentially has the modifiers GRANT and REVOKE.

The definer of a file is fully authorized to the file. The definer of a view gets the "intersection" of the authorizations he has to its components. For example, if a user has only read authorization to a file, then any view he defines based on that file will be (at most) read only.

Each user catalog is really a view of the system catalog file. Each user gets a view of his subset of the catalog and some transactions which display and modify his view of the catalog (DEFINE and GRANT insert entries in the catalog; DROP and REVOKE remove entries from the catalog). The user's view is qualified in that he cannot directly modify some fields in the catalog (e.g. authorization fields). He may be given GRANT authority on individual authorities of his view so that he can grant other users selective access to his view. If he wants to grant access to a subset of his catalog, he can define a new view which sub-sets his catalog and then grant the subset view to others, or he may define a transaction which accesses his catalog and then grant that transaction to others.

Only the system administrator has a view of the entire catalog.

The paper by Chamberlin <2> discusses the virtues and problems of views in detail. Stonebraker <6> presents another approach to views and proposes an interesting implementation.

E. Transaction Authorization

One reason for defining transactions is to encapsulate objects so that others may use them without violating the integrity of the constituent objects.

F. Transactions Have the Additional Authority:

  •   RUN: the ability to run a transaction.

Just as for views, a transaction RUN authority has the modifiers GRANT and REVOKE. If the transaction definition consists entirely of objects grantable by the transaction definer, then the transaction will be grantable. Otherwise, the definer gets the transaction with RUN & ¬GRANT & ¬REVOKE authority.

If a transaction is held RUN & GRANT, the definer can grant RUN & ¬GRANT authority to others, who can then run the trans-action. He can also grant others the ability to grant run authority by granting RUN & GRANT authority.

For example, a banking system provides transactions which credit and debit accounts (according to certain rules) rather than granting direct access to the accounts file. This effectively encapsulates the procedures of the bank and insures that all users of the data follow these procedures. An application programmer would write the transactions and grant run authority to the tellers of the bank and grant RUN & GRANT authority to the branch managers so that they could authorize new tellers at their branches.

G. Authorization Times

The authorization of a transaction can be done at any of three times:

- Definition: The text and environment of the transaction is described by the application programmer.

- Installation: The transaction is made known to the system.

- Invocation: The transaction is "used" by the end user.

For reasons of efficiency, authorization should be done as early as possible in this process. If possible, no authorization tests are performed at invocation time (except for validation that earlier authorization decisions have not been revoked).

When defining a transaction, the application programmer has some notion of what objects the transaction will touch and what operations will be performed on these objects (e.g. get message from queue "A", put record in file "B"). Further, he has some notion of what is allowed on the data (e.g. one should not debit an account to a negative value). The application programmer includes these tests in his program and at invocation the transaction aborts or takes remedial action if the tests are violated.

When the transaction is installed, the ability of the author to access the objects the transaction references is checked. Also the operations themselves are authorized (e.g. read authority is required on the account number and balance fields and update authority is required on the balance field). This checking is done by a program which examines the transaction text, discovering what calls the transaction makes. If everything is ok, the processor enters the transaction in the system catalog along with a descriptor of the transaction domain.

If authorization fails, there are two possible alternatives:
One can abort the operation, or one can defer the operation,
giving a warning message. We propose to defer when authorization
fails at definition or installation time. An attempt to actually
operate on an unauthorized object fails. This philosophy allows
programmers to define and install views and transactions which
make unauthorized calls. These transactions may even be run so
long as the unauthorized calls are not actually executed. As
will be seen, the logic for run-time authorization must be present
anyway so this decision adds little to the system complexity.
The approach has the virtue that it detects many authorization
errors rather than only the first.

When the transaction is invoked, the invoker's authorization
to invoke the transaction is checked. When the transaction runs,
both the system and the application program do value dependent
authorization. For example, if a view is qualified by a selection
criterion then each record which is fetched or stored via the
view must satisfy that criterion. As another example, the
application program may refuse to insert user-provided data
which does not satisfy application-dependent criteria.

Given this motivation, it is clear that the authorization of
the transaction may be different from the authorization of the
invoker of the transaction.

H.   *Authorization Environments*

When an application programmer installs a transaction which is
to be granted to another user, there is some question as to which
authorization environment should be used to authorize the transaction. Candidate authorization environments are:

(a)   Authorize the transaction in the environment of the definer
      (application programmer).
(b)   Authorize the transaction in the environment of the user.
(c)   Sometimes (a), sometimes (b) and sometimes (a) and (b).

It might seem obvious that the transaction should be
authorized in the context of the definer. However, if the
transaction is parameterized then access to parameters must be
authorized in the environment of the invoker of the transaction.
Similarly, if the program is a "snell" which takes in user
commands and executes them, then certain of its actions should
be authorized in the context of the user.

Perhaps the most extreme example of this is a program called User Friendly Interface (UFI) in System R <1>. The UFI is a program which accepts data base requests in symbolic form, translates them into system calls, and executes them against the invoker's data base. It is a combination data-base-editor and report generation language. The authors of UFI have no idea what files it will be used with or what operations may be performed on these files. All its authorization comes from the user of UFI. Clearly, UFI calls to the system must be evaluated entirely in the context of the invoker.

As another example, consider authorization to objects which are created by the transaction at run time. In some cases, (e.g. an internal scratch file) the invoker should not be able to see the object while, in other cases (the report file) the invoker should be allowed to see the object. In general, it seems best to attribute these transient objects to the definer who can then GRANT them to the invoker as part of the transaction logic if he so chooses.

The general rules seem to be:

- Perform authorization tests as soon as possible.

- Authorization of an operation known at installation should be done in the context of the object definer at installation time.

- Authorization to operations not known at installation (e.g. parameters) must be done at transaction invocation.

- The transaction runs in a new authorization context which is a synthesis of objects granted it by the object definer and objects granted by the object invoker.

I. Revocation and Redefinition

As explained above, one may grant another user type "x" authority to an object if the grantor has a grantable version of type "x" authority on the object. Any subset of grantable authorities may be granted together. These authorities may then be revoked individually.

The problem of revoking access to objects is very difficult. When an object is destroyed, it is deleted from the catalog of all users to whom it was granted. This also invalidates all objects which derive from that object and authorizations on them, recursively. When someone with revoke authority modifies the authorization of an object, that modification is propagated to all objects derived from it. One may selectively revoke access to the object. For example:

REVOKE HIRE-EMPLOYEE FROM JONES;

revokes Jones' access to the HIRE-EMPLOYEE transaction.

One may imagine objects organized into a dependency hierarchy.
If one object is defined in terms of another, then changes in the
parent will affect the child and *all* its descendants.

Proper implementation of this notion is very subtle. The
problem is further discussed and a solution is presented by
Griffiths <5>.

References

<1> Astrahan, Blasgen, Chamberlin, Eswaran, Gray, Griffiths,
     King, Lorie, McJones, Mehl, Putzolu, Traiger, Wade, Watson.
     System R: Relational Approach to Database Management, ACM
     TODS, Vol. 1, No. 2, June 1976, pp. 97-137.
<2> Chamberlin, Gray, Traiger. Views, Authorization and
     Locking in a Relational Data Base System. ACM National
     Computer Conference Proceedings, 1975, pp. 425-430.
<3> Dennis, and Van Horn. Programming Semantics for Multi-
     programmed Computations. CACM Vol. 9, No. 7, July 1977,
     pp. 145-155.
<4> Bell, LaPadula. Secure Computer Systems. ESD-TR-73-278.
     (AD 770768, 771543, and 780528). MITRE, Bedford Mass.,
     Nov. 1973.
<5> Griffiths, and Wade. An Authorization Mechanism for a
     Relational Database System. ACM TODS, Vol. 1, No. 3, Sept.
     1976, pp. 242-255.
<6> Stonebraker. Implementation of Integrity Constraints and
     View by Query Modification. ACM SIGMOD Conference. May 1975,
     pp. 554-556.

DISCUSSION

Cohen: I wondered whether the system is running and how much experience you have with kinds of replication that users do.

Griffiths: The authorization subsystem is not yet integrated into our system; so, we have no data on the depth to which grants are typically nested. It appears that people don't expect trees of grants to be very deep. However, I disagree with this. Let's examine how the president of a company issues a memo to all the company's managers down the line. First, the president issues the memo to all the managers immediately under him. And, they in turn issue copies to managers under them, and so on. I believe this analosy holds, that information sharing by granted privileges in a data management system tends to propagate along organizational lines in "real life". Once a multiple level granting mechanism is available in a data management system, I suspect we will find that it is used in surprisingly complex ways which are similar to the ways that information flows between people.

Harrison: These views are actually something that is stored as a relation in the machine.

Griffiths: Views are not a relation copying mechanism; they are not pre-computed and then stored. We store only definitions of the views, and use those definitions to provide dynamic "windows" on the underlying store relations. If someone else is currently examining and changing a relation, then the changes are reflected immediately to all views on that relation. For example, suppose there is a relation containing all the names and salaries of university employees. Then, I can define a view PROFS which contains the names and salaries of those employees who are professors. If someone gives a professor a raise while I am examining the PROFS view, then I will see the update the

MEDIANS AND DATABASE SECURITY

Steven P. Reiss

Brown University
Providence, Rhode Island

I. SECURITY IN DATABASES

Central to the ever-increasing use of computerized databases
is the notion of database security. With computers becoming
more powerful and less expensive, the advantages of placing large
amounts of information in an online computerized database have
led to an increased number of database systems. Such systems
allow a group of users to access large quantities of information
so that both specific pieces of information are rapidly accessible and so that large amounts of data can be correlated to gain
an accurate statistical view. As such, databases are becoming
increasingly important to corporate and university management,
to the many government bureaucracies, to police and related
organizations, as well as to researchers in areas like sociology.

Along with the many benefits of computerized databases,
there are several disadvantages, the most important being the
lack of a guarantee for the security of the stored information.
It is hard to imagine corporations using databases for confidential information if they thought that their competitors or even
their employees would easily gain access to this information.
Moreover, recent actions in the Congress have shown that the
citizens of this country are not going to allow the amassing of
large databases containing privileged information without adequate
guarantees that the information will be kept private. It is
because databases are so important that addressing these serious
concerns about the security of the stored information is such an
important problem.

A. *Research in Database Security*

Most of the research into this problem of database security
has focused on the problem of physical security, i.e. guaranteeing that only authorized persons have access to the computer,
the database system, or the data. These problems represent valid
and important issues in the area but are too crude to handle many
of the essential questions. In particular, it is often the case
that there are users who should be able to use most but not all
of a database.

This latter type of question is addressed more by research
that is aimed at maintaining security for specific privileged
fields of database while allowing general access to the non-
privileged fields. Research here has involved encrypting the
privileged fields, requiring user passwords, as well as physically separating the privileged fields from the remainder of the
database. However, even this approach is still too stringent
for some applications. In particular, there are cases where the
specific elements of a field must be safeguarded, while
statistical access to the same data must be allowed. This is
especially true for databases used in sociological research and
for such items as grades in a university database or salaries in
a corporate database. The problem of allowing such statistical
access while maintaining the security of the individual items
has only recently been studied on a large scale.

B. *A Model for Statistical Security*

Much of this recent research into statistical security has
been based on the simple formal model of a database proposed by
Dobkin, Jones and Lipton [DJL] that was specifically designed
for the purpose. This model considers only the field of the
database that contains the privileged information. By assuming
that all the non-privileged information is available to the user
and that complex queries can be asked to select arbitrary subsets of the privileged data for use in queries, the model allows
one to address and answer the relevant questions concerning
statistical security.

Within this model a database is viewed as a set X of
elements $x_1, \ldots, x_n$ where n is the size of the database. Each of
these elements represents a privileged datum and thus is assigned
a value. The database is said to be compromised if it is
possible to determine the value that is associated with some
element of the database. Similarly, an element is said to be
compromised if its associated value is known. Queries into such
a database consists of applying some statistical function, i.e.
mean, median, max, min, etc, to some subset of the elements.

Finally the model assumes that there is a database policy that attempts to enforce security by limiting the nature of the queries that can be asked. We can determine the effectiveness of such a policy by establishing as a measure of its security the number of queries of the particular type allowed that are required to guarantee that the database can be compromised. If a large number of queries of a certain type are required before the database can be compromised, then the data is relatively secure; if only a small number of queries will suffice, the database is not secure.

There are several ways of limiting the types of queries that can be allowed. First of all, one generally allows only queries involving the same statistical function. Moreover, all queries are required to involve some minimal number of elements. Clearly, if a query asks for the median or average of a set containing a single element, then the value returned is just the value of that element.

C. *Our Study*

In this paper, we study one specific type of statistical query and show that a database system in which it was allowed would not be secure. In particular, we consider queries that ask for the median of sets of exactly k elements. We make the assumption in this study that the elements of the database have unique values, i.e. if elements x_i and x_j in the database X both have the same value, then i = j. This assumption, while not entirely accurate in practice, is probably valid when a small random sample is taken from a large database and when the compromising is done within this sample [DL].

For this model and assumptions, previous results have shown that $O(\sqrt{k})$ queries were sufficient to insure that the database can be compromised [DLR]. Moreover, it was shown that a specific element in the database could be compromised, using an exponential number of queries [DLR]. In this paper, we first present a technique for getting information from median queries in Section 3. In Section 4 and 5, we use this technique to define two methods whereby a database can be compromised using only

$O(\text{Log}^2 k)$ k-median queries. Moreover, we show in Section 6 how a specific element can generally be compromised using $O(k)$ queries and, for the case where something is known about the specific element, compromise can often be achieved using $O(\text{Log } k)$ or fewer queries.

II.   NOTATION

The study of statistical security in databases is interesting both because of its relevance to actual database systems and
because of the mathematics involved.   In this paper we apply
methods from combinatorics, probability and the analysis of
algorithms to answer questions about the security of databases
under queries involving the median of sets of exactly k elements.

Since we deal extensively with sets of elements from the
database, we use the fairly standard set notations of

ε for set membership;

$\subseteq$ for set inclusion;

ϕ for the null or empty set;

$|\ |$ for the size of a set;

$\cup$ for set union;

$\cap$ for set intersection;

$-$ for set difference, $A-B = \{c\,|\,c\varepsilon A,\ c\notin B\}$, $(B\subseteq A)$; and

$+$ for set addition, $A+B = A\cup B$, $(A\cap B = \phi)$.

We only use set difference, $A-B$, when $B \subseteq A$.   Similarly, we only
use set addition, $A+B$, when A and B are disjoint.   We use the
notation $|\ |$ to both denote the size of a set and the absolute
value of a numeric expression.   It will be clear from the context
which case is meant.   Finally, we call a set of k elements a
k-set.

In addition to working with sets, our results involve combinatorics, probability and analysis of algorithms.   We use the
following standard notation from these fields:

$\binom{a}{b}$ binomial coefficient $= \dfrac{a!}{b!\,(a-b)!}$;

$Pr\{E\}$ the probability of event E;

Log   logarithm (base 2);

$\lceil x \rceil$ the smallest integer greater than or equal to x;

$\lfloor x \rfloor$ the largest integer less than or equal to x; and

$O(f)$ on the order of f.

Note here that we use Log consistently throughout this paper to mean the base 2 logarithm.

In addition to these standard notations, we introduce some rather specialized notation for dealing with medians. We denote the median of a set A by m(A) and call the median of a k-set a k-median. Moreover, we often need to refer to the properties of a set with respect to some median M. We say that an element is negative with respect to a median M, or, if M is understood, just negative, if the value of the element is less than M. Similarly, a positive element is one whose value is greater than M. A set is more negative (positive) than another set if if has more negative (positive) elements. Finally, we denote the number of negative elements in a set A by $N_M(A)$ and the number of

elements less than or equal to M by $\bar{N}_N(A)$. When M is understood

here we omit it, writing N(A) and $\bar{N}(A)$ respectively.

Finally, throughout our discussion of security we refer to the concept of a random database. Since we are viewing a database as a set of n elements each of which has a unique value, and since we are only considering queries involving medians and hence only relative values are important, we can assume that there is a fixed n-set of values. Then we define a random database as one in which all of the n! possible assignments of values to elements of the database are equally likely.

III. BALANCING

In order to compromise a database using k-median queries, we must be able to obtain some information from each query or each set of queries. Although several methods have been proposed for doing this [DDL1, DJL, R, DLR], the most efficient is that of balancing where specific information can be extracted using only $O(Log(k))$ queries. In this section, we consider this technique in detail, presenting the relevant algorithms and proving their properties. We then illustrate the technique with an algorithm that determines if the median of a set is an element of a certain subset of that set. We will show in later sections how this algorithm can be used to actually compromise a data base.

The idea behind the technique of balancing is to find a set that has a certain distribution of elements with respect to some median M, that is, one that has precisely some number of elements ℓ less than M and some number of elements h greater than M. Once we have such a set, we can obtain information about specific elements very easily. For example, suppose we have a set $A = A_1 + A_2$ with median M, and we have another set B such that

$|B| = |A_1|$ and B has the same number of elements less than M
that A_1 does. Then by computing the median of $B + A_2$, we can
easily determine if the element with value M is in A_1 or A_2
since it is in A_2 if and only if $m(B + A_2) = M$.

In order to find a set with exactly ℓ negative elements with
respect to some median, we take two sets, one with fewer than ℓ
negative elements and one with more than ℓ negative elements.
We begin with the first set and successively substitute elements
of the latter. In this way, it is assured that one of the
intermediate sets will have the desired distribution or balance
of negative elements. Assuming that we have some way of checking for this proper balance, we are done. This brute force
approach is not directly useful however since it requires a
number of queries proportional to the size of the desired set.
We make it very efficient by using a binary search technique to
locate the desired set in such a way that the number of queries
required is only proportional to the log of the size of the
desired set.

A. Definitions

The object of balancing is to find a set containing a certain
distribution of elements with respect to some median.   In
particular, we define

Definition: A set G is *balanced* with respect to a median M,
a number ℓ and one of the functions $\tilde{N} \, \epsilon \, \{N_M, \bar{N}_M\}$ if and only if

$$N(G) \, \epsilon \, \{\lceil \ell \rceil, \lfloor \ell \rfloor\}.$$

We denote this fact by $\sim G$, where ℓ, M and $\tilde{N}$ will be clear from
the context. If ℓ is an integer here, the number of negative
elements in G must be precisely ℓ. Moreover, as $\tilde{N}(G)$ must be
integral, if ℓ is not an integer, then $\tilde{N}(G)$ must be as close to
ℓ as possible.

When it is possible to find a balanced set from two given
sets, we say that the two sets are balanceable. Formally,

Definition : Two sets G and H where $|G| = |H|$ are *balanceable*
with respect to a median M and a number ℓ if and only if either
$$\tilde{N}(G) \leq \ell \leq \tilde{N}(H)$$

or

$$\tilde{N}(G) \geq \ell \geq \tilde{N}(H).\qquad\qquad \square$$

It is obvious, using the pigeon-hole principle and element-by-element substitution, that

Lemma 3.1   If G and H are balanceable with respect to M and then there is a set $S \subset G \cup H$, $|S| = |G|$, such that ~ S. $\square$

Finally, to properly balance two sets we must be able to test if some set is balanced or not. Because we are going to utilize a binary search technique, we do this in such a way that we indicate whether the set has too many or too few negative elements. To accomplish these goals, we introduce the notion of a balancing function. In particular,

Definition: For equal sized sets G and H, TEST(G,H) is a *balancing function* with respect to a property P, median M, and a value ℓ if and only if

1)   TEST(G,H) = 0 if and only if P(G,H) holds;

2)   TEST(G,H) = + 1 implies $\tilde{N}(G) \leq \ell$; and

3)   TEST(G,H) = - 1 implies $\tilde{N}(G) \geq \ell$. $\square$

Since the object of balancing is to obtain a set with a desired distribution, property P here generally says that this distribution has been achieved and condition 1) insures that this information is returned. Moreover, conditions 2) and 3) insure that TEST indicates how the actual distribution of the set G relates to the desired distribution. We generalize the definition of two sets being balanceable by saying that they are balanceable with respect to a balancing function if and only if they are balanceable with respect to the values of ℓ, M, and $\tilde{N}$ upon which the function is defined.

B.   The Balancing Algorithm

Rather than presenting a separate algorithm for each balancing function, we define an algorithm that uses a binary search technique to balance a set with respect to an arbitrary balancing function. In this way, we are actually defining a whole set of similar algorithms, several of which we will use in this and later sections of this paper. The specific algorithm is:

ALGORITHM: Balance -- Find a balanced set.

GIVEN: A Balancing function TEST with respect to a property P; sets C_o, D_o, B where $|C_o| = |D_o|$, $B \cap (C_o \cup D_o) = \phi$, $|B| + |C_o| = k$, and C_0 and D_0 are balanceable.

FIND: $<G, H, G', H', FG>$ where FG is a binary flag, G, H, G', H' are sets and $|G| = |H| = |G'| = |H'| = |C_0|$, $G \cup H = G' \cup H' = C_0 \cup D_0$, and

    1)   FG = TRUE and P(G,H) holds

    2)   FG = FALSE and either ~G or ~G'.

1)   Set $C = C_0$, $D = D_0$, $X = C - C_0 \cap D_0$, $Y = D - C_0 \cap D_0$,

     v = TEST(C,D). If $v = 0$ then return $<C,D,C,D, \text{TRUE}>$.

2)   Let X_1 be the first $n = \lceil |X|/2 \rceil$ elements of X, $X_2 = X - X_1$.

     Let Y_1 be the first n elements of Y, $Y_2 = Y - Y_1$. Let G =

     $C - X_1 + Y_1$ and $H = D - Y_1 + X_1$.

3)   Set v' = TEST(G,H). If $v' = 0$ then return $<G,H,G,H,\text{TRUE}>$.
     If $|X| \leq 1$ then return $<C,D,G,H, \text{FALSE}>$.

4)   If $v = v'$ then set $X,Y,C,D = X_2$, Y_2, G, H; otherwise set

     $X,Y,C,D = X_1$, Y_1, C, D. Go back to step 2.   □

     Throughout this algorithm C is the set to be balanced and $X \subseteq C$ and $Y \subseteq D$ are the subsets that are used for this balancing. To illustrate why the algorithm works, we note that C and $C - X + Y$ are always balanceable. Then for the limiting case where $|X| = |Y| = 1$, either $C = G$ or $C - X + Y = G'$ or both are balanced. The details are given by

Lemma 3.2   Given balanceable sets C_0 & D_0 and a balancing function TEST as required for BALANCE, the algorithm works as specified and makes only $\lceil \text{Log} |C_0| \rceil + 2$ calls to TEST.

Proof: From the specification of the algorithm, the following properties are obvious:

    1) $X \subseteq C$, $Y \subseteq D$

    2) $|C| = |D| = |G| = |H| = |C_0|$

    3) $|X| = |Y|$

    4) $C \cup D = G \cup H = C_0 \cup D_0$

Thus, any returned value must specify a G, H, G', H' that satisfy the necessary constraints. It is also clear from the algorithm that FG = TRUE is returned if and only if TEST(G,H) = 0 and, as TEST is a balancing function with respect to P, this occurs if and only if P(G,H) holds. Thus, it is sufficient to show that if TEST = 0 never occurs the algorithm halts, uses at most $\lceil \text{Log}|C_o| \rceil + 2$ calls to TEST, and that either ~G or ~G' upon termination.

We first note that each time the algorithm executes the loop containing steps 2, 3, and 4, the set X is divided in about half. As this can occur at most $\lceil \text{Log}|C_o| \rceil$ times before $|X| = 1$ and the algorithm is forced to halt at step 3, and as there is only one call to TEST in this loop, it is clear that the algorithm must halt and make at most $\lceil \text{Log}|C_o| \rceil + 2$ calls to TEST. Hence, we need only show that ~G or ~G' when $|X| = 1$ and FG = FALSE is returned.

We do this by first proving that

CLAIM: C - X + Y and C are balanceable at all times.

For the final case where $|X| = |Y| = 1$, this easily shows that either ~G or ~(C - X + Y) as either $\tilde{N}(G) \leq \ell \leq \tilde{N}(C - X + Y)$ or $N(C) \geq \ell \geq \tilde{N}(C - X + Y)$ must hold, and $|\tilde{N}(C) - \tilde{N}(C - X + Y)| = 1$ implies that either $N(C) = \ell$ or $N(C - X) = \ell$ if ℓ is integral or $N(C), N(C - X + Y) \in \{\lceil \ell \rceil, \lfloor \ell \rfloor\}$ if ℓ is not integral.

To prove this claim, we use induction on the number of times through the loop containing steps 2, 3, and 4. Initially, $X = C_o - C_o \cap D_o$, $Y = D_o - C_o \cap D_o$ and $C_o = C_o$, $C_o - X + Y = D_o$ and the claim holds because C_o and D_o are balanced by assumption. We complete the proof by showing that this property is maintained in the new C, X, Y computed in step 4. Let

$$C = X_1 + X_2 + \bar{C}, \quad C' = Y_1 + X_2 + \bar{C} = G, \quad C'' = Y_1 + Y_2 + \bar{C} = C-X+Y$$

$$D = Y_1 + Y_2 + \bar{D}, \quad D' = X_1 + Y_2 + \bar{D} = H, \quad D'' = X_1 + X_2 + \bar{D} = D-Y+X$$

and suppose without loss of generality that TEST(C,D) = -1. Then it must be the case that $\tilde{N}(C) \geq \ell$ and hence by the inductive hypothesis, $N(C'') \leq \ell$. There are then two cases to consider:

CASE 1:   TEST(C',D') = -1. Here $\tilde{N}(C') \geq \ell \geq \tilde{N}(C'')$ and C' and C''
are balanceable.

CASE 2:   TEST(C',D') = +1. Here $\tilde{N}(C') \leq \ell \leq \tilde{N}(C)$ and C and C'
are balanceable.

But then the claim and the lemma follow as step 4 defines the
new sets C, X, and Y properly in both these cases.   □

The claim we used to prove this lemma is also interesting in
itself. In particular, if the algorithm terminates with
FG = FALSE then G and G' are actually C and C - X + Y and hence
we note

COROLLARY 3.3:   If BALANCE terminates with FG = FALSE, then G
and G' are balanceable.   □

C.   An Example of Balancing -- CHECK

As a simple illustration of this method of balancing and its
uses, we show how it can be used to determine if the median of a
k-set is a member of a specific subset of that set or not.   In
sections 4, 5, and 6, we use this algorithm as a subroutine for
algorithms that actually compromise databases.   In this section
however, we just present the algorithm and prove that it works.

Let E be a k-set, m(E) = M, and let $\chi \in$ E be the unique
element whose value is M.   Suppose E can be separated into disjoint subsets E = A + B and suppose we are given sets C, D dis-
joint from E such that $|C| = |D| = |A|$ and m(C+B) $\leq$ m(A+B) =
M $\leq$ m(D+B).   Then we will define an algorithm CHECK to determine
if $\chi \in$ A or $\chi \in$ B.   This algorithm will operate by balancing C
and D with respect to M such that the resultant set, C', has
exactly N(A) negative elements.   It is easy to see that
m(C'+B) = M if and only if $\chi \in$ B and hence by using one additional query after determining C', we can determine whether
$\chi \in$ A or $\chi \in$ B.

We first define a balancing function CHECKBAL that attempts
to determine if the given set has too many or too few negative
elements.   This function incorporates a predicate to test if the
median of the given set together with the set B is exactly M and
hence if $\chi \in$ B.   In particular:

FUNCTION CHECKBAL (G,H):

GIVEN: Sets G,H along with implicit sets A,B such that
$|G| = |H| = |A|$, m(A+B) = M, ℓ = N(A), and G+B and H+B are
balanceable.

1. Compute M_1 = m(G+B).

2. If M_1 = M then return 0, if M_1 > M then return +1, if M_1 < M then return -1.   □

It is clear that

Lemma 3.4: CHECKBAL (G,H) is a balancing function with respect to the property P + {m(G+B) = M}, the median M and the value N(A).

Proof: This follows immediately as m(G+B) $\geq$ m(A+B) = M if and only if N(G) $\leq$ N(A) and m(G+B) $\leq$ m(A+B) = M if and only if N(G) $\geq$ N(A).   □

We use this balancing function along with the given initial sets C and D to define the algorithm CHECK:

ALGORITHM: CHECK

GIVEN: Given sets A,B,C,D such that $|C|$ = $|D|$ = $|A|$, (A∪B)∩(C∪D) = ϕ, and m(C+B) $\leq$ m(A+B) = M $\leq$ m(D+B).

FIND: Whether the unique element χ ε A+B with value M is in A or in B.

1. Compute BALANCE with CHECKBAL and sets C,D, and A. Let FG be the Boolean flag that results.
2. If FG = TRUE then χ ε B; if FG = FALSE then χ ε A.

   □

We can easily show that this algorithm works and requires only $O(\text{Log}|A|)$ queries by referring to Lemma 3.2.

In particular

Lemma 3.5: CHECK correctly indicates whether χ ε A or χ ε B and uses only $O(\text{Log}|A|)$ queries.

Proof: Since the function CHECKBAL makes only one query, Lemma 3.2 shows that the algorithm CHECK makes at most $\lceil \text{Log}|A| \rceil$+2 queries. Moreover, if FG = TRUE is returned, Lemma 3 shows that P = {m(G+B) = M} must hold and hence, by the uniqueness of χ, χ ε B. Hence, it is sufficient to show that if FG = FALSE is returned, then χ ε A. From Lemma 3.2, we note that one of the returned sets, say G, must be balanced. But then if χ ε B, m(G+B) = M as the median is determined only by the number of negative elements in G+B which by assumption is the same as the number in A+B. But, this cannot be the case as CHECKBAL(G,H) $\neq$ 0 and hence $\chi \notin$ B; thus χ ε A.   □

This example illustrates the usefulness and the power of the method of balancing. In the next section of this paper, we use the technique first to determine some element of a database both probabilistically and deterministically and then to determine the value of particular elements of the database.

IV.   COMPROMISING A DATABASE PROBABILISTICALLY

The technique of balancing and the algorithm CHECK intro-duced in the previous section can be efficiently used to compro-mise a database. In particular, if we are given a k-set of elements S from the database such that $m(S) = M$, CHECK can be used in a binary search that will isolate the unique element $\chi \in S$ whose value is M. To do this, it is first used to deter-mine which half of S χ lies in, then which quarter of S, then which eighth, and so on. This approach requires only $O(\text{Log } k)$ applications of CHECK, and hence only $O(\text{Log}^2 k)$ queries, to compromise a database.

Unfortunately, this straightforward approach cannot be implemented in the obvious way because of the conditions imposed by CHECK on the two sets used to do the balancing. It is generally difficult to find sets C and D for a given set $A \subseteq S$ such that
$$m(C+B) \leq m(A+B) \leq m(D+B)$$
where $B = S - A$. In this and the next section, we demonstrate two methods whereby these sets can be computed at each stage of the binary search from the corresponding sets of the previous stage. The first method is simpler but is probabilistic in nature -- it can use any number of queries, but with probability $1-\varepsilon$ for any $\varepsilon > 0$ it will use only $O(\text{Log }^2 k)$ queries. The second method is more complex, requiring another application of the balancing algorithm, but is guaranteed to always work using $O(\text{Log}^2 k)$ queries.

A.   *The General Approach*

Even without specifying exactly how we are going to compute the necessary sets, we can present an algorithm to implement this divide and conquer approach to compromising a database. We begin by computing the median of three sets, A, C, and D, and then relabeling them so that for $B = \phi$ and $\chi \in A$,
$$m(C+B) \leq m(A+B) \leq m(D+B).$$

This provides the basis for a recursive algorithm which contin-ually splits A in half which maintaining $\chi \in A$ and simultaneously splitting C and D so that condition 4.1 still holds. The basic algorithm is:

ALGORITHM: FINDMEDIAN - compromise a database

GIVEN: A database $\bar{X}$ of $n \geq 3k$ elements.

FIND: An element $\chi \in \bar{X}$ with a known value.

1. {Initialization} Form 3 disjoint k-sets, A, C, D. Compute m(A), m(C), m(D). Relabel the 3 sets so that m(C) < m(A) < m(D). Let M = m(A) and let $\chi \in A$ be the unique element with value M. Let B = ϕ.

2. {Splitting} Apply some splitting algorithm to A, B, C, D to find A' $\subseteq$ A, C' $\subseteq$ C, D' $\subseteq$ D, B' = B + A - A' such that

   2a) $|C'| = |D'| = |A'| \in \{\lfloor |A|/2 \rfloor , \lceil |A|/2 \rceil\}$

   2b) $m(C'+B') \leq m(A'+B') = M \leq m(D' + B')$, and

   2c) $\chi \in A'$.

3. {Recurse} If $|A'| = 1$ then return (χ has value M). Otherwise, set A, B, C, D = A', B', C', D' and go back to step 2. □

From the divide and conquer nature of this algorithm, it is easy to note that

Lemma 4.1: If the splitting algorithm of step 2 requires O(Log k) queries, then FINDMEDIAN will determine the element χ using $O(Log^2 k)$ queries.

Proof: Clearly as $\chi \in A'$ is guaranteed at each step, if $|A'| = 1$, A' = $\{\chi\}$ and the algorithm determines χ correctly. Moreover, as A is originally of size k and is about divided in half each time the splitting algorithm is executed, this algorithm will be executed only O(Log k) times. Hence at most $O(Log^2 k)$ queries will be required. □

In the next section, we provide a simple splitting algorithm that achieves this O(Log k) bound with any fixed probability $0 < \alpha < 1$.

B.   A Probabilistic Splitting Algorithm

The splitting required in step 2 of this algorithm can be accomplished by randomly choosing the subsets A', C', D' until we find one that can be used as input to CHECK to determine if $\chi \in A'$. At each stage, we are given sets A, B, C, D such that

$$m(C+B) \leq m(A+B) \leq m(D+B)$$

and hence, it is reasonable to assume that if we make enough random selections of $C' \subseteq C$, $D' \subseteq D$ and $A' \subseteq A$, we will find one where

$$m(C'+B') \leq m(A' + B') \leq m(D' + B')$$

and

$$m(C'+B'') \leq m(A-A'+B'') \leq m(D'+B'')$$

for appropriate B' and B''. Once this situation occurs, we can apply CHECK to A', using C' and D', to test if $\chi \in A'$ or $\chi \in A-A'$ and hence finish the split.

The exact algorithm we use here is

ALGORITHM PROBSPLIT - probabilistic splitting

GIVEN: Sets C, D, A, B as in FINDMEDIAN step 2.

FIND: Sets $C' \subseteq C$, $D' \subseteq D$, $A' \subseteq A$, B' = B + A-A' such that

    a) $|C'| = |D'| = |A'| \in \{\lceil |A|/2 \rceil, \lfloor |A|/2 \rfloor\}$

    b) $m(C'+B') \leq m(A'+B') = M \leq m(D'+B')$

    c) $\chi \in A'$.

1.   Randomly choose $C' \subseteq C$; $D' \subseteq D$; A', $A'' \subseteq A$ and sets B' = B+A-A', B'' = B+A-A'' such that

    a) $|C'| = |D'| = |A'| = |A''| = \lceil |A|/2 \rceil$,

    b) $A' \cup A'' = A$.

2.   Compute $m(C'+B')$, $m(C'+B'')$, $m(D'+B')$, $m(D'+B'')$. If $m(C'+B') > M$ or $m(C'+B'') > M$ or $m(C'+B') < M$ or $m(D'+B'') < M$ then repeat step 1.

3.   Apply CHECK to A', B', C', D' to test if $\chi \in A'$. If so, return A', B', C', D'. If not, return A'', B'', C', D''.   □

It is clear that this algorithm correctly splits A,C, and D since

Lemma 4.2: If PROBSPLIT halts then the values returned satisfy the requirements of FINDMEDIAN step 2.

Proof: Step 2 of PROBSPLIT insures that both

$$m(C'+B') < m(A'+B') < m(D'+B')$$

and

$$m(C'+B'') < m(A''+B'') < m(D'+B'')$$

hold and hence that either of (A', C', D') or (A'', C', D') satisfy requirements 2a and 2b of FINDMEDIAN. Moreover, lemma 3.5 insures that step 3 will correctly determine if $\chi \in A'$ or not. If it is then (A', C', D') satisfies the conditions. If not, $\chi \in A - A' \subseteq A''$ and hence (A'', C', D') satisfies the condition. $\qquad\qquad\square$

The number of queries required by this splitting algorithm is just $O(\text{Log } k) + 4n$ where n is the number of times that steps 1 and 2 must be executed. In order to determine the expected number of queries required by the algorithm for a random database, we must determine what the expected value is for n. We start by showing that the probability of making a proper selection in step 1 is greater than some constant c_o.

Lemma 4.3: Given that $m(C+B) \leq m(A+B) \leq m(D+B)$, the probability of choosing $C' \subseteq C$; $D' \subseteq D$; A', $A'' \subseteq A$ and setting $B' = B+A-A'$, $B'' = B+A-A''$ such that $A' \cup A'' = A$, $m(C'+B') < m(A'+B') < m(D'+B')$ and $m(C'+B'') < m(A''+B'') < m(D'+B'')$, is greater than some constant c_o.

Proof: Since $m(C+B) \leq m(A+B) \leq m(D+B)$, it follows that $N(C) \geq N(A) \geq N(D)$. It clearly suffices to show that the probability of making a proper selection is $\geq c_o$ for the case $N(C) = N(A) = N(D)$. We define the variation v in each random choice as

$$v(X') = |N(X') - N(X - X')|$$

for $\chi \in \{A,C,D\}$. Then as $|v(A') - v(A'')| \leq 1$ we can guarantee that a proper choice exists if

$$v(C'), v(D') \geq v(A') \geq v(A'')$$

and we choose the "proper" half of C for C' and D for D'. This latter probability is at least $\frac{1}{2} \cdot \frac{1}{2} = \frac{1}{4}$ and the probability that $v(A') \geq v(A'')$ is at least $\frac{1}{2}$. Moreover, as A',C' and D' are chosen independently, the following cases are equally probable:

$$v(C'), \ v(D') \geq v(A')$$

$$v(C'), \ v(A') \geq v(D')$$

$$v(D'), \ v(A') \geq v(C')$$

As these span all possible cases, the probability of each must be at least 1/3, and as the first case represents a proper selection, the probability of step 1 succeeding is at least

$$1/3 \cdot 1/4 \cdot 1/2 = 1/24. \qquad\qquad \square$$

Since the probability of making the proper selection is step 1 is greater than some constant c_o, the expected number of times the step will have to be repeated is at worst $1/c_o$ which is $O(1)$. Hence, the expected number of queries required by PROBSPLIT is $O(\text{Log } k) + O(1) = O(\text{Log } k)$ and hence that FINDMEDIAN can operate with an expected number of queries of $O(\text{Log}^2 k)$.

This demonstrates that the expected number of k-median queries required to compromise a database is $O(\text{Log}^2 k)$, however, it gives us no feel for the distribution of the number of queries required -- it is theoretically possible that many applications will require $O(\text{Log}^3 k)$ or even $O(k)$ queries to compromise a database. We show that this is not the case by proving for any constant $0 < \alpha < 1$ that FINDMEDIAN using PROB-SPLIT will compromise a database using only $O(\text{Log}^2 k)$ queries with probability α. In particular, we show

Lemma 4.4: The number of times that step 1 of PROBSPLIT must be executed during the execution of FINDMEDIAN is $O(\text{Log } k)$ with probability α for any fixed $0 < \alpha < 1$.

Proof: Let c_o be the minimum probability that stage 1 makes a successful choice as determined by lemma 4.3. Since this minimum probability is independent of previous successes or failures and the size of the set being selected, we can view all the executions of step 1 of PROBSPLIT during the execution of FINDMEDIAN in a worst case sense as a sequence of Bernoulli trials [F], each with probability of success c_o and probability of failure $1-c_o$. For the whole algorithm to succeed, it suffices to show that any such sequence of $n = O(\text{Log } k)$ trials will have $\lceil \text{Log } k \rceil + 2$ successes with probability α.

Let $q = 1-c_o$, $r = \text{Log } k + 3 \geq \lceil \text{Log } k \rceil + 2$, $\beta = 1-\alpha$. Let S_n be the number of successes in n trials. Then we must establish that

$$P_R \{S_n \leq r\} \leq 1 - \alpha = \beta.$$

It is known [F] that

$$P_R \{S_n \leq r\} \leq \frac{(n-r)c_o}{(nc_o-r)^2} \text{ for } r < nc_o$$

and hence it suffices to show that

$$\frac{(n-r)c_o}{(nc_o-r)^2} \leq \beta$$

for some $n > \dfrac{r}{c_o}$ which is $0(\text{Log } k)$.

Let

$$n \geq \frac{3\text{Log } k + 9}{c_o} + \frac{1}{\beta c_o} \approx 0(\text{Log } k).$$

Then

$$n \geq \frac{3\beta r + 1}{\beta c_o} = \frac{6\beta r + 2}{2\beta c_o} \geq \frac{6\beta r + 2 - 4\beta r c_o}{2\beta c_o}$$

$$\geq \frac{2\beta r + 1 + 1 + 4\beta r(1-c_o)}{2\beta c_o}$$

$$\geq \frac{2\beta r + 1 + \sqrt{1 + 4\beta r(1-c_o)}}{2\beta c_o} \geq \frac{2\beta r + 1 - \sqrt{1 + 4\beta r(1-c_o)}}{2\beta c_o}$$

But then

$$\left(n - \frac{2\beta r + 1 + \sqrt{1 + 4\beta r(1-c_o)}}{2\beta c_o} \right)\left(n - \frac{2\beta r + 1 - \sqrt{1 + 4\beta r(1-c_o)}}{2\beta c_o} \geq 0 \right)$$

or

$$\beta c_o^2 n - 2\beta c_o rn - nc_o + \beta r^2 + rc_o \geq 0$$

$$\beta (c_o^2 n^2 - 2c_o rn + r^2) \geq nc_o - rc_o$$

and hence

$$\beta \geq \frac{(n - r)\ c_o}{(nc_o - r)^2} .$$ □

From this and the preceding lemmas, it is easy to conclude that:

Theorem 4.5: A database can be compromised using n k—median queries where n is $O(Log^2 k)$ with probability $1 - \varepsilon$ for any $\varepsilon > 0$.   □

V. COMPROMISING A DATABASE

The results of the previous section show that a database can be easily compromised using only $O(Log^2 k)$ queries almost all of the time. The question still remains as to how many queries are required to guarantee that a database can be compromised. Previous results have shown that $O(\sqrt{k})$ k-median queries are sufficient [DLR]. In this section, we improve this bound by developing a deterministic splitting algorithm that uses $O(Log\ k)$ queries. In conjunction with the algorithm FINDMEDIAN of the previous section, this allows us to insure compromise with only $O(Log^2 k)$ queries.

The idea behind this new splitting algorithm is to take an arbitrary division of A, C, and D as in the previous section and then, rather than discarding it if it is not proper, modifying it so that the necessary conditions are met. In the analysis of the probabilistic splitting algorithm, we noted that for a random split of A, C, and D to be proper, it was enough to insure that $C' \subseteq C$ and $D' \subseteq D$ have greater variance than $A' \subseteq A$ and $A'' \subseteq A$ and that this variance is in the proper direction (i.e. C' has more negative elements and D' has more positive elements). Since we are dividing C and D in half, and since we know that one of the halves must have more negative elements and the other more positive elements, rather than just choosing one and hoping it is correct, we try them both and use the proper one. Thus, we need only modify A' and A'' until they have smaller variances than both halves of C and D. This is accomplished by using balancing algorithm of section 3 to modify the two halves of A until they both have about the same number of negative and positive elements.

This simple approach is complicated by two factors. First of all, there are cases where the C' or D' that are selected exhibit little or no variance and the desired relationships between C', D', A' and A'',

$$m(C'+B') \leq m(A'+B') = M \leq m(D'+B')$$

and

$$m(C'+B'') \leq m(A''+B'') = M \leq m(D'+B''),$$

cannot be achieved. We show that this case is easily recognized and that when it occurs we can determine which of $\chi \in A'$ or $\chi \in A''$ holds and are able to use the proper set recursively. The second complication is that the size of A may be odd and hence it is impossible to divide A, C, or D into two equal sets. We handle this by splitting each of these sets into either two sets that overlap by one element or into two equal sets with an extra element. This makes the simple analysis that follows much more complex.

A. *The Splitting Algorithm*

Our particular algorithm operates by first dividing each of A, C, and D into 3 disjoint sets, X_1, X_2, X_3 for $X \in \{A,C,D\}$, such that $|X_1| = |X_2| = \lfloor |X|/2 \rfloor$ and $|X_3| \in \{0,1\}$. We denote such a division function by $DIVIDE(X) \to \langle X_1, X_2, X_3 \rangle$. Using the divided sets, we let $\bar{C}$ be the more negative of $C_1 + C_3$ and $C_2 + C_3$ and we let $\bar{D}$ be the more positive of $D_1 + D_3$ and $D_2 + D_3$. Then, the core of the algorithm consists of balancing A_1 and A_2 until either both satisfy

$$m(\bar{C} + A_i + B) < m(A + B) < m(\bar{D} + A_i + B), \quad i = 1,2 \quad (5.1)$$

or until they have an equal number of negative elements. In the first case, we use CHECK to determine which of $A_i + A_3$ contains the element χ and then return with this set, $\bar{C}$ and $\bar{D}$ for the next stage of FINDMEDIAN. In the latter case, we show that a condition similar to (5.1) must hold for the A_i which contains χ once A_1 and A_2 are balanced. Hence, we apply CHECK to the appropriate sets, determine which of $\chi \in A_1+A_3$ or $\chi \in A_2+A_3$ holds, and return to FINDMEDIAN correctly.

The specific algorithm is:

ALGORITHM SPLIT - deterministic splitting

GIVEN: Sets C, D, A, B as in FINDMEDIAN step 2.

FIND: Sets $C' \subseteq C$, $D' \subseteq D$, $A' \subseteq A$, $B' \subseteq B + A - A'$ such that

    a) $|C'| = |D'| = |A'| \; \varepsilon \; \{\lceil |A|/2 \rceil, \lfloor |A|/2 \rfloor\}$

    b) $m(C'+B') \leq m(A'+B') = M \leq m(D'+B')$

    c) $\chi \; \varepsilon \; A'$.

1. $DIVIDE(A) \rightarrow \langle A_1, A_2, A_3 \rangle$; $DIVIDE(C) \rightarrow \langle C_1, C_2, C_3 \rangle$;

     $DIVIDE(D) \rightarrow \langle D_1, D_2, D_3 \rangle$.

2.   BALANCE A_1 and A_2 yielding A_1, A_2, A_1', A_2' until either

    a) $m(\bar{C}+A_1+B) \leq m(A+B) \leq m(\bar{D}+A_1+B)$ and

        $m(\bar{C}+A_2+B) \leq m(A+B) \leq m(\bar{D}+A_2+B)$ where

        $\bar{C} \; \varepsilon \; \{C_1+C_3, \; C_2+C_3\}$, $\bar{D} \; \varepsilon \; \{D_1+D_3, \; D_2+D_3\}$; or

    b) $|\bar{N}(A_1) - \bar{N}(A_2)| \leq 1$ or $|\bar{N}(A_1') - \bar{N}(A_2')| \leq 1$

3.   If condition a) holds then apply CHECK to $A_2 + A_3$, $A_1 + B$,

     $\bar{C}$ and $\bar{D}$ to test if $\chi \; \varepsilon \; A_2 + B$, or $\chi \; \varepsilon \; A_1 + B$. If

     $\chi \; \varepsilon \; A_2 + A_3$ then return $\langle \bar{C}, \bar{D}, A_2 + A_3, B + A_1 \rangle$

     as $\langle C', D', A', B' \rangle$. Otherwise, return $\langle \bar{C}, \bar{D}, A_1 + A_3, B + A_2 \rangle$

     as $\langle C', D', A', B' \rangle$.

4.   If condition a) fails to hold then if SPLITCHECK

     $(A_1, A_2, A_3, B, C_1, C_2, C_3, D_1, D_2, D_3)$ is not NIL, return its value.

     Otherwise if SPLITCHECK $(A_1', A_2', A_3, B, C_1, C_2, C_3, D_1, D_2, D_3)$ is

     not NIL, return its value. Otherwise, χ is A_3 and we are
     done.

                                                        □

Here the algorithm SPLITCHECK does the necessary tests to determine a new A', C', D' based on the fact that A_1 and A_2 (or A_1' and A_2') are balanced. It is guaranteed to return a satisfactory split if A_1 and A_2 are balanced and $\chi \notin A_3$ and hence, either one of the two calls in step 4 will succeed or we will know that χ is the unique element in A_3.

To show that this algorithm correctly splits A, C, and D and uses no more than 0(Log k) queries, we divide our analysis into three distinct parts. We first note that if condition a) of step 2 holds at any time, the algorithm splits A,C, and D correctly. Secondly, we present the appropriate balancing algorithm for step 2 and prove its properties. Finally, we show that if A_1 and A_2 are balanced by this algorithm so that they have about an equal number of negative elements, then the algorithm SPLITCHECK and hence, step 4 of this algorithm yields a correct split and uses only 0(Log k) queries. Thus, since CHECK in step 3 uses only 0(Log(k)) queries, the whole algorithm must correctly split A, C, and D and use no more than 0(Log k) queries.

B.   The Case Where Step 3 is Executed

The case where condition a) of step 2 holds is essentially the same as the probabilistic splitting algorithm of the previous section with C' = $\bar{C}$, D' = D', A' = $A_1 + A_3$, B' = $A_2 + B$, A'' = $A_2 + A_3$, B'' = $A_1 + B$ and hence from lemma 4.2 we can conclude that

Lemma 5.1: If condition a) of step 2 holds, then SPLIT properly returns A', B', C', D' and uses at most 0(Log k) queries in step 3.

Proof: Lemma 4.2 and the above discussion demonstrates that A', C', and D' represent a proper split of A, C, and D. Moreover, since the only queries involved in step 3 come from a single execution of CHECK, lemma 3.5 shows that at most 0(Log k) queries can be asked.   □

C.   The Balancing Process

The previous lemma demonstrates that if condition a) of step 2 ever holds, then we can easily finish up the splitting process in 0(Log k) steps. Our remaining concern regarding the algorithm SPLIT is to establish what happens if this condition never holds. In particular, we are concerned with the case where the balancing algorithm has terminated so that A_1 and A_2 or A_1' and A_2' have roughly the same number of negative elements and yet have more variance than either C_1 and C_2 or D_1 and D_2. We show that in

this case, the splits of C, D, and A have very specific properties which we can exploit in order to split A.

In order to present and prove the algorithm SPLITCHECK, we
must first establish the balancing algorithm and its properties.
Essentially, this algorithm balances A_1 and A_2 with respect to
condition a) so that the number of negative elements in A_1 is
within one of the number of negative elements in A_2. The
algorithm is

ALGORITHM SPLITBAL - balance A_1 and A_2 for SPLIT

GIVEN: Divided C_1, C_2, C_3 and D_1, D_2, D_3; set B as in algorithm
SPLIT; sets G and H to balance.

ACT: as a balancing function with respect to condition a),
attempting to get the number of negative elements in A_1 equal to
the number in A_2.

1. Evaluate the queries

$$m(C_1 + C_3 + G + B) = M_1$$

$$m(C_2 + C_3 + G + B) = M_2$$

$$m(C_1 + C_3 + H + B) = M_3$$

$$m(C_2 + C_3 + H + B) = M_4$$

$$m(D_1 + D_3 + G + B) = M_5$$

$$m(D_2 + D_3 + G + B) = M_6$$

$$m(D_1 + D_3 + H + B) = M_7$$

$$m(D_2 + D_3 + H + B) = M_8$$

2. If $((M_1 \leq M$ and $M_3 \leq M)$ or $(M_2 \leq M$ and $M_4 \leq M))$ and

$((M_5 \geq M$ and $M_7 \geq M)$ or $(M_6 \geq M$ and $M_8 \geq M))$ then return 0.

3. If $M_1 > M$ and $M_2 > M$ then return +1

    else if $M_3 > M$ and $M_4 > M$ then return -1

    else if $M_5 < M$ and $M_6 < M$ then return -1

    else if $M_7 < M$ and $M_8 < M$ then return +1. $\square$

To prove this is a proper balancing function we show that

Lemma 5.2: SPLITBAL(G,H) returns

a) 0 iff condition a) of step 2 of SPLIT hold;

b) +1 iff $\bar{N}(G) \leq \bar{N}(G)$; and

c) -1 iff $\bar{N}(H) \geq \bar{N}(H)$.

Proof: Clearly step 2 can cause a return of zero if only if condition a) holds for some $\bar{C}$ and $\bar{D}$. Hence, it suffices to show that the tests of step 3 produce a proper result and cover all possible cases.

To show that these tests cover all cases, we assume that no condition at step 3 holds and that step 2 fails as well. Step 2 must fail for either the C's or the D's or both. We assume without loss of generality that it fails at least for the C's. This means that the following must hold:

$$(M_1 > M \vee M_3 > M) \wedge (M_2 > M \vee M_4 > M)$$

Then, as no case of step 3 can hold, it must be the case that either M_1, $M_4 > M$ and M_2, $M_3 \leq M$ or M_2, $M_3 > M$ and M_1, $M_4 \leq M$.

We assume without loss of generality that the first case holds. Let $\alpha = 1$ if $\chi \varepsilon$ GuH and $\alpha = 0$ otherwise. Then, $C_1 + C_3 + G + B$ can have at most $\frac{k-1}{2}$ negative elements and $C_2 + C_3 + H + B$ can have at most $\frac{k-1}{2}$ negative elements and, if $\chi \varepsilon G + H$ one of these must have one fewer. But then

$$N(C_1 + C_2 + C_3 + C_3 + G + H + B + B) \leq \frac{2k-2}{2} - \alpha$$

and since $N(G + H + B) \geq \frac{k-1}{2} - \alpha$, $N(C_3) \geq 0$, we get

$$N(C_1 + C_2 + C_3 + B) \leq \frac{k-1}{2} \ .$$

This is a contradiction since $m(C+B) < m(A+B)$ and hence,

$N(C+B) \geq \frac{k+1}{2} \ .$

Of the four cases in step 3, the first two and the last two are symmetric since one of $\bar{N}(G) \geq \bar{N}(H)$, or $\bar{N}(H) \geq \bar{N}(G)$ must hold. We therefore consider only the first and third cases. Suppose $M_1 > M$ and $M_2 > M$. Then

$$\bar{N}(C_1 + C_3 + G + B) \leq \frac{k-1}{2}$$

and

$$\bar{N}(C_2 + C_3 + G + B) \leq \frac{k-1}{2}$$

and hence

$$\bar{N}(C_1 + C_2 + C_3 + C_3 + G + G + B + B) \leq \frac{2k-2}{2} \ .$$

We have established that $N(C+B) \geq \frac{k+1}{2}$ and hence

$$\bar{N}(C_3 + G + G + B) \leq \frac{k-3}{2}$$

or

$$\bar{N}(G + G + B) \leq \frac{k-1}{2} \ .$$

But then $\bar{N}(G) \leq \bar{N}(H)$ as otherwise

$$\bar{N}(G + H + B) \leq \frac{k-1}{2} - 1$$

which is a contradiction as $\bar{N}(G + H + A_3 + B) = \frac{k+1}{2}$ and hence

$\bar{N}(G+H+B) \geq \frac{k-1}{2} \ .$

The proof for the other two cases is similar. Suppose that $M_5 < M$ and $M_6 < M$. Then $\bar{N}(D_1+D_3+G+B) \geq \frac{k+1}{2}$ and

$\bar{N}(D_2+D_3+G+B) \geq \frac{k+1}{2}$ and hence

$$\bar{N}(D_1 + D_2 + D_3 + G + G + B + B) \geq \frac{2k+2}{2} \ .$$

Now as $\bar{N}(D+B) \leq \frac{k-1}{2}$, and $\bar{N}(D_3) \leq 1$,

$$\bar{N}(G + G + B) \geq \frac{k+1}{2} \ .$$

But then $\bar{N}(G) \geq \bar{N}(H)$ as otherwise

$$\bar{N}(G + H + B) \geq \frac{k+1}{2} + 1$$

which is a contradiction since $\bar{N}(G + H + A_3 + B) = \frac{k+1}{2}$ and hence

$$\bar{N}(G + H + B) \leq \frac{k+1}{2} \ . \qquad \qquad \Box$$

This shows that SPLITBAL is indeed a balancing function with respect to condition a) of step 2 of SPLIT. Moreover, it is clear that it makes only a constant number of queries per execution and hence by lemma 3.2 and corollary 3.3, we get

Lemma 5.3: Let $N(A) = \ell$. Then either we can determine χ directly or χ is in A_i and A_j' as returned from BALANCE, and

$\{N(A_i), N(A_j')\}$ contains

    a) $\{\lceil\frac{\ell}{2}\rceil - 1, \lfloor\frac{\ell}{2}\rfloor - 1\}$ if A_3 is positive or empty; or

    b) $\{\lceil\frac{\ell-1}{2}\rceil - 1, \lfloor\frac{\ell-1}{2}\rfloor - 1\}$ if A_3 is negative.

Proof: We first note that cases a) and b) are symmetric there are ℓ negative elements in $A_1 + A_2$ if A_3 is positive or empty and only $\ell-1$ if A_3 is negative. Hence, we need only prove case a).

Clearly, if ℓ is even, then $\{\lceil\frac{\ell}{2}\rceil - 1, \lfloor\frac{\ell}{2}\rfloor - 1\} =$

$\{\frac{\ell}{2} - 1\}$ and as one of A_i and A_j' must be balanced, it must

satisfy $\bar{N}(X) = \frac{\ell}{2}$ and hence $N(X) = \frac{\ell}{2} - 1$. If ℓ is odd, then the

four sets that are returned by BALANCE are

$$G + X \qquad H + Y$$

$$G + Y \qquad H + X$$

where $|X| = |Y| = 1$, so that

$$\bar{N}(G + X) = \bar{N}(H + X) = \frac{\ell+1}{2} \text{ and } \bar{N}(G + Y) = \bar{N}(H + Y) = \frac{\ell-1}{2}.$$

If $\chi \in G$, then $G + X$ and $G + Y$ satisfy the lemma while if

$\chi \in H$, $H + X$ and $H + Y$ satisfy the lemma. This leaves only the

case that $\chi \in X \cup Y$. But, as $\bar{N}(\chi) = 1$, this implies that $X=\{X\}$

and, since we can tell which of $\bar{N}(G+X) > \bar{N}(G+Y)$ or

$\bar{N}(G+X) < \bar{N}(G+Y)$ holds, we can determine χ. $\square$

D.   The Case Where A_1 and A_2 are Balanced

Having shown in this last lemma what the result of the
balancing process will be with respect to sets containing χ, we
are now ready to describe and verify the algorithm SPLITCHECK.
This algorithm takes advantage of the various conditions that
must be satisfied before step 4 of SPLIT and hence, SPLITCHECK
can be executed. It considers some of the possible sets that
might provide proper splits and then uses CHECK to determine
when a proper split exists. For such a method to succeed, we
need to insure that CHECK is only called with proper arguments,
that at least one of the cases for which CHECK is called will
work, and that CHECK will only be called a constant number of
times.

The algorithm we use is

ALGORITHM SPLITCHECK - test for proper split.

GIVEN: A_1 and A_2 possibly balanced, as well as $A_3, C_1, C_2, C_3,$

D_1, D_2, D_3 from step 4 of SPLIT.

FIND: Sets A', C', D' that form a proper split of A, C, D if possible, NIL if not.

1. For $\bar{C} \in \{C_1 + C_3, C_2 + C_3\}$, $\bar{D} \in \{D_1 + D_3, D_2 + D_3\}$,

   $\bar{A} \in \{A_1 + A_3, A_2 + A_3\}$, $\bar{B} = \{B + A_1 + A_2 + A_3 - \bar{A}\}$, do steps 2-4. If none of these returns a value, return NIL.

2. Compute

$$M_1 = m(\bar{C} + \bar{B})$$

$$M_2 = m(\bar{D} + \bar{B})$$

$$M_3 = m(\bar{C} - C_3 + A_3 + \bar{B})$$

$$M_4 = m(\bar{D} - D_3 + A_3 + \bar{B})$$

3. If $M_1 < M < M_2$ then if CHECK$(\bar{A},\bar{B},\bar{C},\bar{D})$ shows $\chi \in \bar{A}$, return C,D,A as C',D',A'.

4. If $M_3 < M < M_4$ then if CHECK $(\bar{A}-A_3, \bar{B}+A_3, \bar{C}-C_3, \bar{D}-D_3)$ shows

   $\chi \in \bar{A}-A_3$, then return $\bar{C}-C_3$, $\bar{D}-D_3$ and $\bar{A}-A_3$ as C', C', A'. □

It is clear from the specification of SPLITCHECK that the number of queries required is $O(\text{Log } k)$ and that, because of the nature of CHECK, if a value is returned from SPLITCHECK, it must represent a proper split. What remains to be shown is that if $\chi \notin A_3$, then for at least one of the two balanced sets containing χ, one of the calls to SPLITCHECK will return a split. Thus

Lemma 5.4: If $\chi \notin A_3$, then for one of A_i, A_j' such that

$\chi \in A_i \cap A_j'$, the call to SPLITCHECK involving this set must

return a value.

Proof: There are several cases to consider, mainly dependent on the values of A_3, C_3, and D_3. Let $\ell = \bar{N}(A)$ and let $\bar{A}$ be one of $A_i + A_3$, $A'_j + A_3$. From lemma 5.3, we note that $N(\bar{A})$ will take on the values $\{\left\lceil \frac{\ell}{2} \right\rceil - 1, \left\lfloor \frac{\ell}{2} \right\rfloor - 1\}$ if A_3 is empty or positive and the values $\{\left\lceil \frac{\ell-1}{2} \right\rceil, \left\lfloor \frac{\ell-1}{2} \right\rfloor\}$ if A_3 is negative. Hence, it suffices to show that for each case as determined by $|A|$, C_3, D_3 and A_3, that one of these values will cause SPLITCHECK to return a split.

We first note that by simple counting arguments, if we have sets R, S, T and U and an element $\psi \ \varepsilon \ S$ such that ψ is the median element of $A + U$, then

$$N(R) > N(S) \geq N(T)$$

if and only if

$$m(R+U) < m(S+U) < m(T+U).$$

We make extensive use of this fact in the three cases that follow.

Case 1: $|A|$ is even: Then $N(\bar{D}) \leq \left\lfloor \frac{\ell-1}{2} \right\rfloor$ and $N(\bar{C}) \geq \left\lceil \frac{\ell}{2} \right\rceil$ for some $\bar{C}$ and $\bar{D}$ and hence, $N(\bar{A}) = \left\lceil \frac{\ell}{2} \right\rceil - 1$ satisfies $N(\bar{C}) > N(\bar{A}) \geq N(\bar{D})$.

Case 2: $|A|$ is odd, D_3 is positive: Then $N(\bar{D}) \leq \left\lfloor \frac{\ell-1}{2} \right\rfloor$ and $N(\bar{C}) \geq \left\lceil \frac{\ell}{2} \right\rceil$ for some $\bar{C}$ and $\bar{D}$ and hence $N(\bar{A}) = \left\lfloor \frac{\ell}{2} \right\rfloor - 1 = \left\lfloor \frac{\ell-1}{2} \right\rfloor$ satisfies $N(\bar{C}) > N(\bar{A}) \geq N(\bar{D})$.

Case 3: $|A|$ is odd, D_3 is negative: Then $N(\bar{D}-D_3) \leq \left\lfloor \frac{\ell-2}{2} \right\rfloor$ $N(\bar{C}-C_3) \geq \left\lceil \frac{\ell-1}{2} \right\rceil$ and hence $N(\bar{A}-A_3) = \left\lfloor \frac{\ell}{2} \right\rfloor - 1$ if A_3 is positive or $N(\bar{A}-A_3) = \left\lceil \frac{\ell-1}{2} \right\rceil - 1$ if A_3 is negative satisfy $N(\bar{C}-C_3) \geq N(\bar{A}-A_3) \geq N(\bar{D}-D_3)$. □

This completes the specification and verification of the algorithms involved with SPLIT and we can summarize lemmas 5.1 through 5.4 as

Theorem 5.5: Algorithm SPLIT compromises a database using $O(\text{Log}^2 k)$ k-median queries. □

VI. DETERMINING SPECIFIC ELEMENTS

The previous two sections show that it is relatively easy to compromise a database using k-median queries. However, the information that was obtained was about some arbitrary element, and we are often more concerned with determining the value of some specific element. Previous results in this area have shown that if the value of a specific element lies in the α-tile, $0 < \alpha < \frac{1}{2}$, (i.e. in a database of size n, at least αn elements have a smaller value and at least αn elements have a larger value) then it can be compromised using a probabilistic approach with an expected number of queries of $O(k) + \alpha^{-k/2}(1-\alpha)^{-k/2}$. In this section, we improve this exponential bound by showing that for any α and sufficiently large n, there is a probabilistic means of determining the value of any specific element in the α-tile using a expected number of $O(k)$ queries. Moreover, we begin by noting that if a slight amount of extra information is available, compromising a specific element can be done using $O(\text{Log } k)$ or fewer queries.

A. *Using Selector Information*

So far in this paper, we have considered a simplified model of a database in which all selector information has been discarded. While this model may be somewhat unrealistic in the number and type of queries allowed and hence could make a database seem easier to compromise than it actually is, it also ignores a good deal of information that could make compromising a database significantly simpler if not trivial. For example, suppose we wanted to determine the salary of some employee E. Moreover, suppose we know $\frac{k-1}{2}$ other employees who must have smaller salaries than E (i.e. they are mail clerks, secretaries, or assistant professors) and we know $\frac{k-1}{2}$ employees whose salary must be greater than E's. Then by simply asking for the median salary of E and these two groups of employees, we can be assured that the result is E's salary. Hence, using a single query, we can compromise the database.

While it might not be easy to find sets all of whose elements are greater than or less than the element to be determined, it should be considerably easier to find two k-sets, one whose median value is less than the element and one whose median value is greater than the element. We can use these two sets along with the technique of balancing of section 3 to determine the specific element using an expected number of 0(Log k) queries with probability 1-ε for any $0 < ε < 1$.

The algorithm we use here is

ALGORITHM GETVALUE

GIVEN: An element $χ$, two sets of k elements, A, B such that $m(A) < χ < m(B)$.

FIND: The value of $χ$, M.

1. Randomly choose aεA until $M(A-\{a\} + \{χ\}) > M(A)$.

2. Randomly choose bεB until $m(B-\{b\} + \{χ\}) < m(B)$.

3. Balance A-{a} and B-{b} using the following balancing function:

   a) Compute $M_1 = m(G+\{χ\})$, $M_2 = m(G+\{a\})$, $M_3 = m(G+\{b\})$

   b) If $M_1 \neq M_2$ and $M_1 \neq M_3$, then return 0

      else if $M_1 = M_2$ then return +1

      else return -1.

4. If BALANCE returned with FG=FALSE, then $\underline{m}(A) < M < m(B)$ did not hold initially. Otherwise, let $\overline{A}$ be the balanced set that is returned. Then return $m(\overline{A} + \{χ\})$ as the value of $χ$.   □

The method used in this algorithm is straightforward. Step 1 finds an element a in A whose value is $\leq m(A)$ and hence is less than M. Step 2 repeats this process with B to find an element b whose value is $\geq m(B)$ and hence greater than M. Finally, the two sets A-{a} and B-{b} balanced so that the resultant set $\overline{A}$ contains $\frac{k-1}{2}$ negative elements and hence so that

$m(\overline{A} + \{χ\}) = M$ is the value of $χ$. It is clear that steps 3 and 4 use only 0(Log k) median queries. Moreover, if FG = TRUE is returned from BALANCE in step 3, then it must be the case that $M(G + \{χ\}) = M$. Hence, if we can show that the number of queries required in steps 1 and 2 is small and that BALANCE must return with $N(\bar{A}) = \frac{k-1}{2}$ provided that $m(A) < M < m(B)$, then we can prove

Theorem 6.1: Let χ be an element of a database and let A and B be two k-sets of elements, $\chi \neq A \cup B$. Then, GETVALUE will return the value M of χ if $m(A) < M < m(B)$ and moreover, for any constant $0 < \varepsilon < 1$, will use $O(\text{Log } k)$ queries with probability $1-\varepsilon$.

Proof: If $m(A) < M$ then A must have $\frac{k+1}{2}$ negative elements.

Hence, as a is negative, $N(A-\{a\}) \geq \frac{k-1}{2}$. Similarly, as

$m(B) > M$, B must contain at least $\frac{k+1}{2}$ positive elements. Hence

as b is positive, $B-\{b\}$ must have at least $\frac{k-1}{2}$ positive elements.

But then $A-\{a\}$ and $B-\{b\}$ are balanceable with respect to M and

$\frac{k-1}{2}$.

To show that the balancing function of step 3 works, we note that the value of a is less than the value of χ is less than the value of b. Hence, if $m(G+\{\chi\}) < M$, then $m(G+\{\chi\}) = m(G+\{b\})$, while if $m(G+\{\chi\}) > M$ then $m(G+\{\chi\}) = m(G+\{a\})$. Thus, the balancing function returns 0 if and only if $m(G+\{\chi\}) = M$, returns $+1$ if and only if $m(G+\{\chi\}) > M$, and returns -1 if and only if $m(G+\{\chi\}) < M$. But, as $m(G+\{\chi\}) > M$ if and only if

$N(G) < \frac{k-1}{2}$, and as $m(G+\{\chi\}) < M$ if and only if $N(G) > \frac{k-1}{2}$,

lemma 3.2 shows that one of $\bar{A}$ and A' returned from BALANCE using

the balancing function must have $\frac{k-1}{2}$ negative elements. More-

over, because both these sets are tested by the balancing function at some point, this function must return with FG=TRUE. Hence, $m(\bar{A}+\{\chi\}) = M$ and the algorithm is guaranteed to return the proper value.

Finally, since $N(A) \geq \frac{k+1}{2}$ and since B has at least $\frac{k+1}{2}$

positive elements, the probability of choosing a or b correctly

in steps 1 or 2 is greater than $\frac{1}{2}$. Then, let α_n be the

probability of completing either step 1 or step 2 in n or fewer

tests. We need to show that $\alpha_n^2 \geq 1-\varepsilon$ for reasonable n. Let

$c_0 = -\text{Log}(1-\sqrt{1-\varepsilon})$ be a constant dependent on ε. Then choosing

$n \geq c_0$ is sufficient. Hence, at most $0(c_0) = 0(1)$ queries should

be required in steps 1 and 2.   □

B.   The General Case

While it may often be the case that enough information is
known about an element to determine a set of data with a lower
median and a set with a higher median, such an assumption cannot
be made in the general case. We next consider the task of comp-
promising a specific element of a random database where no
selection information is present. Here, we suppose that we are
given an element   which lies in some α-tile of the database and
we are interested in the average number of queries required to
determine its value.

We determine this value by choosing a random set of elements
such that the set is likely to contain at least $\frac{k-1}{2}$ elements

both less than and greater to the value of χ, M. Once we have
such a set, we need only isolate the subsets of elements that
are less than and greater than M to determine the desired value
using the techniques of section 6.1. To efficiently perform
this isolation process, we make use of the theorem of [DJL]:

Lemma: In $3k + 0(1)$ k-median queries, we can determine the
median M' of a set of elements $Y_1 \ldots Y_k$ of a database; and moreover, we can determine for each j, whether $Y_j < M'$, $y_j = M'$, or
$y_j > M'$.   □

To use this lemma to isolate the negative and positive subsets, we start with a set of $\ell(k-1)$ elements for some ℓ, and
apply this method to ℓ disjoint sets of $(k-1)$ elements joined
with the element χ in order to determine a set of

$\frac{\ell}{2}(k-1)$ elements that are all less than the respective median of

the ℓ set. We then repeat this process with the resultant
elements until we find a median whose value is less than the
given element. This terminating condition can easily be determined since χ is in the set to which we apply the method of the
lemma. Once a negative subset is found, we can repeat this
whole process to find a positive subset. This, however, is
generally not necessary since the original set had to have either
a larger or smaller median than M and, hence, the process is
needed only to determine one of the two subsets. Once we have a

set with a larger median than M and a set with a smaller median than M, we can apply the results of the previous section to determine the value of χ with one extra query.

The number of times the method of the lemma must be applied in the process is at most

$$\ell + \frac{\ell}{2} + \frac{\ell}{4} + \ldots + 1 \sim 2\ell$$

and hence, at most $O(\ell k)$ queries are all that is required. Moreover, if e is a negative element, then it is easy to see that e is always used in the next stage of the algorithm provided that the test it is used in at the current stage has a median greater than M. But this must occur since if the median were $\geq$ M, we would be done. Hence, all elements of the original

set <M are gathered together by this process and if there were

more than $\frac{k-1}{2}$ such elements in the original set, a median must

eventually be achieved that is <M. Similarly, a median must be achieved that is >M.

Thus, it is sufficient to determine the value of ℓ to determine the expected number of queries needed to compromise χ. By assuming that χ is in the α-tile for some $0 < \alpha < \frac{1}{2}$, we can show

Lemma 6.2: Let χ be in the α-tile for some α. Then, for any constant $0 < c < 1$, a random set of

$$n \geq \frac{3c\left(\dfrac{k-1}{2}\right) + 1}{c\alpha} \sim O\!\left(\frac{k}{\alpha}\right)$$

will have $\frac{k-1}{2}$ negative elements with probability 1-c.

Proof: We assume that the size of the database is sufficiently large that can estimate the probability of an element being negative as α even as we have chosen about n elements. Then,

the probability of choosing fewer than $r = \frac{k-3}{2}$ negative elements

in a sample of size n can be estimated as [F].

$$P_R \{S_n \leq r\} \leq \frac{(n-r)\alpha}{(n\alpha-r)^2} \quad \text{for } r < n\alpha \ .$$

From the proof of lemma 4.4, when

$$n \geq \frac{3cr + 1}{c\alpha}$$

we have $P_r \{S_n \leq r\} \leq c$.

From this lemma, we can conclude

Theorem 6.3: Let χ be in the α-tile of a large database. Then we can determine the value of χ using $0\left(\frac{k}{\alpha}\right)$ queries with probability $1-\varepsilon$ for any $\varepsilon > 0$.   □

And hence

COROLLARY 6.4: Let χ be in the α-tile of a large database for a fixed α. Then, we can determine the value of χ using $0(k)$ queries with probability $1-\varepsilon$ for any $\varepsilon > 0$.   □

VII.   CONCLUSION

This study shows that it is very difficult to insure security in a database when queries involving the median are allowed. In particular, it is shown that some arbitrary element can be compromised with only $0(Log^2 k)$ queries and that a specific element can generally be determined in $0(k)$ queries unless its value is extreme. Moreover, if outside data is known about a specific element, then it can often be determined in $0(Log k)$ or fewer queries. This suggests the interesting problem of what reasonable and enforceable restrictions can be placed on a database system so that median queries could be allowed while maintaining the privacy of the data.

Another interesting open problem suggested by our results is whether they are the best possible. The best lower bound on the number of median queries required is $0(Log k)$ [DDL2] while the upper bound given in this paper is $0(Log^2 k)$. It seems difficult to insure that a database can be compromised in anything less than $0(Log^2 k)$ queries. Moreover, the results of section 6 demonstrate that proving a lower bound greater than $0(Log k)$ is probably just as difficult.

REFERENCES

[DDL1] R. DeMillo, D. Dobkin, and R. Lipton, "Even Databases
That Lie Can Be Compromised", *IEEE Transactions on Software
Engineering*, Vol. SE-4, No. 1, pp. 73-74.

[DDL2] R. DeMillo, D. Dobkin, and R. Lipton, "Combinatorial
Inference," this volume.

[DJL] D. Dobkin, A. Johns, and R. Lipton, "Secure Databases:
Protection Against User Inference," (submitted for pulica-
tion).

[DL] D. Dobkin and R. Lipton, "Complexity Aspects of Database
Security," (unpublished manuscript).

[DLR] D. Dobkin, R. Lipton, and S. Reiss, "Aspects of the
Database Security Problem," *Proceedings of a Conference on
Theoretical Computer Science*, pp. 262-274, University of
Waterloo, 1977.

[F] William Feller, *An Introduction to Probability Theory and
Its Applications*, Vol. I. John Wiley & Sons, Inc., 1960.

[R] S. Reiss, "Security in Databases: A Combinatorial Study,"
(submitted for publication).

SECTION II. ENCRYPTION AS A SECURITY MECHANISM

Of all the security techniques which are currently under
investigation, encryption and data security has attracted the
most public attention. Perhaps this is because cryptography has
been a favorite activity of amateur mathematicians and has
figured prominently in literature ranging from historical studies
to the exploits of Sherlock Holmes. Indeed, at the time of the
assemblage of these papers (October 1977), events reported in
scientific and public outlets broke so quickly that aspects of
several of the papers in the section were not known in detail
until our gathering in Atlanta.

The five papers presented here are truly representative of
current research in data encryption. George Davida and John Kam
propose a type of substitution - permutation encryption network
design. Their intent is to provide a variant of the NBS data
encryption standard which obviates several of the objections
raised by Hellman and Diffie and others. Richard DeMillo,
Richard Lipton and Larry McNeil raise a novel application for
encryption research: the protection through encryption of
commercial software from overt theft. Gerald Popek and Charles
Kline correctly point out that often times the protocol through
which encryption algorithms are made available have significant
impact on their effectiveness. They examine several encryption
algorithms from this perspective. A surprising probabilistic
method for creating secure digital signatures is the subject of
Michael Rabin's article. He presents a method which can be
based upon any block encoding function that satisfies three
simple axioms. Ronald Rivest, Len Adelman and Michael Dertouzos
address a serious defect in current methods of encrypting data:
coded information must be decoded before it can be manipulated.
Out of all possible privacy transformations, the authors select
the *privacy homomorphisms* which allow data to be operated upon
in its encrypted form.

A STRUCTURED DESIGN OF SUBSTITUTION-PERMUTATION ENCRYPTION NETWORK*

John B. Kam

Department of Electrical Engineering & Computer Science
Columbia University
New York, New York

George I. Davida

Department of Electrical Engineering & Computer Science
University of Wisconsin-Milwaukee
Milwaukee, Wisconsin

I.   INTRODUCTION

The advent of large databases and computer networks has created tremendous interest in the area of data security in general and the field of cryptography in particular [1-8].

* *The research reported in this paper was supported in part by the National Science Foundation under Grant No. MCS 77-02156.*

Recently, a variant of the substitution-permutation encryption scheme developed by IBM [9] was adopted by NBS as the data encryption standard (DES). However, the DES is considered weak by several computer scientists, including Hellman [10-12]. One of the main arguments against DES is the smallness of the key size.

We plan to present a method for designing S-P networks which will ensure that the designed networks may be arbitrarily large and possess certain desirable properties that add more insight to the design of secure encryption devices.

II.   BACKGROUND AND DEFINITIONS

The model we will use for S-P networks is essentially the same as that described by Feistel [13]. In general, each S-P network has three parameters:

(i) $n \equiv$ the number of input (output) bits of the S-P network
(ii) $k \equiv$ the number of input (output) bits for each substitution box
(iii) $\ell \equiv$ the number of substitution-permutation stages.

Figure 1 illustrates an S-P network where $n=9$, $k=3$, $\ell=3$.

In general, each substitution box (S-box) S_{ij} is a logical circuit that implements a one-one correspondence $f: \{0,1\}^k \to \{0,1\}^k$, and different S_{ij}'s may implement different one-one correspondence functions. It is obvious that each S-P network is itself a one-one correspondence function $g: \{0,1\}^n \to \{0,1\}^n$.

In actual applications, we have to guard against the possibility that the internal structures of all S-boxes and permutation may become known to some cryptanalysts. To obtain security even in this situation, we may modify the design of the encryption network by allowing two choices of S-boxes for each S_{ij}, and by including a key register which has as many bits as the number of S-boxes in the network. Before a user encrypts a message, he will first input a binary key to the key register, so that one of the two S-boxes is selected for each S_{ij} according to the values of the corresponding key bit. Figure 2 illustrates an S-P network with the modification and key register incorporated.

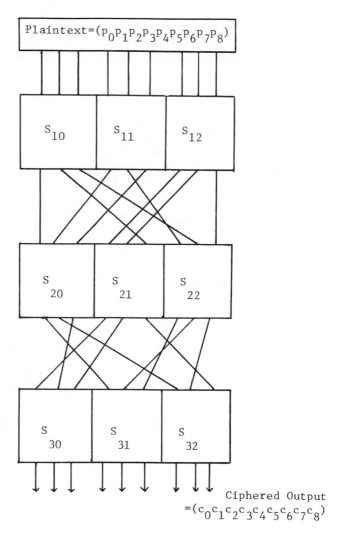

Figure 1.   A Sample S-P Network

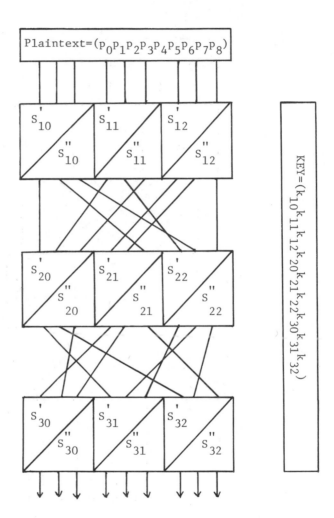

Figure 2.   *A Sample S-P Network With Two Choices Of S-Boxes For Each S_{ij}.*

Several people, including Hellman have recently argued that when the key size is small, this class of encryption schemes is susceptible to attack using exhaustive search of the key values [10]. One obvious remedy to this potential weakness is to enlarge the key size by increasing the number of S-boxes.

In this paper, we are going to present a design scheme for constructing arbitrarily large S-P networks which will always satisfy some desirable properties for all possible key values.

The following notations are useful in describing the networks:

Encryption Key: $K = k_0, \ldots, k_{m-1}$ where $m = \ell \times (n/k)$

Plaintext: $P = P_0, \ldots, P_{n-1}$

Encrypted Output: $C = c_0, \ldots, c_{n-1}$

For brevity, we will denote the encrypted output C of an S-P network as related to the first stage input by SP(P).

III. DESIGN CRITERIA

Following common practice, we may evaluate the strength of an S-P network by its robustness against known plaintext cryptanalytic attacks. The strength of the network is measured by the difficulty in determining the key used, assuming

(i) the internal structure of the S-P network is known to the cryptanalyst and

(ii) the cryptanalyst has obtained some plaintext-cryptogram pairs, with all cryptograms obtained for the corresponding plaintexts, using the same key.

That is, it should be difficult to determine the key directly from plaintext-cryptogram pairs even with the knowledge of the internal structure of the S-P network.

Given the known-plaintext cryptanalytic attack, we can see intuitively that the following property is desirable for S-P networks:

Property Z: For every possible value of the key, every output bit c_i of the S-P network depends on the values of all input bits $P_0, \ldots, P_{n-1}$, not just a proper subset of the input bits.

The following are some arguments indicating why property Z is advantageous. Let us suppose an S-P network does not satisfy the property Z, and for some value of the key, some output bits c_j's depend only on a few input bits. By observing a significant number of plaintext-cryptogram pairs, the cryptanalysts may be able to detect the relations among the c_j's and the corresponding small subsets of input bits. The cryptanalysts may subsequently use this information to facilitate the identification of the key value. However, if a network satisfies property Z, it becomes hard to identify the relation between a particular output bit c_j with the input bits, because c_j depends on all of them.

The formal mathematical definition of property Z follows:

Definition: Give a one-one correspondence $f: \{0,1\}^n \rightarrow \{0,1\}^n$, f is said to be *complete* if, for every $i,j \in \{1,\ldots,n\}$, there exist two n-bit vectors X_1, X_2 such that X_1 and X_2 differ only in the ith bit and $f(X_1)$ differs from $f(X_2)$ at least in the jth bit.

Formally: $(\forall_{i,j})(\exists x_1 x_2, \ldots, x_i, \ldots, x_n) \wedge (\exists x_1 x_2, \ldots, \bar{x}_i, \ldots, x_n)$

$[(f(x_1 x_2, \ldots, x_i, \ldots, x_n) = (y_1, \ldots, y_n)) \wedge (f(x_1 x_2, \ldots, \bar{x}_i, \ldots, x_n) =$

$(z_1, \ldots, z_j, \ldots, z_n)) \wedge (y_j = \bar{z}_j)]$

Definition: A substitution box S is said to be *complete* if the function implemented by S is complete. Similarly, an S-P network is said to be *complete* if the function implemented by the network is complete.

IV. AN ALGORITHM FOR CONSTRUCTING COMPLETE S-P NETWORKS

In this section, we will present a hardware-efficient scheme of implementing arbitrarily large complete S-P networks. In order to minimize unnecessary details in the presentation and proofs, we are going to show only the case where there is only one choice for each S_{ij}. The generalization of the design to the case of two choices for each S_{ij} is straightforward.

Convention 1: The input (output) bits of a single S-box are labeled from 0 through k-1

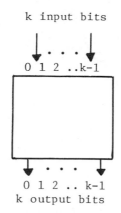

k input bits

0 1 2 ..k-1

0 1 2 .. k-1
k output bits

Convention 2: Given the Ath stage of an S-P network as shown below,

$S_{A,0}$	$S_{A,1}$	...	$S_{A,b}$

the jth input bit of the $S_{A,b}$ box is called the $(b,j)^{IN}_{A^{th}}$ bit of the Ath stage. Similarly, we use $(b,j)^{OUT}_A$ to stand for the jth output bit of $S_{A,b}$.

ALGORITHM COMP

Purpose: To construct an n-bit complete S-P network using k-bit complete substitution boxes, where n is of the form k^{ℓ}, with $\ell \geq 1$ and $k \geq 3$.

Input: ℓ stages of complete S-boxes where the stages are labeled 1 through ℓ and each stage has $k^{\ell-1}$ S-boxes.

Output: A complete n-bit S-P network.

Begin

Integer   STAGE#, GROUP_OFFSET, BIT#, BOX#, PRESENT_BOX#,

LAST_BOX#, LAST_BIT#, BIT_OFFSET;

Comment: The following will connect the inputs in the STAGE#th
stage to the outputs of the (STAGE#-1)st stage.

for STAGE# :=2 *step* 1 *until* ℓ *do*

    Comment: We partition the S-boxes in the STAGE#th stage into
        groups of $k^{STAGE\#-1}$ boxes each.

    for GROUP_OFFSET:=0 *step* $k^{STAGE\#-1}$ *until* $k^{\ell-1} - k^{STAGE\#-1}$ *do*

    Comment: We connect the 0th input bits of the $k^{STAGE\#-1}$
        S-boxes in each group to the first $k^{STAGE\#-1}$ output
        bits of the same group of the previous stage, then
        the 1st input bits of the $k^{STAGE\#-1}$ S-boxes to the
        next $k^{STAGE\#-1}$ output bits of the group of the
        previous stage, etc., as shown in Figure 3.

Final Step:

    for   BIT# :=0 *step* 1 *until* k-1 *do*

    Begin   BIT_OFFSET:=BIT# * $k^{STAGE\#-1}$;

    for   BOX#:=0 *step* 1 *until* $k^{STAGE\#-1} - 1$ *do*

      Begin

            PRESENT_BOX#:=GROUP_OFFSET+BOX#;

$$LAST\_BOX\#:=GROUP\_OFFSET+ \left\lfloor \left(\frac{BOX\#+BIT\_OFFSET}{k} \right) \right\rfloor;$$

$$LAST\_BIT\#:=remainder \left(\frac{\overline{BOX\#}}{k} \right);$$

            connect the (PRESENT BOX#,BIT#)th input bit of the
            STAGE# stage to the (LAST_BOX#,LAST_BIT#)th output
            bit of the (STAGE#-1)th stage.

      END
    END
END

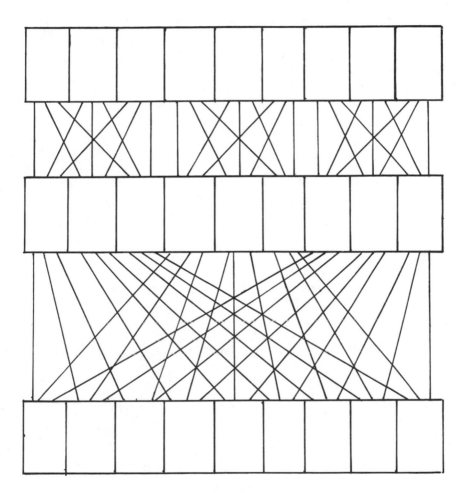

Figure 3.   An Output From Comp

$$n = 3^3 = 27$$

We will now show that the outputs from algorithm COMP are complete S-P networks.

Definition: Given an arbitrary output bit $(a,b)_m^{OUT}$ in an S-P network produced by COMP, we define $AFFECT((a,b)_m^{OUT})$ to be the set of 2^m input bits in the 1st stage that may affect the value of $(a,b)_m^{OUT}$. Formally,

$$AFFECT\left[(a,b)_m^{OUT}\right] \equiv AFFECT\left[(a)_m^{OUT}\right]$$

$$\equiv \text{the } k^m \text{ input bits of } S_{1,p}, S_{1,p+1}, \ldots, S_{1,p+k^{m-1}-1}$$

where

$$p = k^{m-1} \times \left\lfloor \frac{a}{k^{m-1}} \right\rfloor$$

Similarly, given $(a,b)_m^{IN}$, we define

$$AFFECT\left[(a,b)_m^{IN}\right] \equiv AFFECT\left[(a_b)_m^{OUT}\right], \text{ where}$$

$$a_b = (k^{m-1}) \times \left\lfloor \frac{a}{k^{m-1}} \right\rfloor + b(k^{m-2}) + \left\lfloor \left(\frac{rem(\frac{a}{k^{m-1}})}{k} \right) \right\rfloor$$

Definition: A pair of m-vectors is said to be *i-different* if they differ only in the ith bit.

Lemma 1: The value of $(a,b)_m^{OUT}$ depends only on the value of the bits in $AFFECT\ [(a,b)_m^{OUT}]$.

Proof: By induction on m.

Basis   (m=1) obvious.

Induction step (m = r > 1): According to algorithm COMP, each of $(a,o)_r^{IN}, \ldots, (a,k-1)_r^{IN}$ is connected to an output bit from $S_{r-1,a_o}, \ldots S_{r-1,a_{k-1}}$, respectively,

where

$$a_i = k^{r-1} \times \left\lfloor \frac{a}{k^{r-1}} \right\rfloor + \left\lfloor \left(\frac{rem(\frac{a}{k^{r-1}})}{k} \right) \right\rfloor + (k^{r-2})$$

By induction hypothesis, any output bit of S_{r-1,a_i} depends only

on bits in $\text{AFFECT}\left[(a_i)_{r-1}^{OUT}\right]$; hence, the theorem follows from the

definition of AFFECT. □

Lemma 2: For every a, $0 \leq a < \frac{n}{k}$ and for every b, $0 \leq b < k$,

with $1 \leq m \leq \ell$, there are exactly 2^{k^m-1} k^m-bit vectors that can

be used to initialize the k^m bits of $\text{AFFECT}\left[(a,b)_m^{OUT}\right]$ such that

$(a,b)_m^{OUT}$ will be set to 1. Similarly, the remaining 2^{k^m-1} vectors

will set $(a,b)_m^{OUT} = 0$.

Proof: It is obvious that for any j where $0 \leq j \leq m$, half of 2^m

binary m-vectors have 1 in the jth bit.

By definition, any one-one correspondence $f:\{0,2\}^k \to \{0,2\}^k$

maps the set of 2^k k-vectors into the same set of 2^k vectors.
With the preceding two statements and Lemma 1, Lemma 2 follows by
simple induction. □

Definition: Let f be a one-one correspondence mapping $\{0,1\}^n \to$

$\{0,1\}^n$. We define Q_{ij} of f to be the set of pairs and vectors

$Q_{ij} = \{\{V,V'\} \mid (V \text{ and } V' \text{ are i-different}) \wedge (f(V) \text{ and } f(V') \text{ differ}$
in the jth bit)$\}$.

We also define the *multiplicity* of f to be the integer M,

$$M = \min_{0 \leq i,j < n} |Q_{ij}| \text{ of f.}$$

Theorem 1: Let SP be an n-bit S-P network constructed by the

Algorithm COMP, where $n = k^{\ell+1}$. If the multiplicity of $S_{ij} \geq M$

for all i and j, $0 \leq i, j \leq n/k$, then the one-one correspondence

$f: \{0,1\}^n \to \{0,1\}^n$ achieved by the S-P network is complete.

Furthermore, the multiplicity of $f \geq M^{\ell} (\prod_{i=0}^{\ell-1} 2^{(k^i-1)(k-1)}) =$

$M^{\ell} (2^{k^{\ell}-(k-1)(\ell-1)-k})$.

Proof: We want to prove by induction on m that for each $(a,b)_m^{IN}$

and for each i, $0 \leq i < 2^m$, there is a set Q of at least

$M^m(\prod_{i=0}^{m-1} 2^{(k^i-1)(k-1)})$ pairs of i-different 2^m-bit vectors such

that if we pick an $\{V,V'\} \in Q$ and set the bits in $AFFECT[(a,b)_m^{OUT}]$

first according to V and then V', then $(a,b)_m^{OUT}$ will have

distinct values for the two cases.

Basis   (m=1) $M^m(\prod_{i=0}^{m-1} 2^{(k^i-1)(k-1)}) = M$ and the basis follows

directly from the assumption that each S-box in the input to COMP
is complete.

Induction step (m = r > 1)
Let us pick an arbitrary $(a,b)_r^{OUT}$ and an arbitrary $(e,f)_1^{IN} \in$

$AFFECT [(a,b)_\ell^{OUT}]$.

    In the proof of Lemma 1, we showed that among the k input

bits to $S_{r,a}$, only the $(a,z)_r^{IN}$ depends on the value of $(e,f)_1^{IN}$

where

$$z = \left\lfloor \left(\frac{e - \left(\frac{a}{k^{r-1}} \times k^{r-1} \right)}{k^{r-2}} \right) \right\rfloor$$

Let us pick a particular pair of z-different vectors
$V = (v_1 v_2, \ldots, v_z, \ldots, v_k)$ and $V' = (v_1 v_2, \ldots \bar{v}_z, \bar{v}_k)$ which, when used

as inputs to $((a,0)_r^{IN}, \ldots, (a,k-1)_r^{IN})$ will cause $(a,b)_r^{OUT}$ to

change. From Lemma 2, we know that there are 2^{k^r-1} ways to set

$AFFECT [(a,q)_r^{IN}]$ s.t. $(a,q)_r^{IN} = v_q$, for $(0 \leq q \leq k-1)$ and $(q \neq z)$.

Hence, by induction hypothesis, there are at least

$(M^{r-1}) (\prod_{i=0}^{r-2} 2^{(k^i-1)(k-1)}) \times (2^{k^r-1})^{k-1}$ pairs of n-vectors such that

the vectors W, W' in each pair differ only in the bit correspond-

ing to $(e,f)_1^{IN}$ and when the bits in $AFFECT ((a,b)_r^{OUT})$ are set according to W and W', then the values of

$$((a,0)_r^{IN}, \ldots, a(k-1)_r^{IN})$$ will become V, V' respectively.

Finally, the induction hypothesis follows from the assumption that $S_{r,a}$ has multiplicity $\geq$ M. □

To ensure that our design is meaningful, we must show that a complete one-one correspondence function mapping $\{0,1\}^k \to \{0,1\}^k$ exists for some value of k.

Theorem 2: For each $k \geq 3$, there exists a one-one correspondence f: $\{0,1\}^k \to \{0,1\}^k$ which is complete.

Proof: For every $k \geq 1$, the 2^k binary k-vectors may be partitioned into 2^{k-1} pairs of k-bit vectors of the form

$$Y = \{\{Y_i, Y_i'\} | (0 \leq i < 2^{k-1}) \wedge (Y_i' = \bar{Y}_i)\}.$$ If we can use 2^k

distinct vectors to construct k pairs of k-vectors of the form $V = \{\{V_j, V_j'\} | (0 \leq j < k) \wedge (V_j \text{ and } V_j' \text{ are i-different})\}$, then a complete one-one correspondence f can easily be constructed by defining a one-one correspondence f with the property that

$(\forall i, 0 \leq i < k)$
$$f(V_i) = Y_i \qquad \text{where } \{V_i, V_i'\} \in V \text{ and}$$
$$f(V_i') = Y_i' \qquad \qquad \{Y_i, Y_i'\} \in Y$$

We are going to show by induction on k that we can always find V.

Basis   (k-3) the 3 pairs may be chosen as shown in Figure 4.

Induction step: (k = r + 1)

We may partition the 2^{r+1} (r+1)-vectors into 2 groups G_0 and G_1, where

$G_0 = \{x | x \text{ is an } (r+1)\text{-vector with the } (v+1)\text{st bit being } 0\}$

$G_1 = \{y | y \text{ is an } (r+1)\text{-vector with the } (r+1)\text{st bit being } 1\}$

By induction hypothesis, we can find 2r distinct vectors from G_0 to form

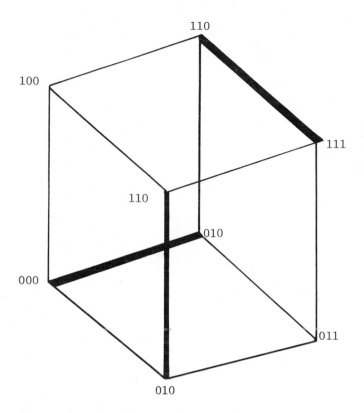

Figure 4.   The Three Pairs For The Case k = 3.

$V_r = \{(v_i, v_i') \mid (1 \le i \le r) \quad (v_i \text{ and } v_i' \text{ are i-different})\}.$

Since $G_0 = (2^{r+1})/2$ vectors and V_r may be formed by using only

2r vectors, there must be vector $X\ G_0$ which is not one of the 2r vectors used when $r \ge 3$. Hence

$V_{r+1} = V_r \cup \{X, X'\}$, where $X' \in G_1$ is $(r+1)$-different from X

forms a V needed for the case m = r+1. □

It is known [11] that linear or affine encryption functions can be broken more easily. In the next theorem, we are going to show that a complete one-one correspondence is neither linear nor affine.

Theorem 3: Let f be a one-one correspondence mapping $\{0,1\}^n \rightarrow \{0,1\}^n$. If f is complete, then f does not satisfy the following property:

(I) $(\exists h \varepsilon (0,1)^n)(\exists n \times n \text{ matrix } M)[f(A \oplus B) = ((A \oplus B)M) \oplus h]$ for all A, B $\varepsilon \{0,1\}^n$.

Proof: We are going to show that f does not satisfy property (I) by contradiction.

Assume f is complete and satisfies (I). By the completeness of f, we know that

$(\forall i, j_1, 0 \le i, j_1 < n)(\exists X, X' \varepsilon \{0,1\}^n)[(X \text{ and } X' \text{ are i-different})$

$\quad \wedge (f(x) \text{ and } f(x') \text{ differ at least in the } j_1\text{st bit})]$

Since $f(x) = f(x' \oplus Y_i)$, where Y_i has 1 only in the ith position

$\quad x'M \oplus Y_i M \oplus h$

This implies the j_1st bit of $Y_i M$ is 1.

Since j_1 is arbitrarily chosen, we conclude that $Y_i M = \underbrace{111 \ldots 1}_{n}.$

Similarly, we may conclude that $Y_j M = \underbrace{111 \ldots 1}_{n}$ for $j \neq i$. This

contradicts the assumption that f is a one-one correspondence. Hence, f does not satisfy property (I).   □

Corollary 1: Let f be a one-one correspondence mapping $\{0,1\}^n \rightarrow \{0,1\}^n$. If f is complete, then f is neither linear nor a bit-permutation function.

    In order to increase the key size of a network, we may modify the S-P network by allowing the output of each ith stage of the network to be exclusive-ored with an arbitrary n-bit vector V_i. In Figure 5, we show a modified version of the S-P network in Figure 3 with the inclusion of exclusive or facility. Before we encrypt a message using the network in Figure 5, we have to initialize the key and all V_i's. Our next results show that the additional facility does not affect the completeness property.

Lemma 3: If f is a complete one-one correspondence mapping $\{0,1\}^k \rightarrow \{0,1\}^k$. Let g be a new function defined as follows

$$(h \varepsilon \{0,1\}^k)(a \varepsilon \{0,1\}^k)[g(a) = f(a) \oplus h]$$

then g is complete and has the same multiplicity as f.

Proof: The proof is obvious and is omitted.   □

Theorem 4: Let SP be an n-bit S-P network constructed by the algorithm COMP. Let SP" be a network obtained from SP by the inclusion of exclusive-or facility. SP" is complete and has the same multiplicity of SP.

Proof: It follows directly from Lemma 3.   □

Definition: For a fixed $k \geq 3$ and $n = k^\ell$, we define $(S-P)^i$ to be the class of all functions realizable by using S-P networks with i-stages, where each stage has $k^{\ell-1}$ S-boxes and each S-box has k-bit input.

Lemma 4: Let f be in $(S-P)^i$, if X and X' are j-different for some $1 \leq j \leq n$ then f(X) and f(X') differ in at most k^i bit.

Proof: Simple induction on i.   □

Theorem 5: $(S-P)^1 \subset (S-P)^2 \subset (S-P)^3 \ldots \subset (S-P)$.

Proof: To prove that $(S-P)^i \subset (S-P)^{i+1}$, for $1 \leq i < \ell$, we only

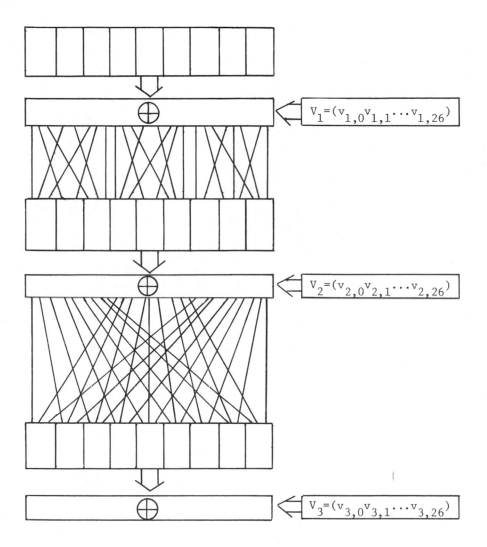

*Figure 5.   The Extension Of An Output From Comp With The
Exclusive-Or Facility Included.*

have to show that there exists f $(S-P)^{i+1}$ such that $f(X)$ differs from $f(X')$ in more than k^i places for some j-different X and X'. The existence of f can be shown by construction a $(\ell + 1)$ stage S-P network using the algorithm COMP, where all input S-boxes are all identical and have the following property:

Input to S	Output to S
00...00	00...00
00...01	11...11
.	.
.	.
.	.

It is easy to show that the function g achieved by the S-P network has the property that

$$g(\underbrace{00...00}_{n}) \text{ differs from } g(\underbrace{00...01}_{n})$$

in exactly $k^{\ell+1}$ bits.   □

V.   CONCLUSION AND OPEN PROBLEMS

In this paper, we have presented a general scheme which enables us to design arbitrarily large complete S-P networks in a hardware-efficient manner. We have also investigated some ramifications of the completeness property. There are a number of open problems that must be examined in order to improve our scheme.

   (1)   What other properties are implied by completeness?
   (2)   What other properties are desirable for S-P networks?
   (3)   What properties do the S-boxes used in Algorithm COMP satisfy in addition to the completeness property?

REFERENCES

[1]   Shannon, C., "Communiation Theory of Secrecy Systems,"
Bell System Technical Journal, Vol. 28, pp. 656–715,
October 1949.

[2]   Diffie, W. and Hellman, M., "New Directions in Cryptography," *IEEE Transaction on Information Theory*, pp. 644–654,
November 1976.

[3]   Davida, G., Mahar, T. and Kam, J., "Design and Analysis of
a Class of Cipher," *IEEE International Symposium on Information Theory*, 1975, Ronneby, Sweden.

[4]   Wyner, A., "The Wiretap Channel," *Bell System Technical
Journal*, Vol. 54, pp. 1355–1387, October 1975.

[5]   Kam, J. and Ullman, J., "A Model of Statistical Databases
and Their Security," *ACM Transaction on Database Systems*,
March, 1977.

[6]   Hoffman, L. and Miller, W., "Getting a Personal Dossier
from a Statistical Databank," *Datamation*, pp. 74–75, May 1970.

[7]   DeMillo, R., Dobkin, D. and Lipton, R., "Even Databases
That Lie Can Be Compromised," Research Report #67, Department
of Computer Science, Yale University, April 1976.

[8]   Rivest, R., Shamir, A. and Adleman, L., "On Digital
Signatures Public Key Cryptosystems," MIT-LCS-TM-82, April
1977.

[9]   *Federal Register*, Vol. 40, No. 149, August 1, 1975.

[10]   Diffie, W. and Hellman, M., "Exhaustive Cryptanalysis of
the NBS Data Encryption Standard," *Computer*, pp. 74–84, 1977.

[11]   Hellman, M. and Diffie, W., "Results of an Initial Attempt
to Cryptanalyze the NBS Data Encryption Standard," Information
System Laboratory Report, Stanford University, November 1976.

[12]   Morris, R., Sloane, N. and Wyner, A., "Assessment of the
National Bureau of Standards Proposed Federal Data Encryption
Standard," Bell Telephone Laboratories Memo, December 1976.

[13]   Feistel, H., "Cryptography and Computer Privacy,"
Scientific American, May 1973.

PROPRIETARY SOFTWARE PROTECTION

Richard DeMillo

Georgia Institute of Technology
and
Management Science America, Inc.

Richard Lipton

Computer Science Department
Yale University

Leonard McNeil

Management Science America, Inc.

I. INTRODUCTION

It is conventional wisdom in academic computer science that
clearly written, readable programs have demonstrable economic
benefit in computing. We were, therefore, very surprised to
learn that the benefits which obviously accrue from good programming practice carry with them problems of such impact that the
computer "software market" may cease to exist in its current form.
At issue is the protection of software from theft and the
establishment of unquestionable proprietary rights on behalf of
the creators of software products. With the lack of adequate
protection mechanisms and with current methods of transacting
business, there is an increased risk associated with the proprietary software market. First, there is the risk that new software
vendors, in an attempt to expedite their entry into the market
with a minimum investment of resources, will incorporate key
concepts from other vendors, either singularly or in combination,
into a new product. Second, new vendors who through independent
research and development manage to create products incorporating
truly original ideas run the risk of having their investments
usurped by resource-rich competitors. Finally, whenever vendors
find themselves in competition with one another, there is the
possibility that one might attempt to recapture a lost market
share by including other vendor's ideas into his existing product.
In each of these scenarios, the manner in which the business of
commercial software is transacted on a day-to-day basis is
responsible for the creation of an environment that encourages
software theft attempts.

In economic terms, such difficulties can tend to affect the
growth potential of the industry either by influencing investment
capitol or redirecting the conduct of business. It is not
difficult to imagine that in order to maintain any sustained
growth in the commercial software industry, mechanisms must be
found to protect the proprietary software vendors. Such
mechanisms could take the form of changes in the manner of con-
ducting day-to-day business, improved legislation, or the development of new technology to *insure* that proprietary rights to
computer software can be established and maintained.

In the sequel, we will discuss at more length the origins and
implications of the proprietary software protection problem and
outline a strategy which can incorporate technical safeguards
into new methods of transacting the sale purchase and maintenance
of proprietary software.

Proprietary Software. The true issues dealing with proprietary software arise in the "computer services" portion of the computer industry. The economic dimensions of this industry segment are staggering; for instance, in computer services alone, the projected 1978 revenues are in the neighborhood of 7.8 billion dollars [1]. The computer services industry may be subdivided along three lines:

(1) hardware specialists dealing in the sale, leasing and maintenance of computer equipment;

(2) direct service organizations, including data processing systems, facilities management, contract programming, and consulting;

(3) proprietary software, the sale or lease of machine-executable instructions often referred to as a software package.

The term "proprietary software" isolates a specific subset of the software market. Specifically, proprietary software refers to "a computer program that has wide potential use and also reflects a better than average level of industry and/or computer expertise, [which is to be sold] at a fraction of the cost it would take for any one computer installation to program themselves" [2].

Within the broad category of proprietary software, it is possible to distinguish products which are primarily application-oriented as opposed to those directed primarily to the operation and efficiency of the computer system itself (i.e., systems software). A quick survey of the primary sources of uniform software product information leads one to the conclusion that software products are widely divergent in their scope, purpose, potential market and technological sophistication. The products range in complexity from single utility programs with limited specific intent to systems of hundreds of loosely connected programs with broadly defined intent and numerous specific features. The range of possible application is similarly diverse, spanning the spectrum of computer applications from commercial computing through scientific applications.

Market Advantages . Using a comprehensive source [3] for a representative sampling of the market, it is possible to identify 1,800 software packages, emanating from 600 vendors, which are in current circulation in the market place. Of these software packages, 1,426 (emanating from 546 vendors) have been classified as software package as follows. About one-third of the software products can be classified as systems software, and the remaining two-thirds fall clearly into application-oriented proprietary software. The lure to potential investors and the attendant benefits to accrue from competition are enormous: for example, the projected 1978 total market for proprietary software is in excess of one million dollars and this represents an annual sales growth rate of 35% [2]. With the resulting increase in pressure brought about by additional competitors comes the hand-in-glove problem of how to gain advantage in a swelling market through a product having an attractive combination of performance features.

Source Distribution. Regardless of the software product involved, successful competition in the market place forces a number of constraints on current and potential software vendors. First, since it is usually desirable that a software product should have the wide potential use, restrictions peculiar to a narrow sector of potential customers must be designed out of the product in the hopes of obtaining a generalized package. Second, with the obvious exception of computing machine manufacturers, it is seldom desirable that a software product be dependent on any specific computer hardware specifications; therefore, to the extent that it is technically possible, programs tend to be produced using standard high-level languages with transparent interfaces to a variety of systems software. Finally - and most critically - it is the practice of over 90% of the application-oriented proprietary software vendors to divulge the contents or to actually issue to their clients proprietary product source code.

A variety of factors convolve to make source code distribution an advantageous arrangement for both vendors and clients. First, when a prospective client weighs the generalized features of a software package against his specific needs, the ultimate decision is often an economic compromise. That is, a customer may realize economic gains in the purchase or lease of a software package, but in doing so, he must be able to adjust the package in the areas which are most significant to him. While the vendor tends to have a broadly based knowledge of the relevant application area, the knowledge can be at best only of a very generalized sort. A potential customer, on the other hand, has intimate day-to-day contact with his application. He knows, in particular, his needs and the effects of meeting those needs on his organization. Since the customer's specific needs ultimately determine later courses of action, the added degree of flexibility given by his ability to modify a generalized software package, is often a key factor in helping a customer decide whether to buy applications software or to build his own. A proprietary software vendor may even use whatever capabilities exist in his products for easy modification as an aid in competing with other vendors of direct services. It is easy to see that the provision of such capabilities might be a determining factor in competition between two proprietary software vendors.

A second consideration that often impacts the decision to distribute source code to customers is the issue of the compatibility of a software package with the confusion of hardware in the typical user community. Since the primary goal of a general purpose software package is to be independent of any particular computing system configuration, a careful design will segregate a software product from any hardware dependency. Thus, in order for a vendor to deliver a working software package for a given computer system, the vendor would necessarily have had to countenance every major combination of computer architecture and operating system. Since such development efforts are prohibitive, the normal course is for the vendor to insure contractually that the software package being sold in source code format performs accurately and as advertised. The problems that arise from hardware and software incompatabilities often wind up as negotiable contract items which are eventually resolved by relying on the customer to correct the problems.

Even though software vendors often warrant their packages against inaccuracies, large computer programs always have errors in them, and these errors are of varying degrees of severity. Since as part of his warranty, the vendor must correct all source code errors within a specific time frame, a method must be established to easily communicate to the customer those corrections that originate with the vendor. One possibility is that the vendor may elect to send a representative to fix problems at every installation of their package. When a vendor has thousands of versions of his package installed at widely separated sites, this is clearly cost prohitive. On the other hand, a client who has access to source code, can receive from the vendor only those changes to the package source code necessary to correct a specific problem.

It may even be a concern to some customers that the vendor will not continue as a successful, functioning organization. A customer who does not have access to the source code for the package in his possession, may find himself with a useless pile of code, should the vendor discontinue support of the product or fail to adequately support the product. In such event, clearly the customer would not have any viable solution that would allow continued processing using the software. With the possession of source code, if the vendor's support of the package every ceases or fails, the vendor can still employ his own resources to fix bugs and thus continue using the software.

The demands to provide customer software source code place an additional burden on the proprietary software vendor. Not only must the vendor provide source code, he must also provide it in such a manner as to identify the inner workings of the program through precise, technical documentation in explanatory program notes. Obviously, with the current practice of distribution of source code, a customer's user and data processing departments must have full access to information on the package components in order to derive full benefit from the package.

Trade Secrets. A key assumption in the definition of proprietary software is that proprietary software is the result of a creative engineering effort and is based in whole (or in part) on the originality and the creative intellectual processes of the vendor. With the creation of an idea, a process, or a computer program comes the issue of the proprietary rights of ownership which are vested in the creator. In the case of computer software, the process of creation generally involves a non-trivial expenditure of resources. These resources can take the form of computer usage, research and development costs, personnel costs, and overhead expenses, which taken together represent a significant economic investment on the part of an individual or an organization. Such investments are entered into with calculated risk. The justification for taking such a risk is an ultimate or indirect economic benefit to the investor. A responsible investor will not take such a risk unless he is reasonably certain that what is to be developed can be protected as an investment.

A rapidly growing market, a highly-competitive environment, and the market demands for complete disclosure of product details will eventually be in direct confrontation with the risk aversion goals of the software developer and his investors. Proprietary software is the market segment most directly affected by the issue of software protection. Indeed, it is the area most susceptable to the consequences of the lack of protection. However, the goals of software protection must be defined prior to the creation of improved protection methods.

The creation of proprietary software is an iterative process by which expertise and knowledge are applied to achieve specific goals. The development cycle generates the concepts and features of the package to be marketed. These in turn manifest themselves in the algorithms and data structures which the package implements. Physically, this logical structure is represented in program source code and to a lesser extent in the documentation supporting the package. It is this underlying structure that is the true result of the investment of expertise and financial resources. Accordingly, these items are the target of any useful protection mechanisms, even though it is in their physical representation where our protection mechanisms are to be found. As software systems become more and more complex, the number of separately identifiable algorithms increases quite rapidly. Ideally, a vendor would like to protect his entire system. However, he will usually admit that within the system, there are a few algorithms or a series of related algorithms that may be considered to be the *heart* of the system. These critical portions of the system may consist of routines within a program or specific programs themselves. Exampls of such key components are the depreciation/ aging programs of a fixed asset system, the taxation routines in a generalized payroll system, the polling strategy in an on-line data management system, or a sorting heuristic to pre-process data for a numerical software package. A key concept may even be a unique data organization methodology which is included as part of every program in the system.

The current protection methods for a vendor's proprietary software do not rely on the underlying logical structure of the package, but rather on its physical representation. It is from this protection gap that software theft becomes a real threat. On the one hand, patent laws are inteded to protect a physical entity, such as a machine part, but the prevailing legal interpretation is that ideas are not patentable, only the end result of the thought processes. As a result, patent laws offer little protection to proprietary software vendors. On the other hand, copyright laws provide protection only from blatant reproduction of program source code. Thus, copyright protection is limited only to the physical aspects of a program, and so, it cannot be stretched to encompass the algorithms and data structures on which a program is based.

A third and most widely-used means of software protection relies on the concept of "trade secret" protection. In essence, trade secret protection derives from the fact that a software vendor does not disseminate those key portions of his package to the *general public*, but rather takes whatever means are required to restrict this distribution. The legal framework within which trade secret protection is applied varies from state to state and at the federal level is only loosely unified. It is embarrasingly

difficult to even formulate a meaningful definition of what constitutes a trade secret. A trade secret is variously defined as
a "feature" or "concept" embodied in the package or specifically
as any combination of algorithms and data structures that address
the specific goals or problems. This, however, makes many of a
vendor's trade secret tools useless since the variability of laws
creates a variety of opinion as to how to apply the notion of a
trade secret to a specific software product.

The tools available to protect a vendor's trade secrets
include such devices as the restrictive lease or sale contracts
that limit distribution and access by the customer, non-disclosure
agreements between the vendor and a prospective customer which in
a pre-sales environment clearly define the proprietary rights
involved, and employee contracts and agreements which stipulate
in some manner the ownership of items produced as a direct or
indirect result of the efforts of an employee of the vendor.

There are, of course, several weaknesses implicit in trade
secret protection mechanisms. The first and most obvious lies
in the notion of secrecy. In the current conduct of business in
the proprietary software market place, secrets are distributed
to N people, all of whom have specific rights to those secrets
by virtue of their purchase of software systems. A natural
question to ask is how large N must become before the secret is
no longer secret.

A second weakness is the assumption that trade secrets can be
isolated for a specific software package. Of course, a reasonable goal is to define a trade secret as narrowly as possibel so
as to make it unique and distinguishable in both approach and
purpose from other trade secrets. There is a problem in the
deciding and composition of a trade secret; that is, the collection of algorithms and data structures into trade secret entities.
If one identifies a trade secret too broadly, it looses its
uniqueness. For example, every payroll system reads input,
edits, calculates payroll factors, and produces payroll checks.
So, these mechanisms cannot be construed as trade secrets. On
the other hand, too restrictive a definition causes a trade
secret's characteristics to be indistinguishable from others.
For instance, in a payroll system, the calculation "ADD A, B
GIVING C" applies to many functions throughout a payroll system.

A third weakness in trade secret protection is that vendors
lack real policing powers, making enforcement of contracts
difficult. Since policing powers apply directly to corporate
entities, the vendor is forced to review customer disclosure
policies from outside the customer's organization. Such review
may be based on questionable marketing intelligence information
since the vendor is at the mercy of its customer's management

and their effectiveness in controlling distribution within their
organization. Furthermore, vendors have very little control over
what ex-employees *of customers* take with them upon termination;
similarly, employees of the vendor carry with them not only
physical representations of programs that they have written, but
also an accumulation of expertise gained at the expense of the
vendor. Of course, in the case of ex-employees *of the vendor*,
there is usually no doubt as to the ex-employees' intimacy with
trade secrets, but demonstrating theft by a former employee will
gain as a result of his direct experience in the industry. The
situation is further complicated by the elapsed time between the
act of theft and the discovery by the vendor that a trade secret
infringement has occurred. During this time lag, the original
vendor has no control of the distribution of the trade secret so
that the once secret idea may have been disseminated to the
general public. In this case, future enforcement is clouded
since it introduces the new concept of "public domain" at which
time the vendor clearly loses his trade secret, his investment,
and possible competitive advantage to public knowledge. In the
case of theft by a client's employees, a vendor will tend to be
cautious of distrupting relationships with his customers by
forcing the issue of distribution of proprietary software
materials within the clients' organization or the issue of the
disposition of proprietary software materials upon the termination of a customer's employees. Software vendors have marketing
concerns, and an undisturbed, satisfied client is a source of
sales references and future sales prospects. A vendor has clearly much to gain by maintaining his distance from the internal
procedures of his clients.

A fourth weakness is that trade secret protection is contin-
uous and costly. An organization's overhead expenses rise to
match the administrative requirements of contract and non-disclosure procedures. But these expenses only represent the continuing fixed cost. Much larger variable expenses come from legal
actions taken when there is the possibility of a breech of an
agreement or a trade secret infringement. A single law suit
based on trade secret infringement can consume many man-years of
effort on the vendor's part and can result in high costs
associated with legal services.

As might be expected, no current protection mechanism totally
protects trade secrets from a calculating computer software
thief who employs "hybrid piracy". A hybrid pirate is someone
who intentionally steals the "heart" of a package (i.e., trade
secrets, but not the entire package), digests the logic knowledge
embodied in the trade secrets, and then reintroduces the trade
secrets as part of a "new", or in addition to an "old" package
through a transformation of its physical representation.

Lacking any strong legal alternatives due to the weaknesses in copyright patent, and trade secret legislation, a proprietary software vendor must seek additional alternatives to gain protection for his products and to protect his investment. Although new legislation has been proposed that solidified and clarifies federal laws on trade secrets and copyrights for proprietary software, the uncertainty over the congressional action that may be taken means that the proprietary software industry can only look to a possible technological solution to the problem.

Software Encryption. The protection problem for proprietary software can be interpreted as either protective protection or detective protection. An ideal solution should treat both interpretations. A trade-secret thief is usually able to alter the macro and micro structure of a software package: he may consolidate and re-order routines within programs and programs within packages, he may alter (either manually or by use of a cross-compiler) the coding of the system, and he may modify the internal and external file organizations for systems whose data-manipulating features are paramount.

Therefore, an appropriated program may appear quite different from the original program in a variety of respects. The overall conception of the program may be much changed, and direct matching of corresponding lines of source code may not be possible. Yet, if theft of trade secrets has really taken place, then there should be aspects of the original program that have been substantially *reproduced* in the appropriate version. In fact, programmers who are able to examine appropriated versions of their own work can frequently detect their unique design concepts. Some of this is clearly based on transferral of programming *style*, but a far greater component is attributable to a thief's inability to recreate the trade secrets. Without completely redesigning a program, it is very difficult to mutilate all aspects of the original design. Therefore, a test of similarity for programs is their "edit distance". If P and P' are programs (say, P' has been obtained from P) then the transformations used to create P' from P should be invertible. That is, it should be possible to proceed from P' to P by undoing the effects of the piracy. Let the *distance* from P' to P be the minimal number of editing transformations needed to identify P and P'. Such transformations will surely involve consolidating blocks of source code into functionally identifiable units, and rearrangement of routines or logically coherent portions of routines which have no significance for the application. If the shortest identification of P and P' is comparatively long, then P and P' are of doubtful similarity. In particular, if P and P' are payroll programs and if in order to identify P and P', we must abstract from all internal structure beyond reading input, editing, calculating payroll factors, and producing checks, then P and P' have not been strongly correlated. If on the other hand we find short distances - i.e., if we are able to expose nearly identically implemented trade secrets - then, we have established positive correlations between P and P'.

In order to protect P from theft and to detect theft when it occurs, we would like to insure that the only way to infer the implementation of trade secrets in P is to solve a problem that is prohibitively expensive to solve. Therefore, since a potential thief cannot *understand* the implementation of a trade secret, he must either:

(1) redesign the solution to the problem solved by the trade secret, or
(2) copy the implementation with minimal change.

Option (1) does not constitute theft, while option (2) leads to detection by edit distance. Because the protection of proprietary software is an economic problem, the thresholds for what constitutes "prohibitive" expense can be set somewhat lower than, say, the type of "prohibitive expense" required to crack a military code. In particular, we need only insure that success-fully appropriating the trade secrets of P is sufficiently more expensive than developing independent solutions that a potential thief will be inclined to spend his resources in original product development. From a technical point of view, it is no longer necessary to encode a protection problem into a problem that is provably *intractable*. A secret with n = 1,000 characterizing parameters can be encoded into a problem with a tractible decision problem of time complexity $O(n^{3.5})$ to obtain a protected secret which involves the analysis of 10^{10} conditions.

This approach is consonant with distribution of source code for P; we want only that P be confusing to a penetrator, not that it be an unreadable program.

Given a program Q, in source form, we want to distribute to customers an *encrypted* program P which has approximately the same performance characteristics as Q so that clients will buy and use it and which protects Q's trade secrets. "Approximately the same performance characteristics" means that P and Q deliver the same results to the same input and that the resources demand of P and Q (e.g., execution time, storage requirements) are comparable. It is not so easy to specify what we mean by pro-tecting trade secrets. Again, any reasonably intuitive rendering should require that the amount of effort required to unravel the details of a trade secret will be so great that a potential thief will be disposed to design his own system.

It is obviously not useful to consider Q to be a piece of
data (bit string) and encrypt it using a secure data encryption
scheme [4]. A program is a dynamic object, and there is nothing
to insure that data encryption will preserve its dynamic
characteristics; in particular, a naively encrypted version of Q
will not even be a well-formed program. This brings up an
essential difference between encrypting data and programs: since
data is static its encrypted form does not have to be useful, but
a program - in *any* form - is *supposed* to leak some information,
namely its output. The key problem is to balance the desired
information leakage with the undesired leakage.

Let us illustrate how such an ecryption scheme might work.

A frequently protected type of program logic consists of
relatively simple computations linked by many layers of decisions.
In the case of a general purpose taxing package, for instance,
tax computations for federal, state and local taxing authorities
may be driven by decision table logic which tests comparatively
few conditions; reducing the many taxing contingencies for two
thousand taxing authorities to 100 or so requires expert tax
knowledge and the investment of many man-years to verify that the
simplifications do not violate federal, state, or local laws and
to maintain the table to reflect recent changes in taxation legislation. This, in fact, qualifies the table as a trade secret,
and makes it a likely candidate for encryption.

A decision rule for such a system may be expressed as follows.
Let us assume that we have N attributes of a given taxing
situation; the presence of the ith attribute is indicated by the
setting of a flag x_i = 1 while its absence is indicated by setting
x_i = 0. If the ith attribute is irrelevant, then x_i is a "don't
care" condition. Then a decision rule is completely determined
by a predicate $P(x_1,...,x_n)$ which holds exactly when some
specified attributes x_i = 1 and some specified attributes x_j = 0.

Now let us represent each boolean flag x_i by k-bit words w_i,
$\tilde{w}_i$ in which m $\ll$ k-bits randomly chosen of w_1 are set high if
x_i = 1 and m randomly chosen m-bits of w_2 are set high if x_1 = 0.
By using a technique known as "superimposed coding" [5], we then
form 2 k-bit words A,B by forming the "inclusive or" of each of
the positive and negative w_i, $\tilde{w}_i$. Then, by associating a bit
pattern of each of A,B with $P(x_1,...,x_n)$, it is possible to
select a correct action based on the value of $P(x_1,...,x_n)$ with-

out ever revealing the method of evaluating the predicate.
(cf. Appendix).

   Superimposed coding originated as a method of retrieving
information based on secondary keys; as a result of one choice
of m bits for w_i, $\tilde{w}_i$, we may find that unintended atttributes
are selected by some A,B. In the searching application, this
condition is called "false drop", and its occurrence cannot be
eliminated but it can be controlled statistically.

   Returning now to our example taxation package, let us
imagine a potential penetrator observing tax computations
occurring in bit patterns A and B. In order to infer
$P(x_1,...,x_n)$ from A,B, he must be able to identify the positive
and negative contributions of the attributes x_i and for even
small choices of N, k this is prohibitive. The end user on the
other hand, has no trouble *executing* the decision table – indeed,
the superimposed coding scheme can be implemented using full-
word bit vector operations so that the running time is only
increased negligibly. The user also has the source code in plain
view, so that changes and updates can be sent directly to the
client; he will be able to determine that decisions are being
made properly but will not have access to the internal working
of the decision-making mechanisms.

   Protection is finally achieved by "padding" the real rules
with a few false rules. The penetrator now must decide whether
to infer the proper taxing rules by either static or dynamic
analysis. In dynamic analysis, the penetrator must be able to
distinguish real responses from false ones. A penetrator
sufficiently expert to make such distinctions will surely be
inclined to design his own solutions. Static analysis reduces
to a covering and partition problem as described in the
appendix. This problem is solvable in polynomial time, but the
superimposed coding scheme gives a decision table predicate
with $\sim 10^6$ degrees of freedom; this is already the same order of
magnitude as the number of state, local and federal taxing
contingencies, so that the economic benefits of theft is doubtful.

It is not clear how to extend this idea to other key computational pieces of a software package, but the point of these methods should be clear. We want to keep tight control over the "clear" interpretation of trade secrets, so that a potential thief will not be able to use hybrid methods without leaving fingerprints. In the case above, he must insure that the decision table operates correctly by copying it; since the structure of the table is determined by a large number of random choices, it may be demonstrated in a court of law that chance duplication is statistically impossible.

REFERENCES

[1]   ADAPSO Data, ADASSO, Vol. VI, No. 5.
[2]   *Bottomline*, International Computer Programs, Inc., October 1975, Vol. 1, No. 1.
[3]   *Data Pro Directory of Software*, Data Pro Research Corp., Vol. 1.
[4]   Rivest, R., Adelman, L. and Shamir, A., "A Method for Obtaining Digital Signatures and Public Key Cryptography Systems", MIT Report, TM-82, Laboratory for Computer Science.
[5]   Knuth, D. E., *Sorting and Searching*, Addison-Wesley, 1973.

APPENDIX. Superimposed Coding

Let $x_1, \ldots, x_N$ be boolean variables and let $P(x_1, \ldots, x_N)$ be the predicate

$$P(x_1, \ldots, x_N) \quad \text{iff} \quad \begin{cases} x_i = 1 & \forall i \in I, \text{ and} \\ \\ x_j = 0 & \forall j \in J, \end{cases}$$

$|I| + |J| \leq N$.

Then by superimposed coding, it is possible to construct $A_1, \ldots, A_N, A, B_1, \ldots, B_N, B$ so that for i, j $\leq$ N

$$|\{\ell: \quad A_{i\ell} = 1\}| \ << \ \text{length of } A_i = k$$
$$|\{\ell: \quad B_{i\ell} = 1\}| \ << \ \text{length of } B_i = k,$$

and

$$P(x_1, \ldots, x_N) \quad \text{iff} \quad \bigvee_{x_i=1} A_i \supseteq A \ \wedge \ \bigvee_{x_i=0} B_i \supseteq B \ .$$

$P(x_1, \ldots, x_N)$ is thus encoded since in order to determine the manner in which P depends on its arguments, it is required to solve a set partition problem which is solvable in time $O(n^{3.5})$. While this is not intractible, it may be sufficient for protecting proprietary software as described in the text.

The statistics of false drops for this algorithm is discussed in Knuth [5].

DISCUSSION

Rabin: The problem is really to make it possible for the original vendor to prove in court, say, that theft really did occur.

DeMillo: The problem also is to insure that someone could not take the protected program and directly sell it because it's not a program that he could modify. It leaves hidden those parts which you've protected, those parts which you consider the heart or the critical inventions of the program.

Lipton: Just a follow-up on that point. What we're really trying to say is that if you could recover the original program which is a clear and understandable structure, you can then modify it according to a number of techniques to come up with a new program that you could then possibly argue that you built. By putting dirty, strange fingerprints throughout the program, we can then make it much more difficult for that to happen.

Millen: There is a story that I think is fairly well-known and is relevant to this. It has to do with the days when books of mathematical tables were produced manually with a calculator. The method for protecting copyrights was to introduce some very small error ... perhaps, one decimal place in ten digits. It probably would not effect anyone who was using the table, but it was a dead give-away to identify copies.

McNeil: I would prefer for a solution to be preventive. It is costly to follow-up a theft. For instance, in one case which we're involved with now, we are spending thousands and thousands of dollars just in the follow-up. It would be much better for us if we had access to a technology in which it was not possible to successfully steal the protected components. That's a solution that completely solves our problem from the beginning.

Minsky: I am intrigued by your remark about the dynamic aspect of these things. Do you mean that one may reproduce the protected program by simply observing how it behaves?

DeMillo: No. The purpose of the comment was to underline the fact that one cannot directly apply data encryption techniques. They may change drastically the dynamic behavior of the program. In particular, the program may not in fact even be a program after it is encrypted. So, you cannot treat the program as a bit string and encrypt it.

Cohen: Not only must it work, but it must have almost the same performance characteristics.

DeMillo: That's right. It has to be competitive with the original. If we can close on a non-technical note, I think it is important to emphasize that the world is just not structured to handle these problems. Some commercial software people are very much at a state of deciding whether or not to abandon traditional ways of dealing with users and competitors.

ENCRYPTION PROTOCOLS, PUBLIC KEY ALGORITHMS
AND DIGITAL SIGNATURES IN COMPUTER NETWORKS*

Gerald J. Popek
Charles S. Kline

University of California at Los Angeles
Los Angeles, California

I. INTRODUCTION

There has been considerable interest recently in the development of encryption methods for computer networks. Activity
falls into two major but related areas: the development of strong
encryption algorithms, and the design of the rules or protocols
by which an algorithm is actually used in an operating network.
As an example of the relation between these two areas, public key
algorithms have been suggested as a superior solution to key
distribution and digital signatures; issues which, it is claimed,
would otherwise require additional protocols. Here we concentrate
on the protocol problems. We examine protocol questions which
arise at various levels of a system, from the low, detailed level
at which the various operating systems in a network communicate,
to the higher, user visible level involving such services as
digital mail. As a result a rather unique perspective is provided,
and we are led to some fairly surprising conclusions.

* *This research was supported by the Advanced Research Projects*
Agency of the Department of Defense under Contract MDA 903-77-
C-0211.

133

The paper is written basically in a bottom up fashion. The
first section considers questions of how encryption "channels"
interact with network software. The next section outlines a
basic protocol for the use of encryption in a network, independent
of the nature of the encryption algorithm (public key, conventional, etc). These two sections show how it is possible to build a
secure network base, on top of which many extensions are directly
possible. At that point attention turns to some of the higher
level, user visible issues, such as public key algorithms and
digital signatures. It is argued that none of the currently
proposed signature methods is satisfactory. We propose an
alternative which we believe satisfies the necessary requirements.
It is based on the existence of the secure lower level protocols
discussed in the earlier sections. Those readers willing to
accept the existence of secure lower level network protocols may
wish to skip to section six, where the discussion of public keys
and digital signatures can be found.

II.   LEVELS OF INTEGRATION

Encryption forms the basis for solutions to computer network
security problems. Basically, a single communications channel can
be multiplexed into a large number of separately protected, secure
communication channels by assigning a separate encryption key
pair for each logical communication channel. When a user requests
the establishment of a new communication, protection policy checks
can be performed, and, if successful, a key can be distributed to
each end of the communication channel.

Several key distribution methods have been studied [Popek 78b].
One method utilizes a key distribution center which receives
requests for communications, and distributes keys accordingly.
The keys are transmitted using previously arranged secret keys
which change only rarely. Other methods allow distributed key
management, with several, or even all, sites participating in key
distribution. Recently, public key encryption algorithms [Rivest
77a] have become available. Originally, such algorithms were
thought to simplify the key distribution problem, but recent
research suggests that no savings result [Needham 77]. This issue
is discussed at length in section six.

One problem which must be resolved in designing a secure network encryption mechanism, regardless of the nature of the
encryption algorithm or the key distribution method, is the level
of integration of the encryption facility. There are many
possible choices for the endpoints of the encryption channel in a
computer network, each with its own tradeoffs. In a packet
switched network, one could encrypt each line between two switches
separately from all other lines. This is a low level choice, and

is often called link encryption. Instead, the endpoints of the
encryption channels could be chosen at a higher architectural
level: at the computer systems, referred to as hosts, which are
connected to the network. Thus, the encryption system would
support host-host channels, and a message would be encrypted only
once as it was sent through the network rather than being decrypted and reencrypted a number of times, as implied by the low level
choice. In fact, one could even choose a higher architectural
level. Endpoints could be individual processes within the
operating systems of the machines that are attached to the network. If the user were employing an intelligent terminal, then
the terminal is a candidate for an endpoint, too. This view
envisions a single encryption channel from the user directly to
the program with which he is interacting, even though that program
might be running on a site other than the one to which the
terminal is connected. This high level choice is endpoints is
sometimes called end-end encryption.

    The choice of architectural level in which the encryption is
to be integrated has many ramifications for the overall architecture. One of the more important is the combinatorics of key
control versus the amount of trusted software.

    In general, as one considers higher and higher levels in most
systems, the number of identifiable and separately protected
entities in the system tends to increase, sometimes dramatically.
For example, while there are less than a hundred hosts attached
to the ARPANET, at a higher level there often are over a thousand
processes concurrently operating, each one separately protected
and controlled. The number of terminals and users is of course
also high. This numerical increase means that the number of
secure channels -- that is the number of separately distributed
matched key pairs required -- is correspondingly larger. Also,
the rate at which keys must be generated and distributed can be
dramatically increased.

    In return for the additional cost and complexity which may
result, there can be significant reduction in the amount of software whose correct functioning must be assured for the protection
of the communication channel. This issue is very important and
must be carefully considered. It arises in the following way.
When the lowest level is chosen, the data being communicated
exists in cleartext form as it is passed from one encrypted link
to the next by the switch. Therefore, the software in the switch
must be trusted not to intermix packets of different channels.
If a higher level is selected, from host to host for example, then
errors in the switches are of no consequence. However, operating
system failures are still serious, since the data exists as
cleartext while it is system resident.

In principle then, the highest level integration of
encryption is most secure. However, it is still the case that
the data must be maintained in clear form in the machine upon
which processing is done. Therefore, the more classical methods
of protection within individual machines are still quite necessary,
and the value of very high level end-end encryption may be somewhat lessened. A rather appealing choice of level that integrates
effectively with kernel structured operating system architectures
is outlined in section four.

Another small but nontrivial drawback to high level encryption
should be pointed out. Once the data is encrypted, it is difficult to perform meaningful operations on it. Many front end
systems provide such functions as packing, character erasures,
transmission on end of line or control character detect, etc. If
the data is encrypted before it reaches the front end, then these
functions cannot be performed. That is, any processing of data
flowing through the channel must be done above the level at which
encryption takes place.

III. ENCRYPTION PROTOCOLS

Network communication protocols concern the discipline
imposed on messages sent throughout the network to control
virtually all aspects of data traffic, both in amount and
direction. It is well recognized that choice of protocol has
dramatic impacts on the utility, flexibility and bandwidth
provided by the network. Since encryption facilities essentially
provide a potentially large set of logical channels, the protocols
by which the operation of those channels is managed also can have
significant impact.

There are several important questions which any encryption
protocol must answer:

(1) How is the initial cleartext/ciphertext/cleartext channel
from sender to receiver and back established?
(2) How are cleartext addresses passed by the sender around the
encryption facilities to the network without providing a path by
which cleartext data can be inadvertently or intentionally leaked
by the same means?
(3) What facilities are provided for error recovery and
resynchronization of the protocol?
(4) How is flow control performed?
(5) How are channels closed?
(6) How do the encryption protocols interact with the rest of the
network protocols?
(7) How much software is needed to implement the encryption
protocols? Does the security of the network depend on this
software?

One wishes a protocol which permits channels to be dynamically opened and closed, allows the traffic flow rate to be controlled (by the receiver presumably), provides reasonable error handling, and all with a minimum of mechanism upon which the security of the network depends. Clearly the more software is involved, the more one must be concerned about the safety of the overall network. The performance resulting from use of the protocol must compare favorably with the attainable performance of the network using other suitable protocols without encryption. Lastly, one would prefer a general protocol which could also be added to existing networks, disturbing the transmission mechanisms already in place as little as possible. Each of these issues must be settled independent of the level of integration of encryption which is selected, the method of key distribution, or the nature of the encryption algorithms employed.

To illustrate the ways in which these considerations interact, in the next section we outline a complete protocol. The case considered employs an end to end architecture in a way that can be added to an existing network.

IV. NETWORK ENCRYPTION PROTOCOL CASE STUDY: PROCESS-PROCESS ENCRYPTION

We outline here a general encryption protocol that operates at the relatively high level of process to process communication. A major goal is the minimization of the software on which the security of the system depends. Network communication protocols often involve fairly large and complex parts of the operating system, sometimes the primary source of complexity and amount of code. This fact results from the variety of tasks which the network protocol must perform, such as connection establishment, flow control, error detection and correction. Thus, this design attempts to eliminate as much as possible the necessity of trusting that software for secure operation.

The design presented here utilizes process-process encryption. In process-process encryption, encoding is performed as data moves from the source process to the system's network software. This approach minimizes the points where data exists in cleartext form, and thus the mechanism which needs to be trusted. While a higher level choice could be made, for example allowing the processes to perform their own encryption within themselves, such a choice does not assure that all data sent over the network is encrypted. Thus, process-process encryption seems to be the highest safe choice. The details of the protocol are applicable either to public key based or conventional algorithms. Any of the key distribution methods discussed in [Popek 78b] can be supported.

It is assumed that the reader is familiar with the ideas of operating system security kernels [Popek 78c]. Briefly, security kernel based systems attempt to isolate the security relevant parts of the system and place them in a nucleus, running on the bare hardware. In that way, the secure operation of the system depends only on that software. By careful design and implementation of a security kernel, it is possible to formally verify the security properties of the system [Popek 78a].

Overview

In this protocol, when a user attempts to send data, a system encrypt function encrypts that data and passes it to the network management software, which is logically part of the local operating system. The network software then attaches headers or other information required by the network protocols and sends the data to the communications facility. Upon reception by the remote network software, the headers and other protocol information are removed from the data and the data is passed, via a system decrypt function, to the appropriate user process.

Initial establishment of the communication channel is also provided in a secure way. When a user process attempts to establish communication, the local network software is informed by the system. The network software then communicates with the network software at the remote site. When the two network software packages have arranged for the new communication, the system at each site is informed. At this point in time, the system software attempts to obtain encryption keys for this communication. This key distribution is accomplished either with local key management software, or via a key distribution center. If a conventional encryption algorithm was employed, then new keys would be chosen and distributed. If a public key encryption algorithm was utilized, then the public key of the recipient and the private key of the sender would be retrieved.

In the public key case, an additional authentication sequence is required, since the public keys may have been used before. This authentication sequence effectively establishes a sequence number to be included in each message to guarantee that previous messages cannot be recorded by an imposter and replayed. The authentication sequence is not required in the conventional encryption case since the new keys effectively form an authentication and prevent any prior messages from being useful.

After the keys have been chosen and distributed (using a previously established secure key distribution channel), the user processes are given capabilities to send and receive data. The operating system calls employed should automatically encrypt and decrypt the data with the appropriate keys. Thus, the communication channel is established.

The above design allows existing network protocols in many cases to be largely left undisturbed, and preserves much existing network software. If desired, user processes can be blocked, in a reliable way, from communicating with any other user processes anywhere in the network unless the protection policy involved in setting up the keys permits it. Each user's communication is protected from every other user's communication. Perhaps most important, the amount of trusted mechanism required in the system nucleus, as we shall see, is quite limited.

The Encyption Connection Protocol

The details of secure communication establishment, briefly described above, are now presented in more detail. To outline this procedure, we first view the operation from the vantage point of the operating system nucleus, or kernel, and then see how host network protocol software operates making use of the kernel facilities. For brevity, in this discussion, a logical communication channel between two processes will be known as a connection. The host network software will be referred to as the network protocol manager (NPM). In general purpose networks, the role of the NPM is quite sophisticated and requires considerable code to implement the necessary protocols, an important reason not to have security depend on the NPM.

In the discussion below, it will be understood that a pair of matching encryption keys, one held by each of the two hosts involved, defines a secure, one way (simplex) channel. A bi-directional (duplex) channel between two hosts therefore employs two pairs of keys [1]. Each kernel of each host in normal operational mode has a secure full duplex channel established with each other kernel in the network. How these channels are established concerns the method by which hosts are intialized, and is discussed later. The kernel-kernel channels are used for exchanging keys that will be used for other channels between the two hosts and for kernel-kernel control messages [2]. The need for these will become apparent as the protocol is outlined. If it is desired, the protocols can be trivially altered to keep the cleartext form of keys only within the encryption units of the hosts. For simplicity of explanation, that requirement is not used here.

---

[1] *The same key could be used for both directions in conventional encryption, but for conceptual clarity here it is not*

[2] *In a centralized key distribution version, these kernel-kernel secure channels would be replaced by kernel-key distribution center secure channels.*

A connection will get established in the following way.
When hosts are initialized, their NPMs will establish connections
through a procedure analogous to the one we outline here, and
described in more detail later. Then, when a user process wishes
to connect to a foreign site, the process executes an "establish
connection" system call which informs the NPM of the request.
The NPM exchanges messages with the foreign NPM using their
already existing channel. This exchange will include any host-
host protocol for establishing communications in the network.
Presumably the NPMs eventually agree that a connection has been
established. At that point the user processes are still unable
to communicate, since so far as the kernel is concerned, nothing
has been done. The content of NPM exchanges is invisible to the
kernel. Rather, at this point, the NPMs must ask the kernel to
establish the channel for the processes. This action is performed
with kernel function calls. Those calls grant capabilities to
the user process so that subsequent requests can be made directly
by the process.

In order to explain in more detail, the following four proto-
type kernel calls are described. The first two are involved in
setting up the encryption channel, and presumably would be issued
only by the NPMs. The second two are the means by which user
processes send and receive data over the connection.

GID (foreign-host, connection-id, process-id, state) Give-id.
This call supplies to the kernel an id which the caller would
like to be used as the name of a channel to be established. The
kernel checks it for uniqueness before accepting it, and also
makes relevant protection checks. If *state* = "init", the kernel
chooses the encryption key to be associated with the id (or
queries key controller for key). The entry <connection-id, key,
process-id, state> is made in the kernel Key Table. Using its
secure channel, the kernel sends <connection-id, key, policy-info>
to the foreign host. The policy-info can be anything, but in the
military case, it should be the security level of the local
process identified by process-id. In a commercial case it might
be the organization by which the user was employed. It might
also be a network-wide global name of the user associated with
the process. If *state* = "complete", then there should already be
an entry in the Key Table (caused by the other host having
executed a GID) so a check for match is made before sending out
the kernel-kernel message and a key is not included. The NPM
process is notified when an id is received from a foreign kernel.

CID (connection-id) Close id. The NPM and the appropriate process at the local site are both notified that the call has been issued. The corresponding entry in the Key Table is deleted. Over the secure kernel-kernel channel, a message is sent telling the other kernel to delete its corresponding Key Table entry. This call should be executable only by NPMs or by the process whose Key Table entry indicates that it is the process associated with this id, to block potential denial of service problems.

Encrypt (connection-id, data) Encrypt data and buffer for NPM. This call adds integrity information, such as sequence numbers, to the data, encrypts the data using the key corresponding to the supplied id (fails unless the process-id associated with the connection-id matches that of the caller) and places the data in an internal buffer. The NPM is informed of the awaiting data.

Decrypt (connection-id, user-buffer) Decrypt data. This call decrypts the data from the system buffer belonging to the connection-id supplied using the appropriate key. The data is moved into the user's buffer. The call fails unless the process-id stored in the Key Table matches the caller and all data integrity checks succeed (such as sequence numbers).

An important new kernel table is the Key Table [1]. It contains some number of entries, each of which have the following information:

<foreign-host, connection-id, key, sequence-no, local-process-id>

There is one additional kernel entry point besides the calls listed above, namely the one caused by control messages from the foreign kernel. There are two types of such messages: one corresponding to the foreign GID call and the other corresponding to a foreign CID. The first makes an incomplete entry in the receiving kernel's Key Table, and the second deletes the appropriate entry.

The following sequence of steps illustrates how a connection would be established using the encryption connection protocol. The host processors involved are numbered 1 and 2. Process A at host 1 wishes to connect to process B at host 2.

---

[1] *In some hardware encryption implementations, the keys are kept internal to the hardware unit. In that case, the key entry in the Key Table can merely be an index into the encryption unit's key table.*

(1)   Process A executes an establish connection call which informs
NPM@1, saying "connect from A to B@2".   This message can be sent
locally in the clear.   If confinement is important, other methods
can be employed to limit the bandwidth between A and the NPM.
(2)   NPM@1 sends control messages to NPM@2 including whatever
Host-Host protocol required [2].
(3)   NPM@2 receives an indication of message arrival, does an I/O
call to retrieve it, examines header, determines that it is
recipient and processes the message.
(4)   NPM@2 initiates step 2 at site 2, leading to step 3 being
executed at site 1 in response.   This exchange continues until
NPM@1 and NPM@2 open the connection, having established whatever
internal local name mappings are required.
(5)   NPM@1 executes GID (connection-id, process-id, "init"), where
connection-id is an agreed upon connection id between the two
NPMs, and process-id is the local name of the process that
requested the connection.
(6)   In executing the GID, the kernel@1 generates or obtains a
key, makes an entry in its Key Table, and sends a message over
its secure channel to Kernel@2, who makes corresponding entry in
its table and interrupts NPM@2, giving it connection-id.
(7)   NPM@2 issues corresponding GID (connection-id, process-id',
"complete") where connection-id is the same and process-id' is
the one local to host 2.   This call interrupts process-id', and
eventually causes the appropriate entry to be made in the kernel
table at host 1.   The making of that entry interrupts NPM@1 and
process-id@1.
(8)   Process-id and process-id' can now use the channel by issu-
ing successive Encrypt and Decrypt calls.

There are a number of places in the mechanisms just described
where failure can occur.   If the network software in either of the
hosts fails or decides not to open the connection, no kernel calls
are involved, and standard protocols operate.   A GID may fail
because the id supplied was already in use, a protection policy
check was not successful or because the kernel table was full.
The caller is notified.   He may try again.   In the case of failure
of a GID, it may be necessary for the kernel to execute most of
the actions of CID to avoid race conditions that can result from
other methods of indicating failure to the foreign site.

---

[2]   *The host-host protocol messages would normally be sent
      encrypted using the NPM-NPM key in most implementations.*

Discussion

The encryption mechanism just outlined contains no error correction facilities. If messages are lost, or sequence numbers are out of order or duplicated, the kernel merely notifies the user and network software of the error and renders the channel unusable. This action is taken on all channels, including the kernel-kernel channels. For every case but the last, CIDs must be issued and a new channel created via GIDs. In the last case, the procedures for bringing up the network must be used.

This simple minded view is acceptable in part because the expected error rate on most networks is quite low. Otherwise, it would be too expensive to reestablish the channel for each error. However, it should be noted that any higher level protocol errors are still handled by that protocol software, so that most failures can be managed by the NPM without affecting the encryption channel. On highly error prone channels, additional protocol at the encryption level may still be necessary. See Kent [Kent 76] for a discussion of resynchronization of the sequencing supported by the encryption channel.

From the protection viewpoint, one can consider the collection of NPMs across the network as forming a single (distributed) domain. They may exchange information freely among them. No user process can send or receive data directly to or from an NPM, except via narrow bandwidth channels through which control information is sent to the NPM and status and error information is returned. These channels can be limited by adding parameterized calls to the kernel to pass the minimum amount of data to the NPMs, and having the kernel post, as much as possible, status reports directly to the processes involved. The channel bandwidth cannot be zero, however.

System Initialization Procedures

The task of bringing up the network software is composed of two important parts. First, it is necessary to establish keys for the secure kernel-kernel channels and the NPM-NPM channels. Next, the NPM can initialize itself and its communications with other NPMs. Finally, the kernel can initialize its communications with other kernels. This latter problem is essentially one of mutual authentication, of each kernel with the other member of the pair, and appropriate solutions depend upon the expected threats against which protection is desired.

The initialization of the kernel-kernel channel and NPM-NPM channel key table entries will require that the kernel maintain initial keys for this purpose. The kernel cannot obtain these keys using the above mechanisms at initialization because they require the prior existence of the NPM–NPM and kernel–kernel channels. Thus, this circularity requires the kernel to maintain at least two key pairs [1]. However, such keys could be kept in read only memory of the encryption unit if desired.

The initialization of the NPM–NPM communications then proceeds as it would if encryption were not present. In most networks, some form of host–host reset command would be sent (encrypted with the proper NPM–NPM key). Once this NPM–NPM initialization is complete, the kernel–kernel connections could be established by the NPM. At this point, the system would be ready for new connection establishment. It should be noted that, if desired, the kernels could then set up new keys for the kernel–kernel and NPM–NPM channels, thus only using the initialization keys for a short time. To avoid overhead at initialization time, and to limit the sizes of kernel Key Tables, NPMs probably should only establish channels with other NPMs when a user wants to connect to that particular foreign site, and perhaps close the NPM–NPM channel after all user channels are closed.

Symmetry

The case study just presented portrayed a basically symmetric protocol suitable for use by intelligent nodes, a fairly general case. However, in some instances, one of the pair lacks algorithmic capacity, as illustrated by simple hardware terminals or simple microprocessors. Then a strongly asymmetric protocol is required, where the burden falls on the more powerful of the pair.

A form of this problem might also occur if encryption is not handled by the system, but rather by the user processes themselves. Then for certain operations, such as sending mail, the receiving user process might not even be present. (Note that such an approach may not guarantee the encryption of all network traffic). Schroeder and Needham have sketched protocols that are similar in spirit to those presented here to deal with such cases.

----

[1] *In a centralized key distribution version, the only keys which would be needed would be those for the key distributor NPM-host NPM channel and for the key distributor kernel-host kernel channel. In a distributed key management system, keys would be needed for each key manager.*

V.   DATAGRAMS

The case of electronic mail illustrates an important variation to the protocols presented earlier. Assume that a user at one site wishes to send mail to a user at another site.

Using conventional encryption algorithms, the first user would request a connection to the second user, and a new key would be chosen and distributed by the key controller for use in the communication. That key is sent using the secret keys of the two users.

However, since the second user may not be signed on at the time, a daemon process is used to receive the mail and deliver it to the user's "mailbox" file for his later inspection. It is desirable that the daemon process not need to access the cleartext form of the mail, for that would require the mail receiver mechanism to be trusted. This feat can be accomplished by sending the mail to the daemon process in encrypted form and having the daemon put that encrypted data directly into the mailbox file. The user can decrypt it when he signs on to read his mail. In that way, the daemon only needs the ability to append to a user's mailbox file.

In order for the user to know the new key used for this mail, however, the key distribution algorithm used earlier must be modified. Rather than sending the key for this connection to both the sender and the receiver, the key controller sends the key twice to the sender, one copy encrypted with the sender's secret key and one copy encrypted with the receiver's. The sender can prepend the copy of the key encrypted in the receiver's secret key to the mail before transmission. When the recipient signs on, his own mail program will examine the mailbox file, find the key message, decrypt it using his secret key, and then use the new key to decrypt the remaining text.

In the case of the public key encryption algorithms, the mail problem is somewhat simplified since the recipient knows what key to use in decryption (his secret key). However, authentication is not possible since the recipient is not present when the message is received. Thus, it may be a replay of a previously sent message. This problem can be prevented in the conventional encryption algorithm case via various protocols with the key managers, for example, by timestamping the mail and having the recipient keep track of recently used mail keys.

Both mechanisms outlined above do guarantee that only the desired recipient of a message will be able to read it. However, as pointed out, they don't guarantee to the recipient the identity of the sender. This problem is essentially that of digital signatures, and is discussed in the next section.

VI. PUBLIC KEY ALGORITHMS AND DIGITAL SIGNATURES

The development of public key based encryption was greeted by a great deal of interest, since the method appears to present considerable advantages over conventional encryption methods, especially with respect to key distribution and digital mail signatures.

However, on closer examination, it seems that public key algorithms possess no particular advantages over conventional algorithms. The reasons for this conclusion are readily seen and are outlined below.

Key Distribution

Let us examine each of the advantages claimed for public key algorithms. The first is key distribution. Simply put, public key advocates argue that an automated "telephone book" of public keys can generally be made available, and therefore whenever user x wishes to communicate with user y, x merely must look up y's public key in the book, encrypt the message with that key, and send it to y [Diffie 76]. Therefore, there is no key distribution problem at all. Further, no central authority is required initially to set up the channel between x and y.

Needham and Schroeder point out however that this viewpoint is incorrect: some form of a central authority is needed and the protocol involved is no simpler nor any more efficient than one based on conventional algorithms [Needham 77]. Their argument may be summarized as follows. First, the safety of the public key scheme depends critically on the correct public key being selected by the sender. If the key listed with a name in the "telephone book" is the wrong one, then there is no security. Furthermore, maintenance of the (by necessity machine supported) book is non-trivial because keys will change; either because of the natural desire to replace a key pair which has been used for high amounts of data transmission, or because a key has been compromised through a variety of ways. There must be some source of carefully maintained "books" with the responsibility of care- fully authenticating any changes and correctly sending out public keys (or entire copies of the book) upon request.

Needham and Schroeder also exhibit protocols to provide the desired properties for public key systems, and show that there are equivalent protocols for conventional algorithms. The protocols are equivalent both in terms of numbers of messages required as well as in the mechanisms which must be trusted. The only observable difference is that the central authority in the conventional case, in addition to being trusted, must also keep its collection of (conventional) keys secret. Based on the work at UCLA on secure operating systems, it appears that the task of constructing a secure central authority is no harder than building the correct one needed for public key systems.

Digital Signatures

The second area in which public key methods are often thought to be superior to conventional ones is digital message signatures. The method, assuming a suitable public key algorithm, is for the sender to encode the mail by "decrypting" it with his private key and then send it. The receiver decodes the message by "encrypting" with the sender's public key. The usual view is that this procedure does not require a central authority, except to adjudicate an authorship challenge. However, two points should be noted. First, a central authority *is* needed by the recipient for aid in deciphering the first message received from any given author (to get the corresponding public key, as above). Second, the central authority must keep all old values of public keys in a reliable way to properly adjudicate conflicts over old signatures (consider the relevant lifetime of a signature on a real estate deed for example) [Needham 77].

Further, and more serious, the unadorned public key signature protocol just described has an important flaw. The author of signed messages can effectively disavow and repudiate his signatures at any time, merely by causing his secret key to be made public, or "compromised". When such an event occurs, either by accident or intention, all messages previously "signed" using the given private key are invalidated, since the only proof of validity has been destroyed. Because the private key is now known, anyone could have created any of the messages sent earlier by the given author. None of the signatures can be relied upon.

Hence, the validity of a signature on a message is only as safe as the *entire* future history of protection of the private key. Further, the ability to remove the protection resides in precisely the individual (the author) who should not hold that right. That is, one important purpose of a signature is to indicate responsibility for the content of the accompanying message in a way that cannot be later disavowed.

Some people may argue that this concern is overly conservative; that existing signature methods are not very reliable, that individuals have considerable incentive not to repudiate their signatures, and so one is justified in constructing a flawed solution. However, in our view this characteristic is clearly unsatisfactory, especially if it is possible to devise suitable digital signature methods which do not suffer from this problem.

The situation with respect to signatures using conventional algorithms initially appears slightly better. Rabin [Rabin 78] proposes elsewhere in this volume a method of digital signatures based on any strong conventional algorithm. Like public key methods, it too requires either a central authority or an explicit agreement between the two parties involved to get matters going [1]. Similarly, an adjudicator is required for challenges. Rabin's method, however, uses a large number of keys, with keys not being reused from message to message. As a result, if a few keys are compromised, other signatures based on other keys are still safe. However, that is not a real advantage over public key methods, since one could easily add a layer of protocol over the public key method to change keys for each message as Rabin does for conventional methods. One could even use a variant of Rabin's scheme itself with public keys, although it is easy to develop a simpler one.

However, *all* of the digital signature methods described or suggested above suffer from the problem of repudiation of signature via key compromise. Rabin's protocol or analogues to it merely limit the damage (or, equivalently, provide selectivity!). It appears that the problem is intrinsic to any approach in which the validity of an author's signature depends on secret information, which can potentially be revealed, either by the author or other interested parties. Surely improvement would be desirable.

---

[1]   *In his paper, Rabin describes an initialization method which involves an explicit contract between each pair of parties that wish to communicate with digitally signed messages. One can easily instead add a central authority to play this role, using suitable authentication protocols, thus obviating any need for two parties to make specific arrangements prior to exchanging signed correspondence.*

A Reliable Digital Signature Method

A simple, obvious solution is to interpose some trusted interpretive layer between the author and his signature keys, whatever their form. For example, suppose the list of keys in Rabin's algorithm were not known to the author, but instead were contained in a secure Unit (hardware or software). Whenever the author wished to send a signed message, he merely submitted the message to the Unit, which selected the appropriate keys and then used the standard algorithm. Each author has access to such a Unit.

The loading of each Unit requires some examination. In particular, the means which are used to select keys and insert them into each Unit must be correct if mail challenges are to be handled satisfactorily. That is, there must be some trusted Source of keys (and matching "standard message" in the Rabin protocol), and the key list for each author/recipient pair must be deliverable in a correct, secret way to the appropriate Units. We will call the collection of Units and the Source(s), together with their internal communication protocols, a Network Registry (NR). Such an NR appears required to solve the problems raised earlier. Note that some secure communication protocol among the components of the Network Registry is required. However, it can be very simple; low level link encryption would suffice.

For safety and efficiency, the NR functions presumably should be decomposed and distributed throughout the network. In particular, the failure or compromise of a local NR would then only have local consequences. One can even construct local NR components of the Network Registry in a decentralized way so that compromise of more than one component would be required before a message signature was affected [1]. The NR architecture issue, while important, is to some degree a digression here and so we put it aside.

The Registry concept is quite common in the paper world. A local government's real estate recorder's office is probably the most commonly known example.

---

[1] *See section 6.6.*

Authentication

We now make an important observation. It is still necessary
that there exist a guaranteed authentication mechanism by which
an individual is authenticated to the NR (presumably directly to
the local Unit). Any reasonable communication system of course
ultimately requires such a facility, for if one user can
masquerade as another, all signature systems will fail. What is
required is some reliable way to identify a user sitting at a
terminal -- some method stronger than the password schemes used
today. Perhaps an unforgeable mechanism based on fingerprints
or other personal characteristics will emerge.

Simplification of the Proposed Signature Architecture:
Specialized Digital Signature Protocols Unnecessary

Once the necessity of a Network Registry is recognized,
including a guaranteed authentication mechanism, it appears that
simplifications in the mechanisms required for digital signatures
can be made that seem to remove the need for specialized digital
signature protocols. Instead, any of a collection of simple
methods will suffice.

In particular, in order for the Network Registry to operate
satisfactorily (including performing user authentication), it
clearly must be distributed, and clearly must be able to
communicate securely internally among the distributed components.
Given that such facilities exist, then the following is an example
of a simple implementation of digital signatures which does not
require a specialized protocol or encryption algorithm:

(1)   The author authenticates with a local Network Registry
component, creates a message, and hands the message to the NR
together with the recipient identifier and an indication that a
registered signature is desired.
(2)   A Network Registry (not necessarily the local component)
computes a simple characteristic function of the message, author,
recipient, and current time, encrypts the result with a key known
only to the Network Registry, and forwards the resulting
"signature block" to the recipient. The NR only retains the
encryption key employed.
(3)   The recipient, when the message is received, can ask the NR
if the message was indeed signed by the claimed author by presenting the signature block and message. Subsequent challenges are
handled in the same way.

This simple protocol involves little additional mechanism beyond that which was needed by the Network Registry anyway. It does require that the Network Registry be involved in every message signature and validation. However, recall that all of the unadorned signature methods reviewed earlier require involvement of some form of a Network Registry for at least the first message between any two parties. Public key protocols must check the "telephone book", and Rabin's method requires either a contract or a Network Registry. Furthermore, when one adds a more complete Network Registry on top of those other signature methods to correct their repudiation problem, all methods involve the NR for each message. Note that this protocol also does not require the NR to maintain any significant storage for signature blocks.

Performance and Safety

Certain elementary precautions should be taken in the design of the Network Registry to avoid unnecessary internal message exchanges and to assure safety of the keys used to encrypt the signature blocks. Performance enhancements presumably would involve distributing the signature block calculation. Safety enhancements could include the use of different keys at each distributed site, replicating sites, and employing a signature block computation which requires the cooperation of multiple sites. Each of these facilities is straightforward to build and so they are not discussed further here.

From the preceding discussion, we conclude that the digital signature algorithms proposed heretofore are unsatisfactory, and the improvements required to correct their inadequacies make the use of a specialized digital signature algorithm unnecessary.

We note here that the safety of signatures in this proposal also depends on the future history of protection of keys as before, in this case those held by the Network Registry. However, there are several crucial differences between this case and previous proposals. First, the authors of messages do not retain the ability to repudiate signatures at will. Second, the Network Registry can be structured so that failure or compromise of several of the components is necessary before signature validity is lost. In the previous methods, a single failure could lead to compromise.

VI.   CONCLUSIONS

We draw a number of specific conclusions, as well as more
general perspectives from the preceding discussions. The
specifics are as follows. First, public key encryption systems,
viewed in the context of the network protocols by which they
must be used, do not seem to provide any significant advantages
over conventional encryption algorithms. Each important function
that has been recognized can be performed at least as easily by
conventional methods with, it appears, no more supporting
mechanism. Therefore, if strong conventional algorithms are
easier to develop, as has been speculated [Rivest 77b], research
would be better devoted to that area rather than public key
systems.

Second, it seems that the digital signature methods which
have been proposed, both public key and conventional algorithm
based, do not adequately protect recipients of signed documents
from repudiation of signatures by the author revealing the secret
key(s) employed. The difficulty appears intrinsic to the
approaches being taken. An alternative is available which over-
comes this problem, however, that involves a small amount of
trusted software.

Third, the necessary underlying mechanism required to support
improved digital signature methods, as well as other user visible
secure network communication protocols, is relatively well understood, and an example is presented in this paper. The example
takes account of the important requirements that the amount of
trusted mechanism involved be minimized for the sake of safety.

In more global terms, this discussion of network security has
been intended to illustrate the current state of the art. It
suggests the following general perspectives.

If one's view of security of data in networks is basically a
common carrier philosophy, then general principles by which
secure, common carrier based, point to point communication can be
provided are reasonably well in hand. Of course, as in any
sophisticated implementation, there will surely be considerable
careful engineering to be done.

However, this conclusion rests on one important assumption
that is not universally valid. Either there exist secure
operating systems to support the individual processes and the
required encryption protocol facilities, or each machine operates
as a single protection domain. A secure implementation of a Key
Distribution Center or Registry is necessary in any case.
Fortunately, reasonably secure operating systems are well on their
way, so that this intrinsic dependency of network security on an

appropriate operating system base should not seriously delay common carrier security.

One could however take a rather different view of the nature of the network security problem: the goal might be to provide a high level extended machine for the user, in which no explicit awareness of the network is required. The underlying facility is trusted to securely move data from site to site as necessary to support whatever data types and operations that are relevant to the user. The facility operates securely and with integrity in the face of unplanned crashes of any nodes in the network. Synchronization of operations on user meaningful objects (such as Withdrawal on Checking Account) is reliably maintained. If one takes such a high level view of the goal of network security, then the simple common carrier solutions respond only to part of the network security problem and more work remains.

REFERENCES

[Diffie 76] Diffie, W. and M. Hellman, "New Directions in Cryptography", *IEEE Transactions on Information Theory*, November 1976, pp. 644-654.
[Kent 76] Kent, S., *Encryption-Based Protection Protocols for Interactive User-Computer Communication*, Laboratory for Computer Science, MIT, TR 162, 1976.
[Needham 77] Needham, R. and M. Schroeder, "Security and Authentication in Large Networks of Computers", Xerox Palo Alto Research Center Technical Report, September 1977.
[Popek 78a] Popek, G. J. and D. Farber, "A Model for Verification of Data Security in Operating Systems", *Communications of the ACM* (to appear).
[Popek 78b] Popek, G. J. and C. S. Kline, "Design Issues for Secure Computer Networks", in *Operating Systems, An Advanced Course*, R. Bayer, R. M. Graham, G. Seegmuller, ed., Springer-Verlag, 1978.
[Popek 78c] Popek, G. J. and C. S. Kline, "Issues in Kernel Design", *Proceedings of the National Computer Conference*, AFIPS Press, 1978.
[Rabin 77] Rabin, M., "Digital Signatures Using Conventional Encryption Algorithms", *Proceedings of the Conference on Foundations of Secure Computation*, Atlanta, Georgia, October 3-5, 1977, Academic Press.
[Rivest 77a] Rivest, R. L., Shamir, A. and L. Adleman, *A Method for Obtaining Digital Signatures and Public-Key Cryptosystems*, MIT Laboratory for Computer Science Technical Memo, LCS/TM82 Cambridge, Massachusetts 02139, April 4, 1977 (revised in August 1977)
[Rivest 77b] Rivest, R., private communications, 1977.

DIGITALIZED SIGNATURES*

Michael O. Rabin

Hebrew University of Jerusalem
Massachusetts Institute of Technology

INTRODUCTION

In many business transactions an essential role is played by
signed messages and by cerification of messages received. A
party to a contract or the issuer of a binding document in
question. The signature, which is assumed to be unique to the
signatory or signer, serves as proof that he was a party to the
document, or that he was its sole originator. If the document
spells out certain obligations for the signer then his signature
signals his agreement to undertake these obligations. The
certification of receipt of a message is effected by the receiver
or some intermediary agent, signing a statement to the effect
that the message was in fact received by him.

Thus signature and certification nowadays involve the production, transfer, and eventual storage of a physical document.

We are moving towards an era of electronic correspondence
when a large bulk of business correspondence will be conducted,
even when humanly generated, from computer to computer. When
corresponding in this mode, there arises the problem of how to
affix a binding signature to a message when this is deemed
necessary.

---

* *This work was done while the author was visiting the IBM
Thomas J. Watson Laboratory during July of 1976, and prepared
for publication during a visit to MIT.*

The problem of digitalized signatures is by no means simple. For example, a telegram bearing somebody's name, cannot by itself serve as full legal proof that it originated with the named sender. The alleged sender can disown the message, claiming that somebody else, maybe even the recipient or his agent, has sent it using a false name. The adjudication of such a dispute is time consuming and costly.

The difficulty may be summed up by noting that in electronic communications a message is just information, i.e., a string of bits devoid of unique physical characteristics. Consequently what will serve as signature must also be information.

In this paper we propose a signature system employing any block-encoding device and based, in one essential aspect, on probabilistic logic. A different signature system can be based on the Diffie-Hellman proposal [1] of public-key cipher systems. An algorithm for such a public key-system employing large prime numbers was discovered by the author (unpublished) and independently by Rivest, Adleman and Shamir [3].

The properties of the encoding function which are needed for rendering the signature system secure are stated in Section 3 in axiomatic form. This enables us to establish properties of the system as provable consequences from the axioms. The advantage of this approach is that in the absence of explicitly stated assumptions and deductions, discussions concerning viability of a security system tend to degenerate into hand waiving non-convergent arguments.

The axioms themselves are assumptions about the intractability of certain computations involving the encoding function. The notion of intractability required for ensuring the soundness of an encoding function is different from and stronger than the existing concept in complexity theory. In Section 10 we briefly touch on the methodological questions pertaining to secure communications and signatures. We introduce the notion of *universal intractability* required for a sound theoretical foundation of this field.

I. Signatures and Their Properties

Denote by M a message such as a contract and by $\sigma_p(M)$ the signature on M by a person P (who may be signing on behalf of a legal entity). This signature must have the following properties:

Property (a):   Only P can produce *any* pairs, M, $\sigma_p(M)$.

Property (b): The recipient of a pair M, W claimed to be signed by P, can check that indeed $W = \sigma_p(M)$.

Note that property (a) is stronger than the assumption that only P can sign a *given* message. Property (a) entails that the signature $\sigma_p(M)$ is characteristic not only of P but also of the entire message M. If when given a signed message N, $\sigma_p(N)$ an adversary could effectively find a message $M \neq N$ such that $\sigma_p(M) = \sigma_p(N)$, then the adversary could produce a signed message M, $\sigma_p(M)$ not authored by P. This would contradict (a). Ordinary signatures do not enjoy this important property of immutability of the message.

II. The Encoding Function

Let k be some fixed word length.

Definition 1: An *encoding function* is a mapping E: $\{0,1\}^k \times \{0,1\}^k \to \{0,1\}^k$. For x, w $\varepsilon \{0,1\}^k$ denote the function value $E_x w$ and call it the *encoding* of w by use of the *key* x.

Such encoding functions are used in block-ciphers for secure commercial communications. One existing commercial device uses k = 64. To serve for encryption E must be supplemented by the *decoding function* D which satisfies $D_x E_x w = w$. For the construction of our signature system, however, only the encoding function is required.

A *message* is a sequence of words

$$M = w_1 w_2 \ldots w_m, \quad \ell(w_i) = k.$$

The encoding function E can be extended to a mapping $E: (\{0,1\}^k)* \times \{0,1\}^k \to \{0,1\}^k$ employing messages as keys, by defining

$$E_M w = E_{w_1} E_{w_2} \ldots E_{w_m} w.$$

Note that we are using parenthesis-free notation. Thus $E_x E_y u = E_x(E_y(u)) = E_{xy} u.$

III.   Assumptions Concerning E

In the spirit of basing the development on a small number of explicitly stated assumptions (axioms) from which subsequent statements are logically derivable, we now proceed to list our assumptions concerning E.

Assumption 1.   The function $E_x w$ is rapidly calculable.

Assumption 2.   For every key x, and any given list
(1) $w_1, E_x w_1, \ldots, w_n, E_x w_n$,

it is intractably hard to produce a pair w, $u = E_x w$ such that $w \neq w_i$; $1 \leq i \leq n$.

The intractable computation is Assumption 2 has as input the sequence (1) (but not x) and the required output is a new pair w, $E_x w$. Note that from these assumptions follows the intractability of computing a key x from the sequence (1). For if it were possible to compute x, then one could choose a $w \neq w_i$, $1 \leq i \leq n$, and by Assumption 1 compute $u = E_x w$.

Assumption 3.   Given any word w it is intractable to compute two messages $N \neq M$ such that $E_N w = E_M w$.

For a fixed w the mapping $M \rightarrow E_M w$ is a hashing-function, mapping messages into words (of length k). Counting arguments imply that there must exist $M \neq N$ so that $E_M w = E_N w$. Assumption 3 just claims that it is computationally hard to find such pairs. The reader can check for himself that even if there exists an easy way to compute the decoding function D, the obvious attempts at finding such a pair M, N, run afoul of Assumption 2. But we need Assumption 3 to rule out all possible algorithms.

IV.   Exchange of Keys

If A and B want to conduct digitalized signed correspondence they get together once for exchanging keys by the following procedure.

A chooses, say, 120 keys $x_1, \ldots, x_{120}$ which he does not devulge.   Similarly B chooses $y_1, \ldots, y_{120}$.

Let $M_0 = 0^k$ be the *standard message* which will be employed by all users of the system. If i is an integer we shall understand $M_0(i)$ to be the word obtained by writing $i = \varepsilon_{e-1} \varepsilon_{e-2} \cdots \varepsilon_0$

in binary notation and setting $M_0(i) = 0^{k-e}\varepsilon_{e-1}\cdots\varepsilon_0$. Thus if $i = 5$ then $M_0(i) = 0^{k-3}101$, so that $\ell(M_0(i)) = k$.

Using the encoding function, A produces the ordered list

$$(2) \qquad \alpha = E_{x_1}M_0(1),\ldots,E_{x_{120}}M_0(120) = \alpha_1,\ldots,\alpha_{120}.$$

Similarly for B:

$$(3) \qquad \beta = E_{y_1}M_0(1),\ldots,E_{y_{120}}M_0(120) = \beta_1,\ldots,\beta_{120}.$$

A and B then sign (by ordinary legal procedure) an agreement stating that α is an encoding of the standard message using A's keys and similarly for B with respect to β.

V. Verification of Keys

Let B or any other party be presented with a word x claimed to be the A's i^{th} key x_i. He can verify the claim by computing $E_x M_0(i)$ and comparing with α_i in the list α. Similarly for B's keys.

VI. Production and Acceptance of Signatures

When signing a message M, A starts by *compressing* M. Namely, he forms

$$(4) \qquad\qquad C(M) = E_M M_0 .$$

The signature is defined as follows.

Definition 2. A's signature on message M using the first block (of 40) keys is

$$\sigma_A(M) = E_{x_1} C(M),\ldots,E_{x_{40}} C(M).$$

Each $E_{x_i} C(M) = E_{x_i}M_0$ will be called a *marking* so that the signature $\sigma_A(M)$ is a sequence of 40 markings. Using 40 markings is, of course, arbitrary. The number of markings employed in an actual implementation depends on security considerations spelled out in Section 8.

Signing the next message, A will employ the second block of keys $x_{41}, \ldots, x_{80}$, etc. Each block of 40 keys is used only *once* and an onward moving marker is kept in the list of keys, or a signature count is maintained, to ensure strict adherence to this rule.

For a purely technical reason A checks, after compressing M, whether $C(M) = M_0(i)$ for some $i \leq 10^7$, i.e., whether $C(M)$ is mostly zeros. In the unlikely event that this occurs, he slightly modifies M before signing it. As a practical matter this contingency never arises. But we impose this restriction that $C(M) \neq M_0(i)$ so that markings $E_{x_i} C(M)$ will not unintention-ally coincide with key encryptions $E_{x_i} M_0(i)$. See Section 8.

When B receives the sequence $M, u_1, \ldots, u_{40}$ from A he verifies that indeed $(u_1, \ldots, u_{40}) = \sigma_A(M)$ by the following procedure.

(i)   B *randomly* chooses 20 different numbers $1 \leq i_j \leq 40$, $1 \leq j \leq 20$.

(ii) Upon request from B, A devulges to him the actual keys $x_{i_1}, \ldots, x_{i_{20}}$.

(iii) B verifies by the method in Section 5 that these are indeed the i_1th,$\ldots,i_{20}$th keys of A.

(iv) B checks that $u_{i_j} = E_{x_{i_j}} C(M)$ $1 \leq j \leq 20$.

(v)   B *accepts* the signed message if and only if *all* the tests in (iii), (iv) resulted positively.

VII.   Adjudication of Disputes

It is inevitable that occasionally a participant A in a signature-system may want to challenge or disown a message claimed to be signed by him. In this situation, B presents a message (contract) $M, v_1, \ldots, v_{40}$, claiming that A signed it using, say, the first block of keys; A denies this claim.

Settlement of such a dispute requires the supervision of an *adjudicator* or judge. Adjudication, however, is not a process of examination of witnesses and evidence but rather the imple-mentation of a certain algorithm.

The adjudicator requests A to reveal his keys $x_1, \ldots, x_{40}$ which allegedly were employed in producing the markings $v_1, \ldots, v_{40}$. He then proceeds to

(i) Verify these keys, i.e., check whether

$$E_{x_1} M_0(1) = \alpha_1, \ldots, E_{x_{40}} M_0(40) = \alpha_{40}.$$

If not *all* keys are verified, the adjudicator right away upholds B's claim that the signature is valid.

(ii) After all keys are verified, the adjudicator tests for each marking v_i, $1 \leq i \leq 40$, whether $E_{x_i} C(M) = v_i$.

(iii) If 20 or fewer of these equalities are true the adjudicator upholds A's challenge. If 21 or more equalities are true, the adjudicator upholds B's claim.

The fact that A challenged the message M, $v_1, \ldots, v_{40}$ and in doing so revealed keys $x_1, \ldots, x_{40}$ is recorded. In the future, if A's challenge was upheld then no message presented by B as signed by use of the first block of keys will be accepted. If B was upheld, then only the message M will be accepted as signed by A using the first block of keys.

VIII. Validity of the System

We now proceed to show that this signature system does satisfy Properties (a) - (b) of Section 1.

Consider the possibility of somebody other than A producing a signed message N, $v_1, \ldots, v_{40}$ employing the mth block of keys, $x_{i+1}, \ldots, x_{i+40}$, $i = 40(m-1)$. To make it easier on the counterfeiter, assume that this block was already used to produce the signed message

$$M, u_1, \ldots, u_{40}, \quad u_j = E_{x_{i+j}} C(M), \quad 1 \leq j \leq 40.$$

Of course, $M \neq N$ for otherwise N is not a forgery. The counterfeiter knows twenty of the keys $x_{i+1}, \ldots, x_{i+40}$, namely, those revealed by A, so that he can correctly produce the markings v_t corresponding to these keys. To produce a signature which will stand up when challenged by A, counterfeiter must produce one correct marking $v_p = E_{x_{i+p}} C(M)$ employing a key x_{i+p} *not* among those revealed.

At this stage the only available information involving x_{i+p} are the pairs $M_0(i+p)$, $E_{x_{i+p}} M_0(i+p) (=\alpha_{i+p})$ and $C(M)$,

$E_{x_{i+p}} C(M) (=u_p)$. For v_p to be a proper marking on N we must have

$v_p = E_{x_{i+p}} C(N)$. By the stipulation about signatures,

$C(N) \neq M_0(i+p)$. Now, if $C(N) \neq C(M)$ then the counterfeiter was

able to compute a third pair $C(N)$, $E_{x_{i+p}} C(N)$ contrary to Assump-

tion 2 in Section 3. If $C(N) = C(M)$ the counterfeiter was able to find an $N \neq M$ with $E_N M_0 = C(N) = C(M) = E_M M_0$, contrary to Assumption 3.

Thus A is protected, nobody can forge messages signed by him. Next we show that Property (b) of signatures holds, i.e., that B can verify that a message was signed by A in a way which bars A from later on disowing his signature.

The only way for A to produce a seemingly signed message $M, u_1, \ldots, u_{40}$ which B will accept and which A can later success-fully challenge, is to produce *exactly* twenty markings $u_{j_1}, \ldots, u_{j_{20}}$ which are proper, i.e., $u_j = E_{x_j} C(M)$. (We again assume that A informs B that the first block of keys was used.) For if fewer than 20 markings are proper, then by steps (iv) – (v) of the acceptance procedure B, will never accept $M, u_1, \ldots, u_{40}$. And if 21 or more markings are proper then, because of the rule (iii) of the adjudication procedure, A cannot successfully challenge this signed message.

Thus assume that A has prepared $M, u_1, \ldots, u_{40}$ so that just $u_{j_1}, \ldots, u_{j_{20}}$ are proper. Now, B will accept the message only if in his random choice of 20 indices $1 \leq i_1, \ldots, i_{20} \leq 40$ he picks exactly the indices $j_1, \ldots, j_{20}$. The probability of this occur-

ring is $1/\binom{40}{20} \sim \sqrt{20\pi}/2^{40} < 10^{-11}$. Thus B can be cheated on the average no more than once in 10^{11} times that he accepts a signed message. For all practical purposes this is an ample margin of safety.

Actually the margin of safety is even larger because in general the correspondents will not try to cheat. This is especially true since it is almost certain (probability $\geq 1 - 10^{-11}$) that if A tries to cheat he will be caught and there may be a penalty involved.

Assume that we use only 16 markings. In this case B will ask for 8 randomly chosen keys. The probability of B accepting an improperly signed message is $1/\binom{16}{8} \sim 13000^{-1}$. We may reasonably assume that even in extensive correspondence, attempts to cheat B will be fewer than once a day. Consequently 13000 days, i.e., 36 years, will pass on the average before B will acept an improperly signed message. We see that the number of markings in the signature depends on the desired level of confidence, and as a partical matter can be chosen to be quite small.

IV. Implementation

The signature system is, of course, implemented by machine. Thus when we say that A chooses keys x_1, x_2,..., or that B randomly selects 20 indices $1 \leq i,...,i_{20} \leq 40$ and A reveals to B the keys $x_{i_1},...,x_{i_{20}}$, etc. we intend all these steps to be executed by machine.

From a practical point of view the best arrangement may be a combination of a signature-machine (SIM) completely controllable by A, with a general computer available to many users.

SIM_A will contain a random number generator (RNG) for producing the keys x_1, x_2,..., used by A, and for the randomized key requests when checking signatures on messages received. For added security it may be preferable to use a physical device as RNG rather than a pseudo-random number generator.

It is preferable not to allow A's keys x_1, x_2,..., to be present in the general computer. To this end, assume that the encoding function E is decodable by D. (Alternatively, if E is not decodable, another pair $\overline{E}$, $\overline{D}$ may be used for the purpose at hand.) A uses a key a stored only in SIM_A. After the keys x_1, x_2,..., are generated inside STM_A, their coded version $E_a(x_1)$, $E_a(x_2)$,..., is stored in the general computer. When

keys are needed by A, he calls into SIM_A a block
$E_a(x_i), \ldots, E_a(x_{i+40})$ and decodes it using D_a.

The initially exchanged lists α and β need not be short.
They can involve tens of thousands of keys x_1, $x_2, \ldots, x_{40p}$,
$y_1, \ldots, y_{40p}$ so that $\alpha = E_{x_1} M_0(1), \ldots, E_{x_{40p}} M_0(40p)$ and similarly
for B. Treating α and β as messages, $C(\alpha)$ and $C(\beta)$ are formed.
A and B now exchange the lists α and β computer to computer, and
sign (by ordinary legal procedure) an agreement identifying $C(\alpha)$
and $C(\beta)$ as the compressed forms of α and β.

When the original lists α, β are about to be exhausted,
additional keys can be exchanged by the system itself in the
form of signed message using the now established protocol. In
order to avoid backtracking of challenged signatures, the
signatures on keylist extensions should involve only keys from
the lists orginally exchanged.

If the system is widely used within some commercial domain
such as banking or stock brokerage, then the bilateral agreement
can be replaced by establishing a central "trustee" with whom
each of the participants deposits lists of the form α.

The legal viability of such a digitalized signature system
does not depend on new laws pertaining to signatures. The
initial agreement between A and B (Section 4) will state that
the participants undertake to correspond and sign by the method
proposed in this paper, specify the dispute adjudication procedure and the (commercial) legal obligations and penalties
involved. Thus the initial agreement becomes a contract governing the digitalized signature procedure.

X.   Universal Intractability

As explained in [2], the viability of a digitalized signature system requires that the relevant system-breaking computations be intractable in a sense stronger than the one usually
defined in complexity theory. Even if the problem were proved
to be exponentially complex (no such result was proved to date)
this would only be a worst case or average complexity result.
It does not preclude the possibility that for one key in a
thousand the system can be broken by an algorithm not known to
the user. This level of hazard is not acceptable in the context
of signatures.

We want the encoding function to have the necessary properties *without exception*. This is, of course, too much to ask for
because an algorithm (program) may, for example, list certain
keys x, y,..., which are tried as a guess. In rare cases the
key used for the signature happens to be the one guessed at in
the algorithm, and forgery becomes possible. We thus want to
capture the idea that the encoding function E is strongly
randomizing and that any conceivable attack works no better than
a random guess at keys.

Take n = 2 in Assumption 2. The problem to be solved for
signature forgery is: Given $(u_1, E_x u_1)$, $(u_2, E_x u_2)$, find a

third pair $(v, E_x v)$, $v \neq u_1$, u_2. The intractability of this
special n = 2 case of Assumption 2 suffices for the proof of

validity of the signature system. Denote by $P \sim 2^{3k}$ the total
number of instances of the problem (k is the key and word

length). A given key x is involved in $2^{-k}P$ problem instances.
If AL is an algorithm for solving the problem then AL can list
at most $\ell(AL)$ keys. If AL runs N steps it can generate and try
at most N keys. Thus saying that given (u_1, w_1), (u_2, w_2), no
algorithm is better than "guessing" at keys x, trying if
$w_i = E_x u_i$, i = 1, 2, and if yes encoding a word v to produce
$v, E_x v$, is elucidated by

Definition 3. The list-extension problem of Assumption 2
is called *universally intractable* for an encoding function E if
any algorithm AL running N steps solves no more than

$(\ell(AL)+N)2^{-k}P$ instances.

For example, if k = 100, we restrict ourselves to algorithms
of size at most 10^{12}, and run on each instance at most 10^{12}

steps, the *fraction* of instances solved is $2 \cdot 10^{12} \cdot 2^{-100}$. Thus
the likelihood that for any given instance the problem will be
solvable in practical time is negligible. From the practical
point of view the problem can indeed be considered universally
intractable.

XI. Discussion

A comparison between the method proposed here and other
systems is in order.

One possibility which is considered is the digitalization,
by analogue to digital converstion, of paper and ink signatures.

This process is reported to have an about 95% reliability in terms of reproducibility and resistence to forgery. Once a physical signature was digitalized and affixed to a message, it can be lifted off and affixed to any other message. Thus a method employing physical signatures affords little protection in digitalized correspondence.

Signatures based on public-key ciphers (PKC) have some obvious advantages in terms of simplicity of protocol and avodicence of storage of lists of keys. In detailed comparison, the following points come up.

The signature protocol proposed here is implemented machine to machine so that the "work" involved is not a serious issue. In fact, the one-way functions used in PKC are considerably slower to compute than the encoding functions which can serve in this system.

Compared to the total volume of messages such as letters, contracts, etc., the total length of keys used in signatures is not large. Also, messages requiring signatures can often be batched and signed together.

The one-time use of a block of keys in the SIM system has advantages over the public-key. If the security of the public key is breached through some error or accident, then an avalanche of pre-dated counterfeit documents can ensue. The SIM system is much more stable under the effect of inadvertent disclosure of a block of keys.

Finally and most importantly, the PKC System is completely dependent on two or three known one-way functions having very special properties. If an algorithm for the decoding of the function in question is found, then the users of signatures based on PKC will have no substitute. The method proposed here can employ any block-encoding function as soon as it satisfies Assumptions 1 - 3. Thus unless a method is found to break all block-encoding devices, which would mean that secure communications other than by one time pads is impossible, our signature system is always implementable.

BIBLIOGRAPHY

[1]   Diffie, W., and Hellman, M., New Directions in Cryptograph, IEEE Trans. on Information Theory (November, 1976).
[2]   Rabin, M.O., Complexity of Computations, Comm. ACM, Vol. 20 (1977), 625-633.
[3]   Rivest, R.L., Shamir, A., and Adleman, L., A Method for Obtaining Digital Signatures and Public-key Cryptosystems, MIT Lab. for Comp. Sci. TM-82 (1977).

DISCUSSION

Shapiro: I'd like to comment on the simplicity and elegance of your solution. The core of it is the idea to randomize. It's not unlike a technique of probabilistic mathematical proof in which you allow a receiver to select one of two cases.

Rabin: Yes, you're right. B is, in fact, proving that the message came from A. And, in a way, similar to what occurs in my algorithm for testing primality, the proof is not a complete proof, but the residue of doubt is provably, negligibly small. The adversary, A in this case, cannot arrange things so that B's security is less than 1 - 1/2000. Or, if he wants to be safer, he does a little more and gets even a smaller number. The real assumption about these encoding systems is that they randomize in a very complete way. That is supported by experimental evidence, but only by experimental evidence. This sort of randomness says that there is no discernable connection between the w's and the u's, and that should really hold for all keys. One could try to do it for a subset of the keys; but, however, the state of the science here is that we really know nothing about this. We don't even know whether P = NP is true, but of course, if it is solvable then all of these keys are not good. A point I want to make is that even if we know that NP is provably exponential, then we are still not in the clear because we need a much stronger concept of complexity.

Cohen: Do you have a name for it?

Rabin: No, but that is a good question. Maybe I'll try to coin a name.

Rivest: I think it's worth pointing out that your system has an advantage with respect to key lossage over public key systems. In a public key system, if you've lost your key, you've lost it

with respect to everyone using the system; whereas, in this
system, if you lose your key, you've only lost it with respect to
the particular person that you are doing business with.

   Rabin: Now, there are some final remarks on physical
security.   This can be worked out by various obvious devices.
For example, keys are never stored in raw form; rathern encoded
forms of the keys are stored.   Then, of course, you use another
key to discipher it, but you do that within the confines of a
secure area.

ON DATA BANKS AND PRIVACY HOMOMORPHISMS

Ronald L. Rivest
Len Adleman
Michael L. Dertouzos

Massachusetts Institute of Technology
Cambridge, Massachusetts

I. INTRODUCTION

Encryption is a well-known technique for preserving the privacy of sensitive information. One of the basic, apparently inherent, limitations of this technique is that an information system working with encrypted data can at most store or retrieve the data for the user; any more complicated operations seem to require that the data be decrypted before being operated on. This limitation follows from the choice of encryption functions used, however, and although there are some truly inherent limitations on what can be accomplished, we shall see that it appears likely that there exist encryption functions which permit encrypted data to be operated on without preliminary decryption of the operands, for many sets of interesting operations. These special encryption functions we call "privacy homomorphisms"; they form an interesting subset of arbitrary encryption schemes (called "privacy transformations").

As a sample application, consider a small loan company which uses a commercial time-sharing service to store its records. The loan company's "data bank" obviously contains sensitive information which should be kept private. On the other hand, suppose that the information protection techniques employed by the time-sharing service are not considered adequate by the loan company. In particular, the systems programmers would presumably have access to the sensitive information. The loan company therefore decides to encrypt all of its data kept in the data bank and to maintain a policy of only decrypting data at the home office -- data will never be decrypted by the time-shared computer. The situation is thus that of Figure 1, where the wavy line encircles the physically secure premises of the loan company.

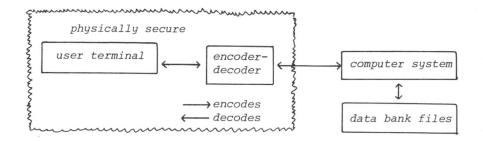

Figure 1

This organization permits the loan company to utilize the storage facilities of the time-sharing service, but generally makes it difficult to utilize the computational facilities without compromising the privacy of the stored data. The loan company, however, wishes to be able to answer such questions as:

- What is the size of the average loan outstanding?
- How much income from loan payments is expected next month?
- How many loans over $5,000 have been granted?

These questions require computation for their answers.

There are four possibilities that the loan company may pursue:

(1) Give up the idea of using the time-shared service and purchase an in-house computer system.

(2) Use the storage facilities of the time-sharing service only to store the encrypted data, and use an "intelligent terminal" at the loan company office to do the necessary decryption and computation.

(3) Persuade the time-sharing company to make hardware modifications to its computer allowing the data to exist in decrypted form for brief moments inside its CPU, but such that the decrypted data is not externally accessible.

(4) Use a special privacy homomorphism to encrypt its data so that the time-shared computer can operate on the data without the necessity of decrypting it first.

Option (1) can be very expensive, and does not necessarily solve the problem -- some form of encryption may be desired to protect the stored information against theft or malicious tampering by the in-house systems programmers. Option (2) will work, but entails rather large communications costs in general. Option (3) is also workable, but requires the cooperation of the time-sharing company. In section 2, we discuss this solution briefly. Option (4) requires only that a suitable privacy homomorphism

exist and that the loan company obtain an encryption/decryption
device implementing this homomorphism. In sections 3 to 5, we
examine the mathematical requirements for such a solution, some
limitations on its applicability, and some potentially useful
privacy homomorphisms, respectively.

II. SOLUTION BY HARDWARE MODIFICATION

In figure 2, we present a sketch of how a computer system
might be modified to solve the problem of performing operations
on encrypted data securely. In addition to the standard register
set and ALU (A,B), a physically secure register set and ALU (C,D)
are added. All communication of data between main memory and the
physically secure register set passes through an encoder-decoder
(E) supplied with the user's key, so that unencrypted data can
exist only within the physically secure register set. All sensitive data in main memory, in the data bank files, in the ordinary
register set, and on the communications channel will be encrypted.
During operation, a load/store instruction between main memory
and the secure register set will automatically cause the appropriate decryption/encryption operations to be performed.

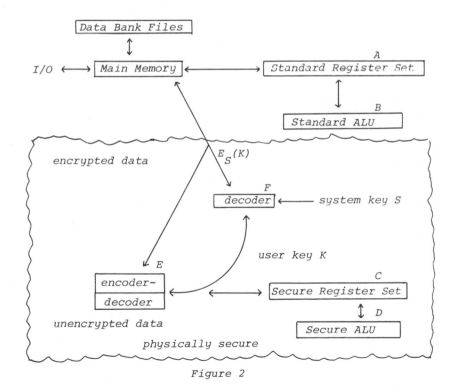

Figure 2

An obvious problem is getting the encoder/decoder (E) loaded with the user's key K without compromising the security of the user's key. One possible approach is to keep the user's key encrypted under control of a system key S. The encrypted form of K, $E_S(K)$, can be transmitted over the insecure channel to the system, decrypted by the physically secure decoder (F), and loaded into the encoder-decoder (E). The user knows K and $E_S(K)$; the latter is obtained during a visit to the time-shared services manager, who is the only one who knows the system key S.

Besides the problems of key management, there are questions of the speed degradation caused by invoking the encryption/ decryption with every load or store. However, it appears that suitably secure encryption (e.g. DES) can be performed on a time scale comparable to that of the instruction execution of many machines (e.g. 10 m sec).

The most severe restriction on this solution, however, is one that will turn out to be a restriction on *any* solution to the problem (even privacy homomorphisms): it is not possible to simultaneously preserve security and give the system the operation of performing comparisons against known constants. That is, we may not give the computer system a means of performing operations sufficiently powerful to enable someone who knows only $E_S(K)$ to decrypt the data. The ability to perform comparisons against constants would allow someone to perform a simple binary search procedure to determine the decoded value of any datum. We examine this restriction in more detail in section 4.

III. PRIVACY HOMOMORPHISMS

One might prefer a solution which did not require decryption of the user's data (except of course at the user's terminal). That is, the hardware configuration will be that of Figure 1, but the encryption function used will permit the computer system to operate on the data without decrypting it.

The unencoded data and the operations to be performed on it, we assume to be drawn from some algebraic system. An algebraic system consists of a set S, some operations f_1, f_2, ... , some predicates p_1, p_2, ..., and some distinguished constants s_1, s_2, ... We denote this system by $<S; f_1, f_2, ... ; p_1, p_2, ... ; s_1, s_2, ... >$. For example, the system consisting of the integers under the usual set of operations might be denoted $<Z; +, -, x, \div; \leq; 0, 1>$; where Z is the set of integers.

In addition to the algebraic system of the user (let's call it U), we shall need another algebraic system C to be used by the computer system. Encoding and decoding shall then mean mapping elements from U to C or vice versa, respectively. More formally, if

$$U = \langle S; f_1, \ldots, f_k; P_1, \ldots, P_\ell; s_1, \ldots, s_m \rangle$$

then

$$C = \langle S'; f'_1, \ldots, f'_k; P_1', \ldots, P'_\ell; s_1', \ldots, s'_m \rangle$$

and we must have a decoding function ϕ: $S' \rightarrow S$ and its inverse, the encoding function ϕ^{-1}: $S \rightarrow S'$.

In operation, the user gives the computer system a description of the algebraic system C; in practice this means that the system has a subroutine to compute each of the operations f_i' and predicates p_i', as well as representations of the distinguished constants s_i'. The users actual data base we denote as the sequence d_1, d_2, $\ldots$, each d_1 is an element of S. However, the user encodes each datum before giving it to the system; the encoded data base $\phi^{-1}(d_1)$, $\phi^{-1}(d_2)$, $\ldots$.

In order for the system to be able to operate on the (encoded) data base without decrypting it, the decoding function ϕ must be a homomorphism from C onto U. Formally, this means that

$$(\forall i)(\ a,b,c,\ldots)\ [f'_i(a,b,\ldots) = c \Rightarrow f_i(\phi(a),\phi(b),\ldots)=\phi(c)],$$

$$(\forall i)(\ a,b,\ldots)\ p'(a,b,\ldots) \equiv p(\phi(a),\ \phi(b),\ldots),$$

and

$$(\forall i)\ \phi(s_i') = s_i\ ;$$

ϕ carries each operation in C into the corresponding operation in U. Suppose now that the user wants to know the value of $f_1(d_1,\ d_2)$. He asks the system to compute $f_1'(\phi^{-1}(d_1),\ \phi^{-1}(d_2))$. Since ϕ is a homomorphism,

$$\phi(f_1'(\phi^{-1}(d_1),\ \phi^{-1}(d_2))) = f_1(d_1,\ d_2)$$

so that the system arrives at the encrypted form of the answer without having to decrypt the intermediate results. In general, an arbitrary computer program using the operations of U to compute some function of the user's data base can be transformed into another computer program suitable for operation on the encoded data merely by changing all f_i 's to f'_i 's, all p_i 's to p'_i 's, and all s_i 's to s'_i 's.

The requirements on the choice of the algebraic system C and the functions ϕ, ϕ^{-1} are:

(1) ϕ and ϕ^{-1}, the decoding and encoding functions, should be easy to compute.

(2)   The operations f'_i and predicates p_i' in C should be efficiently computable.

(3)   An encoded version of a datum d_i, $\phi^{-1}(d_i)$, should not require much more space to represent than a representation of d_i.

(4)   Knowledge of $\phi^{-1}(d_i)$ for many data d_i should not be sufficient to reveal ϕ. (Ciphertext only only attack).

(5)   Knowledge of d_i *and* $\phi^{-1}(d_i)$ for several values of d_i should not reveal ϕ. (Chosen plaintext attack).

(6)   The operations and predicates in C should not be sufficient to yield an efficient computation of ϕ. (This relates primarily to the use of comparisons).

IV.   SOME SIMPLE OBSERVATIONS

Some inherent restrictions limit the utility of privacy homomorphisms as we have described. The most severe is probably the following.

Fact.   If the operations available in C allow the computer system to determine the encoded version of arbitrary constants, and a predicate "$\leq$" for a total order is available, then there is no secure privacy homomorphism from C to U.

This follows from a simple "binary search" strategy. For example, for the system of natural numbers

$U = \langle N; +; \leq; 0, 1\rangle$

and

$C = \langle W; +'; \leq'; 0', 1'\rangle$

for some set W, the malicious systems programmer on the computer system can decode $\phi^{-1}(d_i)$ by computing $\phi^{-1}(1) = 1'$, $\phi^{-1}(2) = 1' +' 1'$, $\phi^{-1}(4) = \phi^{-1}(2) +' \phi^{-1}(2)$, and so on until he finds a k such that $\phi^{-1}(2^k) \geq '\phi^{-1}(d_i)$. Continuing, similar strategy enables him to compute d_i exactly.

Other facts about the ability of one system to simulate another are not quite so easy to see, but can be found. For example, we have the following.

Fact. If C is over the natural numbers and has the operations of addition, multiplication, and a binary equality predicate and a unary predicate "equal" to zero, then it has the capability to test for equality to an arbitrary constant.

The proof follows from $x=k \iff (x \neq 0) \wedge \underbrace{(x^2 = x+\cdots+x)}_{k \text{ times}}$.

Lynch [1] gives an excellent study of the relationships between one algebraic system and another which simulates +.

V. SOME SAMPLE PRIVACY HOMOMORPHISMS

We give here four sample privacy homomorphisms. These are intended primarily as examples to support the hypothesis that useful privacy homomorphisms may exist for many applications. Some of them are rather weak cryptographically; a "chosen plaintext attack" may break them. We list them anyway to illustrate the kinds of privacy homomorphisms that may exist.

Example 1.   Suppose $U = \langle Z_{p-1}; +_{p-1}, -_{p-1} \rangle$, the system of integers modulo p-1 with the operations of addition and subtraction, where p is a prime number. We may choose $C = \langle Z_n; x_n, \div_n \rangle$, the integers modulo n where $n = p \cdot q$, the product of p and a large prime q. Let g be a generator modulo p. Then we choose

$$\phi^{-1}(x) \equiv g^x (\text{modulo } n)$$

and the decoding function is the inverse "mod(p) logarithm, base g" function. by the laws of exponents, ϕ is a homomorphism. If n is difficult to factor (both p and q are large) and the prime p is such that logarithms modulo p can be efficiently computed (see [2]), then the computer system can be given both g and n without fear of compromising the security of the data.

Example 2.   Suppose $U = \langle Z_p; x_p; \equiv_p \rangle$, the integers modulo p with multiplication and test for equality. Again, letting $n=p \cdot q$, where q is a large prime and supposing that n is difficult to factor, we may take

$$\phi^{-1}(x) = x^e (\text{mod } n).$$

Since $(x^e)(y^e) = (xy)^e$, this is a homomorphism. This is, in fact,
the encoding function used by Rivest, Shamir, and Adleman in
their method of implementing public-key cryptosystems [3]. The
security of this system should be very good, even if the computer
system is given both e and n.

Example 3. $U = <Z_n; +_n, -_n, x_n>$, where n is again the product
of two large primes p and q such that n is difficult to factor.
We choose to represent each element of Z_n by a pair of numbers:

$$\phi^{-1}(x) = (x \bmod p, x \bmod q).$$

The computer system forms the sum, difference, or product of two
encodings by performing the operations componentwise, modulo n.
Without knowing p and q, the system is not able to decode any
numbers. Since there are several possible encodings of a given
number, test for equality is not possible.

Example 4.   Suppose $U = <Z; +, -, x>$, the system of integers
under the usual operations of addition, subtraction, and multiplication. The user chooses an integer n and represents all of
his data in radix-n notation. The computer system can operate on
these values without knowing n (and thus without knowing the
unencoded data) by allowing individual coordinate positions to
exceed n. For example, if n = 17, we have

$$\phi^{-1}(23) = (1,4)$$

$$\phi^{-1}(44) = (2,10)$$

$$\phi^{-1}(1012) = \phi^{-1}(23 \cdot 44) = (2,18,40).$$

Again, test for equality are not possible since a given number
might have several representations. The computer system can also
find an encoding of any given constant by just using that constant
in the units position.

By combining two systems of the above sort, one can implement
the rational numbers using "fractions". This system is not
really secure against a "chosen plaintext attack", although it
has many good properties otherwise.

Example 5.   Suppose we again have $U = <Z; +, -, x>$, the system
of integers under the operations of addition, subtraction, and
multiplication. Let k be chosen so that all intermediate results
used in any calculation are less than 2^k, and let $a_0, a_1, \ldots ,$
a_{k-1} be k randomly chosen integers. The encoding of the integer
x, where $x = x_{k-1} \cdots x_1 x_0$ in binary notation (each x_i is 0 or 1)

is the k-tuple $(f_x(a_0), f_x(a_1), \ldots, f_x(a_{k-1}))$ where

$$f_x(Z) = \sum_{i=0}^{k-1} x_i \cdot Z^i .$$

The encoded representations can be operated upon componentwise.
Decoding means interpolating a polynomial through the given
values and then evaluating that polynomial at the point Z=2.
This privacy homomorphism is not very space efficient. The
security of the system, even against a chosen plaintext attack,
looks like it involves solving high-order nonlinear equations
for the a_i 's, but there are possibly cryptanalytic shortcuts.

VI. CONCLUSIONS

Privacy homomorphisms provide a novel way of ensuring the
privacy of data which must be operated on. They are of
inherently limited applicability, since comparisons may not in
general be included in the set of operations to be used. In
addition, it remains to be seen whether it is possible to have
a privacy homomorphism with a large set of operations which is
highly secure. The results presented here give a basis for some
optimism about finding useful privacy homomorphisms; the examples
given here are suggestive if not very practical. The open
questions are

- Does this approach have enough utility to make it
  worthwhile in practice?

- For what algebraic systems U does a useful privacy
  homomorphism exist?

REFERENCES

[1] Lynch, N. and E. Blum, "Efficient Reducibility Between
    Programming Systems", *Proc. 9th Annual ACM Symposium on
    Theory of Computing,* (Boulder, May 1977), pp. 228-238.
[2] Pohlig, S. and M. Hellman, "An Improved Algorithm for
    Computing Logarithms Over GF(p) and Its Cryptographic
    Significance" (to appear IEEE *Trans. Info. Theory*).
[3] Rivest, R., A. Shamir, and L. Adleman, "A Method For
    Obtaining Digital Signatures and Public-Key Crypto Systems",
    Massachusetts Institute of Technology, Laboratory for
    Computer Science, Technical Memo, TM-82, April 1977. (to
    appear in *CACM*).

DISCUSSION

Rabin: I would like to mention an additional consideration concerning safety. One of the most attractive proposals here was really doing the arithmetic modulo. When n is the product of p and q and when you do the component-wise modular arithmetic, you don't do it modulo p and q separately, you do it in modulo n arithmetic. That looks pretty good because we don't know how to factor numbers. However, a possibility for cracking any of these systems, is that the adversary has a special knowledge. Sometimes the adversary has under his control, part of the input data. He is the depositor in a bank which is manipulating his bank account. So, he actually knows the values of A, B, C and so on which are being encoded. Now, one would have to consider the possibility of looking at the encoding, one might be able to find the factorization of n in this particular case.

Rivest: It's quite plausible that one might be able to break it, then.

Rabin: Yes, and there are similar considerations of challenging the system by feeding it known information and following its course within the encrypted version, feeding it encrypted information and following its course must be taken into account when we're evaluating its safety.

Gaines: Maybe I misunderstood, but I thought that p and q would be chosen outside the system. Separately for each individual. So that no one would have the opportunity to do what you said.

Rabin: May I add a remark? If you then propose to have different p and q for each customer, which is quite difficult and impractical, sometimes a non-innocent by-stander has knowledge of how much money you deposited. The other problem again exists. You must assume at least spotty partial information about the data which is going to be protected.

Rivest: All the systems I've presented, I think, are susceptible to variations of that kind of attack. I do not consider any of them very satisfactory for precisely those kinds of reasons.

SECTION III.   DESIGN-ORIENTED MODELS
OF OPERATING SYSTEM SECURITY

By its very nature, system software is mostly hidden from
users. This creates a special problem in security, for if the
"invisible" operating system of a computer system is not secure,
all of the remaining security measures may be of little use.
Operating system security is a world of authorization and access,
rights and privileges, a world where theoreticians and the
pragmatic designers are -- if they are not the same people -- in
constant dialog. They must be convinced that their theoretical
models are at least consistent with reality. On the other hand,
reality is so complex that frequently the only way to study a
security issue is to abstract away from the inessential detail,
to carry out a theoretical analysis. In this section and in
section IV, the interplay between the practical and the theoretical is apparent.

In Robert Fabry's article, we see a designer struggling to
come to grips with the real-world implications of a theoretical
result: the Harrison-Ruzzo-Ullman decidability theorem. The
two-part paper by Frederick Furtek and Jonathan Millen attempts
a simplification of several design concepts; they represent a
system as "prime constraints", a concept similar to prime
implicants of switching theory. Stockton Gaines and Norman
Shapiro take a step back from detailed considerations to give us
an overview. They provide us with some general perspective on
the state of security research based on some fairly pragmatic
insights. The contribution by Anita Jones is indicative of the
fertile interplay of theory and practice in security research;
her article is the outcome of a designer assessing the usefulness
of the take-grant system which has been the object of extensive
theoretical analysis. In the final paper of this section,
Naftaly Minsky addresses Peter Denning's "principle of attenuation of privilege" and presents an authorization scheme which
satisfies the principle.

ONE PERSPECTIVE ON THE RESULTS
ABOUT THE DECIDABILITY OF SYSTEM SAFETY

R. S. Fabry

University of California
Berkeley, California

On the one hand, we have the fact that we have produced systems whose security properties are hard to understand. On the other hand, we have the Harrison, Ruzzo, and Ullman decidability result about system safety [1]. It would be useful to know how these two things are related, if at all.

One refinement is that if the original six primitive operations (enter right, delete right, create subject, destroy subject, create object, and destroy object) are reduced to three by eliminating the delete and destroy operations, the resulting system, which is said to be monotonic, is still not decidable. This result corresponds to my intuition concerning the difficulties we have with real systems: leaving out the delete and destroy operations in a real system would not simplify the job of understanding the protection it provides. In fact, the opposite is more likely; by leaving objects and rights which are no longer required, we make it more difficult to understand the protection situation.

The effect in real systems is related to the amount of information in the protection matrix, however, and brings to mind the result that if the protection matrix is constrained to be finite the safety question is decidable.

Another refinement to the basic decidability result is that
if each command contains but a single primitive operation, the
resulting system, said to be mono-operational, has decidable
safety. This is an intriguing result because it might be taken
to be analogous to the generally believed notion that a system
composed of small modules is easier to understand than a system
composed of larger modules. It is often said that the fine
grained protection provided by capability systems such as Hydra
and Cap allows the construction of systems which are easier to
understand than a monolithic supervisor/user system.

These analogies are at best tenuous, and rather than suggesting they are true, I suggest merely that such relationships would
make the decidability results useful to a designer of real
systems.

A second way to approach the question of the relevance of the
decidability results to real systems is to look at real systems
that are understood and to try to argue that various interesting
safety questions are decidable for those systems.

In fact, it is my hunch that in all well designed protection
systems, the simple safety questions are trivially decidable, at
least for users who follow certain reasonable and normal
conventions. This has happened because designers have intuitively
considered safety in choosing the set of commands they provide.

Two well understood cases which are often used as test cases
for modern protection systems are a file system and a type
manager.

Looking first at a file system, it is natural to ask about
the safety of some particular file. For example, suppose I trust
some of the users and do not trust the rest and I want to make
sure that none of the users I do not trust can ever get access
rights for a certain file. I must make sure that:

- There are no access rights which will allow direct
  access to the file by any user I do not trust.

- There are no access rights which will allow any user
  I do not trust to directly change the access rights
  for the file.

- There are no access rights which allow a trusted user
  to directly change the access rights for the file
  unless he or she has agreed to abide by the same
  three constraints.

I believe one could easily show that these three constraints imply safety. There is a simple linear algorithm for determining whether or not the constraints hold for a given protection matrix.

Turning to the case of a type manager, a vital safety issue is whether or not a subject other than the type manager can access directly the implementation objects. Again, such a question is clearly decidable so long as the type manager follows certain reasonable guidelines: Never give away access rights for implementation objects and never give away the right to give away rights to implementation objects.

In considering the file system and a type manager, I have not been specific about formal meaning, but I believe it would be simple to fill in the formalism.

REFERENCES

[1] Harrison, M. A., Ruzzo, W. L., and Ullman, J. D., "Protection in Operating Systems", CACM 19, 8 (Aug 1976), pp. 461-470.

DISCUSSION

Ruzzo: I think you've made a fair statement of the results
to some extent, but I would like to amplify a few points. The
first concerns your comment about decidability in the finite
case. I think you said that systems, although they are finite,
tend to be so large and complex that you can't understand them
anyway. I would like to add that although the finite cases are
decidable, the computational complexity turns out to be enormous,
probably requiring exponential time for the types of things we
have looked at. Again, this supports the idea that you can't
understand things just because they are finite.

Fabry: Good point.

Ruzzo: The second point I wanted to make is about the
decidability of the mono-operation case and your comments about
that. You are right in stating that the decidability of these
systems stems from the fact that the commands we're using are
simple. However, the threshold between where those commands are
simple enough to be decidable, and where they slip over to being
undecidable, is very low. For instance, syst-ms with one
operation per command are decidable, but I think that allowing
two or three operations per command is enough to make the systems
undecidable. It is not that the modules be simple. Even though
they are simple and individually very transparent, they can
interact in complicated ways. I agree with modularization. You
do want modular systems with simple modules. But our results
show that having simple modules is not sufficient.

Lipton: I'd like to follow-up on both of these comments.
I think that all of the undecidability results point to danger
spots and, therefore, are interesting. I'd just like to know if
anybody has ever looked at the kinds of access mechanisms that
people actually use in real systems. I would be curious to know

if the dangers signaled by these results are real. If one runs naive algorithms, does one unravel things well or do they fail miserably? One is reminded of Knuth's analysis of Fortran programs. He explained how he was always thinking about very complicated arithmetic expressions and about parsing them, and he was surprised to see that "a <- b" was the most common.

Gaines: I'd like to comment about that. I can think of two kinds of exploitation of the results. One can exploit the un-decidability to cause information to flow where because of the initial state of control, you would hope that it would not. I don't think that there's any evidence that anybody has ever tried to do that. My point is it could easily happen by accident. In the course of the normal functioning of the systems, somebody will find suddenly that they have access where they didn't or shouldn't. Through some complicated sequence of actions, some user may find a path by which he can get access to data. The manager of the system will have a hard time deciding whether he is putting the system in a good initial state, or a bad one.

Jones: I have a number of observations. First, these access-control mechansims are nothing but little databases with a set of commands. Those commands were designed to be a protection mechanism, and not a vehicle by which I could get an undecid-ability result. It's just not cler that real mechanisms are undecidable. A second point is one that I made in my talk: that for every new access right gained in a real system, there is some subject that caused that to happen. You can build an arc from a to b, so that a can perform an operation on b. That takes the collusion of everybody in the system, and that's just not realistic. So, when I look at the finiteness result, I say, "that's neat", because most questions I want to answer only involve a few users and lost of subjects. But, all of those subjects were, in fact, programs invoked by just these couple of users that were in collusion. In fact, the access matrix may be not only finite, but small and finite. Maybe the only kinds of questions in real systems that I want to answer involve only a very restricted piece of protected database. And, you just don't care whether the general problem is decidable or not.

Minsky: One may construct a system (set of commands) which is decidable and easy to analyze even if it is not mono-operational. On the other hand, mono-operational systems, which by the HRU result are decidable, may be nevertheless very hard to analyze. In short, I do not think that the HRU result has much to say about the simplicity, or undecidability of any specific system.

Fabry: If it turns out that all existing systems are special cases which are decidable, then I will lose interest in all of this theory. The theory is useful for me as a practitioner only if it helps me understand that there are some systems that I can build that will get me into trouble, other systems I can build that won't get me into trouble, and which are which.

Jones: Let me just comment on another sort of gulf between theory and practitioners. I have difficulty in mapping the theoretician's definitions of safety into things that I see in real systems. I don't know whether or not the model is asking the same question that I ask of a real system.

Gaines: One of the important things about this work is that it points out a particular problem area which previously was completely ignored: You could have a well-functioning access control system and still have problems as to whether or not the system was secure.

CONSTRAINTS

PART I   CONSTRAINTS AND COMPROMISE

Frederick C. Furtek

The Mitre Corporation
Bedford, Massachusetts

I.   INTRODUCTION

A new concept is proposed for dealing with the *logical dependencies* inherent in system behavior. The *prime constraints* of a system are derived from, and provide an alternative to, the traditional state-vector representation of a system. There are several reasons for being interested in prime constraints.

1.   They provide a compact and transparent representation for a system.
2.   They are especially well suited to systems exhibiting either concurrency or nondeterminacy, or both.
3.   They appear to be closely related to intuitive ideas of information flow.
4.   They have the potential of providing a practical representation for the 'external behavior' of a system.
5.   They provide a simple condition that is both necessary and sufficient for the ability to make a deduction about the values assumed by a collection of variables.

II.   CONDITIONS, VARIABLES, STATES, AND SIMULATIONS

Although the concepts of 'value' and 'variable' are taken as the basic elements of many theories, they do not quite suit our purposes. We will instead be dealing with 'conditions'. A condition may be viewed as the assignment of a value to a variable. Thus, a condition is associated with a *unique* variable, a useful property not shared by values.

Postulate.   Associated with a system is a finite set of primitive objects called *conditions* and a partition on this set, the blocks of which are called *variables*.[†]

[†] *We have taken the liberty of referring to the set of conditions associated with a variable as the variable itself.*

(Distinct conditions belonging to the same
variables are said to be *alternative*.)

In the theory developed below, conditions are the only primitive
objects we deal with -- all other objects being constructed from
them.

Our requirement that each value belong to a unique variable
permits us to formalize the notion of state in a simple way.

Definition: A system *state* is any set of conditions containing
exactly one representative from each variable.

To obtain the condition that a state assigns to a variable it is
only necessary to intersect the state with the variable. Note
that because a condition never belongs to more than one variable
there is a one-to-one correspondence between the conditions in a
state and the system variables.

The behavior of a system is embodied in the set of allowable
state sequences for that system. In what follows, we shall
assume that these system 'simulations' can be characterized by a
finite set of 'state transitions'.

Postulate: A system has associated with it a set of ordered
state pairs called (*state*) *transitions*.

Definition: A system *simulation* is any finite state sequence in
which every ordered pair of consecutive states is a state transition.

These ideas are easier to visualize when the states and state
transitions are interpreted as the nodes and arcs, respectively,
of a graph. The set of simulations is then just the set of finite
paths (including the null path) in this 'state graph'. Note that
any state can serve as an 'initial state'. (The question of
initialization will be considered in a subsequent paper).

Example: Consider the following system. (Do not be put off by its apparent complexity. As we shall see later, the system is nothing more than a three-stage shift register).

conditions = $\{a_0, a_1, b_0, b_1, c_0, c_1\}^\dagger$

variables = $\{\{a_0, a_1\}, \{b_0, b_1\}, \{c_0, c_1\}\}$

transitions = $\{<\{a_0, b_0, c_0\}, \{a_0, b_0, c_0\}>$, $<\{a_0, b_0, c_0\}, \{a_1, b_0, c_0\}>$,

$<\{a_0, b_0, c_1\}, \{a_0, b_0, c_0\}>$, $<\{a_0, b_0, c_1\}, \{a_1, b_0, c_0\}>$,

$<\{a_0 \; b_1 \; c_0\}, \{a_0 \; b_0 \; c_1\}>$, $<\{a_0 \; b_1 \; c_0\}, \{a_1 \; b_0 \; c_1\}>$,

$<\{a_0 \; b_1 \; c_1\}, \{a_0 \; b_0 \; c_1\}>$, $<\{a_0 \; b_1 \; c_1\}, \{a_1 \; b_0 \; c_1\}>$,

$<\{a_1 \; b_0 \; c_0\}, \{a_0 \; b_1 \; c_0\}>$, $<\{a_1 \; b_0 \; c_0\}, \{a_1 \; b_1 \; c_0\}>$,

$<\{a_1 \; b_0 \; c_1\}, \{a_0 \; b_1 \; c_0\}>$, $<\{a_1 \; b_0 \; c_1\}, \{a_1 \; b_1 \; c_0\}>$,

$<\{a_1 \; b_1 \; c_0\}, \{a_0 \; b_1 \; c_1\}>$, $<\{a_1 \; b_1 \; c_0\}, \{a_1 \; b_1 \; c_1\}>$,

$<\{a_1 \; b_1 \; c_1\}, \{a_0 \; b_1 \; c_1\}>$, $<\{a_1 \; b_1 \; c_1\}, \{a_1 \; b_1 \; c_1\}>\}$

$\dagger$ *As a notational convenience we will often associate a lower case letter with each variable and distinguish between alternative values with subscripts. It must be emphasized that there is no formal significance to the fact that two values may share the same letter or the same subscript.*

The state-transition graph for this system is:

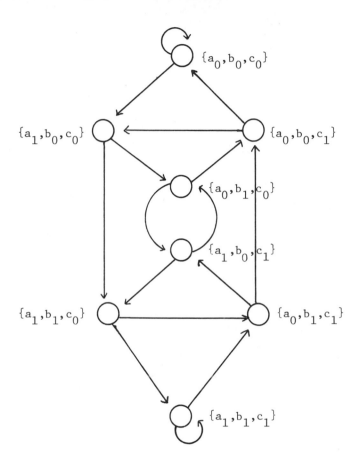

State Graph

Any path in this graph is a simulation. A few of these simulations are represented here in a convenient tabular form:

a_0	b_1	c_0

a_1	b_0	c_1
a_1	b_1	c_0
a_0	b_1	c_1
a_0	b_0	c_1

a_1	b_1	c_1
a_1	b_1	c_1
a_1	b_1	c_1

Simulations

III.   TERMS AND CLAUSES

An objective of this work is to develop mathematical tools for characterizing and analyzing system behavior. So far, the only finite characterization we have for system behavior is the set of state transitions, from which we can generate the set of system simulations. However, it is not practical to deal directly with transitions. Besides the obvious problem of complexity (the number of states and the number of transitions are usually astonomical), there is the problem of transparency. This is the problem of presenting in as clear and as compact a way as possible the principles governing a system's behavior. The set of state transitions, unfortunately, tends to obscure these principles. We shall describe an approach that offers a major improvement in reducing complexity and increasing transparency -- without sacrificing any generality.

Rather than dealing directly with states, transitions, and simulations, we shall be dealing with 'terms' and 'clauses'. A term will be used to represent a set of states, and a clause a set of state sequences. (Note that a transition is a state sequence).

Definition: A *term* is any set of conditions not containing an entire variable.

Example: Consider a system in which,

$$\text{conditions} = \{a_0, a_1, b_0, b_1, b_2\}$$

$$\text{variables} = \{\{a_0, a_1\}, \{b_0, b_1, b_2\}\}$$

The terms that we get are:

$$\{\emptyset, \{a_0\}, \{a_1\}, \{b_0\}, \{b_1\}, \{b_2\}, \{b_0, b_1\}, \{b_0', b_2\}, \{b_1, b_2\},$$

$$\{a_0, b_0\}, \{a_0, b_1\}, \{a_0, b_2\}, \{a_1, b_0\}, \{a_1, b_1\}, \{a_1, b_2\}, \{a_0, b_0, b_1\},$$

$$\{a_0, b_0, b_2\}, \{a_0, b_1, b_2\}, \{a_1, b_0, b_1\}, \{a_1, b_0, b_2\}, \{a_1, b_1, b_2\}\}$$

We now present a method for associating a set of states with a term. It is this mapping that provides the bridge between the constructs of our theory and system behavior.

Notation: In what follows we shall be considering a system in which

C   denotes the set of conditions,
V   denotes the set of variables,
S   denotes the set of states,
T   denotes the set of terms, and
S   denotes the set of simulations.

Definition: For $t \in T$,

$$\pi(t) = \{s \in S \,|\, \forall v \in V: (t \cap v \neq \phi) \Rightarrow (s \cap v \subseteq t \cap v)\}$$

'$\pi(t)$ consists of those states s such that every variable having conditions in t is assigned one of those conditions by s.'

We list here some of the basic properties of π.

Property 3.1: $\pi(\phi) = S$

'π applied to the empty set yields the state set.'

Property 3.2: $\forall s \in S: \pi(s) = \{s\}$

'π applied to a state yields the singleton set containing that state.'

Property 3.3: $\forall t_1, t_2 \in T:$

$$\pi(t_1) \subseteq \pi(t_2) \quad \Leftrightarrow \quad \forall v \in V: (t_2 \cap v \neq \phi) \Rightarrow (t_1 \cap v \neq \phi \wedge t_1 \cap v \subseteq t_2 \cap v)$$

'$\pi(t_1) \subseteq \pi(t_2)$ if and only if for each variable v with conditions in t_2, $t_1 \cap v$ is nonempty and $t_1 \cap v \subseteq t_2 \cap v$.'

Property 3.4: $\forall t_1, t_2 \varepsilon T$: $\pi(t_1) = \pi(t_2) \Rightarrow t_1 = t_2$

'π is one-to-one.'

Example: For a system in which,

conditions = $\{a_0, a_1, a_2, b_0, b_1, b_2\}$

variables = $\{\{a_0, a_1, a_2\}, \{b_0, b_1, b_2\}$

we have,

$\pi(\{a_0\}) = \{s \varepsilon S | a_0 \varepsilon s\} = \{\{a_0, b_0\}, \{a_0, b_1\}, \{a_0, b_2\}\}$

$\pi(\{b_0, b_1\}) = \{s \varepsilon S | b_0 \varepsilon s \lor b_1 \varepsilon s\} = \{\{a_0, b_0\}, \{a_1, b_0\}, \{a_2, b_0\}$

$\{a_0, b_1\}, \{a_1, b_1\}, \{a_2, b_1\}\}$

$\pi(\{a_0, b_2\}) = \{s \varepsilon S | a_0 \varepsilon s \land b_2 \varepsilon s\} = \{\{a_0, b_2\}\}$

$\pi(\{a_0, a_2, b_0, b_2\}) = \{s \varepsilon S | (a_0 \varepsilon s \lor a_2 \varepsilon s) \land (b_0 \varepsilon s \lor b_2 \varepsilon s)\}$

$= \{\{a_0, b_0\}, \{a_0, b_2\}, \{a_2, b_0\}, \{a_2, b_2\}\}$

Notice that $\pi(\{a_0, b_2\}) \subseteq \pi(\{a_0\})$ and $\pi(\{a_0, b_2\}) \subseteq \pi(\{a_0, a_2, b_0, b_2\})$, in accordance with Property 3.3.

We turn now to clauses.

Definition: A *clause* is a sequence of terms.

A clause is used to generate a set of state sequences by first applying π to each of the terms in the clause and then taking the Cartesian product of the resulting sets of states.

Notation: For a sequence α, we use $|\alpha|$ to denote the length of α, and $\alpha(i)$ to denote the i'th component of α.

Definition: For $\alpha\epsilon T*$: †

$$\pi(\alpha) = \overset{|\alpha|}{\underset{i=1}{\times}} \pi(\alpha(i))$$

Property 3.5: $\forall\omega\epsilon S*$: $\pi(\omega) = \{\omega\}$

'π applied to a state sequence yields the singleton set containing that state sequence.'

Property 3.6:   For clauses α and β of the same length,

$$\pi(\alpha) \subseteq \pi(\beta) <=> \forall i:\ \pi(\alpha(i)) \subseteq \pi(\beta(i))$$

'$\pi(\alpha) \subseteq \pi(\beta)$ if and only if for each pair of corresponding terms $\alpha(i)$ and $\beta(i)$, $\pi(\alpha(i)) \subseteq \pi(\beta(i))$.'

Property 3.7: $\forall\alpha,\beta\epsilon T*$:

$$\pi(\alpha)=\pi(\beta) => \alpha=\beta$$

'The extension of π to clauses is also one-to-one.'

Example: Consider a system in which:

conditions = $\{a_0,a_1,b_0,b_1,b_2\}$

variables = $\{\{a_0,a_1\},\ \{b_0,b_1,b_2\}\}$

Let $\alpha = <\{a_1,b_0,b_2\},\ \{a_0,b_1\},\ \{b_1,b_2\}>$

Then $\pi(\alpha)=\{\{a_1,b_0\},\ \{a_1,b_2\}\} \times \{\{a_0,b_1\}\} \times \{\{a_0,b_1\},\ \{a_0,b_2\},$

$\{a_1,b_1\},\ \{a_1,b_2\}\}$

$=\{<\{a_1,b_0\},\ \{a_0,b_1\},\ \{a_0,b_1\}>,\ <\{a_1,b_0\},\{a_0,b_1\},\{a_0,b_2\}>,$

$<\{a_1,b_0\},\ \{a_0,b_1\},\ \{a_1,b_1\}>,\ <\{a_1,b_0\},\{a_0,b_1\},\{a_1,b_2\}>,$

$<\{a_1,b_2\},\ \{a_0,b_1\},\ \{a_0,b_1\}>,\ <\{a_1,b_2\},\{a_0,b_1\},\{a_0,b_2\}>,$

$<\{a_1,b_2\},\ \{a_0,b_1\},\ \{a_1,b_1\}>,\ <\{a_1,b_2\},\{a_0,b_1\},\{a_1,b_2\}>\}$

---

† *If A is a set, then A* denotes the set of finite sequences over A.*

IV. CONSTRAINTS

The function π introduced in the preceding section maps a clause into a set of state sequences. We now focus our attention on those clauses that map only into 'nonsimulations'.

Definition: $C = \{\alpha \varepsilon \text{ T*} \mid \pi(\alpha) \cap S = \phi\}$

'C is the set of those clauses α such that $\pi(\alpha)$ contains no simulations.'

C is the set of *constraints*. A constraint of length n is called an *n-place constraint*.

Our choice for the definition of a constraint is motivated in part by a useful property of non-simulations.

Property 4.1: $\forall R \subseteq S*$:

$$R \cap S = \phi \Rightarrow (S*RS*) \cap S = \phi$$

'Any extension of a nonsimulation is also a nonsimulation.'

Let us now introduce a relationship on the set of clauses.

Definition: For $\alpha, \beta \varepsilon$ T*,

$$\alpha \leq \cdot \beta \iff (S*\pi(\alpha)S*) \subseteq (S*\pi(\beta)S*)$$

'$\alpha \leq \cdot \beta$ if and only if every extension of a state sequence in $\pi(\alpha)$ is also an extension of a state sequence in $\pi(\beta)$.'

The clause β is said to *cover* the clause α if and only if $\alpha \leq \cdot \beta$.

The next result follows from Property 4.1, and it provides us with the justification for considering just a special subset of constraints.

Property 4.2: $\forall \alpha \varepsilon$ T*: $\forall \beta \varepsilon C$:

$$\alpha \leq \cdot \beta \Rightarrow \alpha \varepsilon C$$

'Every clause covered by a constraint must itself be a constraint.'

To help us better understand the nature of the relation $\leq \cdot$, we provide a formulation that is equivalent to the definition above.

Property 4.3: $\forall \alpha, \beta \epsilon T^*$:

$$\alpha \underline{<} \cdot \beta \iff \exists \gamma \underline{\subseteq} \alpha: \; |\gamma| = |\beta| \; \wedge \; \pi(\gamma) \subseteq \pi(\beta) \quad ^\dagger$$

'$\alpha \underline{<} \cdot \beta$ if and only if α contains a subsequence γ the same length as β such that $\pi(\gamma) \subseteq \pi(\beta)$.'

From the definition of $\underline{<} \cdot$ it follows immediately that $\underline{<} \cdot$ is reflexive and transitive. From Properties 3.7 and 4.3 it follows that $\underline{<} \cdot$ is also antisymmetric and, therefore, a partial order.

Now in order to take advantage of Property 4.2, we must first establish that a clause has only a finite number of superiors with respect to $\underline{<} \cdot$.

Property 4.4: $\forall \alpha, \beta \epsilon T^*$: $\alpha \underline{<} \cdot \beta \Rightarrow |\beta| \underline{<} |\alpha|$

'Every superior of the clause α is either shorter than or the same length as α.'

This last result means that the set of 'maximal constraints' is well-defined.

Definition: $C' = \max_{\underline{<} \cdot} (C) \quad ^\ddagger$

         C' is the set of *prime constraints*.

From Property 4.2 we see that the set of *prime* constraints determines the set of *all* constraints.

Example: Consider the system whose state graph is given in Section II.

Although there are an infinite number of constraints for this system (which is the usual case), there are just six prime constraints.

$$C' = \{ <\{a_0\}, \{b_1\}>, \;\; <\{a_1\}, \{b_0\}>,$$
$$<\{b_0\}, \{c_1\}>, \;\; <\{b_1\}, \{c_0\}>,$$
$$<\{a_0\}, \phi, \{c_1\}>, \;\; <\{a_1\}, \phi, \{c_0\}> \}$$

---

† *For sequences* μ_1 *and* μ_2, $\mu_1 \subseteq \mu_2$ *indicates that* μ_1 *is a (consecutive) subsequence of* μ_2.

‡ *If* $\underline{<}$ *is a partial order on a set* Q *and if* $P \subseteq Q$, *then*
$$max_{\underline{<}} \; (P) = \{ r\epsilon P \,|\, \exists p \epsilon P: \; p > r \}$$

(A method for constructing prime constraints will be given in a subsequent paper).

With these prime constraints, we now see that the state graph describes nothing more than a three-stage shirt register. For example, the prime constraint $<\{a_0\}, \{b_1\}>$ tells us that if a particular state in a simulation contains an a_0, then the next state -- if there is any -- cannot contain a b_1. In other words, the next state must contain a b_0. (Otherwise, we would have a nonsimulation). The prime constraint $<\{a_0\}, \emptyset, \{c_1\}>$ says that if a state contains an a_0, then two states later we cannot have a c_1 -- we must have a c_0. (We might note that the prime constraint $<\{a_0\}, \emptyset, \{c_1\}>$ is a direct consequence of the prime constraints $<\{a_0\}, \{b_1\}>$ and $<\{b_0\}, \{c_1\}>$). Although we're discussing prime constraints in terms of their 'predicative' abilities, it should be clear from symmetry that prime constraints can also be used for 'postdiction'. For example, the prime constraint $<\{a_0\}, \{b_1\}>$ tells us that if a particular state in a simulation contains a b_1, then the preceding state, if any, cannot contain an a_0 and must, therefore, contain an a_1.

In the preceding example there were an infinite number of constraints but only a finite number of prime constraints. So it might be supposed that the number of prime constraints is always finite. However, this is not the case as the next example shows.

Example: Consider this system,

$$\text{values} = \{a_0, a_1\}$$
$$\text{variables} = \{\{a_0, a_1\}\}$$

state graph: $\{a_0\}$ $\{a_1\}$

In spite of its simplicity, this system has an infinite number of prime constraints. Each one is of the form $<\{a_0\}, \emptyset^n, \{a_1\}>$ where $n \geq 0$. There are two ways to interpret this set of prime constraints,

1. Once we have an a_0, we will always have an a_0.

2. If we have an a_1, then we must always have had an a_1.

The following two results establish the equivalence of the set of two-place prime constraints and the set of state transitions.

Theorem 4.1: $S_2 = \{\omega \varepsilon S^2 | \not\exists \alpha \varepsilon C_2' : \quad \omega \underline{<} \bullet \alpha\}$ [†]

'A state transition is any ordered pair of states not covered by a two-place prime constraint.'

Theorem 4.2: $C_2' = \max_{\underline{<} \bullet} (\{\alpha \varepsilon T^2 | \pi(\alpha) \cap S_2 = \phi\})$

'A two-place prime constraint is a maximal clause of length two that does not cover any state transitions.'

V. DEDUCTION

To illustrate the utility of prime constraints, we shall show how they can be used to provide a necessary and sufficient condition for the ability to *access* a set of variables.

Consider the following problem: We are given two disjoint subset of variables for some system. We assume that an agent knows the values taken on by the variables in one of those subsets. We would like to know under what circumstances this knowledge can be used to deduce something about the values taken on by the variables in the other subset.

To help formulate the problem a littler better, let the two subsets of variables be denoted A and B, with A the set of variables to which our mythical agent has access. We shall assume that this agent knows the constraints of the system. On the basis of this particular knowledge, the agent is able to determine *a priori* that only certain *patterns* of values are possible for the variables in B. We shall say that the agent is able to deduce something about Set B using Set A if and only if there exists a simulation in which the pattern of values for the variables in A can be used to *further restrict* the set of possible patterns in that simulation for the variables in B. Thus, a deduction about B based on A can occur if and only if there exist two patterns, one *restricted* to A and the other to B, that are possible separately, but not together. The presence of one pattern excludes the other. These ideas are formalized as follows.

[†] *If A is a set of sequence and n a non-negative integer, then A_n denotes the set of those sequences in A of length n.*

Definition: A pattern is a clause in which each term contains no more than one value per variable.

Notation: If α and β are sequences of sets of the same length, then $\alpha.\cup\beta$ is the componentwise union of α and β and $\alpha.\cap\beta$ the componentwise intersection of α and β.

Definition: Two patterns α and β are said to be *mutually-exclusive* if and only if,

    1. α and β are the same length
    2. $\alpha.\cup\beta$ is a constraint
    3. neither α nor β is a constraint by itself.

Definition: If α is a clause and A a set of variables, then α_A, the *restriction of α to A*, is the clause obtained by deleting from each term of α all conditions not belonging to a variable in A. We say that α *is restricted to A* if and only if $\alpha=\alpha_A$.

Lemma 5.1: If α and β are clauses of the same length, then,

$$\alpha\underline{<}\cdot\beta <=> \pi(\alpha)\subseteq\pi(\beta)$$

Lemma 5.2: If α and β are clauses of the same length, then,

$$\alpha\underline{<}\cdot\beta => \alpha\underline{<}\cdot\ \alpha.\ \cap\ \beta\ \underline{<}\cdot\ \beta$$

Lemma 5.3: If α and β are clauses and A a set of variables, then,

$$\alpha=\alpha_A \wedge \alpha\underline{<}\cdot\beta => \beta=\beta_A$$

Theorem 5.1: If A and B are disjoint sets of variables, then: There exists two mutually-exclusive patterns, one restricted to A and the other to B.

    if and only if

There exists a prime constraint restricted to $A\cup B$ that is not restricted to either A or B individually.

Proof: 'If' Let θ be a prime constraint satisfying the indicated properties. From Properties 3.3 and 3.6 and Lemma 5.1 it follows that,

$$\theta\underline{<}\cdot\theta_A \text{ and } \theta\underline{<}\cdot\theta_B$$

But because θ is not restricted to either A or B individually, we know that $\theta \neq \theta_A$ and $\theta \neq \theta_B$. Thus,

$$\theta<\cdot\theta_A \text{ and } \theta<\cdot\theta_B$$

These two relationships together with the fact that Θ is a prime constraint mean that neither Θ_A nor Θ_B is a constraint. There must exist, therefore, two simulations ω_A and ω_B such that,

$$\omega_A \ \varepsilon \ \pi(\Theta_A) \ \text{ and } \ \omega_B \ \varepsilon \ \pi(\Theta_B) \tag{a}$$

Now let,

$$\mu_A = \omega_A \cdot \cap \Theta_A \ \text{ and } \ \mu_B = \omega_B \cdot \cap \Theta_B$$

Because ω_A and ω_B are both simulations, μ_A and μ_B are both patterns. And because Θ_A is restricted to A and Θ_B to B, μ_A is restricted to A and μ_B to B. Now from Line (a) it follows that $\omega_A \leq^\bullet \Theta_A$ and $\omega_B \leq^\bullet \Theta_B$. Applying Lemma 5.2 to these two relationships and using the definitions of μ_A and μ_B, we get,

$$\omega_A \leq^\bullet \mu_A \quad \text{ and } \quad \omega_B \leq^\bullet \mu_B \tag{b}$$

$$\mu_A \leq^\bullet \Theta_A \quad \text{ and } \quad \mu_B \leq^\bullet \Theta_B \tag{c}$$

Line (b) tells us that neither μ_A nor μ_B is a constraint (since ω_A and ω_B are simulations). From Line (c) and the fact that $\Theta = \Theta_A \cdot \cup \Theta_B$ we have (by Properties 3.3 and 3.6 and Lemma 5.1),

$$\mu_A \cdot \cup \mu_B \leq^\bullet \Theta$$

Since Θ is a constraint it follows that $\mu_A \cdot \cup \mu_B$ is also (Property 4.2). Hence, μ_A and μ_B are mutually-exclusive patterns.

'Only If'   Let α and β be two mutually-exclusive patterns, α being restricted to A and β to B. Thus, $\alpha \cdot \cup \beta$ is a constraint, and so there must exist a prime constraint Θ such that

$$\alpha \cdot \cup \beta \leq^\bullet \Theta$$

This relationship means that there is a subsequence δ of $\alpha \cdot \cup \beta$ such that $|\delta| = |\Theta|$ and $\delta \leq^\bullet \Theta$ (Property 4.3). We then have $\delta = \delta_A \cdot \cup \delta_{.B}$ and,

$$\delta_A \cdot \cup \delta_B \leq^\bullet \Theta$$

Because $\delta_A \cdot \cup \delta_B$ is restricted to $A \cup B$, it follows that Θ is also restricted to $A \cup B$ (Lemma 5.3). Suppose now that θ is restricted to A. Then $(\delta_A \cdot \cup \delta_B) \cdot \cap \theta = \delta_A \cdot \cap \theta$, and by Lemma 5.2. $\delta_A \cdot \cap \theta \underline{\leq} \cdot \theta$. Furthermore, since δ_A is a pattern, $\delta_A \underline{\leq} \cdot \delta_A \cdot \cap \theta$ (Properties 3.3 and 3.6 and Lemma 5.1). Thus, $\delta_A \underline{\leq} \cdot \theta$, and by Property 4.2 δ_A must be a constraint. And, so too must be μ_A since δ_A is a subsequence of μ_A. But this contradicts our initial assumption that μ_A and μ_B are mutually-exclusive patterns. We must conclude that θ is not restricted to A. A similar argument shows that θ is not restricted to B. □

Example: Consider the following system,

variables = $\{a, b, c\}$

where $a = \{a_0, a_1\}$, $b = \{b_0, b_1\}$, and $c = \{c_0, c_1\}$

two-place prime constraints = $\{<\{a_0, b_0\}, \{c_0\}>,$

$$<\{c_1, b_1\}, \{a_1, b_0\}>\}$$

Now let $A = \{a\}$ and $B = \{b\}$. Question: Can anything ever be deduced about the values assumed by Variable b by observing the values assumed by Variable a. Answer: Yes, because there is a prime constraint restricted to $\{a,b\}$ but not to either $\{a\}$ or $\{b\}$ individually. That prime constraint is,

$$<\{a_0, b_0\}, \{b_1\}, \{a_1, b_0\}>$$

From Theorem 5.1 we know that there must exist two mutually-exclusive patterns, one restricted to $\{a\}$ and the other to $\{b\}$. They are,

	a	b	c			a	b	c
a_0							b_0	
							b_1	
a_1							b_0	

With Theorem 5.1 we've attempted to show that prime constraints can be used in formulating and answering an important question about system behavior. We, of course, are not done since we must now provide an effective (and efficient) procedure for determining whether a prime constraint of the prescribed type exists [†]. Work is now progressing in that area, and in other areas related to answering a broad class of questions about system behavior using prime constraints.

ACKNOWLEDGMENT

The work reported on in this paper is the result of a joint effort by the author and Jonathan K. Millen. The work was supported by the Electronic Systems Division of the Air Force Systems Command under Contract F19628-78-C-0001.

[†] *In subsequent work, the author has shown this problem to be decidable by showing that the set of prime constraints for a system is regular.*

CONSTRAINTS

PART II CONSTRAINTS AND MULTILEVEL SECURITY

Jonathan K. Millen

The Mitre Corporation
Bedford, Massachusetts

I. INTRODUCTION

In its early days, the theory of information security in computer systems was regarded solely as a matter of access control. Subjects had a natural interpretation in a manual data-processing environment as people, and objects as documents. When this philosophy was transferred to computer systems, subjects became processes and objects became files. The process/file level of granularity was acceptable for ordinary user programs, but turned out to be too coarse for system programs where efficiency is of great importance. The operating system software that handles access requests, and changes in access authorization, was found to be a prime source of the need to work at a finer-grained level. The subject/object approach is awkward at this level because there is no natural interpretation for subjects.

The reason that processes no longer suffice as subjects can be illustrated with an example. Consider a program with the two assignment statements:

$$U2 := U1;$$
$$S2 := S1;$$

and let us assume that information flow from S1 to U2 is not authorized. The process evidently needs read access to S1 and write access to U2. From a subject-object-access point of view, the situation is insecure. What makes the difference here is the fact that we know what the program is, and we can see that it causes no information flow from S1 to U2. How can we formalize this argument?

One way is to introduce new, more abstract, subjects, and say that the two statements could, in principle, be executed by two distinct subjects. When subjects are reinterpreted, however, access also has to be viewed differently, and there is less intuitive assurance that read and write accesses are being interpreted appropriately in any but the simplest situations.

If the primary objective of the analysis is to detect unauthorized disclosure of information, an appealing alternative
is to formalize the notion of information flow from one object
or variable to another.

Shannon's theory of communication does not seem to be directly applicable here, primarily because it deals with a single
communication channel. In a computer or computer program, there
is potentially a channel between any pair of variables, and the
usefulness of the channel often depends on the current values of
other variables. In this context, also, probability distributions
are usually not known.

There have recently been several papers that have taken information flow approaches to computer security. Their common setting
is a deterministic abstract machine whose current state is
embodied in a set of state variables. Information flow from each
state variable to others may result from each transition of the
machine.

Jones and Lipton [1] consider a transition as the result of
invoking a program. A program is a function from its inputs --
which include global variables and data structures as well as
arguments -- to its outputs, which can be stored in global
variables or just viewed. If an output can be determined from
some proper subset of the inputs, then there is no information
flow from the inputs not in that subset to that output.

D. Denning and P. Denning [2] classify program statements
according to the information flows that can occur between the
variables that participate in the statement. An assignment
statement potentially transfers information from its right hand
variables to its left hand variable. A conditional statement
potentially transfers information from the condition variables
to any variables that can be modified in its sequel. The flow
characteristics or "certification semantics" of a wide variety of
statements are given.

Feiertag, et al [3] has a functional definition like Jones
and Lipton, but considers the flow only from the past succession
of external inputs to a given external output. This yields the
most immediate application to multilevel computer security, since
levels are known a priori only for external variables. It is
then shown that a per-transition policy based on assigning
security levels to internal state variables is sufficient to
protect against unauthorized disclosure.

Cohen [4] gives a sufficient as well as necessary condition
for information flow, suggested by Shannon's probabilistic theory.
A variable B is "strongly dependent" on a variable A over
execution of an operation if variety in the value of A beforehand
forces variety in the value of B afterward. This definition
satisfies the requirement of a functional approach: if an output
is determined by a certain set of variables, it is not strongly
dependent on any variables not in that set, with the exception
of those linked by some relation or invariant to a variable in
the set.

Our approach uses a particular static representation of a
system in terms of "prime constraints", which are analogous to
prime implicants in switching theory. A prime constraint
characterization:

1. describes the system as a whole, rather than single
   operations, programs, or statements;
2. exhibits security compromises transparently;
3. exists for nondeterministic systems.

The prime constraints of a system are derivable from non-
procedural transition specifications such as those introduced by
Parnas and used by MITRE and SRI in security verifications. A
way to generate a set of prime constraints sufficient for
security analysis will be suggested.

The main result in this paper is the proof that a certain
condition on transitions, similar to the *-property, is sufficient
to guarantee security against unauthorized disclosure.

II. PRELIMINARIES

Notation. In what follows, we shall be dealing with only one
system at a time and we shall use fixed symbols for the state
set, variables, etc., as indicated in this section.

A is the finite set of *variables* (or objects). V(a) is the
finite set of possible *values* (or local states) for a variable a.
The set of all *states* is denoted by unity, 1. Each state is a
function q assigning a value to each variable. Thus, $q(a) \varepsilon V(a)$.

T is the set of *transitions*; it is a relation on 1. If
$(q,q') \varepsilon T$, we write $q \rightarrow q'$ and say that there is a transition from
q to q', in which q is the old state and q' is the new state. We
require that *every state must have at least one transition from
it.*

F is the set of *free* variables, those whose value in the new state after any transition is unconstrained by the old state. F is determined from T by:

$$F = \{a \,|\, \text{if } q \to q' \text{ and } q'(b) = q''(b) \text{ for all } b \neq a \text{ then } q \to q''\}.$$

X and Y are the *input* and *output* sets, respectively. They are of no significance structurally, but they play a necessary part in the definition of security. Inputs are required to be free.*

A *causal* (discrete) system can be described completely by its set of transitions. A sequence of states is a *simulation* if and only if each state is followed by one to which there is a transition, except the last.

Constraints. The concept of "constraint" in this paper is essentially the same as in the paper by F. C. Furtek in this volume. There are some technical differences, however, of which two stand out: the characterization of constraints as sets of state sequences of a given length, and the limitation of one value per variable per state position.

This section introduces some preliminary definitions in a version of switching theory based on state sequences instead of states, and which deals with variables that are not necessarily binary. Constraints are like implicants, except that they are sets of state sequences that are *not* simulations.

Constraints are built up from *conditions*. A condition is the set of states assigning the same value to a particular variable. The condition fixing the value v for the variable a is denoted a_v. Thus, $q \,\varepsilon\, a_v$ if and only if $q(a) = v$.

A *term* is a nonempty intersection of conditions. Terms are written multiplicatively, like $a_1 b_1 c_0$. The set of all terms is denoted P. By convention, the set 1 of all states is considered a term.

---

* *Free variables are unconstrained by even their own past values. Hence, a free variable that is not an input must get its value from some process that is unpredictable except perhaps probabilistically. We assume that probability distributions of such variables are not known to prospective penetrators.*

So far, we have only been talking about sets of states. A cartesian product of terms is a set of state sequences. These are just called *products*. Let P_n be the set of n-place products.

$$P_n = \{p_1 \times \ldots \times p_n \mid p_i \in P \text{ for all } i\}.$$

A *constraint* is a product that contains no simulations. Let C_n be the set of n-place constraints. An n-place constraint is *prime* if it is maximal in C_n.

As an example, consider the system with two binary variables whose transition set is described by the assignment statement

$$b := a$$

with the understanding that a is free. The system has four possible states:

$$q_0 \; \varepsilon \; a_0 b_0 \qquad\qquad q_2 \; \varepsilon \; a_1 b_0$$

$$q_1 \; \varepsilon \; a_0 b_1 \qquad\qquad q_3 \; \varepsilon \; a_1 b_1$$

Each of the terms above, because it has a condition from every variable, contains exactly one state; it is often convenient to use such terms to represent states.

The product

$$a_0 b_1 \times a_1 b_1,$$

which contains just one state pair, is a constraint because $a_0 b_1 \not\vdash a_1 b_1$. It is not prime, however, because

$$a_0 \times b_1$$

is also a constraint, and, being a product of a proper subset of the conditions in each term of the former constraint, it properly includes it. In fact, $a_0 \times b_1$ is prime.

III. DEFINITION OF SECURITY

One can use a constraint, plus knowledge of the values of all but one of the variables appearing in it, to deduce something about the value of the remaining variable. For example, the constraint

$$a_0 b_1 \times c_0 \; ,$$

together with the knowledge that $q(b) = 1$ in state q and $q'(c) = 0$ in the next state q', permits the deduction that $q(a) \neq 0$.

Knowledge about b and c has led to a conclusion about a.

If the constraint is prime, we can guarantee that the events $q(b) = 1$, $q'(c) = 0$ are possible, since

$$b_1 \times c_0$$

cannot be a constraint. Thus, a prime constraint is sufficient to make a deduction about any one of the variables occuring in it, if one can control or observe the others.

Prime constraints are also necessary for a deduction of this type. Suppose that one observes and/or causes a series of events expressed by the product

$$p_1 \times \ldots \times p_n .$$

We shall say that one can "deduce something about" a variable a if he can exclude at least one possible value u for a at some time i (relative to the series of events). If the deduction about a concerns its value at some time before the first event or after the last, one can extend the product with $\times$ 1's to ensure that i is between 1 and n. The conclusion that a cannot have value u at time i implies that

$$p_1 \times \ldots \times p_i a_u \times \ldots \times p_n$$

is a constraint. This constraint might not be prime, but there is some prime constraint covering it. Furthermore, any prime constraint covering it still contains the occurence of a_u, since $p_1 \times \ldots \times p_n$ is not a constraint -- it expresses events that have occured in some simulation.

In summary, a necessary and sufficient condition to deduce something about the value of a variable on the basis of access to other variables is the existence of a prime constraint with an occurence of the variable in question, such that all other variables occuring in it are accessible. (This statement would have to be refined somewhat to take into consideration access capabilities that change in time).

In defining security, we consider only those constraints involving solely input and output variables. Any control or observation of system variables by a user must be managed via inputs and outputs, and those are the only variables for which security levels are given.

Although a user can directly observe outputs only at his own
level or lower, he can sometimes control inputs at higher or
incomparable levels. One way to do so is by introducing a "Trojan
Horse" into the system software. This higher-level control
ability can be limited or eliminated in some environments, but
only the worst case of unlimited ability to control all inputs is
treated below.

Of course, it does not help a penetrator to control *all* the
inputs to a system, since he will learn nothing he did not already
know, but we do not exclude the possibility that he will control
all but one, or as many as he needs, to learn something about one
particular input still controlled by a high level user.

Security compromises are not limited to deductions involving
two consecutive states. A value entered in some input at the
"Secret" level should not predictably reappear as the value of an
"Unclassified" output at *any* later time. The definition of
security, therefore, involves n-place rather than just two-place
constraints.

Security levels are defined for inputs and outputs only, and,
in this paper, are assumed constant in time. Security levels do
change in real systems, but it is possible to regard a variable
as a collection of "virtual" variables of constant security
level, and then prove later that the virtual variables are multiplexed correctly into the single real one. The ability to
virtualize away certain complexities for purposes of security
analysis is one of the advantages of using a high level, formal
transition specification [5].

We define an *external security level assignment* as a function

$$\lambda: \quad X \cup Y \to L$$

where L is a finite lattice of security levels.

A system is *secure against unauthorized disclosure in a*
Trojan Horse environment if no user at level $s \in L$ can deduce
something about the value of an input of a higher or incomparable
level, on the basis of observations of external variables at
level s or lower and/or control of inputs at any level. By the
above arguments, a system is secure in this sense if and only if
the following situation is impossible:

1. $p_1 \times \ldots \times p_i a_u \times \ldots \times p_n$ is a prime constraint
2. $p_j \subset b_v$ implies $b \in X \cup Y$
3. $(p_j \subset b_v$ and $b \notin X)$ implies $\lambda(b) \le s$
4. $a \in X$
5. $\lambda(a) \not\le s$.

IV.   A SUFFICIENT CONDITION FOR SECURITY

Covers. In practice, it is desirable to draw conclusions
about security by analyzing some small-as-possible presentation
of a system, such as a program listing or a formal specification.
In more abstract terms, we wish to analyze the transition set of
a system without having to generate simulations (or constraints)
of greater length than two. Rather than look at the transition
set directly, we shall work with some set of two-place prime
constraints called a *cover*, whose union is the set of all non-
transitions. That is, $R \subset C_2$ is a cover if

$$(1 \times 1) - T = \cup R.$$

A cover consisting of prime constraints is called a prime
cover.

Covers, even prime covers, are not unique, but one can always
produce a cover simply by listing all state pairs that are not
transitions, representing each state by the intersection of the
conditions that contain it. Then a prime cover can be found by
replacing each constraint by a prime constraint that covers it.

The results in this paper apply to systems coverable by
constraints of a restricted form: those with single conditions
on the right. We call a constraint *simple* if it is of the form

$$p \times a_v.$$

A simple system is one possessing a simple cover (a cover consisting of simple constraints). This category of systems includes
all systems that would be considered deterministic. Let us
define a system to be *structurally deterministic* if the value of
every non-free variable is determined by the previous state.
That is,

if $q \to q'$ and $q \to q''$

and $q'(a) \neq q''(a)$

then $a \in F$.

The unqualified term "deterministic" should probably be
reserved, in a security context, for structurally deterministic
systems whose free variables are all inputs. A structurally
deterministic system has the following simple prime cover:

$$R = \{p \times a_v \,|\, a \notin F \text{ and } p \text{ is maximal in } \{p' \in P \,|\, p' \subset 1 - \cdot a_v\}\}$$

where $\cdot a_v$ is the inverse image of a_v, namely,

$$\cdot a_v = \{q \,|\, \text{ for some } q', \ q \to q' \in a_v\}.$$

This cover works because, if (q,q') is not a transition, there must be some non--input a such that $q \not\subset \cdot a_{q'(a)}$. Otherwise, any state q'' such that $q \rightarrow q''$ would have to match q' on all non-inputs, and hence $q \rightarrow q'$ since inputs can be changed freely.

Further evidence that simple constraints are an "interesting" category, is the fact that there is a close connection between simple two-place constraints and strong dependency. To be precise, the following two statements are equivalent:

1. There exist $q,q' \varepsilon 1$ such that $q(c) = q'(c)$ for all $c \neq a$ and $\{q''(b) \mid q \rightarrow q''\} \neq \{q''(b) \mid q' \rightarrow q''\}$;

2. There is a prime constraint $p \times b_v \varepsilon C_2$ such that $p \subset a_u$ for some $u \varepsilon V(a)$.

Statement 1 is Cohen's definition of strong dependency of b on a, modified somewhat to be applicable to nondeterministic systems.

The Monotonicity Condition. The Bell-LaPadula *-property [6] required that if a subject has read access to an object a and write access to an object b in the same state, the security level of a must be dominated by the level of b. The idea is that no information could be transferred from a to b in a single transition without the accesses indicated.

The nearest equivalent in the present context is the following *monotonicity condition.* Given an external security level assignment λ, an extension $\hat{\lambda}$ of λ to A is *monotone* with respect to a simple cover R if, for all generators a_u and constraints $p \times b_v \varepsilon R$,

$$\text{if } p \subset a_u$$
$$\text{then } \hat{\lambda}(a) \leq \hat{\lambda}(b).$$

It is shown below that a system is secure if there exists a monotone extension of the external level assignment.

The argument will proceed roughly as follows, in three steps. First, it is shown easily that any prime constraint $p_1 \times \ldots \times p_n$ is generated by the two-place constraints in a cover. Second, there is a major result, called the Factor Lemma, that there is a chain of variables, joined by constraints in the generating set, between any free variable in each p_i and some non-free variable in a later p_j. Finally, the monotonicity condition applied in a trivial induction to the chain establishes the desired inequality in security levels.

Generation of Prime Constraints from a Cover. If p is a product, $1 \times p$ and $p \times 1$ are called *extensions* of p, as are $1 \times 1 \times p$, $1 \times p \times 1$, and in general $1^i \times p \times 1^j$. If R is a cover, any n-place constraint is covered by extensions to length n of elements of R. For, if p is a constraint, any state sequence in p is a non-simulation, and must contain at least one non-transition, which is included in some element of R. That element can be extended to a constraint that contains the state sequence.

Given a prime constraint p, let Z be a minimal set of extensions of a cover R such that

$$p \subset \cup\, Z.$$

The inclusion is irredundant on the right in the sense that Z is minimal, and irredundant on the left in the sense that no conditions can be removed from p because p is prime. In this situation, p is called the *extended consensus* of Z, and we write

$$p \subset \cup\, Z \text{ (irr.)}$$

after Tison [7]. Thus, any prime constraint is an extended consensus of elements of a cover.

It can be shown that every condition in p appears, in the corresponding state position, in some element of Z. In fact, p is exactly the product of conditions whose variables appear only once in each state position among the elements of Z. Other variables appear with all possible values and get "cancelled" as in this example, assuming b is binary:

$$Z \quad \begin{cases} a_0 \times b_0 c_1 \times 1 \\ 1 \times b_1 d_0 \times a_0 \end{cases}$$

$$\overline{}$$

$$p = a_0 \times c_1 d_0 \times a_0$$

The Factor Lemma. The two-place constraints in R are like links that can be chained together to form any prime constraint. There are, in general, several links in each position along such a chain, as suggested below.

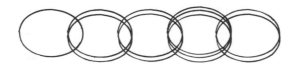

A link is coupled with a link in the following position by sharing a variable. The right-hand variable in each "link" appears as a left-hand variable in one of the links in the next position, except when it "drops out" and appears in the final prime constraint. This is stated formally and proved below as the Factor Lemma. The Factor Lemma serves essentially the same purpose as Cohen's Theorem 4-1 and Feiertag's proof of the sufficiency of "strong security properties".

Consider an n-place prime constraint $p_1 \times \ldots \times p_n$ and a classical prime cover R. There is, as we have seen, a collection Z of constraints from R, which we shall exhibit in the form

$$f_{ij} \times g_{ij}$$

for $i = 1,\ldots,n-1$ and various j, such that the extensions

$$h_{ij} = 1^{i-1} \times f_{ij} \times g_{ij} \times 1^{n-i-1}$$

cover $p_1 \times \ldots \times p_n$ irredundantly. See the accompanying figure.

Suppose that $g_{i_o j_o} = a_v$, and that $p_{i_0+1} \not\subseteq a_u$ for any u.

In this situation, the *Factor Lemma* asserts that there exist j and u such that

$$f_{i_o+1, j} \subset a_u$$

The proof will make repeated use of the argument that, if p is a term that contains a state q but not q', then $p \subset a_v$ for some condition a_v such that $q \in a_v$ but $q' \not\subseteq a_v$. We say in this case that p *distinguishes* q from q', and that p is *a-dependent*. Thus, the Factor Lemma says that if $g_{i_o j_o}$ is a-dependent and p_{i_o+1} is not a-dependent then $f_{i_o+1, j}$ is a-dependent, for some j.

The proof begins by noting that, by irredundancy of the inclusion $p \subset \cup Z$, there is a state sequence

$$s = (q_1,\ldots,q_n)$$

such that

$$s \ \varepsilon \ p_1 \times \ldots \times p_n$$

and

$$s \ \varepsilon \ h_{i_o j_o}$$

but

$$s \not\varepsilon \ h_{ij} \text{ for any } (i,j) \neq (i_o, j_o).$$

Since $s \ \varepsilon \ h_{i_o j_o}$, we have $q_{i_o+1} \ \varepsilon \ g_{i_o j_o} = a_v$. That is,
$q_{i_o+1}(a) = v$. Now, let q'_{i_o+1} be the state identical to q_{i_o+1}
except that $q'_{i_o+1}(a) = u \neq v$, where u is found as follows.
Produce a state q'' such that $q_{i_o} \rightarrow q''$, and let $u = q''(a)$. This
$u \neq v$ because $q_{i_o} \ \varepsilon \ f_{i_o j_o}$, and $f_{i_o j_o} \times a_v$ is a constraint.

Let s' be identical to s except that q_{i_o+1} is replaced by
q'_{i_o+1}. Since p_{i_o+1} is not a-dependent, it cannot distinguish
q'_{i_o+1} from q_{i_o+1}, so

$$s' \ \varepsilon \ p_1 \times \ldots \times p_n.$$

But $s' \not\varepsilon \ h_{i_o j_o}$, because $q'_{i_o+1} \not\varepsilon \ a_v$, hence

$$s' \ \varepsilon \ h_{ij} \text{ for some } (i,j) \neq (i_o, j_o).$$

Since $s \not\varepsilon \ h_{ij}$, h_{ij} *does* distinguish q'_{i_o+1} from q_{i_o} in position
i_o+1, hence position i_o+1 of h_{ij} must be a-dependent; in fact,
it must be included in a_u.

$$h_{1j} \qquad f_{1j} \times g_{1j}$$

$$\cdots$$

$$h_{i_o j_o} \qquad\qquad f_{i_o j_o} \times a_v$$

$$\vdots$$

$$h_{i_o j} \qquad\qquad f_{i_o j} \times g_{i_o j}$$

$$\cdots$$

$$h_{i_o+1,j} \qquad\qquad f_{i_o+1,j} \times g_{i_o+1,j}$$

$$\cdots$$

$$p \qquad p_1 \times p_2 \times \cdots \times p_{i_o} \times \quad p_{i_o+1} \times p_{i_o+2} \times \cdots$$

$$s \qquad (q_1 , q_2 , \cdots , q_{i_o} , \quad q_{i_o+1} , q_{i_o+2} , \cdots \quad)$$

$$s' \qquad (q_1 , q_2 , \cdots , q_{i_o} , \quad q'_{i_o+1} , q_{i_o+2} , \cdots \quad)$$

Factor Lemma Illustration. 1's have been omitted from h_{ij}'s for clarity. The box encloses the i_o+1 position.

If a_u appears on the left, in f_{ij}, then $i = i_o + 1$ and we are done. If a_u appears in the right, in g_{ij}, then $i = i_o$ and $f_{ij} \times g_{ij} = f_{i_o j} \times a_u$. But $q_{i_o} \varepsilon f_{i_o j}$ (since $s' \varepsilon h_{ij}$) and $q_{i_o} \to q'' \varepsilon a_u$, so $f_{i_o j} \times a_u$ cannot be a constraint, yielding a contradiction. This completes the proof.

Security Theorem. Now, consider a prime constraint p as in the definition of security, in which a condition a_u of some input a appears. By using the Factor Lemma and the monotonicity condition, we shall find in p a condition of some non-input which dominates a in level. Assume that $p \subset \cup Z$ (irr.), where Z is a subset of extensions of elements of R, a simple prime cover.

We know that a_u appears in some element of Z. Inputs appear only on the left (in the original two-place prime constraint). A condition b_v, which cannot be an input, appears on the right of that constraint. Note that b dominates a in level, by the monotonicity condition. If b appears in the final prime constraint, we are done. Otherwise, by the Factor lemma, a condition of b appears in the same state position on the left of a constraint in Z. Now apply the same argument to the condition on the right of that constraint, etc. (See figure below). Eventually, a non-input condition dominating a in level will be found in p. This proves the sufficiency of the monotonicity condition when there is a simple prime cover.

$$a_u f \times b_v$$

$$b_v f' \times c_w$$

$$\cdots$$

$$p = \cdots \times a_u \times \cdots \times c_w \times \cdots$$

V. CONCLUSIONS

Application. To test a system for security using the monotonicity condition, a simple prime cover must be found. While a "constructive" proof of the existence of such a cover was given for structurally deterministic systems, a practical technique for producing them has not yet been developed. The prospects for doing so are not bad, as this section will try to show.

Constraints can be viewed as a means of expressing the
semantics of other, more convenient, specification languages.
Formal transition specifications, like some of those suggested
by Parnas, lend themselves to this treatment.

A simple, but not untypical, transition specification for an
operation to copy one element of an array into another with a
greater or equal index is given below:

$$0\text{-function copy } (i,j)$$

$$\text{exception}$$

$$i > j$$

$$\text{effect}$$

$$m(j) := m(i)$$

The first step in translating this type of specification into
a simple prime cover is to identify the variables. First, the
arguments i and j are stored in some variables, say a and b. The
array m is composed of the variables m(1), m(2), ...

The assignment statement in the effect, considered in isolation, suggests the constraints

$$m(i)_u \times m(j)_v \cdot (u \neq v) \tag{1}$$

where $u \in V(m(i))$ and $v \in V(m(j))$ is understood, and it is
assumed that $m(k)$ exists for all $k \in V(a) = V(b)$.

The constraints specified by (1) apply only when i and j are
the argument values, and the exception condition does not hold.
Hence, the function as a whole has constraints

$$a_i b_j m(i)_u \times m(j)_v \qquad (u \neq v, i \leq j) \tag{2}$$

When the exception condition holds, $m(j)$ is not modified.
Hence, we have also:

$$a_i b_j m(j)_u \times m(j)_v \qquad (u \neq v,\ i > j) \tag{3}$$

Finally, no element of m other than $m(j)$ is ever modified;
this gives

$$b_j m(k)_u \times m(k)_v \qquad (u \neq v,\ k \neq j) \tag{4}$$

There are no constraints with a or b on the right because a
and b, which hold arguments of the call, are inputs, and could
change arbitrarily for the next call.

The fact that a constraint cover is for a whole system, while
formal specifications are presented function by function, is not
an obstacle. Assume that we have a collection of covers
$R_1,\ldots,R_n$, each of which specifies one function. Let us introduce a new variable e with values $1,\ldots,n$ to "choose" the function.
Replace each constraint $f \times g$ in R_i by $e_i f \times g$. The collection
of all of the new constraints is a cover for a system in which
any one of the n functions may be chosen freely.

The copy example above also provides an easy demonstration
of a security validation. Suppose that a and b are at the
minimum security level and that the level of m(k) is k. The
monotonicity condition can be verified by inspection of (2)-(4).

Summary. A system comprises variables, whose combined values
express the system state, and transitions. Systems are not
necessarily deterministic or even structurally deterministic.
Products have been defined as certain sets of state sequences.
A constraint is a product containing no simulations. The transition set of a system can be expressed with a cover, a set of two-
place constraints. A cover of simple prime constraints, which
express strong dependencies, can be found for structurally
deterministic systems. A prime constraint of any length is the
extended consensus of extensions of elements of a cover.

Security is defined in terms of prime constraints, regardless
of length, involving inputs and outputs, relative to a given
constant external security level assignment. A monotonicity
condition for any extension of the level assignment, applied to
a simple prime cover, is sufficient for security. The proof
rests mainly on the Factor Lemma.

A possible way of constructing simple prime covers in
practice starts with a formal transition specification.

Extensions. Three simplifying assumptions were made that
could be relaxed to extend the theory in natural directions.

Nothing was assumed known about the initial state of a system.
In practice, however, there are typically some "invariants" of
the system state that are guaranteed initially and preserved by
every transition. As Cohen points out, this additional knowledge
can affect information flow, and hence security, since it makes
certain observations unnecessary. Invariants could be expressed
as constraints of length one, i.e., boolean products containing

only "illegal" states. Such constraints would have to be included in a cover, and the monotonicity condition would probably have to insist that variables in the same one-place constraint have the same level. Actual validations have not used such invariants to estimate information flow, but have used them in connection with non-constant security level assignments.

Non-constant security level assignments allow the security level of a variable to be a function of the current state. They can be handled by defining security in terms of simulations, and expressing the monotonicity condition in terms of transitions. High level specifications can be used to trade this complication for a proof of correct implementation, but such proofs can be very difficult if the system has not been designed to facilitate them.

The worst-case assumption of complete control of arbitrarily high level inputs by uncleared users can be relaxed by weakening the definition of security. If there were no Trojan Horses, for example, one could admit a compromise of an input variable only when all other variables in a prime constraint, rather than just all non-inputs, are bounded by a lower or incomparable security level. The monotonicity condition would then still be sufficient, but one might look for a weaker condition of comparable simplicity.

ACKNOWLEDGMENT

The work reported in this paper is the joint effort of the author and Frederick C. Furtek. The work was supported by the U. S. Air Force under Contract F19628-77-C-0001.

REFERENCES

[1] A. K. Jones and R. J. Lipton, "The Enforcement of Security
     Policies for Computation", *Proc. of the Fifth Symposium on
     Operating Systems Principles*, November 1975, pp. 197-206.
[2] D. E. Denning and P. J. Denning, "Certification of Programs
     for Secure Information Flow", *Comm. ACM*, Vol. 20, No. 7
     (July 1977) pp. 504-513.
[3] P. G. Neumann, R. S. Boyer, R. J. Feiertag, K. N. Levitt and
     L. Robinson, *A Provably Secure Operating System: The System,
     Its Applications, and Proofs*, (Final Report), 11 Feb 1977,
     Stanford Research Institute, Menlo Park, California (also see
     Proc. Sixth ACM Symposium on O. S. Principles, Nov. 1977).
[4] E. S. Cohen, *Strong Dependency: A Formalism for Describing
     Information Transmission in Computational Systems,* Dept. of
     Computer Science, Carnegie-Mellon Univ., Pittsburgh, Pa.,
     August 1976.
[5] J. K. Millen, "Formal Specifications for Security", *Proc. of
     Trends and Applications 1977: Computer Security and Integrity,*
     May 1977, IEEE Computer Society.
[6] D. E. Bell and L. J. LaPadula, *Secure Computer System:
     Unified Exposition and Multics Interpretation*, The MITRE
     Corporation, July 1975, ESD-TR-75-306.
[7] P. Tison, "Generalization of Consensus Theory and Application
     to the Minimization of Boolean Functions", *IEEE Transactions
     on Electronic Computers*, Vol. EC-16, No. 4, Aug 1967, pp.
     446-456.

SOME SECURITY PRINCIPLES
AND THEIR APPLICATION
TO COMPUTER SECURITY*

R. Stockton Gaines
Norman Z. Shapiro

The Rand Corporation
Santa Monica, California

I. INTRODUCTION

This study examines some of the general concepts which apply
to security. It is motivated by a desire to place ideas relevant
to the protection of information stored in a computer system in
the context of other concepts about the protection of physical
objects and of information. An examination of the literature on
protection and security reveals little other than ad hoc ideas
about how to provide protection in various contexts. We document
here our attempts to identify the underlying concepts of security
by generalizing from specific pragmatic ideas, and to relate
these concepts to each other. We then show how they synergisti-
cally combine to result in security greater than that of separate
specific techniques. Since our motivation is the application of
these ideas to computer security, we will emphasize those security
aspects that particularly pertain to it.

* *This research was supported by the National Science Foundation
under Grant No. MCS76-00720.*

As a preliminary matter, it is necessary to point out that the notion of security is fundamentally one of judgment rather then measurement. Security is achieved by means of procedures, mechanisms and computer programs. While for some specific techniques a "work factor" (a quantitative estimate of the effort needed to defeat a protection mechanism or procedure) or some other quantitative measure may be meaningful, many aspects of security depend on qualitative judgments for which quantitative measures probably cannot be obtained. For example, we do not know how to estimate the likelihood that a new, clever attack which defeats a particular security measure will be developed, much less measure the amount of effort it would involve.

Generally, security is a system problem. That is, it is rare to find that a single security mechanism or procedure is used in isolation. Instead, several different elements working together usually compose a security system to protect something. Any judgment regarding the degree of protection or security afforded by a particular security system involves a fairly complex set of interrelated factors. These include the relations among the security measures and procedures, consideration of factors concerning the violator* of a security system, and the properties of the thing being protected. First, we will discuss a number of mechanisms and procedures for achieving security, identifying what we believe to be some underlying principles concerning security measures. We then show the interrelationship among various elements in a security system when the violator and the object being protected are taken into account.

II. GENERAL SECURITY CONCEPTS

The first notion that comes to most people's minds when they think of security is a barrier, which is some sort of a physically strong system that resists penetration. This can range from a strongbox or a safe to a fortress and includes ideas such as making automobiles with good locks. A comparable idea in computer systems is that access control mechanisms can be built into computer systems which cannot be defeated, thereby providing a logical barrier which restricts access to information stored in the computer. Both physical barriers and computer access control mechanisms share two properties: they attempt to prevent something from happening directly, and they are passive.

----

* No single term satisfactorily describes the person who defeats the security of a system; we will use the term "violator" throughout this discussion and intend it to apply in the case of accidental as well as deliberate actions.

The second central notion is that a violator may be detected in his activities. Detection may be obtained by direct surveillance, by the use of alarms, or by the use of accounting or auditing procedures. Detection alone is often considered a sufficient security measure. Sensitive papers may be left on a desk if the office is under surveillance. The defense against a person walking into a bank and taking money from a teller's drawer is based on detection.

The value of detection depends on its consequences. In the case of alarms and the forms of surveillance which provide immediate evidence of a violation, one immediate consequence may be apprehension. Other potential consequences are identification of the violator, and, at the other end of the spectrum, initiation of a search for the violator.

A concept having some overlap with the notions we have already discussed is that of a guard. A guard is far more than just a means of detection or apprehension, although a guard can carry out these functions. Two other aspects of a guard are particularly important. One is that he can use counterforce to actively resist a violator. The other is that a guard has reasoning and deductive powers and is an active observer. He may notice that something is wrong (i.e., perform detection) in ways that may be difficult to predict ahead of time. This aspect of the guard is what lead to the detection of the Watergate burglars. The weaknesses of a guard must also be considered. For example, he may be overcome by force (as can a barrier), or be defeated by trickery.

The above concepts constitute what we may call direct protection mechanisms. In addition, there are some useful indirect protection concepts. One of these is concealment, which applies both to physical and abstract objects. One may hide money, or encrypt data. The protection mechanisms themselves may be concealed or kept secret. The object here is to keep information needed by a violator from him, so that he will not know all he needs to know to mount an attack.

In summary, we have introduced the notions of a barrier, detection, concealment, and a guard to achieve security, and mentioned the ancillary notions of identification, apprehension and couterforce. There are a wide variety of techniques and mechanisms which embody some or all of these principles. Furthermore, in many systems a degree of security can be achieved by using several mechanisms, which provides much greater security than that provided by the individual mechanisms used alone. One of the best examples is that of a safe in an area that is under surveillance. The combination of surveillance and a safe provides a much greater degree of security than either alone would provide. The opportunity for detection is greatly enhanced by the

presence of the safe since the time it takes to break into the
safe increases the opportunity for detection. On the other hand,
the fact that the safe is, or may be, under surveillance limits
the attacks that can be mounted on it since the violator no longer
has undisturbed access to it.

People are often an integral part of the protection mechanisms
in a security system. There is a class of vulnerabilities
associated with people; they are subject to physical attack by
the violator, and they can be subverted or deceived. In addition,
a person who is involved in security can himself become a violator
of the system. Special precautions are often taken to insure
that the people in the system will function correctly. A particularly good example of this is the design of systems so that for
critical elements two people must be involved in any attempt to
defeat the system. Some vaults, for instance, require both a key
and a combination, both of which are not possessed by the same
individual. It is intended that a conspiracy be required to
defeat the system, on the grounds that a conspiracy is much less
likely than an attempted violation on the part of a single
individual.

It is important to consider security from the point of view
of the potential violator. He may seek to obtain information of
value to him or to modify information that somebody else will use
because there is some expected value to him as a consequence of
the modification. He may be dissuaded from doing so because he
estimates that the costs are unacceptable. The first cost is the
direct cost in time, effort, and money of carrying out his plans.
Both strong protection mechanisms and concealment mechanisms, such
as cryptography, may impose unacceptable costs in one or more of
these measures. In addition, detection and apprehension may have
costs associated with them that are uncertain to the violator but
whose deterrence value may be substantial. The violator may
be deterred by the social stigma associated with the detection
or by the penalties which may follow as a consequence of
detection.

Detection may occur while the violation of security is in
progress or afterwards. If detection does occur, it can cause
the violator to fail to achieve his objective even if he is not
identified. Because the penalties we mentioned above occur only
if the violator is correctly identified, identification itself
becomes an important topic. In addition, if the violation is
detected, it may have other consequences for the violator. For
example, the detection of a violation or attempted violation may
cause the security and protection measures to be increased so
that the violator will find it more costly to attempt future
violations of the system.

Another class of problems which the violator must take into account under certain circumstances is detection involving an immediate cost, such as physical harm. For instance, if a person tries to open a vault at an incorrect time, it may explode. The idea hehind this is that anybody opening the vault at that time is attempting an unauthorized entry. The identification of a particular violator is not important; the detection of the violation is sufficient evidence to warrant harmful actions directed at the violator.

The possible motivations of the violator are relevant, and involve the incentives or disincentives which may affect human behavior. Such issues as morale, patriotism, and loyalty play a role. Banks, for example, do not normally allow tellers who have recently received termination notices to handle money, even though security procedures theoretically provide protection against dishonest tellers.

An important notion in security is that of premeditation. The individual who, on the spur of the moment, decides to violate the security of a system generally has far fewer such opportunities than the person who plans in advance to do it. The lead time which the premeditating violator provides himself can be very important. Suppose, for instance, that a building is to be built with security alarms in it. A violator who knows at the time the building is being built that he will want to penetrate the security of the system may more easily interfere with the alarms than he will be able to when the building is complete. This does not erode our confidence in alarms in buildings because that degree of premeditation appears to be quite rare, and correspondingly, the probability of loss associated with it becomes very small.

The possibility of a premeditated attack involving a component of a security system substantially decreases when that component is designed and constructed before its use has been decided upon. For instance, during construction it is very easy to plant bugs in buildings. But if the use of that building has not been decided upon until after it has been completed, it is extremely unlikely to contain any listening devices. The only reason to plant any would be the vague hope that the building might be occupied by tenants against whom the bugs might be useful.

In forming a judgment concerning security, one must take into account not only the protection mechanisms and the attributes of the potential violator but also the attributes of the object being protected. This may be a physical object or information.

The most important characteristic of an object is its value.
The value to the potential violator may come from possession of
the object (knowledge of the information), or because the violator
can use the object. It may be of value to the violator to modify
or destroy the object.

Value may be quantifiable, generally in monetary terms, or it
may be determined subjectively and thus be difficult to quantify.
If the value is well understood, then some sort of cost benefit
analysis may be made to decide what effort and expense is
warranted for protection. For objects of unquantifiable value,
only a subjective estimate of the required degree of protection
can be made.

The value of an object may be relatively constant or it may
be a function of time or other parameters. For instance, a theatre
ticket or information about the stock market is usually only
valuable for a short time. Value may be based on scarcity; the
value of a postage stamp printed in error is a function of the
number of such stamps which fall into public hands. Sometimes the
results of a violation are only valuable to the violator if it is
not known that he succeeded in violating the system. For instance,
if a violator obtains information through his violation it may
only be of value to him if it is not known that he has obtained
the information. When information is being protected, it may be
of more value to the violator to obtain only a portion of the
information or to find out something about the information.
Sometimes all of the information may be required before anything
of value is obtained.

The value of an object to its protector may be different from
its value to a potential violator.

In the foregoing, we have examined a number of security
concepts. The need for security and the effort one is willing to
expend to achieve it depend on several other factors as well.
Basically, security is a state of mind. The degree of security
that exists cannot be proved, although evidence of a breach of
security provides a kind of negative estimate of it. The measures
that one will take to provide security depend on a complex
balancing of judgments. These include effectiveness of the protection mechanisms, estimation of the value of what is being
protected, and judgments concerning the existence, intentions,
motives, values, and capabilities of violators.

III. COMPUTER SECURITY

The main problem in computer security is that of controlling access to data stored in a computer. Occasionally, it is of interest to guarantee the reliable performance of the system and to provide protection against sabotage and physical disaster; these problems will not concern us here. One can, of course, obtain security by limiting physical access to the computer, but the difficult case arises when users who are not authorized access to all the information in the computer are allowed direct access to the computer. The problem is the control of access so that a user or his programs only access authorized data.

One might hope that many of the same principles and techniques (or analogs of the techniques) which apply to other areas would also apply to computer security. Surprisingly, there is very little use of most of these concepts. The main idea in computer security has been the computer version of a barrier: logically correct access control mechanisms in the operating system software. This might be termed the Maginot Line approach to computer security.

To understand the state of computer security today and how it might be enhanced, we first analyze computer systems from a system point of view. A person attempting to use a computer system either by submitting a job or accessing the computer through a terminal must identify himself to the computer and then be authenticated. Once authenticated, the user or his program may attempt to access data stored in the system. Such access must be appropriately restricted by the access control mechanisms of the operating system. The rights of the user or his programs are determined by the security policies enforced in the computer and the data describing the security aspects of users and objects being protected. Other aspects of a computer system which are relevant to security are the hardware itself and the operating and management procedures for the computer.

This broad view of the nature of a computer system and the security problems associated with it is not what has motivated most of the research on computer security. Rather, this work was motivated by the narrower question: Can a program access an object in the system it is not supposed to have access to? In this latter form, the question of computer security appears to be a question of the correctness of the access control mechanismm in the operating system. When the question of the security of information stored in a computer system was first raised, over a decade ago, it was immediately discovered that from a security point of view operating systems were full of flaws (and many of them still are today). In some systems, these flaws were so serious that it was possible for a user to gain control of the operating system, that is, to have code prepared by the user executed as if it were the supervisor code. Furthermore, flaws in the operating system, once discovered, turned out to be easy to exploit. Given the power that resulted from exploitation of flaws in the operating sytem and the ease of exploiting them once they were discovered, it is easy to see why this became a prime focus for computer security research.

The initial reaction to the discovery of the weakness of computer system security was to try to correct the flaws. This meant rewriting the access control code so that it would work correctly and trying to rework those parts of systems for which flaws were due to bad design. Such efforts did not work out well; systems so enhanced were shown to have many flaws remaining. Because these flaws were easy to exploit, covering up only a few of them did not appear to be very advantageous. As a result of these failures, recent research has been directed to finding new operating system designs which take security into account in a fundamental way during the design process (e.g., see [1-3]). It seems likely that this research will have more success than previous efforts to enhance systems by repairing flaws.

The current attempts to provide new operating system designs which are secure will be helpful but will still leave many substantial computer security problems. These problems remain because (1) the correct functioning of the operating system it-self takes care of only part of the problem of security in computer systems and (2) most current and future systems will not be based on these designs (at least for a considerable time), and thus effective means for achieving security in systems not based on such designs is still badly needed.

The first point above -- that even if the operating system access control mechanisms work correctly, a high degree of security is not necessarily achieved in the computer system -- is worth further elaboration. We have mentioned that one aspect of computer security is the authentication process. If this process fails, and a violator manages to log into a system with incorrect identity, the correct functioning of the access control mechanisms cannot prevent a violation of the security of the system. We have no means of detecting the activities of a violator under these circumstances, or any way of making it difficult for him to proceed with his violation. This points out how critical the authentication process is. It also shows that even a good barrier is not sufficient by itself.

A second difficulty concerns the hardware in the computer system. Correct functioning of the access control software depends on correct operation of the hardware. The exact characteristics of the hardware must be taken into account in verifying the correctness of the software composing the security kernel or other access control mechanisms. No reasonable methods for verifying that the computer system hardware is functioning correctly are known. It appears to be a relatively straightforward matter to modify the hardware so as to invalidate the access control mechanisms of a computer system. We are, therefore, dependent upon whatever restraints we may feel are in operation that prevent a violator from modifying the computer. Even the possibility of a violator or his programs systematically searching for and awaiting hardware malfunctions cannot be ignored.

Another difficulty is that while the access control mechanisms of the system may be correct, they may not be used properly. The mechanisms depend, for their correct functioning, on access control data in the system. The data may not define a correct security policy. That is, when the access controls are applied, certain sequences of requests for access to data may result in information being accessible by a user who is not supposed to access that information. (For example, see Harrison [4]). If only very simple policies are embodied in the access control data and these policies are followed rigorously, then the possibility of this kind of flaw is minimized. For instance, if we suppose that there are only four categories of information (let us say unclassified, confidential, secret, and top secret) and that no flow of information between these categories is ever possible, then the access control mechanism might operate correctly. The user would be required to log in at the appropriate security level, do all his work at that level, and if he wishes to work at another level, log off and log in again at the new security level. If, however, the user is allowed to decide that some of the information that is stored in the system as "confidential" is, in fact, unclassified and mechanisms are provided by which he can change the designation or copy that information into an unclassified file, then the opportunity exists for violations of the security of the system in spite of the access control mechanisms.

Compared with the research which has gone into the problem of constructing highly secure operating systems, relatively little work has been done on most other aspects of computer security. We want to mention two areas in particular. One is the assessment of security in computer systems, and the other is the enhancement of security.

It is difficult to assess security, whether we are talking about computers, buildings, or other situations in which security is required. The language used often implies that security is a binary-valued attribute -- we say that something is secure or that it is not. The fact that there are degrees of security is often ignored, in part because it is hard to find meaningful measures. The problem is particularly acute in the computer security area, perhaps as a result of the common fixation on highly secure operating systems. In the previous section, we pointed out that security judgments are, or should be, a complex weighing of many factors involving the protection mechanisms that apply, the potential violator, and the assets being protected. Through long (and often painful) experience some ad hoc ideas and rules of thumb have been developed in a few areas, but it is fair to say that the art of assessing the security of computer systems is in its infancy.

The enchancement of security in computer systems has, undeservingly, come to be viewed rather negatively by those working in the field, probably because one particular way of enhancing security failed rather badly in the early stages of work in this area. These were the attempts, discussed above, to find and remove flaws in operating systems. However, other methods of enhancing security may produce better results. In particular, we wish to recommend that efforts be made to enhance security in computers in ways analogous to those used in other areas. The concepts discussed in the previous section, and others not mentioned, may be sources of ideas for enhancing computer system security. It would seem worthwhile, for example, to try and find security mechanisms which offer some opportunity for detection of a violation, rather than depending exclusively on the passive barriers of the access control mechanisms. It is worth noting that in many situations detection seems to be depended upon more heavily than barriers, especially where assets of considerable value are being protected.

There are currently few examples of the use of detection in computers. One that is frequently used in systems providing remote access via terminals is to report to the user at each log-in the time of his previous log-in. Thus providing him the opportunity to notice if this report differs from what he remembers. This technique may cause the detection of unauthorized use of the account. There are some weaknesses. For instance, users who repeatedly see the log-in message reporting time of last use soon fail to read this information. Weak though this technique may be, it is one of the best that can be found, thus indicating the paucity of ideas that exist in this area.

We can give an example of the suggested approach that illustrates that there can be an advantage to security enhancements which are theoretically easy to defeat, but which in practice can cause difficulty for a violator. Some years ago Conway, Maxwell, and Morgan [5] suggested the following approach to achieving security in a database system. They designed a system which incorporated encryption and decryption routines. This system was intended to run in a batch processing environment in which only the data was stored in the computer between runs of the program. Decks were submitted containing the program (including the encryption and decryption routines) and jobs were flushed from the system at the end of each run. Therefore, during normal operation the encryption and decryption algorithms were not available inside the system. In addition, the keys controlling the encryption and decryption routines were known only to the user and were supplied as a parameter to the job. The idea was that data would always be stored in encrypted form on the disk and information about the encryption algorithm that would be useful to a violator was not available to others using the system who might try to access the data stored on the disk.

At the time the suggestion was made, it was vigorously attacked by many working in the computer security area. It was pointed out that given the extensive nature of flaws in computer systems, it would be a relatively simple matter for somebody who wished to defeat this defense to break into the operating sytem, trap the database job when it ran, and then either remove the decrypted data directly or pick up the encryption algorithm and its keys from the job. This is, however, analogous to claiming that a safe is completely insecure because somebody with the proper tools can break into it with no trouble. In fact, it may take some effort to carry out the plan described. The violator must know when the program he is interested in is being run, which may require adding something to the system that will check for this (possibly exposing him to some risk of detection), and he must be able to analyze the object form of the program sufficiently well to pick out the information that he is interested in. The point is not that it cannot be done, but that in fact the amount of work is not negligible. Furthermore, if the system were designed to have some capability of detecting those who manage to get their own code executed in supervisor mode, then there would be an additional deterrent to the potential exploiter of this attack.

It seems likely that once some attention is devoted to the subject, we may be able to develop a reasonable set of ideas concerning how to enhance the security of systems and how to use detection and its consequences to increase security. Such methods need not be impossible to defeat; instead they must have the property that even if they can be defeated, nevertheless they serve, to some degree, as a deterrent to a potential violator.

We have already remarked that the notion of detection has received very little attention. As an example of the kinds of techniques that might be used, we will consider one idea -- that a record be maintained of all accesses to a file owned by an individual that are made by others, or of only those accesses that are made by others when he is not logged into the system; and that this information be reported to him. Ultimately, the user may provide a list of those he expects to access his files and the report may consist of information concerning all accesses by those not on that list. If such information is stored in a way that a violator cannot get at it, then the information can be relied upon a great deal of the time. One way of recording information so that it cannot be destroyed is to write it on a tape that has no backspace provisions. The violator who wishes to defeat this mechanism must do so by preventing the information from being recorded, which may involve substantial effort on his part and there may be opportunities to detect an attempt to do so. It is not our purpose here to work such ideas out completely; rather we intend only to illustrate the possibility of develop-ments along this line.

REFERENCES

[1] Popek, Gerald J. and Charles S. Kline, "Issues in Kernel Design", (to appear in the Proceedings of the 1978 NCC).
[2] Neumann, P. G., R. S. Boyer, R. J. Feiertag, K. N. Levitt, and L. Robinson, "A Provably Secure Operating System: The System, It's Applications and Proofs", SRI Final Report, Project 4332, 11 Feb., 1977.
[3] Millen, J. K., "Security Kernel Validation in Practice", Communications of the ACM, Vol. 19, No. 5, May 1976.
[4] Harrison, Michael A., Walter L. Ruzzo, and Jeffrey D. Ullman, "Protection in Operating Systems", Communications of the ACM, Vol. 19, No. 8, August 1976.
[5] Conway, R. W., W. L. Maxwell, and H. L. Morgan, "On the Implementation of Security Measures in Information Systems", Communications of the ACM, Vol. 15, No. 4, April 1972, pp. 211-220.

DISCUSSION

Fabry: One of the points that you made was that one need
not strive for perfect software since no system is ever perfect.
Is that a good characterization of what you are saying?

Gaines: Yes, I guess that is a good characterization.

Fabry: There is a difference between breaking into software
and breaking into a safe. In the case of the safe, you can look
at the safe and see how many ways there are to get in, how long
each of them will take, and what's involved: manipulate the
dial, blow up the safe, whatever the possibilities are. But,
when you are dealing with a program that is assumed to be
imperfect, you do not have any handle on the imperfections.
You cannot know how many ways there are to break in, how hard
each way is, and so on. It seems to me that we're driven to
make programs perfect.

Gaines: We want to use reasonable efforts to try to
make programs correct; there is no argument about that. But,
unreasonable efforts are another matter. You picked about the
only area where we can have enough detailed knowledge about how
successful penetration attepmts are. We know what tools are
avaiable to seomeone who wants to crack a safe, and through long
experience, we have some information about how to manipulate
combination locks. But, that knowledge is not available in
other areas. For instance, if we were worried about frauds in
a bank, we do not know how to go about looking for frauds that
have occurred before. We've no way of estimating the likelihood
that someone will discover a cleaver way of defrauding a bank.
The disadvantage of guards is that they are easily conned so
we do not necessarily try to cover all of the bets. So, the
question is not really whether or not you need perfect software,
but how far you go in getting correct software.

Shapiro: I'd question whether or not you can get perfect software. It must function in the real world, not in a mere model of perfect software. I'm sure your model would not necessarily include magnetic tapes that fail or sleepers that can be in programs waiting for magnetic tapes to fail.

Dobkin: I like to think back to college when people did not buy bicycle chains that were big enough to protect their bikes, but were big enough so that you would have to carry around a pretty large set of wire cutters to break them. Michael Rabin is talking about a set of wire cutters that would take many, many lifetimes to build. How big are the wire cutters that you plan on using? You're saying that it won't be perfect, so presumably, there will be wire cutters, but will they be big?

Gaines: There have been two security kernels that have been produced. One by Charlie Kline and the other by the Mitre people. Contractors are looking at both these security kernels to decide which, if either of these two, approaches to adopt. They will proceed to reimplement if necessary those two kernels and do the right things to prepare for generating assertions about relevant security properties and have those verified. Or, at least be verifiable. It's funny, but we have been reduced to talk about terms like verifiable and that is supposed to mean that we're supposed to have more confidence than if the program wasn't produced to be verifiable. We're on shaky ground here, hoping that all of this effort is a kind of good engineering practice that makes it less likely that there will be exploitable flaws in the software.

DeMillo: I'd just like to add that it might be the case that being verified or verifiable actually indicates a lack of good engineering practice and good sense. As Norman Shapiro pointed out, correctness is not with respect to the real world, but to a model. Being verified or even verifiable may unreasonably raise your expectations about the performance of a piece of software in the real world. As a result, you may fail to include either in the software or in the physical protocols the kinds of remedial security measures that it would take to make sure that the system was really secure.

PROTECTION MECHANISM MODELS:
THEIR USEFULNESS

Anita K. Jones

Department of Computer Science
Carnegie-Mellon University
Pittsburgh, Pennsylvania

I. INTRODUCTION

Attempts to formally and precisely express the notions of
security and protection are of recent vintage. Though designers
of programmed systems have been concerned with making their
systems impervious to misuse, it is only recently that researchers
have attempted to precisely define the phenomena of information
flow, security policies which govern how information can flow,
and the requisite protection mechanisms used to enforce security
policies.[1]

There are two sources of knowledge being brought to bear in
the quest to understand security and protection in the context of
computer systems. The first source is the experience of pragmatic
system designers, who have experimented with the implementation
and the application of a range of protection mechanisms. The
second source is the experience of theoreticians, who have
developed tools and techniques for abstraction in an attempt to
understand the essence of many different kinds of phenomena.

---

[1] *The research reported in the paper was supported under
National Science Foundation grant MCS78-00717.*

237

Knowledge from both sources is required to understand
information flow and to design both security policies and the
protection mechanisms to enforce them. One question is essential
to bridging the gulf between those interested primarily in
theoretical analysis, and those whose main objective is to design
and build programmed systems to solve the "real world" problems.
That question is, "Are the abstract models of security and
protection useful?". Do they accurately and productively
represent the problems it is necessary for computer science to
solve? An elegant, aesthetically pleasing theory can be beautiful
to behold; but, in the case of security, it should also be
accurate and consequently useful. In what follows, I ask this
question of usefulness about a particular, restricted model called
the Take-Grant system [4].

II.   THE TAKE-GRANT SYSTEM

The Take-Grant system is interpreted to model a class of
access control protection mechanisms in which each entity is
protected independently of all others. The technical term for
such an entity is *object*. Objects are of interest because they
"contain information". Some objects are active (for example,
objects that are interpreted to represent a human beings or
executing computer programs). These objects are called *subjects*
and are notated with filled circles,●. Objects may be passive
(for example, objects interpreted only to contain information
such as a file). Passive objects are notated by unfilled
circles,○. Objects not known to be either active or passive are
notated with slashed circles,⊘. In the Take-Grant system a
protection state is the set of privileges, or rights, that each
object has. Graphically, a right is notated by a directed edge,
labeled with a name. It is interpreted to mean that the object
at the tail of the edge has the named right to the object at the
head of the edge. Passive, as well as active, objects may have
rights to objects. The protection state of a collection of
objects is represented as a finite graph constructed of objects
connected by labeled edges; the graph is called a *protection
graph*.

The following graph models a protection state in which subject
A has the right to perform operation α on subject B, which in
turn has the right to perform β on passive objects X and Y. In
addition, B has χ right to Y.

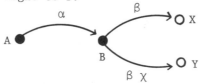

Arcs can be labeled with multiple labels. The distinction between a singleton label and a set of labels should be clear by context. In particular, if a directed edge is to be added between two objects for which an edge with the same direction already exists, I use a single edge labeled with the union of the existing label(s) and the new label(s).

The Take-Grant system is intended to model the access control protection mechanisms that are found in existing programmed systems. In such systems, the protection state changes only when some subject invokes an operation that is defined as part of the protection mechanism. In the Take-Grant system, these operations are modeled by a set of rewriting rules for protection graph transitions. Because the protection state changes only by action of a subject, I will speak of a subject *exercising* its rights or privileges. Consequently, in the model any graph rewriting rules will always require at least the presence of a subject; usually a subject must have a particular right to some object as a prerequisite for a graph transition.

Graph rewrite rules have the form r: $\alpha \Rightarrow \beta$, where r is the name of the rule. A graph transition is defined as follows. If α matches some subgraph of a protection graph G, then rule r can be applied to G, yielding a new graph G'. The shorthand for applying rule r is G $\vdash$ r G'.

Protection graphs are quite general, and could be used to model many different access control mechanisms. The Take-Grant system is made specific by its rewrite rules, but it is but representative of mechanisms commonly found in operating systems and file systems. For the purposes of defining the Take-Grant rewriting rules, I distinguish two rights "take", denoted by the label "t", and "grant", denoted by the label "g". The Take-Grant system has four rewrite rules. For defining the rules, let A, X, and Y be three distinct vertices in a protection graph, such that A is a subject.

Take: Let there be an edge from A to X with at least a label t and an edge from X to Y with any label or set of labels α. Then applying the Take rule adds an edge from A to Y having label α. Graphically,

Intuitively, A takes the right to perform α to Y
from X.

Grant: Let there be an edge from A to X with at least a
         label g, and an edge from A to Y labeled α. Then
         applying the Grant rule adds an edge from X to Y
         having label α. Graphically,

Intuitively, A grants the right to perform α to Y
to X.

Create: Let A be a subject and α be a subset of rights.
         Applying the Create Rule adds a new vertex N such
         that α labels the edge from A to N. Graphically,

Intuitively, A creates the subject or object N with
α rights.

Remove: Let there be an edge labeled γ from subject A to X.
         Let α be any subset of rights. Applying the Remove
         rule causes deletion of the α labels from γ. If
         γ = α, then the edge itself is deleted.
         Graphically,

Intuitively, A removes its right to α X.

This concludes the basic definition of the Take-Grant system. We have used the simplified formulation of the system exhibited in [11].

The possibilities for rewriting a protection graph are amply illustrated in [4], [11], so only a single illustration will be presented here. The kind of question that one might ask about a given protection state, modeled by a protection graph is the following. Can some subject, A -- interpreted to be some user or alternatively some program acting on behalf of a user or class of users -- get access to a particular object. If A can do so, it may compromise the information encoded in that object. In the Take-Grant system such a question is modeled as: Given the protection graph G:

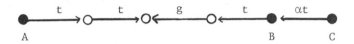

can a sequence of rewrite rules be applied to reach a new state in which A can perform α on B? In this example, the answer is "yes". Using dotted lines to indicate the most recently added edge in a graph, the rewrite sequence is

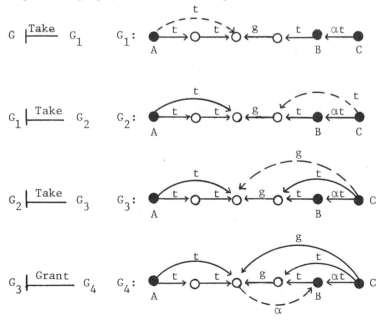

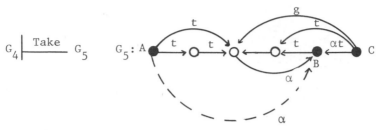

$$G_4 \vdash \frac{\text{Take}}{} G_5 \qquad G_5 : A$$

In the final protection Graph G_5 subject A does, indeed, have α access to object B.

Having a model that permits one to ask the question "given a certain protection state, can a subject ever obtain a certain access to an object" is useful. Using it one can ask whether a change to the protection state yields a new state for which a desired security policy still holds. For example, a system manager might model his system. Then, before granting a right he possesses, the manager consults his model to determine if giving out the right will have some unexpected and undesirable consequences. In particular, he can determine if there is a way for some user to then gain a right to access an object that he should not be able to access. Security policies are generally formulated as predicates relating the subjects and passive objects of a protection state. In contrast, most protection mechanisms, and the Take-Grant system, are phrased in a procedural, not a predicate, form. Though procedural definitions make individual system state transitions easy to understand and to implement, they combine to form a system that exhibits complex behavior. It is difficult to intuit and to express the behavior of a procedurally defined system. Models, such as the Take-Grant system, provide the basis for determining whether the procedurally described system exhibits behavior defined by a predicate -- and in this case the predicate defines a security policy. Thus, we bridge the gap between mechanism and policy.

Now, I have defined the Take-Grant system and illustrated one administrative use to which it may be put. Before exploring the Take-Grant further, I will define some criteria for the usefulness of a model.

III. A USEFUL MODEL

As an operating system designer and implementor, I am only
interested in a model if it helps me with the design, implementation or the administration of a system. I will define a model to
be useful if it

(1) accurately and concisely expresses the essence of the
    phenomena of interest, and
(2) tells a system designer or user something he did not
    know or understand without the model.

The first property ensures that phenomena of interest is captured
by the model. The second property ensures that modeling is not
just an empty exercise; it produces new information. Certainly,
subjective judgement is required to determine if the second usefulness property holds. So, there may be room for debate in some
cases; yet in other cases, the second property should eliminate
aesthetic, but useless models. In the remainder of this paper, I
will consider whether the Take-Grant System meets the criteria
for a useful model.

First, consider the accuracy with which the model represents
protection mechanisms found in extant systems. I have already
claimed that the Take-Grant system is accurate. Now, I want to
demonstrate that it is. The protection mechanisms in operating
and file systems such as those found in Multics [9], CAL-TSS [6],
Hydra [12], StarOS [3], SRI Secure System [8] and OS/370 [2] are
object-oriented. Protected entities are distinguishable, usually
separately nameable and assumed to have non-overlapping physical
representations. Protection of each object is performed
independently of other objects. These attributes are all reflected in the model. The distinction between active subjects (for
example, users, processes, or even programs executing on a user's
behalf) and passive objects (for example, files) is found in real
systems.

Information can flow between two objects as a result of an
operation. For example, information flows between two file
objects if a subject copies the data from one to the other.
Similarly, information flows from a file object to a subject if
the subject is a program that branches, depending on the value
of a datum read from the file. For the purpose of controlling
information flow, operations are partitioned into mutually
exclusive classes. In a simple case, there may only be two
classes; a "read" class and an "alter" class. Operations in the
"read" class only permit information to flow from the object that
is read to the reading subject; operations in the "alter" class
permit information flow in both directions. The writing subject
may acquire information from the object being written as well as
transmit information to it. A typical example is the file

system's update program. One might believe it only writes the
file to be updated. In reality, most file update programs first
read the most recent date-of-update, and perhaps even the
redundantly written file name that is placed in the file to
enhance file system reliability. Thus, information is transmitted
in both directions. If the security policy to be enforced is
confinement of information, even such seemingly innocuous
information transmissions are relevant.

Both the systems cited above and the Take-Grant system use
rights to control information flow. In addition, both use rights
to control what protection operations a particular subject can
exercise. In the Take-Grant system, only "take" and "grant"
rights have been used. Most systems use four or less such
rights. Some capability-based systems, such as Hydra, use many
more. Note that rewrite rules would have to be devised for each
different operating system to be modeled.

There are two types of protection mechanisms found in today's
systems. One is called an *authority list* or *access control list
mechanism* [9]; the other is a *capability-based mechanism* [5].
Both are used to control access to objects. The mechanisms differ
in where data that records permissible accesses is stored. For
the authority list mechanism, the access information is stored
with the object being protected. In contrast, the capability-
based protection mechanism relies on the protection information
being stored with the accessor, not the accessed object.
Theoretically, the two mechanisms have identical functionality.
Graph models, like the Take-Grant system, can be used to model
both.

In reality, the two mechanisms are used differently because
of cost considerations. For example, it is useful to know what
objects a subject can access so that memory can be managed in
such a way that the representation of these objects is readily
available, perhaps in primary memory. For this purpose, the
capability-based systems are convenient. In constrast, it is
sometimes useful to know if any subject can access a particular
object. The authority list mechanism is more convenient; in lieu
of interrogating the protection state of every subject, one need
only scan the protection data associated with the object. Graph
models may be used for computing the cost of certain protection
operations. I do not consider such issues here.

Hopefully, the above arguments are sufficient to convince the
reader that the Take-Grant system accurately reflects the basic
attributes of extant protection mechanisms. The next issue is to
determine whether the modeled phenomena is that which we want to
understand better. To investigate this, consider how security
models have been used to date.

IV. APPLICATION OF THE TAKE-GRANT MODEL

The original formulation of the Take-Grant system modeled
only active entities, say users, or the programs executing on the
behalf of users [7]. Actual systems designs do differ in how one
user or process may access or control another, but the variety of
possible relations is not rich. Said differently, there are very
few different security policies that can be investigated in a
subject-only model. Managers and users of computer installations
have used and understood such policies and their implementation
for a long time. For example, a system manager may decree a
policy that each user may

- create, read and write private files,
- read files created by others in the same project, and
- read system files.

In a subject-only graph model of this system each node would
represent a user; and each user would be associated with one or
more projects. The only operations defined would be CreateSubject
and DeleteSubject to introduce new subjects and remove them from
the systems. Only the system-subject would be able to perform
these two operations. Each user would have "read" access to the
system-subject and to other subjects in the same project. A user
would have no access to subjects outside his project(s). Such a
system is so simple, a model of it does not add to one's understanding.

It is distinguishing between passive, information-containing
objects and subjects that introduces a richer variety of
phenomena. Consequently, the Take-Grant system was extended [4].
For example, compare the model of a catalog system to the subject-
only model of the file system discussed above. A catalog is a
passive object containing name mapping information and rights to
access files and other catalogs. In contrast to the subject-only
file system, catalog system users have protection operations
defined for them. They explicitly give access to individual
files or catalogs to other subjects in the system. It is such
contexts that questions like "Can subject A obtain α access to
object X?" become interesting. The ramifications of granting
access to a catalog may not be clear, because the catalog may in
turn contain rights to access yet other catalogs and files. Using
the model, the ramifications can be investigated. Indeed, the
question can be answered in linear time. Note that this linear
time result contrasts with the results of Harrison, Ruzzo and
Ullman [1]. They showed that a very general formulation of the
access control protection mechanisms is undecidable. In contrast,
by modeling a much less rich class of protection mechanisms, yet
yet mechanisms that accurately reflect those used in practice, we
have shown that some questions about security policy enforcement
can be answered in linear time.

Another application of the Take-Grant system appears in [11]. Snyder synthesizes a couple of example protection and communication structures:

(1) a supervisor that creates one communication object for each user, grants that user "read" rights to the object, but maintains "write" rights to the object and copies data between pairs of communication objects as requested by the users,

(2) a supervisor that creates a communication object for each pair of communicating users (on demand or automatically), and grants the pair of users "read" and "write" rights to the communication object, then divests itself of all rights to access the communication object.

His models satisfy the first usefulness criterion; they are accurate and, indeed, they provide a terse expression of the system protection and communication relations under consideration. But, operating systems designers have been building such structures into systems for many years. And teachers have successfully, and easily I believe, conveyed such structures to their students without benefit of abstract models. These commonly understood examples of subject interconnections do not argue sufficiently well that the Take-Grant system meets the second criterion for usefulness.

V.   A USEFUL EXTENSION

In this section I explore an extension to the Take-Grant system that I believe is useful. It can be used to model system behavior that was demonstrably not understood until many years after the development of a particular system. The system was Multics [9]. Its design contains a security flaw that is due to the way a user was forced to use certain I/O devices, such as the card reader. The flaw was first recognized by its designers [10]. To model the attributes of the Multics design with enough accuracy to make the security flaw discernable, I first extend the Take-Grant system.

The extension is based on the observation that subjects do not act erratically. Users do not grant the right to destroy their files to arbitrary other users, though they may have the right to do so. Processes executing on behalf of a user follow their programs. With the emergence of verification technology, one may expect to see programs routinely characterized by properties that describe actions taken at execution time. The accuracy with which a model reflects the "real world" is enhanced if we can state the properties that characterize a subject's actions. Of course, if nothing is known about the actions of a subject, one must assume that any permissible action might be taken.

Recall the first substantive example in which a subject A could acquire α rights to an object. But, A could gain those rights only with the assistance of another subject, C. We can say that C acted in collusion with A. However, in some cases programs and people will not act in collusion to achieve some objective. We can often prove, or assume, that a subject will not act in collusion to help a particular class of subjects gain a new right. It is this restraint in the behavior of subjects that I wish to express.

I will associate an (unordered) set of behavioral properties with each subject. Properties are described by naming the protection operations the subject may invoke together with some indication of parameters, if any:

- Grant $X \longrightarrow \alpha \longrightarrow Y$
- Take $X \longrightarrow \alpha \longrightarrow Y$
- Remove $X \longrightarrow \alpha \longrightarrow Y$
- Create Y.

The associated semantics are (respectively):

- subject may grant to object X the α access to object Y
- subject may take from object X the α access to object Y
- subject may remove its α access to object Y
- subject may create a new object named Y such that subject has all access to this new object

Note that to exercise a right a subject must have that right. The property set does not contain rights; it specifies intended behavior. The property set will be elided for subjects whose activity is unknown. It must be assumed that such subjects may perform any protection action for which they have appropriate rights. I will use "?" in place of an object name when the name is not bound to a particular object. An example use of the property set is

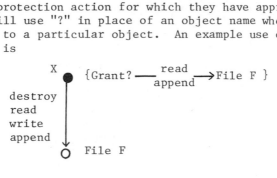

This protection graph is to be interpreted to mean that subject
X may possibly grant "read" or "append" access to File F to any
object.   The "?" notation is used because the receiver of a Grant
is unspecified.   One observation that can be made from this
property set is that the subject, who may be thought of as owning
File F, will not give "write" or "destroy" rights to any other
object under any circumstances.   Because subjects are assumed to
be autonomous, it is reasonable to expect the subject to exercise
only the protection operations as specified in their property
set, no matter what other subjects may be doing.   Note that if a
system administrator, subject SA, can Take rights from X, then
SA might "forceably" wrest "destroy" rights to File F from X.

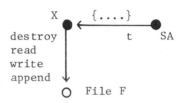

The system administrator might do this if X is vastly over quota
in file space usage and stubbornly refuses to release file space.
If the system administrator has such powers, we would have to
consider both the above graph models of the situation.

    Subjects that represent executing programs also do not act
arbitrarily; they are constrained by the programs they execute.
I introduce a passive object called a *procedure*, notated by □.
A procedure may have a single formal parameter.   It is specified
within the procedure symbol in the following form: ─── α ───→X,
where α is a set of rights and X is the formal name by which the
actual parameter can be named in the property set.   By convention
the formal parameter names will never be names of graph nodes.
I introduce a new right called "fork", and notated as "f" that is
used for procedure invocation.   To illustrate the use of procedures, I define a procedure object, Sort.   It accepts one argument to which "readfile" access is required, and whose property
set indicates that only "readfile" operations are performed on
the parameter object.   The invoker of Sort should be wary,
because Sort may Grant "readfile" access to X to another object.

Sort

The Take-Grant system is augmented by extending the notion of
object creation to include procedure creating using the CreateP
operation and adding a new operation, Fork. For defining these
rewrite rules, let A, X and P be three distinct vertices in a
protection graph such that A is a subject and P is a procedure.

CreateP: Let A be a subject and C be a property set, and S
be a parameter specification. Applying the CreateP
rule adds a new procedure vertex N such that S is
N's parameter specification, C is its property set
and "f" labels the edge from A to N. Graphically,

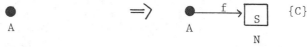

Fork: Let there be an edge from subject A to procedure P
that is labeled f, and an edge from A to X labeled
β. Let P have a property set C and a parameter
specification of the form $- \alpha \rightarrow Y$ such that α is a
subset of β. Then, applying the Fork rule adds a
new vertex N with an edge from N to X labeled α.
N's property set is the same as C, except that the
formal parameter name Y is systematically replaced
by X. This is notated as $C\begin{vmatrix} X \\ Y \end{vmatrix}$

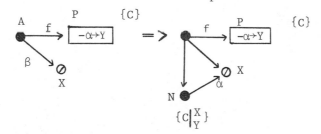

Intuitively, A invokes a procedure P causing
creation of a subject N whose behavio is delimited
by properties specified in C with Y replaced by the
name X.

I will also extend the notion of removal of rights. Using
the RemoveI rewrite rule defined below, a subject can delete
rights from passive objects. The right "r" meaning "remove" is
used to control rights removal.

RemoveI: Let there be an edge from subject A to object X
that is labeled r, and an edge from X to Y labeled
β. Let α be any subset of rights. Applying the
RemoveI rule causes deletion of the α labels from
β. If α = β, then the edge itself is deleted.
Graphically,

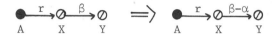

Intuitively, A removes the right to α Y from X.

The Multics Card Reader Daemon Problem

Now I will use the property set extension to describe the
Multics security flaw. First, I describe the flaw intuitively:
The card reader device is permanently allocated to a process
called the Card Reader daemon. It is responsible for reading
card decks, creating files containing the read-in data and then
cataloging the files in the appropriate user catalog. To catalog
a file, the Card Reader daemon requires access to the user's
catalog. In particular, the Card Reader daemon needs "grant"
access to the user's catalog object. Herein lies the problem,
although it may not be obvious.

To render this scenario in the extended Take-Grant system,
let A be a (user) subject with f access to a (procedure) object
CD, as well as to A's catalog object, C. Note that C is the long-
term repository for all the rights to the files A can access.
Let procedure CD have a parameter specification —t,r→Y and a
property set { Grant Y—?—↛?, CreateP}.

If A invokes CD with its catalog C as a parameter, the
resulting protection state is modeled by the following graph,

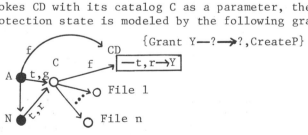

Consider what N might do. It might create a new procedure with the name EDIT. That new procedure has one parameter specified —t,r→ Y, and the property set {Grant Y--?-->?, Create, RemoveI Y—?→ ?, CreateP}. Note that EDIT can Grant and RemoveI rights from the parameter object formally known as Y.

Then, N completes execution by including the right to invoke EDIT into the caller's catalog, C. Sometime later A invokes EDIT with actual parameter —t,r→ C, intending to invoke the system editor. The parameter permitting "take" and "remove" rights to the user's catalog is appropriate; an editor, of course, needs to be able to obtain access to files in a user's catalog and to remove temporary files built during an editing session. The Multics name resolution algorithm first attempts to resolve the name "EDIT" using the local catalog; only later is the system catalog consulted. In this example, the invoked EDIT procedure is found in the user catalog, C. The scene is complete. EDIT, now has the ability to grant to others the content of the user catalog, or to destroy user files at will. Meanwhile, the user believes that the editing program is the system editor. Indeed, it may appear to be the system editor because it invokes the system editor after causing the havoc designed into it by its creator.

Using an abstracted model of subject interactions, the power invested in the Card Reader daemon is apparent. It gained control over the user's catalog and thus his file naming space. Thus, it could add programs at will to the user's catalog. These programs might exhibit any behavior. For example, they may masquerade as system utilities while acting with the full power of the user (because of the rights to the user catalog).

VI. SUMMARY

In this paper, I have tried to place the abstract modeling of protection mechanisms in a pragmatic light to ascertain whether it is useful. My conclusion is that to date the Take-Grant model has been used in too simple a fashion to produce any new information that could affect the design, implementation or administration of actual systems. The model is accurate in that it is faithful to the major attributes of extant protection mechanisms. But, the model must be extended to be powerful enough to satisfy the criteria of usefulness defined in this paper. I suggest one extension to the Take-Grant model. It enables one to model a security flaw that went unnoticed in the Multics system for a long time after the system had been built. To model the desired system behavior, I extended the Take-Grant model so that property sets could be associated with subjects and with passive procedure objects that act as templates for subject creation. These

property sets characterize the behavior of subjects. I believe
that this extension is only one of a number of extensions that
can be used to increase the sensitivity with which the Take-Grant
system models protection mechanisms.

ACKNOWLEDGMENTS

I would like to thank Ellis Cohen and Michael Rabin for
suggestions that led to simplifications of the extensions
described in this paper.

REFERENCES

[1] Harrison, M., L. Ruzzo and J. Ullman, "Protection in
     Operating Systems,"*Communications of the ACM*, 19, 8 (1976).
[2] IBM, IBM System/370 *Principles of Operation*, GA22-7000-1.
[3] Jones, A. K., R. J. Chansler, Jr., I. Durham, P. Feiler and
     K. Schwans, "Software Management of Cm* -- A Distributed
     Multiprocessor, *AFIPS Conference Proceedings*, Vol. 46, (1977),
     pp. 657-663.
[4] Jones, A. K., R. J. Lipton, L. Snyder, "A Linear Time
     Algorithm for Deciding Security", *Foundations of Computer
     Science*, November 1976.
[5] Lampson, B. W., "Protection", *Proceedings Fifth Annual
     Princeton Conference on Information Sciences and Systems*,
     1971, pp. 437-443, (reprinted in *ACM Operating Systems Review*,
     January 1974.
[6] Lampson, B. and H. Sturgis, "Reflections on an Operating
     System Design", *Communications of the ACM*, 19, 5 (May 1976),
     pp. 251-265.
[7] Lipton, R. J. and L. Snyder, "A Linear Time Algorithm for
     Deciding Subject Security", *Journal of the ACM*, 19:8 (1977).
[8] Neumann, P. S., R. S. Fabry, K. N. Levitt, L. Robinson and
     J. H. Wensley, "On the Design of a Provably Secure Operating
     System, *Proceedings Workshop on Protection in Operating
     Systems*, *IRIA*, Rocquencourt, France (August 1974), pp. 161-
     175.
[9] Organick, E., The Multics System: An Examination of Its
     Structure, MIT Press (1972).
[10] Saltzer, J., Private communication.
[11] Snyder, L., "On the Synthesis and Analysis of Protection
     Systems", *Sixth Symposium on Operating System Principles*,
     November 1977.
[12] Wulf, Wm. A., E. Cohen, W. Corwin, A. Jones, R. Levin, C.
     Pierson and R. Pollack, "HYDRA: The Kernel of a Multiprocessc
     Operating System, *Communications of the ACM*, 17, 6, pp. 337-
     345 (1974).

DISCUSSION

Budd: One nice feature about the Take/Grant system was that, given an arbitrary graph, one could decide in linear time whether or not a right can pass from any one of the vertices to any other. It is not clear that this holds true when you add these new rewriting rules. Does the same result apply to your system?

Jones: I do not know whether it's still linear. Certainly, in the example I gave, I think that one can argue that it's still very easy, but I haven't proven the extended system is linear.

Rabin: I have a question about the nature of the T and G operators. They seem to be operators whereby a given node can take any subsets of the sets of all privileges or capabilities from another node, or grant any subset of the capabilities that a given node may grant. Have you considered the possibility of having restricted T and G operators so that a given node has, for instance, a G operator, and that he himself is restricted to granting a certain subset of all possible privileges; and similarly, for the T operator? It may be that using the extended model, you could simulate, or implement, any such restricted T and G operator, matters may be simplified and you may eliminate the need for using some of these predicates and procedures.

Jones: Using that extension, a subject or procedure cannot differentiate between two different subjects that might be recipients of a Grant, for example. With my extension using property sets, I can.

Gaines: Anita, something I hope we all are thinking about as we go through this conference is how accurately the models and theories we develop affect "real world" situations. Can you say in what respects you have tried to choose certain aspects of real world situations?

Jones: I'd be very grateful if we could get anywhere near the "real world". I think that introducing property sets in the model takes it away from being a toy in which things are so general that it's not possible to talk about real problems.

Gaines: When can we start believing real world conclusions from abstract models? We would like to be able to make some inferences about security in the real world based on observations we make on our models.

Jones: That is the very issue I am addressing.

THE PRINCIPLE OF ATTENUATION
OF PRIVILEGES
AND ITS RAMIFICATIONS*

Naftaly Minsky

Rutgers University
The State University of New Jersey

1. INTRODUCTION

Authorization in computer systems is a discipline under which
it is possible to impose restrictions on the kind of action which
can be carried out by the various subjects (actors) of a system.
Such a discipline serves as the basis for any protection
mechanism, and is vital for our ability to produce large scale
reliable software. One can distinguish between the "statics" and
the "dynamics" of an authorization scheme. By the term *statics*
we mean the method used for the representation of the authority
of the various subjects, as well as the technique for the enforcement of such authority. What we call the *dynamics* of an authorization scheme is the technique used for the manipulation of the
"authority-state" of a system. It has to do with the flow of
"privileges" between the various components of a system.

One of the objectives of research in authorization should be
to identify a type of dynamics which is restrictive enough to
allow for the verification of various properties of a given
authority-state, and yet is flexible enough to support a desired
class of policies and authority-structures. The need to restrict
the dynamics of authorization as much as possible has been
recently emphasized by the undecidability of the "Safety Problem"
in the context of the Harrison, Ruzzo and Ullman model of
protection [Har 76]. A step in this direction is the "principle
of attentuation of privileges" recently proposed by Peter Denning
[Den 76]. Informally speaking, this principle states that

* *This work was partially supported by Grant DAHCIS-73-G6 of the
Advanced Research Project Agency.*

privileges should not be allowed to grow when they are transported
from one place in the system to another. In spite of the intuitive
appeal of this principle and the benefits which seem to accrue
from it, it is not widely accepted. In particular, the Hydra
system [Wul 74] allows for *amplification of privileges*, in direct
violation of the principle of attenuation. In responding to
Denning's proposal, Levin, who is one of the designers of Hydra,
writes [Lev 77]: "The existence of amplification in Hydra derives
....from a fundamental protection philosophy that happens to be in
conflict with the attenuation of privileges notion". What Levin
has in mind, in particular, is the important concept of type-
extension for which, he claims, amplification of privileges is
crucial.

In this paper we argue that the difficulty to satisfy the
principle of attenuation of privileges in Hydra (and in related
systems) is not due to a conflict between this principle and the
type of authority structures which Hydra wishes to support, but
due to a fundamental deficiency in the access-control (AC) scheme
on which Hydra is based. Indeed, we will show that the recently
proposed operation-control (OC) scheme for authorization [Min 77]
does satisfy the principle of attenuation without losing the
ability to represent extended-types. The new scheme is based on
an improved technique for representation of privileges which seems
to provide a better approximation to real-life authority structures.

In the next section, the capability-based version of the AC
scheme is described. The principle of attenuation is formally
defined, in the context of this scheme, and the inability to
satisfy it is demonstrated. The underlying reasons for the
incompatibility of the access-control scheme with the principle
of attenuation is discussed in Section 3. In Section 4, some
aspects of the OC (operation-control) scheme are introduced; just
enough to show its compatibility with the principle of attenuation.
A comparison between the OC scheme and the scheme used in the
Hydra system is made in Section 5, and the implementation of
"type extension" under the two schemes is discussed in Section 6.

2. THE ACCESS-CONTROL (AC) SCHEME

The access-control approach to authorization is well documented
in the literature. In particular, the reader is referred to the
work of Lampson [Lam 69, Lam 71], Graham and Denning [Gra 72], and
to recent review articles by Saltzer [Sal 75], and Linden [Lin 76].
Here we outline the main features of a class of AC schemes called
"capability-based", using a somewhat non-standard terminology
which is more suitable for the rest of the paper. (The scheme to
be described here differs in an essential way from the scheme
used in Hydra. Hydra itself is discussed in Section 5).

The objects to be protected by the AC scheme are classified into *types*. An object of type T is called a T-object. (For the moment, we assume that every object belongs to a unique type). For every type T there is a fixed set of *operators* (procedures)

$$op(T) = Pi$$

called the T-operators. It is assumed that the T-operators are the only subjects(*) in the system which can directly manipulate and observe T-objects. For all other subjects, the only way to manipulate or observe T-objects is indirectly, by applying to them T-operators. (We will see later how this rule can be enforced by the authorization scheme itself, for all but a fixed set of primitive types).

Also, for every type T there is a fixed set of symbols

$$rt(T) = \{ri\}$$

called *T-rights*, or simply rights. Objects of type T (T-objects) are addressed by special kind of objects called *tickets*(**) which have the form

$$(b;R)$$

where *b* is the identifier of a T-object, and *R* is a subset of rt(T). There may be several tickets in the system with the same component b, they are called *b-tickets*. The right-symbols contained in a b-ticket t serve to determine which T-operators can be applied(***) to b, when the ticket t is used to address it. It is in this sense that a ticket represents privileges with respect to the object addressed by it. For example, one may have the following one to one correspondence between T-rights and the T-operators which they authorize:

> The T-operator Pi can be applied to a ticket (b;R) of a T-object b, only if R contains the right-symbol ri.

In such a case ri may be called "the right for Pi". Although, in general, the correspondence between rights and operators may be more complex than that, it is always *monotone* in the following sense:

(*) *Note that a subject may be either a procedure (operator) built into the system, or a user of the system.*
(**) *We are using the term "ticket" for what is more commonly called "capability". The reason for this deviation from the, more or less, standard terminology will be clarified later.*
(***) *Since objects are always addressed by their tickets, we will frequently use the phrase "application of an operator to a ticket", to mean the application of the operator to the object which is addressed by the ticket.*

If an operator can be applied to a ticket t=(b;R), then it can be applied to any ticket t'=(b;R') such that R' includes R.

This monotone property suggests the following relation, which defines a partial order, between tickets.

Definition: A ticket t=(b;R) is *weaker* than t=(b;R'), if R' includes R.

Clearly, a weaker ticket carries fewer privileges.

Now, every *subject* (actor) in the system is associated with a special kind of object which we call *domain*. The domain D of a subject S contains tickets of various objects in the system, and it is assumed that a subject can operate only on tickets in his domain. In this way, the domain of a subject determines his authority. The distribution of tickets throughout the system is called the *authority state* of the system.

2.1: On the Dynamics of the AC Scheme. Although there is no general agreement as to the ways in which the authority state of the system is to be changed, the dynamics of most AC schemes is governed by the following rules.

Rule 1: An existing ticket cannot be modified.
Rule 2: When a T-object *b* is created, a ticket (b;R) is created with it, with all its possible rights. (Namely R=rt(T)). We call it the *primary* b-ticket.
Rule 3: There is an operator, *transport*, which when applied to a b-ticket *t*, creates another b-ticket *t'* in some other place in the system. *t'* is called a *direct derivative* of t. (We will use the term "derivative" of a ticket t for a direct or indirect derivative of t.)

To these, practically standard rules, we now add another rule which is essentially Denning's *principle of attenuation of privileges:*

Rule 4: The direct derivative of a ticket t cannot be stronger than t.

As has already been pointed out this principle is not satisfied by a number of AC schemes, notably by Hydra [Wul 74, Coh 75]. One of the main features of Hydra is an operator *amplify* which when applied to a ticket t, creates a ticket t' which is stronger than t(*). Even Denning who was the first to suggest explicitly the principle of attenuation, qualifies himself by requiring it only "under normal circumstances" [Den 76, p. 372]. Indeed, it turns out that the *principle of attenuation is compatible with the AC scheme*. To see this consider the following example.

Example 1: Let P1, P2 be T-operators for a given type T, and let r1, r2 be the corresponding rights. Namely, Pi can be applied only to a ticket with the right ri, for i=1,2. Now, consider S1, S2 and a T-object b.

U1: The subject S1 is allowed to apply *only* P1 to b, and he is the only one who has any privilege with respect to b.

U2: The subject S2 is allowed to apply P2 to b.

The question is, can there be a transition of the system from state U1 to U2? In other words, can S1 authorize S2 to apply the operator P2 to b, which S1 himself is not allowed to do? As we will see next, under the AC scheme the answer to this question is negative, if this scheme is to satisfy the principle of attenuation.

Indeed, in the state U1, S1 must have the ticket t = (b;r1) in his domain. The ticket t cannot contain the right r2, because this would enable S1 to apply P2 to b. Moreover, in U1 nobody else has any right for b. In the state U2, on the other hand, S2 must have a ticket t' = (b;r2) in his domain, but under the rules 1 to 4 there is no way to generate such a ticket.

Since this kind of transition from one authority state to another turns out to be essential for many applications (see example 2 below) one may conclude that the AC scheme is incompatible with the principle of attenuation of privileges. Hydra's response to this situation has been to introduce the amplification operator, which can add a right to a ticket, thus violating the principle of attenuation. We take the opposite approach: using the attenuation of privileges as a fundamental principle of authorization, we conclude that the AC scheme itself is unsatisfactory and should be replaced by a scheme which is compatible with this principle. To see how this can be done we must gain a deeper understanding of the reason for the incompatibility between the AC scheme and the principle of attenuation.

(*) *Actually, Hydra allows only a restricted use of the operator amplify. We will discuss Hydra specifically in a later section.*

3. PRIVILEGES VERSUS ABILITIES

Authority transformations such as in Example 1 are very common in the real world, and it would be instructive to see how they are handled there. Let us consider one such real-life example.

Example 2: When buying a car one automatically gets the right to drive and to sell it. Suppose that these rights are formally represented by a ticket-like structure (c;drive,sell) which stands for the ownership document for the car c. Now, consider a subject S1 who owns a car c, but who does not have a driving license. This person cannot exercise his right to drive his own car. However, S1 can hire a driver, who does have a driving license, authorizing him to drive the car c by granting him his own right to drive it. Such authorization may be formally represented by the ticket-like structure (c;drive) to be given to S2. No process which even remotely resembles amplification is taking place in this real-life situation. The driver S2 can drive the car owned by S1 not because he has more privileges for it than its owner, but because he has another *independent* privilege, a driving license.

The crux of the matter is that in the real world, there is a distinction between the concept of *privilege*, or right, and the concept of *ability*. The ability to perform a certain action may depend on the availability of several privileges(*). In this case: the ability to drive a car is formed by the availability of a driving license as well as of the right to drive this particular car. The problem with the access-control scheme is its failure to recognize this difference between privileges and abilities. Under this scheme, the availability of a b-ticket with the right rl in it is sufficient to give a subject the ability to apply the operator P1 to b. Thus, rights are being equated with abilities.

We maintain that to satisfy the principle of attenuation of privileges one must *distinguish between privileges and abilities*. Such a distinction is being made by the operation-control (OC) scheme to be discussed next. In fact, the Hydra system [Wul 74] also makes such a distinction, but in a less fundamental and not quite satisfactory way, as we will see in Section 5.

(*) In the real world, the ability of a subject to perform a certain action may also depend on such things as his skill and stamina, which we have no intention to model.

4. THE OPERATION-CONTROL (OC) SCHEME

Under the OC scheme, [Min 77] the ability to perform an operation $P(q_1,\ldots,q_k)$ is formed by the availability of two kinds of privileges: a privilege with respect to the operator P, and compatible privileges(*) with respect to the operands $q_1,\ldots,q_k$. Privileges with respect to operands are represented by means of tickets, just as under the AC scheme. However, to represent privileges with respect to operators, the OC scheme is using a new device called *activator*. In this paper, only a simplified version of the activator is described.

An *activator* is a (k+1) tuple

$$\langle P, c_1, \ldots, c_k \rangle$$

where P is an identifier of a k-ary operator, and c_i, for $i = 1,\ldots,k$, is a condition defined on the i-th operand of P. The conditions c_i are called the *operand-patterns* of the activator. The existence of such activator in a domain $D(S)$ serves as a permission for the subject S to apply operator P to a sequence of objects $q_1,\ldots,q_k$ in $D(S)$, which "match" the respective activation patterns (or satisfy the conditions) $c_1,\ldots,c_k$. As a notational devise, we may give a name, say "A", to an activator by writing

$$A = \langle P, c_1, \ldots, c_k \rangle$$

When an activator A is used to authorize the operation $P(q_1,\ldots,q_k)$ we say that the activator A is *applied* to the objects $q_1,\ldots,q_k$, denoting such an application by $A(q_1,\ldots,q_k)$.

An operand-pattern has the form(**)

$$[T;R]$$

where T is a type and R is a set of T-rights. This pattern matches (is satisfied by) any ticket (b;R1) where b is a T-object and R1 includes R.

In order to illustrate the authorization role of the activators, and their relevance to our subject matter, we show next how the authority structure of example 2 can be represented under the OC scheme.

(*) The phrase "compatible privileges" will be clarified later.
(**)This is a simplified form of the operand-patterns introduced in [Min 77].

Example 2': Consider a type CAR. Let op(CAR) be {SELL,DRIVE},
representing the action of selling and driving a car, and let
rt(CAR) = {sell,drive}. Let the primary activators of the CAR-
operators be:

$$\langle\, \text{SELL}, [\text{CAR}; \text{sell}]\, \rangle$$

$$\langle\, \text{DRIVE}, [\text{CAR}; \text{drive}]\, \rangle$$

This means, in particular, that in order to drive a car (by
applying the operator DRIVE to it) one needs a ticket with the
"drive" right for it. Now, consider the subjects S1 and S2
whose domains D1, D2 are described in Figure 1. S1 who owns the
car b1 has the ticket t1 = (b1;sell,drive) for it. However, since
S1 has no DRIVE-activator in his domain he is unable to drive his
own car in spite of the fact that he has all the possible right-
symbols for it. The inability of S1 to drive his own car does
not make the "drive" right that he has for it useless. This
right can be used by S1 to authorize somebody else, S2 in this
case, to drive his car. This is done by giving S2 a derivative
t1' = (b1;drive) of his ticket t1. S2 who has the DRIVE-activator
⟨DRIVE, [CAR;drive]⟩, representing a driving license, would now be
able to drive the car b1. Thus, the requirements of example 2
are satisfied, without amplification.

Note also that although both subjects have the SELL-activator
⟨SELL, [CAR;sell]⟩, which means that both are allowed in
principle to sell cars, the driver S2 is unable to sell the car
b1 because his b1-ticket does not contain the "sell" right.
[End-of-example].

Just as there may be several different b-tickets which
represent different privileges with respect to a given object b,
we allow for several different P-activators which represent
different privileges with respect to a given operator P. In order
to compare different P-activators with each other, we introduce
the following concepts:

Let A be an *activator* of order k (with k operand-patterns).
We define *range(A)* to be the set of all possible k-tuples
(q1,...,qk) of objects, which can be matched with the corresponding activation-patterns of A.

Let A and A' be two P-activators for a given operator P. We
say that A' is *weaker* than A (or, equivalently, A is *stronger*
than A') if range(A) *includes* range(A'). Such an A' is also
called a *reduction* of A.

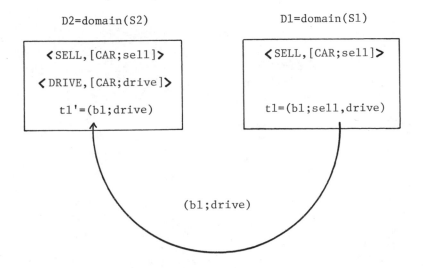

Fig. 1

Clearly, the relation *weaker* between activators defines a
partial order, which is analogous to the partial order defined by
the relation *weaker* between tickets. Due to this and other
similarities between tickets and activators, we sometimes refer
to both kinds of objects by the common name "control-objects", or
"cobjects", for short. Every cobject represents privileges with
respect to the object addressed by it, which may be either an
operator (in the case of an activator) or a "passive object" (in
the case of a ticket).

Note that the two types of cobjects play complementary roles
in our scheme. Neither a ticket nor an activator alone represents
an ability to perform any action. Such an ability is formed by
the availability of an activator, and one or more matching tickets.
To emphasize this complementarity we will use the following
terminology.

Let D(S) be the domain of a given subject S. We will use the
phrase "ower of S" for the set of activators in D(S), and the
phrase "range of S" for the set of tickets in D(S).

Thus, the *ability* of a subject depends on its *range*, which
defines his access rights to various objects, as well as on his
power which defines the kind of operations which he can use.

In spite of the (hopefully) intuitive appeal of these terms,
they do not mean much without specifying the dynamic behavior of
the control objects. This issue is discussed next.

4.1: On the Dynamics of the Operation-Control Scheme. Here are
the rules which govern the transport of cobjects, which are a
generalization of the rules previously formulated for tickets.

Rule 1:   An existing cobject cannot be modified.
Rule 2:   Whenever an object o is created, a cobject is created
          for it, to be called the primary o-cobject. (It
          would be the primary b-ticket if o is a passive
          object b, or the primary P-activator, if o is an
          operator P).
Rule 3:   There is an operator *"transport"* which, when applied
          to a cobject c creates another cobject c' in some
          other place in the system. c' is called a *direct
          derivative* of c. (By the phrase "derivative of c"
          we mean direct or indirect derivative of c).
Rule 4:   The derivative c' of a cobject c is weaker than or
          identical to c.

The last rule is the *principle of attenuation of privileges,* now
extended to activators. An important corollary of this principle
is that a cobject is stronger than, or identical to, every one of
its derivatives. In particular, *the primary o-cobject is the*

strongest o-cobject, for any object o.

Note that the above rules do not define completely the
dynamics of our authorization scheme. In particular, one must
define the operator "transport" and its activators. This is done
in [Min 77] but not repeated here. To facilitate the following
discussion, we will make the simplifying assumption that the set
of activators in a given domain is fixed. In other words: the
"power"of a subject is assumed to be fixed while its range may
vary. Although this assumption cannot be strictly correct for
all the domains in a aystem, it is likely to be correct in many
if not most cases (see [Min 77]). In particular, the "power" of
a *procedure* is likely to be fixed while its range varies from one
invocation to another.

4.2: The Privileges Carried by the Right-Symbols. The privileges
carried by a given right symbol r are best defined in terms of
the affect that the absence of r from a ticket t has on one's
ability to apply operators to the object addressed by t. We will
see in this section that this effect depends on the principle of
attenuation. To facilitate our discussion we start with an
example.

   Example 3: Sharing Memoranda

        Let MEMO by a type of objects which carry memoranda in an
information system. Let

                op(MEMO) = {READ, UPDATE, DELETE}
                   rt(MEMO) = {d,r1,r2}

Let the following be the primary activators of the MEMO-operators:

                < READ, [MEMO] >

                <UPDATE, [MEMO], [TEXT]>(*)

                < DELETE, [MEMO;d] >

Note that the rights r1 and r2 are not used by any of these
activators. The significance of this will be clarified later.

Now, consider a group of subjects G = {S,S1,S2,S3} who are
working on the same project but have different responsibilities
and authority. They communicate with each other by means of a
pool of memoranda whose tickets are contained in a file f. A
ticket of a memo may be stored in f by members of the group G as
well as by other subjects in the system, such as S'. It is also
assumed that every member of G can transport tickets from the
file f to its own domain. Now all the subjects in G are to be

---

(*) *The second operand of the operator UPDATE should be a TEXT-
object which serves to update the memo.*

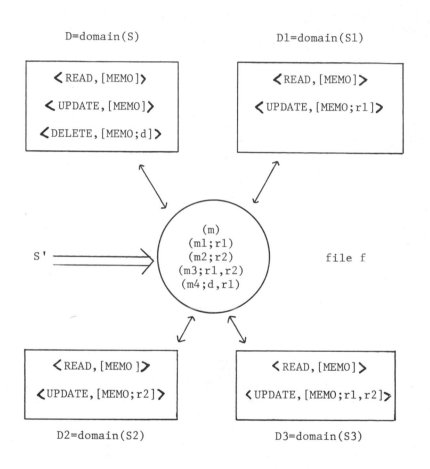

Fig. 2

allowed to read all the memos in f (namely, all the memos whose
tickets are stored in f). However, not every subject is to be
allowed to update all the memos, or to delete them. Figure 2
describes part(*) of the domains of the subjects in G as well as
a sample of the file f.

Now, note that all the subjects in G have a copy of the
primary READ-activator. This enables them to read all memos in f.
However, they have different versions of the UPDATE-activator:
The UPDATE-activator of S does not require any rights in the MEMO-
ticket it is applied to. thus, S can update all the memos in f.
On the other hand, the UPDATE-activator of S1 can be applied only
to tickets with the right r1, which means that, given the current
content of f, S1 can update only the memos m1,m3,m4. Similarly,
S2 can update only m2 and m3, for which the tickets in f have the
right r2. Finally, S3 whose UPDATE-activator requires the rights
r1 and r2, can update only the memo m3.

Note also that only S has a DELETE-activator, so that he is
the only one who can delete memoranda. *Not all of them, however.*
Given the content of the file f described in Figure 2, S can
delete only m4 whose ticket has the d right.

Thus, the four subjects in group G have different "power"
with respect to the MEMO-tickets, due to the different activators
in their domains. Knowing about the power of the various subjects
in G, the originator S' of a memo can control its disposition, as
follows: When S' creates a new memo m', he gets the primary
ticket t = (m';d,r1,r2) for it. If, for example, he wants to
allow everybody in group G to update m' but he does not want them
to delete it, he would insert the reduction (m';r1,r2) of t in the
file f. If he wants only S and S1 to update m', then he would
insert (m';r1) into f, etc. [end-of-example].

Among other things, this example demonstrates that a right-
symbol might have different meaning for different subjects, which
allows our four subjects to share the same pool of MEMO-tickets
and still have different *abilities* with respect to the memos. In
order to formalize this phenomena, we will define the concept of
the "privilege content" of a right-symbol. In fact, two related
concepts of privilege-content will be defined.

---

*(*) The description of the domain in Figure 2 is incomplete in
the following sense. We did not try to account for the assumed
ability of the four subjects in G to transport MEMO-tickets from
f into their own domains. (This ability can be properly formulated only by means of the complete OC scheme [Min 77]).*

Definition: The *absolute privilege content* of a given right-symbol r, to be denoted by U(r), is the set of operators whose primary-activators require r.

For instance, in Example 3   U(d) = {DELETE}, while U(r1) and U(r2) are empty.

The significance of U(r) is due to the principle of attenuation: First, due to the attenuation of activators, if the primary P-activator, for a given operator P, has a pattern which requires r, then all P-activators in the system would require r. Thus, *the absence of r from a ticket t inhibits the application of P to this ticket.* Moreover, because of the attenuation of tickets, if t does not contain r then no derivative of t would contain r. Therefore, we can make the following statement, which we introduce as a corollary of the principle of attenuation:

Corollary 1: The *absence* of a right r from a ticket t *inhibits* the application of operators in U(r) to t itself as well as to all its derivatives.

For example, consider a MEMO-object m and an m-ticket t which does not have the right d. One can put t in the public domain and remain confident that this ticket cannot be used to delete the memo m, neither directly or indirectly. Such is not the case under the AC scheme where there is the danger of somebody adding a right to t by amplification.

Note that by the above definition, the MEMO-rights r1,r2 does not carry any privileges. Indeed, the absence of R1 from a MEMO-ticket t cannot inhibit the application of any MEMO-operator to it. Yet, it is the existence of r1 which allows S1 to apply UPDATE to a ticket. In order to account for this phenomena, we now introduce the concept of *relative privilege content* of a right-symbol.

Definition: The privilege-content of a right symbol r, *relative to a domain D,* to be denoted by U(r/D), is the set of operators for which there is an activator in D which requires r.

For example, U(r1/D1) = {UPDATE}, although U(r1) is empty. The meaning of the concept of relative-privilege-content is summarized by the following statement:

Corollary 2: The absence of r from a ticket t = (b;R) in D = domain(S) inhibits S from applying the operators in the set U(r/D) to t and to its derivatives.

To understand the significance of this statement, note the following: First, suppose that P belongs to U(r/D) but not to U(r). Let t = (b;R) be a ticket in D = domain(S) which does not contain the right r. It is clear that S *himself* cannot apply P to t. However, S may be able to *cause* the application of P to

the object b, by giving a derivative of t to some other domain D'
such that P is not contained in U(r/D').

Secondly, consider an operator P which belongs to U(r) but
not to U(r/D) (which, due to the attenuation of activators, can
happen only if D contains no P-activators). Obviously, the
absence of r from a ticket t = (b;R) in D = domain(S) has no
effect on the ability of S to apply P to object b, because anyway
D has no P-activators. However, this absence does prevent S from
causing the application of P to b by giving a derivative of t to
a subject which does have a P-activator. For example, suppose
that the domain D1 of Example 3 contains the tickets t1 = (m1;d),
t2 = (m2). Since U(d/D1) is empty, the right d does not provide
S1 with any direct ability. Indeed, exactly the same set of
operators can be applied by S1 to t1 and t2. However, S1 can
enable S to delete m1, by placing t1 in the file f, which he can
not do for m2.

In conclusion, the main benefit which accrues from the
principle of attenuation is that it provides us with a definite
measure for the privileges represented by a given control-object,
privileges which can never be increased. In particular, the
concept of the privilege-content of a right-symbol is of utmost
importance. Another, indirect, consequence of the principle and
of the scheme which we used to realize it, is the concept of
relative-privilege-content which allows for more economical
utilization of tickets. In Example 3, for instance, all the
subjects in G were able to use the same directory file. To implement a similar authority structure under the AC scheme one
would need four separate directory files, one for each subject in
G, which would result in larger number of tickets and additional
complexity in their distribution (see also [Min 77, Section 4]).

5. AMPLIFICATION IN HYDRA

Although the authorization scheme of the Hydra system
[Wul 74, Coh 75] is usually considered to be an access-control
scheme, it differs from the AC-scheme outlined in Section 2 in
one important way: Under Hydra, the availability of a ticket
(capability) for an object is not, by itself, sufficient for the
application of an operator to it. One must also have the permission to call the operator. In Hydra, this permission is
represented by a ticket for the operator with the "call" right in
it. In fact, a ticket (P;call) for the operator P, together with
the formal-parameter-specification (FPS) in P itself is equivalent
to the primary P-activator under the OC scheme. Thus, as under
the OC scheme, abilities in Hydra are formed by the availability
of privileges with respect to both operands and operators.
However, Hydra lacks the formal means to represent varying degree

of privileges with respect to one operator P, which, under the OC
scheme, can be represented by *different* P-activators. We maintain
that the ability to represent different privileges with respect to
one operator is necessary if an authorization scheme is to satisfy
the principle of attenuation. In particular, as we will see in
Section 6, it is crucial for the implementation of type-extensions
without the use of amplification.

It should be pointed out that in some sense the effect of
having different P-activators for the same operator P can be
simulated in Hydra, as follows: Let Al...Ak be a set of P-
activators. One can form in Hydra a corresponding set of operators
Pl...Pk, which are identical to P in all but their formal-
parameter-specifications. The FPC of Pi should impose the same
condition on its arguments that are imposed by the corresponding
activator Ai. However, for this facility to be used as part of
an authorization scheme, one must impose a discipline on the
formation of the operators Pi from the original operator P,
similar to our rules concerning the generation of activators.
Since Hydra does not feature any such discipline, there is a
genuine need for amplification in it.

Recognizing the harmful effects of amplification, Hydra
restricted its use to the subsystems which implement type-extension [Coh 75]. Unfortunately, this restriction is not satisfactory, on two accounts:

a) In the context of Hydra, amplification is necessary in
other circumstances besides type-extension. Thus, the restricted
use of amplification in Hydra leaves a class of policies
unsupported.

b) The Hydra's restriction on the use of amplification does
not eliminate all its harmful effects.

The second claim will be discussed in the next section where we
also show that under the OC scheme type-extension can be implemented without amplifications. To substantiate our first claim,
let us return to Example 2. We will show that although the
authority structure of Example 2 can be supported in Hydra,
without amplification, a simple modification of it cannot be so
supported.

The owner-driver situation of Example 2 can be implemented in
Hydra simply by representing a driving license by a ticket
(DRIVE;call) for the operator DRIVE. This ticket should be given
to the driver S2 but not to S1. What makes this case manageable
in Hydra is the fact that S1 is not allowed to drive at all. But
what about a situation where S1 is allowed to drive some car, but
not his own? For example, suppose that S1 is a disabled person
who needs a special permission to drive any specific car,
permission which may be based on the safety features of that car.

The Hydra solution for Example 2 would not work here because both subjects must have the right to call the operator DRIVE.

Under the OC-scheme, this authority structure can be represented as follows: Supposed that S1 has the following DRIVE-activator

$$\langle DRIVE, \; [CAR;drive,sd] \rangle$$

which means that S1 can drive only such a car c' for which it has a ticket (c';drive,sd...), "sd" being this special driving permission. If S1 does not have the "sd" right for his own car c he cannot drive it. The driver, S2, on the other hand, not being disabled, has the more powerful DRIVE-activator $\langle DRIVE,[CAR;drive] \rangle$. Thus, if S1 gives a ticket (c;drive) to S2, the latter would be able to drive the car c. A similar effect can be achieved in Hydra only by amplification, unless one gives the two subjects two different operators for driving cars.

6.   THE ISSUE OF TYPE-EXTENSION

In this section, we show how type-extension can be achieved under the OC-scheme, without violating the principle of attenuation. Moreover, we will argue that the Hydra implementation of type-extension has some drawbacks dur to the amplifications on which it is based. But first, let us define the concept of type-extension.

Definition: Consider a type T' such that op(T')={Qi} and rt(T')={si}. Let T be a type with op(T)={Pi}, T is called an *extension of T'* if the following conditions are satisfied.

1)   Every T-object is also a T'-object. (Note that this partially removes the restriction made in Section 2 that every object belongs to a unique type).
2)   The only subjects which are able to apply T'-operators to a T-object are the T-operators Pi. For any other subject, the only way to manipulate and observe T-objects is indirectly by means of the T-operators, which have the exclusive ability to "see the bare representation of T-objects".
3)   The set of T-rights is

$$rt(T)=rt(T')U\{ri\}$$

We refer to T' as the *representation* type of T, and to the set op(T') as the *representation-operators*. Note that every T-ticket may carry T'-rights, to be called representation-rights, as well as the symbols ri which we call the *intrinsic T-rights*.

In Hydra [Coh 75], all extended types are extensions of a single primitive type T'=SEGMENT. The SEGMENT-operators in Hydra are called "generic operators", which include such operators as GETDATA and PUTDATA. The rights rt(SEGMENT) are called "generic rights". The module which contains the definition of op(T) and rt(T), for a given type T, is called the T-subsystem.

The main difficulty in the implementation of type-extension is requirement (2) of its definition. Here is how the designers of Hydra see this problem ([Coh 75] p. 147).

> "Hydra must somehow guarantee that ordinary users cannot access or manipulate an object's represen-tation...*This implies that ordinary users do not have capabilities [tickets] containing the various generic rights*...Yet a subsystem procedure must be able to gain these rights when a capability for an object of the type it supports is passed to it as an argument".

Hydra's solution to this dilemma is an exclusive ability of the representation-operators of a type T to *amplify* T-tickets (or capabilities, in Hydra's terminology) by adding to them desired representation-rights. Under the OC scheme this dilemma does not arise in the first place, because rights are not identical to abilities. Indeed, if the ordinary users do not have activators for the representation operators, then they may have tickets which contain representation-rights without being able to invoke the corresponding operators. Moreover, we will see below that in most cases, there is *no need to carry representation-rights* in the tickets of extended-type objects.

6.1: The Implementation of Type-Extension Under the OC Scheme. Consider a type T' which, like the type SEGMENT in Hydra, serves as a representation-type for a number of extended types. Let

$$AQ = \langle\, Q, [T']\,\rangle$$

be the primary Q-activator of an arbitrary T'-operators Q. AQ is very powerful as it can be applied to any T'-object, regardless of the extended type it hosts. We assume, however, that these powerful primary Q-activators exist only in the module which generates new type-subsystems. Appropriate reductions of these activators are distributed among the various type-subsystems, as follows:

Let T be an extension of T' and let P be a T-operator which needs to apply a representation-operator Q to its argument. We insert in the domain of P the following reduction of AQ:

$$AQT = \langle\, Q, [T]\,\rangle$$

AQT is weaker than AQ because it can be applied only to T-objects.
Namely, only to such a T'-object which hosts a T-object.

Now, since the activators AQT exist only in the domains of
T-operators, no other subject would be able to apply T-operators
to T-objects, as is required by the definition of type-extension.

Of course, the invocation of the T-operators themselves should
be controlled by their own activators, using the intrinsic T-rights
ri.   For example, the primary P-activator for a T-operator P may
be:

$$\langle P,[T;r]\rangle$$

where r is one of the T-rights.   This means that one needs the
right r in a ticket in order to apply T to it.

Note that this suggests that there is no need to have the
representation rights {si} in T-tickets.   Because, the only way
for ordinary users to cause the invocation of T
invoking T-operators, and such invocation is controlled by the
intrinsic T-rights.   The representation operators, in turn, do not
need any representation-rights for their arguments, because the
representation-activators which they have, such as AQT, do not
require any.   And yet, as we will see below, there is a role to be
played by the representation rights in T-tickets.

6.2:   The Role of the Representation-Rights.   Consider a T-operator
P whose primary activator is $\langle P,[T;r]\rangle$.   Suppose that P is
designed to use a certain T'-operator Q *only on some of its invo-*
cations.   For example, let the type T be FILE and let P be the
operator DELETE, which deletes a record from a file.   Suppose
that normally the operator DELETE only marks the record to be
deleted as an "inactive" record, without actually removing it from
the file.   Occasionally, however, DELETE performs garbage
collection returning the space occupied by inactive records to the
free-storage pool.   To do this, DELETE has to use the representation-operator RETURN-STORAGE.   In this case, one may want to allow
a subject S to apply DELETE to a file f provided that such an
application does not cause physical loss of information which
would result from garbage collection.   In general, *one would like*
to be able to restrict a T-operator, as to which representation-
operators it can apply to its arguments, once it is called.   We
propose to use the representation-rights for this purpose, as is
explained below.

Recall that previously we assumed that a T-operator P would
have in its domain an activator $\langle Q,[T]\rangle$ for every T'-operator Q.
We now suggest that if an operator Q does not have to be used by
P on *every* invocation, then P should have the following activator
for it

$$\langle Q, [T;s] \rangle$$

where s belongs to rt(T'). This means that P cannot apply Q to
its argument unless it has a ticket for it with the representation-
right s.

As before, the primary P-activator is

$$AP = \langle P, [T;r] \rangle$$

so that the representation-right s is not required in the ticket
t=(b;R) in order to apply P to it. However, P itself cannot apply
Q to its argument unless R contains s as well.

In general, the T'-rights can be used in the tickets of T-
object as a means to control the internal operation of T-operators.
In the sense that the absence of such a right can prevent a T-
operator from applying a certain T' operator to its argument.

Note that this important use of the representation-rights
would be disabled by amplification. If an operator P has the
ability to amplify its argument by adding representation-rights
to it, as is the case in Hydra, then it does not matter if the
operand ticket did not have such a right originally. It should
be pointed out that the designers of Hydra recognized this
problem, but only with respect to certain representation-
operators (see [Coh 75] p. 152). Indeed, their solution has been
to, effectively, cancel the amplificatoin for the representation-
rights which control these operators. However, they failed to
see the more general nature of the problem which requires the
complete elimination of amplification.

7. CONCLUSION

The primary result of this paper is the demonstration that an
authorization scheme can be based on the principle of attenuation
of privileges. The obvious advantage of this principle is that
it makes it easier to foresee the consequences of the act of
granting somebody a certain privilege, due to the assurance given
by the principle of attenuation that this privilege cannot be
amplified. Moreover, the need to satisfy the principle of
attenuation gave as an insight into the general problem of
authorization, which may be more valuable than the original
principle itself.

First, the analysis of the incompatibility between the access-
control scheme and the principle of attenuation revealed a need
to make a distinction between "privileges" and "abilities". This
distinction has an intrinsic importance since it seems to be

essential for many real-life authority-structures that have to be
built into computer systems. Secondly, the fundamental difference
between privileges and abilities led us to the two complementary
types of control-objects which represent privileges with respect
to operators and their operands. This complementary of privileges
has a number of important implications which are farther discussed
in [Min 77, Min 77a]. Finally, it should be pointed out that the
operation-control scheme has been originally introduced for a
number of different reasons, including the principle of attenuation, and that it is much more general than the version introduced
in this paper.

REFERENCES

[Coh 75] Cohen, E., and Jefferson, D. "Protection in the Hydra
   Operating System," in Proc. Fifth ACM Symposium on Operating
   Systems Principles; ACM Operating System Review 9,5, (Nov.
   1975), pp. 141-160, ACM, New York, 1975.
[Den 76] Denning, P. J., "Fault-Tolerant Operating Systems",
   Computing Surveys, Dec. 1976.
[Fab 68] Fabry, R. S. "Preliminary Description of a Supervisor
   for a Machine-Oriented Around Capabilities", ICR Quarterly
   Report 18, Univ. of Chicago, Chicago, Ill., 1968.
[Gra 72] Graham, G. S., and Denning, P. J., "Protection --
   Principle and Practice", in Proc. 1972 AFIPS Spring Jt.
   Computer Conf. Vol. 40, AFIPS Press, Montvale, N. J., 1972,
   pp. 417-424.
[Jon 73] Jones, A. J., "Protection in Programmed Systems", Ph.D.
   Thesis, Carnegie-Mellon Univ., Pittsburgh, Pa., June 1973.
[Har 76] Harrison, M. A., Ruzzo, W. L., Ullman, J. D, "Protec-
   tion in Operating Systems", CACM, Aug. 1976.
[Lam 69] Lampson, B. W., "Dynamic Protection Structures", in
   Proc. 1969 AFIPS Fall Jt. Computer Conf., Vol. 35, AFIPS
   Press, Montvale, N. J., 1969, pp. 27-38.
[Lam 71] Lampson, B. W., "Protection", in Proc. Fifth Annual
   Princton Conf. on Information Sciences and Systems 1971, pp.
   437-443. Reprinted in ACM Operating Systems Review (Jan.
   1974).
[Lam 76] Lampson, B. W., and Sturgis, H. E., "Reflections on An
   Operating System Design", Comm. ACM 19, 5 (May 1976), pp.
   251-266.
[Lev 77] Levin, R., A letter to Computing Surveys, June 77.
[Lip 77] Lipton, R. J., and Snyder, L., "A Linear Time
   Algorithm for Deciding Subject Security", in J. of the ACM,
   July 1977, pp. 455-469.
[Lis 75] Liskov, B., and Zilles, S., "Specification Techniques
   for Data Abstractions", IEEE Trans. on Software Engineering
   1, 1 (March 1975), pp. 7-18.

[Min 77] Minsky, N., "An Operation-Control Scheme for Authoriza-
    tion in Computer Systems", to be published in the Int. J. of
    Computer and Information Sci., 1978.
[Min 77a] Minsky, N., "Cooperative Authorization", Proc. of the
    COMPSAC 77 (Computer Software & Applications Conference),
    Nov. 77.
[Neu 75] Neumann, P. G., Robinson, L., Levitt, K. N., Boyer,
    R. S., and Saxena, A. R., "A Provably Secure Operating
    System", Stanford Research Inst. Final Report, Menlo Park,
    Calif., June 1975.
[Red 74a] Redell, D. R., and Fabry, R. S., "Selective Revocation
    of Capabilities", IRIA Internat. Workshop on Protection in
    Operating Systems, Institut de Recherche d'Informatique et
    D'Automatique, 1974 France, pp. 197-210.
[Sal 75] Saltzer, J. H., and Schroeder, M. D., "The Protection
    of Information in Computer Systems", in Proc. of the IEEE 63,
    9 (Sept. 1975), pp. 1278-1308.
[Wul 74a] Wulf, W. A.,; et al. "HYDRA: The Kernel of a Multi-
    processor Operating System", Comm. ACM 17, 6 (June 1974),
    pp. 337-345.

DISCUSSION

Lipton: I've always had very strong reservations about Take/Grant Systems. If you formally change your words, substituting for example colors for the rights, then to the formal machinery, it makes no difference. That clearly means that something is missing in these theorems. We are reading in the semantics of the situation. Do you think that is justified on the basis of the model?

Minsky: I don't know. But maybe someone else has something to add.

Rabin: Yes, my question is also concerned with semantics. If you consider the system that was previously presented by Anita Jones and now what you are doing, there is something which is lacking. We are treating the alphas, betas and gammas as sets of tokens of the sort. But, when Naftaly Minsky's presentation came, we saw that the meaning of these tokens play a role. But actually, I think that the basic issue is the issue of semantics. Take, for example, the business of the right to drive and the right to sell. Now the main problem there was the semantic meaning of drive is not completely explicated. You really have the right to drive and the right to grant the right to drive. Now, I don't want to carry it on, but that is still different from the right to grant the right to grant the right to drive; and, these are entirely different situations. You must have semantics for the token, semantics of which abilities and which privileges of which these are special cases. For example, we would have the ability to drive and the privilege of the right to grant the right to drive. But, that is just an instance of semantics, and I think that for full ramifications, they necessarily would become much more complicated, as all real life situations are.

Minsky: I first don't have any real hope that we can model all real life situations. My own interest in this model comes not from operating systems, but from information systems, which are much more complex. However, I don't believe that you can approximate very well that sort of complexity.

SECTION IV. THEORETICAL MODELS OF OPERATING SYSTEM SECURITY

All of the issues addressed here can be traced to the concepts discussed in section III. If the point of a design is a system, the point of a theoretical study is insight; the kind of insight that flows from answering questions that are very carefully posed. In this section, there are four papers treating theoretical issues; they pose questions concerning security in computing systems and give some rigorous answers. As we saw in section III, the theoretical answers are not always what our practical intuitions say they should be. But then, intuition is often faulty, and that's what helps to make the theory so interesting.

In this final section, Richard Lipton and Timothy Budd open the selection of theoretical contributions by showing us that there is an efficient way to decide safety for a wide variety of protection systems. The requirement is that the systems must be related in certain ways. Ellis Cohen notes the various possibilities for information flow in sequential programs and gives an elegant formal treatment of his ideas. Michael Harrison and Larry Ruzzo extend their well-known investigations into a particular security model by giving a characterization of the relative "power" of different operations allowed in the model. In the final paper, Richard Lipton and Larry Snyder prove the surprising equivalence of a well-studied security model and an *apparently* unrelated model for synchronizing parallel processes.

ON CLASSES OF PROTECTION SYSTEMS

Richard J. Lipton
Timothy A. Budd

Yale University
New Haven, Connecticut

I.   INTRODUCTION

Interest in the modeling and formal analysis of operating
system protection mechanisms has increased in the last few years
[2-7, 11-14].   In [7], it was shown that for arbitrary systems
the sort of questions we are interested in asking, such as whether
rights can be passed to unauthorized persons, are generally
undecidable.   On the other hand, in [12] it was shown that for a
system which had previously been proposed in the literature
[4,11], such questions could be decided in linear time.

In this paper, we will show that the ability to decide the
safety question quickly can be proved for a very large class of
operating system protection models.

II.   THE MODEL

Our paradigm of a protection system will be as follows:

We are given V objects in the system $(X_1, \ldots, X_v)$.   In a
specific instantiation of the model each object could represent,
for example, a file or a process; however, we abstract this idea
by simply stating that each X_i is of type T_i, which is an element
of some finite alphabet T.

Between any two objects, there may be an arbitrary number
(possibly empty) of *rights*, where each right is indicated by an
element from some finite alphabet Σ.

At any time, we indicate the current status of the system by a graph G where each object is represented by a vertex and each right by a labeled directed arc.

The differences we will emphasize in classifying protection systems will be in the rules they use for adding or deleting arcs from an existing graph. These we will call the *transition rules*.

If starting from initial configuration by a finite number of applications of the transition rules, we can connect a vertex X to a vertex Y by an arc labeled α, we will say that in the initial configuration X can α Y.

We will not consider systems which have rules roughly equivalent to "If I have a right to something, I can give it to anyone I choose", or graphically,

Such systems we can refer to as "loose". For these systems, the safety question tends to be either trivial or nonsensical. For example, if I can obtain the α right to Z, then anybody can obtain the α right to Z.

The hazardous effects of having a loose protection system have generally not been recognized; for instance, all the examples given in [4,7] suffer from being loose.

Notice that there is a simple isomorphism between systems represented in this graphical format and systems represented in the *access matrix* format of [4,6,7].

III. SAFETY

There are two questions we can ask with respect to protection system [7].

Question 1: The *safety* question.

Given a protection system G and two objects X_i and X_j in that system, if we introduce the right of X_i to α X_j, what other objects can thereby obtain the rights to α X_j.

Question 2: The *extended safety* question.

Given a protection system G and two objects X_i and X_j in that system, if we introduce the right of X_i to α X_j, what potential changes will this produce in the entire system.

In [7] it was shown that for arbitrary protection systems these problems are undecidable. For certain restricted types of systems they were able to give decision procedures for the safety problem, however their procedures worked in exponential time.

On the other hand, in [12] a specific system is described for which these questions can be decided very quickly.

The remainder of this paper will be devoted to the classifications of differing protection systems, indicating some classes for which polynomial or linear time results can be shown for the above-mentioned problems.

IV. GRAMMATICAL PROTECTION SYSTEMS

We will call a protection system *grammatical* if for each right $\alpha\epsilon\Sigma$, there is a grammar L and start symbol S such that given two vertices X and Y, X can α Y *iff* X and Y are connected by a path such that the concatenation of the right symbols on that path form a word in L(S).

We will illustrate this concept by demonstrating a class of protection and showing them to be grammatical, from this we can obtain a polynomial time solution to the extended safety question.

Working within the model described previously, we will define a General Arc Moving system to be a protection system with transition rules of the following form

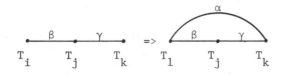

Figure 1

where the types of T_i, T_j and T_k indicate the necessary types for the vertices and α, β and γ are rights. The directionality on the arcs must be specified, but they are here omitted for generality.

We obtain a grammar L by defining a new production for each rewriting rule. For each rule such as that in figure 1, we define a production of L as follows. If they do not already exist, we introduce three nonterminals, A, B and C ε T×R×T such that A corresponds to an arc labeled α between vertices of type T_i and T_k, and in a similar fashion, B and C are defined. We then have the production

$$A \rightarrow BC$$

Note that the nonterminals A, B and C encode both the nature of the right and the type of vertices that the right connects. For each nonterminal A, we create its terminal counterpart a and add the production $A \rightarrow a$.

We then have the following lemma:

Lemma 1: Given two vertices P and Q of types T_p and T_q, respectively, P can α Q *iff* there exists a path between P and Q in $L((T_p, \alpha, T_q))$.

Proof: If P and Q are connected by a path with word in $L((T_p, \alpha, T_q))$, then the derivation of that word gives us a construction method by which we can join P to Q by an arc labeled α, hence P can α Q.

The proof the other way will be by induction on the number of applications of the transition rules which lead to P being able to α Q.

If this number is zero, that is, P had the rights to α Q in the original graph, then we trivially have our result. Hence, we assume P did not originally have the rights to Q, and that it took n applications of the transition rules for P to obtain that right.

The very last application of a transition rule must have been for P to get the ability to α Q from some vertex X (see figure 2). This must have been permitted in virtue of some right β between P and X and some right γ between X and Q and there being a transition rule as shown in figure 1.

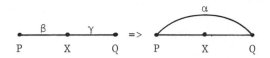

Figure 2

Now it took less than n applications of the transition to form the arcs between Q and X and between X and P, hence by the induction hypothesis there must have been a path between P and X in $L(T_p, \beta, T_x)$ and between X and Q in $L(T_x, \gamma, T_q)$. But associated with the transition rule shown in figure 2 is the production $(T_p, \alpha, T_q) \rightarrow (T_p, \beta, T_x)(T_x, \gamma, T_q)$. Hence, it must be the case that Q and P were connected by a path with word in (T_p, α, T_q).

We can note the similarity between grammars in this form and context-free grammars in Chomsky Normal Form [9]. In view of this, and the relationship between parsing and protection systems demonstrated by lemma 1, it is too much to expect the safety question for arbitrary arc passing systems to be answered in linear time. However, we can demonstrate a polynomial time result as shown by the following theorem.

Theorem 1: The extended safety question can be answered for a general arc moving protection system in $O(V^{2.81})$.

Proof: For this example, we assume the protection network is kept in a V by V matrix (call it M), similar to the access matrix of [3,6,5]. We then define a matrix "multiplication" operation by substituting production reduction (BC = A *iff* $A \rightarrow BC$) for scalar multiplication and set union for scalar addition in the standard matrix multiplication algorithm.

We next observe that since the lower triangular portion of M is the inverse of the upper triangular part, by suitably adding production rules, we can just work with the upper triangular part of M. Hence, we have reduced the problem to that of finding the transitive closure of an upper triangular matrix with respect to our matrix multiplication operation. Valiant [15] has shown how this can be accomplished in $O(V^{2.81})$ operations.

To give a solution to the extended safety question, we simply perform this operation twice, once with and once without the additional arcs. Comparing the results then gives us our answer.

Example 1:   A non-regular Arc Passing System.

In this example, we are just concerned with the movement of
read privileges. Assume we have a right called the *indirect*
right to Y, and Y can read Z, then in effect X can read Z. Next,
there is the *request* right, which says that if X can *request* of
Y, and Y has indirect rights to Z, then X can obtain indirect
rights to Z. (Notice here, as in the take grant system [12], we
take the worst case approach by assuming requests are always
granted). Finally, if X has read rights to Y, and Y has request
rights to Z, X can obtain request rights to Z.

The transition rules are shown in Figure 3. If we let A
represent *read*, B *indirect* and C, we obtain the following grammar:

$$A \rightarrow BA$$

$$B \rightarrow CB$$

$$C \rightarrow AC$$

This obviously is an arc passing grammar, hence theorem 7
gives us a method for solving the safety question. Furthermore,
it can be shown [8] that this grammar is not regular, hence the
$V^{2.81}$ is asymptotically the best upper bound we have on the
safety question for this system.

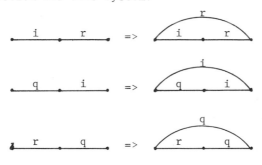

Figure 3

V. REGULAR GRAMMATICAL SYSTEMS

If it happens that for each right the language generated by the grammar associated with a grammatical protection system is regular, we will say the system is a *regular grammatical system*.

Regular grammatical systems are important on account of the following theorem.

Theorem 2: For regular grammatical systems, the *safety* question can be answered in linear time in the size of the protection graph.

Proof: We prove this result by appealing to the fact that regular grammars can be recognized by finite state automata. Assume for a given G, we have an automata with U states that recognize L(G). We then construct a new graph with U×V vertices, where there is an arc from (X_i, U_j) to (X_k, U_ℓ) *iff* there was an arc from X_i to X_k in the original graph, and if we were in state U_j at the point X_i that arc would carry us to state U_ℓ.

Starting from the vertex X and using depth first search on the original graph, we see we can construct this new graph in $O(E)$ operations. Again, using a depth first search on the new graph, we mark those vertices we encounter which are in designated final states for the automata. These are then the only vertices which can obtain rights to X. Again, we have a complexity of $O(E)$ operations.

We wish then to characterize protection systems which have regular languages.

A class of grammars which seem to arise quite frequently are what we call *non-discriminating* grammars. Informally, we will say a protection system is non-discriminating if all the transition rules are of the form "If X and Y are connected by an arc with some right γ, and Y has any right to Z, then X can obtain that right to Z."

The name is meant to imply the fact that we don't discriminate between rights in the second context.

Formally, we will say a protection system is non-discriminating if it has a non-discriminating grammar. We define a non-discriminating grammar as follows.

There are five types of nonterminals, $A_1, \ldots, A_{ka}, B_1, \ldots, B_{kb}, C_1, \ldots, C_{kc}, D_1, \ldots, D_{kd}$ and Z. We allow productions of the following forms (greek letters represent strings of terminal symbols).

Any nonterminals of type A, B, C or D can produce a finite string of terminal symbols.

$$A_i \to \alpha_{aij} \quad B_i \to \alpha_{bij} \quad C_i \to \alpha_{cij} \quad D_i \to \alpha_{dij}$$

A's, B's, C's and D's are allowed productions of the following forms:

$$A_i \to \beta A_j \qquad B_i \to B_j \gamma$$

$$C_i \to Z A_j \qquad C_i \to Z B_j$$

$$C_i \to A_j \qquad C_i \to B_j$$

$$D_i \to A_j Z \qquad D_i \to B_j Z$$

$$D_i \to A_j \qquad D_i \to B_j$$

For Z, we allow productions of the following form:

$$Z \to A_i \qquad Z \to B_j$$

$$Z \to C_i \qquad Z \to D_i$$

$$Z \to C_i D_j$$

$$Z \to ZZ$$

$$A \to A$$

Theorem 3: Non-discriminating grammars are regular.

Proof: We wish to show that starting from any nonterminal, the language produced from this grammar is a regular event. The proof for nonterminal of the first four classes quickly reduces to showing the language produced from Z is a regular event, hence we show only this case.

Notice first, that the nonterminals A (B) form by themselves a right linear (left linear) language and hence associated with every nonterminal A_i or B_i, we have a regular event which represents the language that can be generated from that start symbol.

Let us consider first the set of sentential forms that can be generated from Z using only productions of the type $Z \rightarrow A_i$, $Z \rightarrow B_i$, $Z \rightarrow C_i$ and $Z \rightarrow D_i$.

Let us construct a regular event L as follows. If there are productions $Z \rightarrow D_i$, $D_i \rightarrow A_jZ$ or $D_i \rightarrow B_jZ$ and $A_j \Rightarrow \omega$, $B_j \Rightarrow \nu$ then both ω and ν are in L, and nothing else is in L. We can do a similar trick with C_i to form a regular event R; finally, we can define a regular event F as follows: If there are productions $Z \rightarrow A_i$ and $A_i \Rightarrow \omega$ then ω is in F, similarly for B_i, C_i and D_i.

It should be obvious that the set of sentential forms Z can generate is $L^*(Z!F)R^*$. That is, everything in this form can be generated from Z (using only the productions we have indicated) and nothing else can.

Now assume we have a production $Z \rightarrow ZZ$ (the proof in the case where we don't have this production is easier and won't be given here). Consider what can happen with one application of this rule.

$$Z \Rightarrow L^*ZR^*$$
$$\Rightarrow L^*ZZR^*$$
$$\Rightarrow L^*(L^*(Z!F)R^*)(L^*(Z!F)R^*)R^*$$
$$\Rightarrow (L^*(Z!F)R^*)(L^*(Z!F)R^*)$$

A simple induction argument can be used to show that the set of sentential forms Z can generate is then $(L^*(Z!F)R^*)^*$.

We now wish to add the productions $Z \rightarrow C_iB_j$.

Let us look at what we can generate with one application of this rule.

$$Z \Rightarrow (L^*(Z!F)R^*)^* L^* ZR^* (L^*(Z!F)R^*)^*$$

$$\Rightarrow (L^*(Z!F)R^*)^* L^* C_i D_j R^* (L^*(Z!F)R^*)^*$$

$$\Rightarrow (L^*(Z!F)R^*)^* L^* ZN_1 N_2 ZR^* (L^*(Z!F)R^*)^*$$

$$\Rightarrow (L^*(Z!F)R^*)^* (L^*(Z!F)R^*)^* N_1 N_2 (L^*(Z!F)R^*)^* (L^*(Z!F)R^*)^*$$

$$\Rightarrow (L^*(Z!F)R^*)^* N_1 N_2 (L^*(Z!F)R^*)^*$$

Associated with each nonterminal pair $N_1 N_2$ is a regular event. Let us call the union of all such regular events W. Hence, we have that the set of sentential forms Z can generate with one application of a production $Z \rightarrow C_i D_j$ is simply

$$(L^*(Z!F)R^*)^* W (L^*(Z!F)R^*)^*$$

Let A^r be A repeated r times, with $A^0 = \Lambda$. We now want to show that the set of sentential forms generated by Z using n applications of productions of the form $Z \rightarrow C_i B_j$ is

$$((L^*(Z!F)R^*)^* W)^n (L^*(Z!F)R^*)^*$$

Which is equal to

$$= (L^*(Z!F)R^*)^* (W(L(Z!F)R^*)^*)^n$$

The proof is by induction. We have just shown it true for 1, hence we assume it is true for n and show it is true for n+1.

First, we note that if $P,Q \le n$ then the set of sentential forms we can derive from

$$(L^* ZR^*)(L^* ZR^*)$$

where the left Z is expanded using p applications of the rule and question and the right Z using q, is just

$$L^*(L^*(Z!F)R^*)^* (W(L^*(Z!F)R^*)^*)^P R^* L^*(L^*(Z!F)R^*)^* (W(L^*(Z!F)R^*)^*)^q R^*$$

$$= ((L^*(Z!F)R^*)^* W)^P (L^*(Z!F)R^*)^* (W(L^*(Z!F)R^*)^*)^q$$

$$= (L^*(Z!F)R^*)^* (W(L^*(Z!F)R^*)^*)^{p+q}$$

From this we see that the set of sentential forms that can be generated using n applications of the productions starting from $(L^*(Z!F)R^*)^*$ is just $(L^*(Z!F)R^*)^*(W(L^*(Z!F)R^*)^*)^n$.

To show the induction step, we note that there must be a first time a production $Z \rightarrow C_i D_j$ is applied. Following this, as we previously observed, we will have a sentential form in

$$Z \Rightarrow (L^*(Z!F)R^*)^* W(L^*(Z!F)R^*)^*$$

Now let us assume there are p applications of the productions in question to the left of the W and q to the right and p+q=n. From what we have seen before, this means the set of sentential forms we can generate is

$$L^*(L^*(Z!F)R^*)^*(W(L^*(Z!F)R^*)^*)^P R^*)^* W(L^*(Z!F)R^*)^*(W(L^*(Z!F)R^*)^*)^q R^*)^*$$

$$= ((L^*(Z!F)R^*)^*W)^P(L^*(Z!F)R^*)W(L^*(Z!F)R^*)^*(W(L^*(Z!F)R^*)^*)^*)^q$$

$$= ((L^*(Z!F)R^*)^*W)^{p+1}((L^*(Z!F)R^*)^*W)^q(L^*(Z!F)R^*)^*$$

$$= ((L^*(Z!F)R^*)^*W)^{p+q+1}(L^*(Z!F)R^*)^*$$

Hence, the hypothesis holds.

Since we cannot bound the number of times productions of the form $Z \rightarrow C_i B_j$ will be used, we replace the exponent by a star. Adding the final production $Z \rightarrow \Lambda$, we then have that the set of words which Z can produce lie in the regular expression

$$((L^*(\Lambda!F)R^*)^*W)^*(L^*(\Lambda!F)R^*)^*$$

We note that L's, F's, R's and W's can be computed in any quantity in any order, hence the regular event we derive is just

$$(L!F!R!W)^*$$

Example 2: The grammar associated with the subject/object take and grant system [12] is an example of a nondiscriminating grammar. Given the definition of the nonterminals shown in figure 6, it can be demonstrated that we have the grammar shown in figure 7. If we assume A is our starting symbol, we can eliminate productions 3, 4, 6, 8, 11, 12, 14 and 16, thereby giving us a nondiscriminating grammar.

Following the mechanical transformations used in the proof of the theorem, we see the regular expression associated with A is as follows:

$$(bd^*p \mid bd^*ph^*g \mid jh^*g \mid bd^*\ell h*g \mid e \mid bd^*c \mid e \mid fh^*g \mid j \mid bd^*k \mid m \mid nh^*g)^*(a \mid bd^*c)$$

These methods provide us with a means for giving an alternative proof of the theorem 2 in [12].

A = (S,r,S)	B = (S,r,0)	C = (0,r,S)	D = (0,r,0)
E = (S,r,S)	F = (S,r,0)	G = (0,r,S)	H = (0,r,0)
I = (S,w,S)	J = (S,w,0)	K = (0,w,S)	L = (0,w,0)
M = (S,w,S)	N = (S,w,0)	O = (0,w,S)	P = (0,w,0)

Figure 6

1. $A \to ZR_a \quad R_a \to a \quad R_a \to R_b c$

2. $B \to ZR_b \quad R_b \to R_b d \quad R_b \to b$

3. $C \to OA$

4. $D \to OB$

5. $E \to L_e Z \quad L_e \to e \quad L_e \to fL_g$

6. $F \to EJ$

7. $G \to L_g Z \quad L_g \to hL_g \quad L_g \to g$

8. $H \to GJ$

9. $I \to ZR_i \quad R_i \to i \quad R_i \to R_b k$

10. $J \to ZR_j \quad R_j \to j \quad R_j \to R_b \ell$

11. $K \to OI$

12. $L \to OJ$

13. $M \rightarrow L_m Z$ $L_m \rightarrow m$ $L_m \rightarrow nL_g$

14. $N \rightarrow MJ$

15. $O \rightarrow L_o Z$ $L_o \rightarrow g$ $L_o \rightarrow pL_g$

16. $P \rightarrow OJ$

17. $Z \rightarrow ZZ$ $Z \rightarrow A$ $Z \rightarrow E$ $Z \rightarrow I$ $Z \rightarrow M$ $Z \rightarrow JG$ $Z \rightarrow BO$ $Z \rightarrow A$

Figure 7

Non-Grammatical Protection Systems

As useful as the concept of grammatical protection systems is to obtain linear time results to the safety question, a great many systems described in the literature fail to possess this property [2,5,13].

In this section, we wish to show that certain systems, while failing to be truly grammatical, are sufficiently close to grammatical systems to enable us to utilize the results of the last section.

We will say a protection systems is *near-grammatical* if for each right α there is some regular expression E_α such that a necessary condition for a vertex X to α a vertex Y is that they be connected by a path with word in E_α; furthermore, this condition becomes sufficient if at certain identifiable points in the regular expression we check that certain more global conditions are satisfied. We assume these conditions do not involve the vertex X, and they can be verified in constant time (i.e., independent of the number of edges in the graph).

Theorem 4: The safety question for Near-Grammatical systems can be answered in linear time in the size of the protection graph.

Proof: This theorem is proved in a similar fashion to the previous theorem 8. We place "finger" symbols in the places in the regular expression where the conditions are to be verified. Again, we assume to have a finite state automaton with T states and a protection graph with B vertices. Again, we construct a new graph with B×T vertices, only this time we connect an arc from (G_i, T_j) to (G_k, T_i) *iff*

1) there was an arc from G_i to G_k in the original graph, and if we were in state T_j at the point G_i that arc would carry us to state T_ℓ, or,

2) one of the "finger conditions" is true for G_i. In this case, $k = i$ and T_ℓ is the state we would transfer to having accepted that "finger" in the state T_j.

Again, having constructed the graph the result is then a standard reachability argument from automata theory.

Example 3: In many current protection systems having a right to an object does not, as we have been assuming, automatically allow you to pass that right on to another individual. For instance, in the Multics system an individual can have access to a file only if his name is written on a list of individuals who are permitted to have that right. Therefore, if X has certain access privileges, another vertex Y, no matter what relationship it may have with X, cannot obtain those privileges without somehow getting its name on the list of permitted individuals.

We model this situation by means of a special right called *control* [2]. Having control rights over X could, for instance, mean having the ability to write on the list of people who can access X.

We will use the subject-only take and grant transition rules of [12], only we include the concept of control. The control privilege cannot be passed. The rules are shown in Figure 8.

That the system is not grammatical can be easily demonstrated. In the first graph in Figure 9, X can obtain the read rights to Z, but it cannot do so in either of the two following graphs, thereby demonstrating that the ability to obtain rights does not depend solely upon the nature of the path between the two vertices.

We can observe that for $\alpha \ \epsilon \ \{r,w\}$, X can obtain α rights to Y *iff*
1) X and Y are connected by a path in $(\vec{r}\overset{*}{\underset{\leftarrow}{!}}w)$ and
2) every vertex on that path has control rights to Y.

This system is obviously near-grammatical. Hence, the safety question can be answered in linear time.

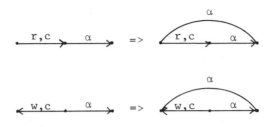

Figure 8

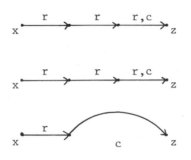

Figure 9

CONCLUSIONS

The security of computer systems is a topic which appears will be of increasing concern in the near future. We feel that true understanding and trust in access privilege mechanisms which are proposed can only be achieved by formal analysis of the capabilities of these systems.

We have attempted to form a basis for the study of protection systems by classifying transformation rules which allow for formal analysis. In doing so, we are trying to fill in the gap between a specific system for which linear time results can be demonstrated [12], and very general systems for which problems are known to be undecidable [7].

We hope that further research will bear out the utility of these studies by allowing us to model protection systems which are actually being used today. We feel the concept of a grammatical or near-grammatical system is natural and justified, since, disregarding those systems which we are labeling "loose", if I have a right and I wish to give it to you, I can only do so in a sense by passing it from hand to hand until it reaches you. Hence, to a certain extent, my ability to pass rights must depend upon the nature of the path between us.

It appears that further research along these lines will have important consequences not only for the formal analysis of abstract protection system models, but also for the practitioner who must design and implement actual access privilege mechanisms.

REFERENCES

[1] Aho, A. V., Hopcroft, J. E. and Ullman, J. D., *The Design and Analysis of Computer Algorithms*, Addison-Wesley, Reading, Mass., 1974.

[2] Bell, D. E. and LaPadula, L. J., *Secure Computer Systems, Vol. I. Mathematical Foundations, Vol. II. A Mathematical Model,* MITRE Corporation Technical Report MTR-2547, 1973.

[3] Dennis, J. B. and Van Horne, E. C.,"Programming Semantics for Multiprogrammed Computations", *Comm. ACM 9,* 3 (March 1966), pp. 143-155.

[4] Graham, G. S. and Denning, P. J., "Protection Principles and Practice", *AFIPS Conference Proceedings,* 40:417-429, 1972.

[5] Graham, R. M., "Protection in an Information Processing Utility", *Comm. ACM 11,* 5 (May 1968) pp. 365-369.

[6] Harrison, M. A., "On Models of Protection in Operating Systems", *4th Symposium on Mathematical Foundations of Computer Science*, (1975). Reprinted in *Lecture Notes in Comp. Science* No. 32, Springer-Verlag.

[7] Harrison, M. A., Ruzzo, W. L. and Ullman, J. D., "Protection in Operating Systems", *Comm. ACM 19,* 8, (August 1976), pp. 461-471.

[8] Harrison, M. A., Private communication.

[9] Hopcroft, J. E. and Ullman, J. D., *Formal Languages and Their Relation To Automata,* Addison-Wesley, Reading, Mass., 1969.

[10] Johnson, D. B., *Algorithms for Shortest Paths,* Ph.D. Thesis, Cornell University, 1973.

[11] Jones, A. K., *Protection in Programmed Systems,* Ph.D. Thesis, Carnegie-Mellon University, 1973.

[12] Jones, A. K., Lipton, R. J. and Snyder, L., "A Linear Time Algorithm for Deciding Security", *Proc. 17th FOCS* (1976).

[13] Saltzer, J. H., "Protection and The Control of Information Sharing in MULTICS", *Comm. ACM 17,* 7 (July 1974), pp. 388-402.

[14] Tsichritzis, D., "Protection in Operating Systems", *Infor. Proc. Letters 1* (1972), pp. 127-131.

[15] Valiant, Leslie G., "General Context-Free Recognition in Less Than Cubic Time", *JCSS 10* (1975), pp. 305-315.

INFORMATION TRANSMISSION
IN SEQUENTIAL PROGRAMS

Ellis Cohen

University of Newcastle upon Tyne
Newcastle upon Tyne
England

I. INTRODUCTION

As the result of executing a sequential program, information can be transmitted from certain variables to other variables. A number of authors have considered the problem of determining the information paths in a program. Their methods have largely been intuitionist. This paper provides a formal approach to information transmission so that information paths can be determined precisely given the formal semantics of a program.

More importantly, the formal approach permits us to answer more selective questions about information transmission. For example, we may not care if output variable b reflects whether input variable a is odd or even. However, we might like to show that b depends upon a in *no other way*. To show this, we assume first that a is even - and then, that a is odd - and show that under neither assumption is information transmitted from a to b. This requires a formal method for describing information transmission given an initial constraint (assumption) concerning the value of the input.

Actually, this paper describes two such formal approaches. The first, *Strong Dependency*, is based on classical information theory, and has been used [Cohen 76, 78] to show that undesirable information paths can be eliminated (e.g. enforcement of confinement [Lampson 73]) in multi-access computer utilities.

The Strong Dependency approach considers whether *variety* can be conveyed as the result of program execution. For example, in executing the program P

P: b ← a div 10 (integer division)

297

information is transmitted from a to b since variety (i.e.
possible different values) in a (e.g. 17 or 34) is conveyed
(i.e. resulting in different values) to b (e.g. 1 or 3, respectively).

The second approach is a deductive one. To determine whether
P transmits information from a to b, we ask whether an observer
of b (seeing the *resulting* value) of b after P's execution can,
armed with a listing of P, deduce anything about the *initial*
value of a. In the example above, if b's result is observed to
be 3, it can be deduced that a initially lies between 30 and 39.
Given an appropriate definition of what it means to deduce something about a's initial value (a point to which I will return
below), strong dependency and the deductive approach can be shown
to be formally equivalent.

The appendix is concerned with proof rules for proving the
absence of information paths in sequential programs. Such rules
have previously been discussed by Denning and Denning [77],
however, as noted above, these have been derived intuitively.
Many of their ideas have impacted the development of the proof
rules in this paper. However, the proof rules discussed here
have been derived formally from the basic definition of strong
dependency. Moreover, the proof rules take into account the fact
that statements may be executed in contexts where certain constraints are known to hold.

Millen [76] has previously noted that assertions can eliminate
certain information paths. In particular, if an assertion
guarantees that the Boolean test in a conditional statement always
evaluates to the same truth value, then possible information
transmission corresponding to the branch that will never be taken
can safely be ignored. This rule is formally derived from strong
dependency in this paper, and in fact, can easily be incorporated
in the Dennings' system as well.

But, this paper shows that assertions may eliminate information paths in a more general way. A variable, actually accessed,
may be ignored as an information source, if the constraint imposed
by the assertion ensures that its value will have no effect on
some result. For example, execution of [b ← a*m] cannot transmit information from a to b if m is constrained to be zero. The
proof rules discussed in this paper allow such information sources
to be eliminated.

The strong dependency formalism yields a theory that is mathematically tractable and can be used to derive the intuitionistic axioms used by Millen and Denning and Denning. Unfortunately, the theory has a number of drawbacks. When certain sorts of initial constraints are used (those formally described as relatively non-autonomous) – strong dependency indicates an absence of information transmission when our intuition indicates that information is indeed transmitted. We'll find that the difficulty is inherent in the information theoretic approach – however, it is possible to produce an alternate deductive approach based on projective logic that eliminates the difficulty.

A closer look at the deductive approach raises additional questions and forces us to distinguish between *definitive* and *contingent* information transmission. An observation of b may permit a definitive deduction concerning a. In the example above, the observation that b was 3 permitted the deduction that $30 \leq a \leq 39$ which does indicate something *definitive* about a's value. However, the program

    P: *if* a = m *then* b ← 3 *else* b ← 0 *fi*

the observation that b is 3 only allows the deduction that [a = m] which does not give any definitive information about a, but it only gives information about a's relationship to other variables (in particular, m). Any information discovered about a alone must be *contingent* on additional knowledge about other variables (e.g. $30 \leq m \leq 39$ would allow the definitive deduction that $30 \leq a \leq 39$). This paper will formalize the notions of definitive and contingent information transmission and will show that in instances where strong dependency can be appropriately applied (i.e. with relatively autonomous constraints), its definition is equivalent to one based on *contingent* information transmission.

The paper closes by considering deductions based on partial or incomplete information and by reflecting briefly on the difficulties of measuring information transmission.

II. SYNTAX AND SEMANTICS

This paper is concerned with defining information transmission in sequential programs, based on formal semantic methods. The semantics are based on a denotational model, following the style to Scott and Strachey [71]. In particular, the entity σ is used to represent the entire data state; execution of a statement is modelled by application of a function operating on σ to yield a new state.

A very simple programming language will be defined. It uses
integer variables only, though expressions may yield Boolean
values for use in Boolean tests. Constructs are provided for
assignment, sequencing, conditional evaluation and for while loops.
There are no procedures.

Since the naming context cannot change, variable names always
refer to the same object. As a result, the state may be divided
into components, each representing a variable. σ.a represents the
value of variable a in state σ, and we write σ1 $=_a$ σ2 to mean that

states σ1 and σ2 are identical except possibly for the value of a
(a similar notation may be found in Hoare and Lauer [74]).

More generally, if A is a set of variables, then σ.A is a
list of the values of each variable a ε A, (according to some
fixed ordering - e.g. lexicographically by variable name) so that

σ1.A = σ2.A   *iff* $(\forall a\varepsilon A)(\sigma1.a = \sigma2.a)$

Also σ1 $=_{\overline{A}}$ σ2 indicates that σ1 and σ2 are identical except

possibly for the values of any number of the variables named in
the set A. Formally

Definition 2-1   σ1 $=_{\overline{A}}$ σ2

$(\forall a\notin A)(\sigma1.a = \sigma2.a)$

Given two states σ1 and σ2, we will find it useful to define a
state σ*, very much like σ1, except that its value for variable
a (or more generally some set of variables A) is taken from σ2.
Formally

Definition 2-2   σ1 $\bigg/$A σ2

σ*   *where* σ* $=_{\overline{A}}$ σ1 &   σ*.A = σ2.A

We will ignore issues of handling exceptions such as overflow
(for example, by assuming modulo arithmetic). Their effects on
information transmission are discussed in Denning & Denning [77]
and Denning, Denning & Graham [74].

The syntax of our simple programming language is:

```
<program> ::= <sequence>
<sequence> ::= <statement>
               <statement> ; <sequence>
<statement> ::= <assignment>
                <conditional>
                <loop>
<assignment> ::= <variable> ← <intexpr>
<conditional> ::= if <boolexpr> then <sequence> fi
                  if <boolexpr> then <sequence>else<sequence>fi
<loop> ::= while <boolexpr> do <sequence> od
```

We won't explain the semantics of evaluating integer and Boolean expressions in detail. Their evaluation is presumed to involve no side effects which alter the state. We write $[E](\sigma)$ to mean the value of expression E in state σ, so for example,

$[b > a+3](\sigma) = \sigma.b > \sigma.a + 3$

If P is a program, the $[P]$ is the corresponding function whose application to an initial state σ results in the final state $[P](\sigma)$ resulting from P's execution. The brackets will be elided where no confusion will result. $P(\sigma)$ may be determined by the following rules:

$[S1; S2] = [S2] \circ [S1]$

("o" is ordinary function composition)

$[v \leftarrow E](\sigma) = \sigma / v \ [E](\sigma)$

$[if\ t\ then\ S1\ else\ S2\ fi](\sigma) =$

$[t](\sigma) \rightarrow [S1](\sigma), [S2](\sigma)$

$[if\ t\ then\ S\ fi](\sigma) =$

$[t](\sigma) \rightarrow [S](\sigma), \sigma$

Intuitively, execution of *while* t *do* S *od* is equivalent to sequentially executing *if* t *then* S *fi* as long as t evaluates *true*. Subsequent (even infinite) execution of *if* t *then* S *fi* will have no further effect on the state. Thus, we can define *while* t *do* S *od* to be the *optimal* fixed point [Manna & Shamir 76] of

$\tau(f) \leq [if\ t\ then\ S\ fi] \circ f$

(Note: The optimal fixed point is required since the least fixed point is undefined. The more usual least fixed point definition can be written as

$$\tau(f) \; <= \; \lambda\sigma.([t](\sigma) \; \rightarrow \; (fo[S])(\sigma), \; \sigma) \qquad\qquad .)$$

Finally, we note that if an assertion ϕ (e.g.[b > a + 3]) is to be satisfied after execution of statement S, then ϕoS must be satisfied prior to execution of S. This follows since, for an initial state σ, $\phi(S(\sigma))$ (equivalently $(\phi oS)(\sigma)$) means that ϕ holds after S is execution. ϕoS is thus the corresponding constraint on the initial state and is the weakest precondition that permits ϕ to hold after execution of S. As a result, Hoare's notation [Hoare 69], $\phi 1 \; \{S\} \; \phi 2$, may be written as $\phi 1 \supset \phi 2 oS$.

III.   STRONG DEPENDENCY

In information theory, information can be transmitted from a source a to a destination b if variety can be conveyed from a to b. If a may initially take on a number of different values, resulting in a number of different values in b after execution of P, then variety is conveyed from a to b as a result of P's execution.

To show that information transmission is possible, we need only find *two* different values of a that yield different values for b after execution of P. We find the different values by finding two states $\sigma 1$ and $\sigma 2$ that differ at a alone, that is, $\sigma 1 \underset{a}{=} \sigma 2$. If they differed elsewhere, we could not be sure that

any resulting difference in b after execution of P was due to a.

b takes on different values after execution of P if $P(\sigma 1).b \neq P(\sigma 2).b$. Formally we say b *strongly depends* on a over execution of P, writing it as

Definition 3-1 $a \; \underset{b}{\overset{P}{\triangleright}}$

$(\exists\sigma 1, \; \sigma 2)(\sigma 1 \underset{a}{=} \sigma 2 \quad P(\sigma 1).b \neq P(\sigma 2).b)$

More generally, we may be concerned whether information can be transmitted from a *set* of variables A to b. In this case, we will look for two states whose values may differ at one or more of the variables in A. Formally

Definition 3-2 $A \; \underset{b}{\overset{P}{\triangleright}}$

$(\exists\sigma 1, \; \sigma 2)(\sigma 1 \underset{A}{=} \sigma 2 \; \wedge \; P(\sigma 1).b \neq P(\sigma 2).b)$

Programs may be guaranteed to execute in an environment in which some entry assertion is known to initially hold true. We have noted that such a guarantee may eliminate certain information paths. For example, consider the program

P: *if* a1 > a2 *then* b ← a *fi*

Information can be transmitted from a to b. However, if the entry assertion [a1 < a2] is known to hold, the "then" part can never be executed and information from a to b is prevented. Formally, we define

Definition 3-3 $\sigma1 \overset{\phi}{\underset{A}{}} \sigma2$

$$\phi(\sigma1) \wedge (\sigma1 \underset{A}{=} \sigma2) \wedge \phi(\sigma2)$$

Definition 3-4 $A \overset{P}{\underset{\phi}{\triangleright}} b$

$$(\sigma1, \sigma2)(\sigma1 \overset{\phi}{\underset{A}{}} \sigma2 \ \bigwedge \ P(\sigma1).b \neq P(\sigma2).b)$$

The difference between this definition and the previous one is that in looking for two states that initially differ at A and produce different results in b, we only consider states that satisfy the entry assertion ϕ.

In the example

P: *if* a1 > a2 *then* b ← a *fi*

ϕ: a1 < a2

we can show $a \neg \overset{P}{\underset{\phi}{\triangleright}} b$

even though $a \overset{P}{\triangleright} b$

Adding an entry assertion reduced the information transmitted. In general, *any* addition or strengthening of an entry assertion may reduce (and can never increase) information transmission.

Formally

> *Theorem 3-1:*
>
> If $\phi1 \supset \phi2$
>
>
> Then $A \underset{\phi1}{\overset{P}{\triangleright}} b \supset A \underset{\phi2}{\overset{P}{\triangleright}} b$

A. *Selective Dependency*

Often, we are not concerned if information can be transmitted from one object to another as long as specific "portions" of the information are protected. Consider the program

  P: b ← x + (a mod 4)

Note that b *does* depend on a (a $\overset{P}{\triangleright}$ b), but only upon the low order two bits of a. We can prove that the rest of a is protected from b by using strong dependency with a constraint.

Suppose we fix the value of the 2 low order bits of a, for example, to 3. Formally, assert

  ϕ: (a mod 4) = 3

We can show that $\neg$ a $\underset{\phi}{\overset{P}{\triangleright}}$ b.

Even though P does convey variety from a to b, ϕ eliminates all the variety that is conveyed.

There are four possible values that may be taken by the 2 lower order bits of a – 0,1,2 and 3 – and this expresses the total variety in these 2 low order bits. To show that this is all the variety in a that is transmitted to b, we must show that no matter how this variety is eliminated (i.e. by constraining the two lower bits of a to be any one of these 4 values), no information can be transmitted from a to b. The four possible values correspond to four constraints

  ϕ_i: (a mod 4) = i   (i – 0,1,2,3)

We have to show that

$$(\forall i)(\quad \neg a \overset{P}{\underset{\phi_i}{\triangleright}} b \quad)$$

In general, $\{\phi_i\}$ might represent a set of constraints that cover the variety in some portion of a source a. Over execution of P, b is *selectively independent* of A given $\{\phi_i\}$ if

$$\neg A \overset{P}{\underset{\phi_i}{\triangleright}} b$$

for each ϕ_i. There are two requirements for selective independence which can be formalized. First, the ϕ_i's must cover all the variety in the selected portion of the source (just as in the example above, (a mod 4) ranged from 0 to 3). A way of guaranteeing this is to ensure that given any system state, the value of the selected portion in that state must be covered by one of the ϕ_i's. Formally

Definition 3-5 $\{\phi_i\}$ is a cover

$$(\forall \sigma \,\exists\, i)(\phi_i(\sigma))$$

Second, if A is an information source, and if $\{\phi_i\}$ covers the variety in some portion of A, then each of the ϕ_i's must *only* name variables in A. In the example above, the ϕ_i's only con-strained the value of a, not the value of any other variables. Formally

Definition 3-6 ρ is A-strict

$$(\forall \sigma1, \sigma2)(\sigma1.A = \sigma2.A \quad \supset \quad \rho(\sigma1) = \rho(\sigma2))$$

That is, ρ is A-strict if changing the value of variables not in A ($\sigma1.A = \sigma2.A$) has no effect on the truth value of ρ.

Finally we define

Definition 3-7   b is selectively independent of
A over P wrt $\{\phi_i\}$.

(1) $\{\phi_i\}$ is a cover

(2) $(\forall i)(\phi_i$ is A-strict)

(3) $(\forall i)(\neg A \;\overset{P}{\underset{\phi_i}{\rhd}}\; b)$

B.   Separation of Variety

As the example above illustrated, b may be selectively
independent of A wrt $\{\phi_i\}$ even though

$A \;\overset{P}{\rhd}\; b$ - in effect, because the ϕ_i's eliminate the variety in

A. If the ϕ_i's did not eliminate any variety in A, then

$(\forall_i)(\neg A \;\overset{P}{\underset{\phi_i}{\rhd}}\; b)$ should guarantee $\neg A \;\overset{P}{\rhd}\; b$. This argument is

made more forcefully in [Cohen 76] and is the basis of a technique called Separation of Variety.

If the ϕ_i's do not eliminate any variety in A, then we can

say that they are A-independent. Formally

Definition 3-8 ρ is A-independent

$$(\forall \sigma1, \; \sigma2)(\sigma1 \underset{A}{=} \sigma2 \supset \rho(\sigma1) = \rho(\sigma2))$$

In other words, ρ is A-independent if changing the value of
A in *any* state $(\sigma1 \underset{A}{=} \sigma2)$ has no effect on the truth value of ρ.

Now we can state

Theorem 3-2: (Separation of Variety)

If $\{\phi_i\}$ is a cover

and $(\forall i)(\phi_i$ is A-independent)

then $(\forall i)(\neg A \,\,\vartriangleright^P_{\phi_i}\, b) \supset \neg A \,\,\vartriangleright^P\, b$

[A more general version of this theorem would replace the last line with

$(\forall i)(\neg A \,\,\vartriangleright^P_{\phi_i}\, b) \supset \neg A \,\,\vartriangleright^P_{\phi}\, b$

This theorem will prove useful in analyzing information transmission in programs with sequential control constructs (Section 4b).

C. *Relative Autonomy*

The strong dependency formalism is not appropriate for certain classes of constraints. In particular, consider the program

P: b ← a1

constrained by the entry assertion

ϕ: a1 = a2

Formally, $\neg$ (a1 $\vartriangleright^P_{\phi}$ b). By definition 3-3, two states $\sigma 1$ and $\sigma 2$ must be found which both satisfy ϕ, yet differ only at a1. This condition cannot be met since ϕ requires that a difference in a1 must be mirrored in a2 as well. Thus, b does not strongly depend upon a1. And yet, intuitively, information is transmitted from a1 to b. What's the problem?

If we had constrained a1 to be a particular constant, for example

ϕ: a1 = 8

we would have similarly found that no information is transmitted
from al to b, that is,

$\neg$(al $\underset{\phi}{\boxed{\rhd}^P}$ b). And with good reason. (Remembering our dis-

cussion about selective dependency). Once al has been constrained
to be 8, there is no other information that can be squeezed out
of al to be transmitted to b.

Now, in asking about al $\boxed{\rhd}$ b, we are implicitly creating a

view of a system having al as a source and b as a destination.
a2 is wholly outside the system. So, constraining al to be the
same as a2 is, with respect to the system where al is sole source,
just like constraining al to be constant.

If we want to get the "intuitively" right answer about
information transmission, we had better include a2 in the system
as well, and in fact, we do find that

{al, a2} $\underset{\phi}{\boxed{\rhd}^P}$ b

More generally, we have to make sure in determining A $\underset{\phi}{\boxed{\rhd}}$ b,

that ϕ does not relate the values of variables in A to the value
of variables outside of A. Formally, we require ϕ to be
A-autonomous, defining

Definition 3-9 ϕ is A-autonomous

$(\forall \sigma 1, \sigma 2)(\phi(\sigma 1) \quad \wedge \quad \phi(\sigma 2) \quad \supset \quad \phi(\sigma 1/\ A\sigma 2))$

It can be shown [Cohen 76] that this definition requires ϕ to be
of the form $\phi 1 \wedge \phi 2$ (either $\phi 1$ or $\phi 2$ may be absent) where $\phi 1$ only
concerns variables in A (that is, $\phi 1$ is A-strict), and $\phi 2$ only
concerns variables outside of A (that is, $\phi 2$ is A-independent).

By matching the sources autonomously to the initial
constraint, strong dependency can be used to accurately reflect
information transmission. However, in the latter part of the
paper, we will see how the insistance on relatively autonomous
constraints can be eliminated through use of a different
formalism.

IV.   THE DEDUCTIVE VIEWPOINT

The last section concentrated on an information theoretic (in the classical sense) approach to information transmission. From this section on, the focus switches to a deductive viewpoint. This section shows that a particular deductive approach is equivalent to the approach based on strong dependency.

The deductive viewpoint argues that information can be transmitted from A to b over execution of program P if a value of b after execution of P can be used to deduce properties of the initial values of variables in A. For example, if P is the program

P: b ← a + 4

and b's final value is 12, then we can deduce that a's initial value was 8. In effect, we have taken the exit assertion [b=12] and have backsubstituted it through P to obtain the weakest precondition

[b=12]oP   =   [a=8]

It is not the case that every final value of b must provide information about a. Consider

P: *if* m > 0 *then* b ← abs(a)

else b ← -1 *fi*

If b's final value is observed to be -1, then no information can be deduced about a, only about m, since [b = -1]oP = [m ≤ 0]. We only require that *some* final value of b yield information about a in order to demonstrate the possibility of information transmission from a to b. In this case

[b = 7]oP = [m > 0 ∧ (a = 7 ∨ a = -7)]

We may say that information can be transmitted from A to b over execution of P if

(∃v)([b = v]oP "says something about" A)

We shall find that different deductive approaches crucially differ, depending upon the interpretation of: an assertion ρ "says something about" A.

We might choose a syntactic definition - looking to see whether any variable in A appears in ρ [or *any* equivalent predicate - which eliminates the problem of [a = a]]. Fortunately, there is an equivalent semantic definition.

If variables in A are used in determining the truth value of ρ, then some change in the values of A must affect the truth value of ρ. Formally,

Definition 4-1 ρ is A-independent

$$(\exists \sigma 1, \sigma 2)(\sigma 1 \underset{A}{=} \sigma 2 \ \wedge \ \rho(\sigma 1) \neq \rho(\sigma 2))$$

Formally then, we can say that information can be transmitted from A to b if

$$(\exists v)(\ [b = v]oP \text{ is A-dependent })$$

Next, we consider the effect of an entry assertion. Consider the example

P: $b \leftarrow b + a*m$

with the assertion ϕ: [m = 0]. Clearly, no information can be transmitted from a to b since b's value never changes if ϕ holds.

For any final value v to b,

$$[b = v]oP = [a*m = (b-v)]$$

which is a-dependent. However, if this precondition is evaluated only for those states satisfying ϕ, then changing the value of a has no effect on the resulting truth value (since a*m is always 0). Formally, [b = v]oP is a-independent given ϕ. We define

Definition 4-2 ρ is A-dependent given ϕ

$$(\exists \sigma 1, \sigma 2)(\sigma 1 \underset{A}{\overset{\phi}{=}} \sigma 2 \ \wedge \ \rho(\sigma 1) \neq \rho(\sigma 2))$$

Thus, in the presence of an initial constraint ϕ, the definition for deductive information transmission from A to b over execution of P is

$$(\exists v)(\ [b = v]oP \text{ is A-dependent given } \phi \ )$$

It is very easy to prove that this definition is equivalent to the one for strong dependency.

Theorem 4-1

$$A \ \underset{\phi}{\triangleright}^{P} \ b \ \textit{iff} \ (\exists v)(\ [b=v]oP \ \text{is A-dependent given } \phi)$$

Consider the example

P: b ← al

ϕ: al = 8

According to strong dependency, al $\underset{\phi}{\triangleright}^{P}$ b, for ϕ eliminates

variety from al – none remains to be transmitted to b. This situation is analyzed in terms of the deductive viewpoint in the following way:

After execution of P, b will be observed to have the value 8. The weakest precondition of [b=8] for P is, of course, [al=8]. This is *not* al-dependent given ϕ. Essentially it provides no *more* information about al than ϕ already provides.

In essence, the deductive viewpoint argues, that if P is executed in an environment *known* to be constrained by ϕ, then information can be transmitted from A to b only if some observation of b permits a deduction that provides more information than ϕ about A's initial value.

In discussing separation of variety, we noted that information might be transmitted from a to b even though all but a *portion of* a was protected. A similar phenomena is illustrated by the following program

P: b ← abs(b)*sign(a)

(sign(x) <= *if* x < 0 *then* –1 *else* 1 *fi*)

Information from a is transmitted to b, a $\triangleright^{P}$ b, but only

a *portion of* b is affected – in this case, b's sign. Imagine if an observer of b could only observe b's absolute value and not b's sign. That is, after P's execution, one could only assert [abs(b)=k]. Note that its precondition is the same.

[abs(b) = k]oP = [abs(b) = k]

which is certainly not a-dependent.

In general, suppose $\bar{\phi}_{b}$ is some post-condition that involves

b alone (that is, $\bar{\phi}_{b}$ is b-strict) which characterizes an observation of b - for example

$$\bar{\phi}_b : \quad abs(b) = k$$

The example above illustrates that A $\rhd_{\phi}^{P}$ b does not necessarily

ensure that

$\bar{\phi}_b oP$ is A-dependent given ϕ

$\bar{\phi}_b$ may need to be stricter to ensure that the precondition is

A-dependent. In particular, it may have to be of the form

$$\bar{\phi}_b : \quad b = v$$

Theorem 4-1 guarantees that some such $\bar{\phi}_b$ can always be found, if

information is transmitted from A to b.

V.   PROJECTIVE INFERENCE

Since the deductive viewpoint (as described in the previous
section) is equivalent to the strong dependency formalism, it
naturally has the same difficulties when used with non-autonomous
constraints. This section shows how these difficulties can be
eliminated by basing the deductive definition of information
transmission on a formalism derived from projective logic.

Consider the program

P: b ← al

ϕ: al = a2

Suppose that execution of P results in a value of 8 for b.
Then we can deduce [b=8]oP = [al=8]. Intuitively, this provides
us with more information about al than [al=a2] and yet, [al=8] is
not al-dependent *given* [al=a2].

The reason is similar to that described in Section 3c - asking
about al-dependence is akin to treating the system as though a2
were outside of it - and therefore treats a2 as containing a value
that might as well be constant. In that case, the example reduces
to the one following theorem 4-1 (for if a2 is constant, it must
be 8) and no information is transmitted from al to b.

In this section, we will pursue another approach and find a
formal way of expressing the fact that [al=8] *is* more informative
about al than [al=a2]. The formalism is based on projective logic.

A. Projective Logic

In this section, we will answer the following question: Given an arbitrary predicate ρ constraining the values of variables both in and out of the set A, what is the strongest deduction that can be made constraining variables in A alone? That deduction will be written as ρ_A.

Consider the predicate

$$\rho: \quad a1 = 2 \lor (a1 = 3 \land a2 = 3)$$

The strongest thing that can be said about a1 is that

$$\rho_A: \quad a1 = 2 \lor a1 = 3$$

This can best be illustrated by the diagram below that graphs possible values of a1 and a2.

ρ	a2 = 0	1	2	3	4	5	...		ρ_{a1}
0									
1									
2	X	X	X	X	X	X..			X
3				X					X
4									
5									
6									
.									.
.									.
.									.

(left column label: al)

In the left graph, the X's represent possible values of \<a1, a2\> pairs. A value of a1 can occur if some \<a1, a2\> value can occur. The strongest deduction that constrains a1 alone describes the possible values of a1. The diagram indicates that

it is just the projection of ρ onto a1. Formally, it can be
defined as

> *Definition 5-1* $\rho_A(\sigma)$

$$(\exists\sigma')(\rho(\ \sigma'\ \overline{/A}\ \sigma)\ )$$

Similarly, it is possible to consider the strongest deduction,
given   , that can be made about variables *not* in A. I write this
as $\rho/_A$. It can be defined as

> *Definition 5-2* $\rho/_A$

$$(\exists\sigma')(\rho(\ \sigma\ \overline{/A}\ \sigma'))$$

The following table presents some examples.

ρ	ρ_{a1}	$\rho/_{a1}$
true	true	true
false	false	false
a1 = 9	a1 = 9	true
a1 = 9 ∧ a2 = 4	a1 = 9	a2 = 4
a1 = 9 ∨ a2 = 4	true	true
a1 = a2	true	true
2*a1 = 3*a2	a1 ≡ 0 (mod 3)	Even(a2)
(a1,a2 are integers)		

The fact that $[a1 = a2]_{a1}$ is true follows from the fact that

[a1 = a2] constrains the particular value of a1 in no way. No
matter what value of a1 is chosen, a value of a2 can be chosen
(i.e. equal to a1) that makes the predicate hold. The projection
of the graph of [a1 = a2] onto a1 illustrates this fact

a2 \ a1	0	1	2	3	4	5		ρ_{a1}
0	X							X
1		X						X
2			X					X
3				X				X
4					X			X
5						X		X

ρ $a1$

It should be clear that ρ_A is always A-strict and that $\rho/_A$ is always A-independent. And, in fact

Theorem 5-1

$\rho = \rho_A \wedge \rho/_A$ *iff* ρ is A-autonomous as is illustrated by the example of

$[a1 = 9 \wedge a2 = 4]$

The use of projections allows an elegant alternate definition of strong dependency based on the discussion at the end of Section 4. It was noted that $A \,\vartriangleright^P_{\phi}\, b$ ensured that for some b-strict post-condition,

$\bar{\phi}_b \circ P$ is A-dependent given ϕ

In general, $\bar{\phi}_b$ can be thought of as the projection onto b of a broader post-condition $\bar{\phi}$, and we can define strong dependency as

Definition 5-3 $A \,\vartriangleright^P_{\phi}\, b$

$(\bar{\exists\phi})(\bar{\phi}_b \circ P$ is A-dependent given $\phi)$

B. Definitive Dependency

We can now return to the question of whether [a1 = 8] provides more information about a1 than [a1 = a2] – or more generally, whether ρ provides more information about A than ϕ.

Whether or not we know ρ, we know ϕ, thus, we really ask – does $\rho \wedge \phi$ provide more information about A than ϕ alone? The last section indicates that a predicate provides information about A if it (or more precisely, its projection onto A) determines the values that A might have taken. The more precisely A's values can be determined, the more information about A is provided. $\rho \wedge \phi$ provides more information about A than ϕ if $(\rho \wedge \phi)_A$

determines A's possible value more precisely than ϕ_A – that is – if

$$(\rho \wedge \phi)_A \subset \phi_A$$

(Interpret "$\subset$" as proper set inclusion, relating the sets characterized by the predicates $(\rho \wedge \phi)_A$ and ϕ_A).

In the example above, where ρ: [a1 = 8] and ϕ: [a1 = a2],

ϕ_A: true $(\rho \wedge \phi)_A$: [a1 = 8].

Therefore

$$(\rho \wedge \phi)_A \subset \phi_A,$$

so,

ρ does provide more information about a1 than ϕ.

Before supplying a formal definition, there is one last difficulty to be avoided – that of using preconditions, derived from *impossible* observations.

Consider the system

P: b ← a

ϕ: a = 8

Obviously, no information can be transmitted from a to b. However, suppose (ignoring for a moment the fact that ϕ initially is guaranteed to hold) that b is observed to be 37 after execution of P. The precondition ρ is [b = 37]oP = [a = 37].

Now, $\rho \wedge \phi$ is false, so

$$(\rho \wedge \phi)_a = \text{false} \subset \phi_a = [a = 8]$$

Obviously, we have to exclude illegal observations by requiring that $(\rho \wedge \phi)_A$ not be false. We formally define

   Definition 5-4 ρ is A-definitive given ϕ

$$\text{false} \subset (\rho \wedge \phi)_A \subset \phi_A$$

If no initial constraint is given, ϕ can be taken as true and we define

   Definition 5-5 ρ is A-definitive

$$\text{false} \subset \rho_A \subset \text{true}$$

We can now use A-definitive-ness to replace A-dependence (in Definition 5-3) to produce a new formalism for information transmission - *definitive* dependency.

   Definition 5-6   b definitively depends on A over P given ϕ

$$(\overline{\exists \phi})(\overline{\phi}_b \text{oP is A-definitive given } \phi)$$

   Definition 5-7   b definitively depends on A over P

$$(\overline{\exists \phi})(\overline{\phi}_b \text{oP is A-definitive})$$

VI. CONTINGENT DEPENDENCY

The previous section closed with a new definition of information transmission - *definitive* dependency. This section will show how it differs from strong dependency. In addition, a new variant, *contingent* dependency, will be defined. For autonomous constraints, it is shown to be equivalent to strong dependency.

Consider the program

P: *if* al $\neq$ a2 *then* b $\leftarrow$ 0 *else* b $\leftarrow$ 1 *fi*

Is information transmitted from al to b? Strong dependency would
indicate that the answer is yes - it is easy to show that

al $\triangleright^P$ b. Definitive dependency indicates that the answer is
no.

If b is observed to be 1, then we obtain the precondition

[b=1]oP = [al=a2]

But its projection onto al is *true*; [al=a2] is hardly al-
definitive. In effect, an observation of b can tell us whether
or not al equals a2, but indicates nothing *definitive* about the
value of al.

Consider another example

P: b ← (al + a2) mod 2^{16}

It is easy to see that al $\triangleright^P$ b. However, the observation
[b=k] leads to the precondition [(al + a2) mod 2^{16} = k]. Its
projection onto al is also *true*; it is not al-definitive. Given
any value of al, a value of a2 can be found such that the sum
(modulo 2^{16}) is k.

In both of the cases above, b does not definitively depend
upon either al or a2, though it does depend on the set {al, a2}.
That is

al *does not* definitively depend on b over P, though {al, a2}
does definitively depend on b over P.

Should b depend upon al or not? The hard line answer is no.
But let's pursue the alternative for a bit.

The predicate [al=a2], while not al-definitive does give some
information about al, but only *contingent* on some (perhaps fuzzy)
information about a2. For example, if we know something about the
distribution of values that a2 takes, [al = a2] provides the same
distribution information about al, and that can be considered to
be definitive information about al.

Consider another example: [al=4 ∨ a2=7] is not al-definitive
its projection onto al yields *true*. But given additional information that implies that a2 is not 7, we can determine that al
must be 4. It is more likely that we might know that a2 is (only)
probably not 7, and thus that al is *probably* 4. In a sense,

contingency pushes the probability to the limit.

In general, we can say that a predicate is A-contingent if *given* additional information, not concerning A (i.e. A-independent), we can determine that the predicate *is* A-definitive. $\hat{\phi}/_A$ can indicate the additional information (it represents a broader assertion $\hat{\phi}$ that has constraints concerning A removed from it (Section 5A) - and is therefore A-independent) and we can define

Definition 6-1   ρ is A-contingent

$$(\exists\hat{\phi})(\rho \text{ is A-definitive given } \hat{\phi}/_A)$$

In the example above, ρ was [a1 = 4 ∨ a2 = 7] and we chose $\hat{\phi} = \hat{\phi}/_{a1} = $ [a2 ≠ 7] to show that ρ was a1-contingent.

Next, taking an initial constraint into account, define

Definition 6-2   ρ is A-contingent given φ

$$(\exists\hat{\phi})(\rho \text{ is A-definitive given } \hat{\phi}/_A \wedge \hat{\phi})$$

Using these definitions, we can define *contingent* dependency as

Definition 6-3   A ▷ b (with P above, b at right)

$$(\exists\bar{\hat{\phi}})(\bar{\phi}_b\text{oP is A-contingent})$$

Definition 6-4   A ▷ b (with P above, φ below)

$$(\exists\bar{\hat{\phi}})(\phi_b\text{oP is A-contingent given }\phi)$$

The good news is that in the absence of a constraint, or given a relatively autonomous constraint, contingent dependency and strong dependency are equivalent. The crucial theorem is

Theorem 6-1

If   φ is A-autonomous
then
       ρ is A-dependent given φ
   iff ρ is A-contingent given φ

It follows directly that

Theorem 6-2

If ϕ is A-autonomous

then A $\triangleright_\phi^P$ b *iff* A$\triangleright_\phi^P$ b

Contingent dependency thus has all of the advantages of strong dependency yet it deals with non-autonomous constraints as well. Consider a final example

P: b ← a1 + a2

ϕ: a1 = a3

Using either strong, definitive or contingent dependency, we can show that execution of P given ϕ transmits information from {a1, a2, a3} to b. We might, however, like to show that information is transmitted from a1 (alone) to b. Only contingent dependency indicates that such transmission takes place.

Strong dependency fails immediately, since in a system with a1 as sole potential source, a3 is treated as a constant (Section 5), and ϕ therefore effectively eliminates all variety from a1.

An observation of b yields the precondition ρ: [a1+a2=k] for some observed value k. It provides no definitive information about a1, even given ϕ, and thus definitive dependency fails as well. However, ρ is a1-contingent, and thus

a1 $\triangleright_\phi^P$ b.

In general, whenever information is transmitted from a set A to b, information to b is transmitted from at least one object in A. Formally

Theorem 6-3

A $\triangleright_\phi^P$ b ⊃ (∃a∈A)(a $\triangleright_\phi^P$ b)

No such theorem holds for either strong or definitive dependency as past examples have indicated.

VII. CONCLUDING NOTES

Ordinarily, questions of information transmission are quantitative rather than qualitative. This paper (and previous formal
work in this area) has concentrated on purely qualitative results
– has information been transmitted from a to b at all? This
section briefly touches on qualitative questions - how much information is transmitted, and what is its value?

Consider the program

P: *if* a > 0 *then* b ← m *else* b ← -m *fi*

According to definitive dependency, information *cannot* be transmitted from a to b. If b is observed to be 27, a might be greater
than 0 (if m were 27), but might equally likely be less than or
equal to 0 (if m were -27). According to contingent dependency,
information *can* be transmitted from a to b, contingent, or course,
on information about m - its sign.

If m's sign is known with certainty, information can certainly
be transmitted from a to b; our conclusions are less certain if we
know less about m. If, we are only 70% certain that m is (say)
positive, then we can be 70% certain about the sign of a.

In information theoretic terms, we can argue that complete
uncertainty of m's sign means that *zero* bits of information are
transmitted from a to b; complete knowledge of m's sign allows *one*
bit of information (representing a's sign) to be transmitted;
partial or probabilistic knowledge permits an intermediate amount
of information transmission. More generally, by using the weakest
precondition derived from a final observation, in conjunction with
statistical information, an information theoretic measure of the
information transmitted can be determined. The presumption is
that arbitrary contingent information can be replaced by more
precise statistical information regarding what is already known.

Information theoretic computations will presumably be useful
in statistical data bases. For example, as part of a census, a
respondent may supply his/her sex. Presumably the information
will only be used for statistical purposes. However, the potential
for misuse is certainly present.

Legitimate use of the data should provide very little opportunity for information to be gained about the respondent's sex.
A secure system might only allow a history of queries that transmitted at most .1 bits of information from data about any
respondent's sex. More interestingly, a respondent might have
the option of determining the level of information that could be
discovered about data he/she provided.

Except for very simple sorts of data, a strict information theoretic measure may not be appropriate; all bits are not equal. For example, the high order bits of a variable containing salary information is likely to be more valuable than the low order bits, and a suitable measure might be weighted accordingly.

REFERENCES

Cohen 76.   E. Cohen, "Strong Dependency: A Formalism for Describing Information Transmission in Computational Systems", CMU-C.S.T.R. August 1976.

Cohen 77.   E. Cohen, "Information Transmission in Computational Systems" Proc. 6th Symp. on Op. Sys. Princ., November 1977.

Cohen 78.   E. Cohen, "Proof of a Solution to the Confinement Problem". (Available from author).

Denning & Denning 77.   D. Denning, P. Denning, "Certification of Programs for Secure Information Flow", CACM 20, 7 (July 1977).

Denning, Denning & Graham 74.   D. Denning, P. Denning, G. S. Graham, "Selectively Confined Subsystems", Proc. Intl. Workshop on Protection in Operating Systems, IRIA Laboria (France), August 1974.

Hoare 69.   C.A.R. Hoare, "An Axiomatic Basis for Computer Programming", CACM 2, 10 (October 1969).

Hoare & Lauer 74.   C.A.R. Hoare, P. Lauer, "Consistent and Complementary Formal Theories of the Semantics of Programming Languages", Acta Informatica 3 (1974).

Jones & Lipton 75.   A. Jones, R. Lipton, "The Enforcement of Security Policies for Computations", Proc. 5th Symp. on Operating System Principles, November 1975.

Lampson 73.   B. Lampson, "A Note on the Confinement Problem", CACM 16, 10 (October 1973).

Manna & Shamir 76.   Z. Manna, A. Shamir, "The Theoretical Aspects of the Optimal Fixedpoint", Stanford AIM-277, March 1976.

Millen 76.   J. Millen, "Security Kernel Validation in Practice", CACM 19, 5 (May 1976).

Scott & Strachey 71.   D. Scott, C. Strachey, "Towards a Mathematical Semantics for Computer Languages", Oxford Univ. PRG-6, August 1971.

A. Appendix. Proof Rules for Sequential Programs

Section 2 described a programming language with four constructs
- assignment, sequential execution, conditionals and loops. This
appendix will develop proof rules for each construct, derived from
the definition of strong dependency, so that absence of information
paths can be determined by incrementally considering each construct
of a program.

A. Assignment

In general, an assignment changes the value of its target
variable. As a result, information may be transmitted from
variables appearing in the source expression to the target
variable. However, entry assertions may eliminate information
paths. Consider the example

$$P: \quad b \leftarrow a*m + 8$$

With the entry assertion [m=0], no information can be transmitted
from a to b. In fact, execution of P will always result in an
assignment of the value 8 to b. In general, if *every* execution
of a program P (satisfying an entry assertion ϕ) sets b to the
same constant value, then no information from any source is transmitted to it.

Definition A-1   P makes b constant given ϕ

$$(\exists v \forall \sigma)(\phi(\sigma) \supset P(\sigma).b = v)$$

Theorem A-1

If P makes b constant given ϕ

then $(\forall A)(\neg A \mathrel{\vcenter{\hbox{$\triangleright$}}}_{\phi}^{P} b)$

If a variable is not the target of an assignment, it retains
its original value. Its useful to think that the information it
contains is retransmitted to it so that in execution of

$$P: \quad b \leftarrow a$$

$m \mathrel{\vcenter{\hbox{$\triangleright$}}}^{P} m$ for every m, m $\neq$ b.

Even the target of an assignment may have information
"retransmitted" to it if it appears in the source expression as
well, so that in

P: b ← b + a*m

we find that b $\triangleright^P$ b as well as a $\triangleright^P$ b.

Note that if the above program were executed in an environment where [m=0], no information could be transmitted from a to b. No matter what a's value were, b's value would not change as the result of P's execution. In general, *some* execution of P (satisfying an entry assertion φ) must change the value of a variable if information is to be transmitted to it from any other variables. Formally

Definition A-2   P changes b given φ

(∃σ)(φ(σ) ∧ σ.b ≠ P(σ).b)

Theorem A-2

If A $\triangleright^P_φ$ b (b ∉ A)

then P changes b given φ

B. *Sequential Execution*

The proof fules for sequential execution are based on the idea of *accumulating* the set of variables to which information from some source may be transmitted after execution of the *initial* part of a sequence of statements – and then determining whether information can be transmitted from this set to some final target as the result of executing the *remainder* of the sequence (whew – an example illustrating this will be found below). Jones and Lipton [75] used this idea as part of a dynamic mechanism for preventing information transmission. In this section, a static version is derived from the definition of strong dependency, and which takes initial and intermediate assertions into account.

Consider the two programs

P1:   m ← a; b ← m

P2:   m ← a; b ← a

Both programs transmit information from a to b. In both cases, the *initial* statement of the sequence is [m ← a], and its execution results in transmission of information from a to m and also in "retransmission of information" from a to a. Information originally in a is now held in both a and m. If we define

Definition A-3   A $\triangleright^{P}$ *

$\{m \mid A \ \triangleright^{P} \ m\}$

then, if S is [m ← a], a $\triangleright^{S}$ * = {a, m}

Now, take S1 and S2 respectively, as

S1: b ← m

S2: b ← a

These are the respective *remainders* of the programs P1 and P2.
P1 or P2 transmits information from a to b if information from the
intermediate *accumulated* set {a, m} is transmitted to b by
execution of S1 or S2 respectively. And in fact, we do find that
both

{a, m} $\triangleright^{S1}$ b and {a, m} $\triangleright^{S2}$ b.

More precisely, m $\triangleright^{S1}$ b and a $\triangleright^{S2}$ b. However, if information is transmitted from a subset or element (e.g. m) of a set
(e.g. {a, m}), then information is transmitted from the whole set
as well. Formally

Theorem A-3

If   A1 ⊆ A2

then A1 $\triangleright^{P}_{\phi}$ b ⊃ A2 $\triangleright^{P}_{\phi}$ b

The example above suggests the following rule: If P is [S;S']

and A $\triangleright^{S}$ * = M, then

M $\triangleright^{S'}$ b *iff* A $\triangleright^{P}$ b

Unfortunately, this does not hold. The forward implication is not true - an example will be discussed below. The reverse implication *does* hold, and is the more important part since we are usually more concerned with showing the absence rather than the presence of an information path. Formally

Theorem A-4

If P is [S; S']

and M = A $\triangleright^S$ *

then ⌐ M $\triangleright^{S'}_{} b \supset \urcorner A \triangleright^P b$

Next we consider the effect of initial constraints. In particular, initial constraints may give rise to intermediate assertions which prevent information transmission in the remainder of a sequence as the next example indicates. Consider the program P: [S; S'] where

S: *if* m1 > 4 *then* m2 ← m1 *fi*

S': *if* m1 ≠ m2 *then* b ← 1 *fi*

with the entry assertion

φ: m1 > 19

After execution of S, the intermediate assertion φ' holds, where

φ: m1 = m2

that is, φ ⊃ φ' oS, or in Hoare's notation, φ{S}φ'. Since S' is executed in an environment in which φ' holds, then "then" part of S' is not executed and

(a $\triangleright^{S'}_{\phi'} b$). The earlier theorem can be extended in the

following way:

Definition A-4   A $\triangleright^P_{\phi}$ *

{m | A $\triangleright^P_{\phi}$ m}

Theorem A-5

> If P is S; S'
>
> and $\phi \supset \phi' \circ S$
>
> and $M = A \triangleright_\phi^S$ *
>
> then $\neg\, M \triangleright_{\phi'}^{S'} b \supset \neg A \triangleright_\phi^P b$

The use of intermediate assertions allows for some sloppiness (overestimation) in determining

$A \triangleright_\phi^S$ * . Consider the program

P = [S; S'], where

S: ml ← a; m2 ← ml; *if* a > 0 *then* ml ← 0 *fi*

S':   b ← ml   and

ϕ: a > 0

We might guess that $A \triangleright_\phi^S$ * is {a, ml, m2}. Actually, it is just {a, m2} by theorem A-1, since ϕ guarantees that ml is always set to zero. However, picking ϕ' to be [ml=0]($\phi \supset \phi' \circ S$), we can immediately show that

$\{a,\ ml,\ m2\} \triangleright_{\phi'}^{S'} b$ which also follows from theorem A-1

since S' makes b constant (i.e. zero) given ϕ'.

I indicated earlier that the converse of theorem A-4 does not hold. More generally, there exist programs P of the form [S; S'] where $M = A \triangleright_\phi^S$ *, such that for *any* ϕ' such that $\phi \supset \phi' \circ S$,

$M \triangleright_{\phi'}^{S'} b$ even though $\neg A \triangleright_\phi^P b$. For example, consider

S: *if* q ≠ 0 *then* m ← a *fi*

S':   *if* q = 0 *then* b ← m *if*

with ϕ taken as the always true predicate. The strictest possible choice for ϕ' is

$[q = 0 \wedge m = a]$, yet

$(a \; \triangleright_{\phi}^{S} \; *) = \{a, m\}$ and $\{a, m\} \; \triangleright_{\phi'}^{S'} \; b$ even though $\neg a \; \triangleright_{\phi}^{P} \; b.$

This example is discussed more fully in [Cohen 76,77], where it is shown that the technique of *Separation of Variety* (Section 3B) can be used in conjunction with (the equivalent of) theorem A-5 to prove the absence of an information path.

Define $\phi1$: $[q = 0]$ and $\phi2$: $[q \neq 0]$. $\{\phi1, \phi2\}$ form a cover

and are both independent of a. By separation of variety

(theorem 3-2), $\neg a \; \triangleright^{P} \; b$ follows from $\neg a \; \triangleright_{\phi1}^{P}$ and $\neg a \; \triangleright_{\phi2}^{P} \; b.$

Considering $\phi1$ first, note that

$(a \; \triangleright_{\phi1}^{S} \; *) = \{a\}$ and $\neg\{a\} \; \triangleright^{S'} \; b.$

Considering $\phi2$ then, pick $\phi2'$: $[q \neq 0]$ (note $\phi2 \supset \phi2'$ oS)

and though $(a \; \triangleright_{\phi2}^{S} \; *) = \{a, m\}, \neg\{a, m\} \; \triangleright_{\phi2'}^{S'} \; b.$

In both cases, theorem A-5 can be applied to show

$\neg a \; \triangleright_{\phi i}^{P} \; b$ $(i = 1, 2)$. By Separation of Variety (Theorem A-5)

$\neg a \; \triangleright^{P} \; b.$

C. *Conditionals*

In earlier examples, we saw that an entry assertion ϕ could guarantee that the Boolean test t in the conditional

P: *if* t *then* S' *fi*

might never be satisfied and as a result, S' would never be executed. More generally, S' is executed only in states in which ϕ and t both hold. Information transmission due to P

(with entry assertion ϕ) can be determined by considering transmission due to S' with entry conditions derived from both ϕ and
t.

The general case is demonstrated by the program

    P: *if* m = ml *then* b ← a*(ml = m2) *fi*

The "then" part is only executed when [m - ml] holds. If the
entry assertion is [m = m2], the "then" part is executed when
both [m - ml] and]m = m2] hold, thus [ml = m2] holds. In that
case, ml - m2 = 0, and b is always assigned the constant value 0,
so by theorem A-1 no information about a can be transmitted to b.

We *might like to show* that if P were

    P: *if* t *then* S' *fi*

and $\phi \wedge t \supset \phi'$

then $\neg(A \mathrel{\vcenter{\hbox{$\triangleright$}}}_{\phi'}^{S'} b) \supset \neg (A \mathrel{\vcenter{\hbox{$\triangleright$}}}_{\phi}^{P} b)$

However, as noted elsewhere [Cohen 76, Denning & Denning 77,
Jones & Lipton 75], information can be transmitted in other ways.
For example, in the program

    P: *if* a > 0 *then* b ← 8 *fi*

information can be transmitted from a to b.

The value in b resulting from execution of P does carry
information about a's initial value. Suppose b is initially 17.
If b remains 17 after P executes, then initially [a = 0], if
b is 8, initially [a > 0]. to Prevent information transmission
from a to b, in executing

    P: *if* t *then* S' *fi*

we must further guarantee that *either* t does not depend upon the
value of a *or* that S' does not make any assignment to b. In fact,
consideration of the relevant assertions allows a weakening of
these conditions.

First consider the program

    P: *if* a = 0 ∨ m = 4 *then* b ← 8 *fi*

with entry assertion ϕ: [a = 9]. Even though the test does depend upon a, the entry assertion effectively nullifies that dependency. While [a = 0 ∨ m = 4] is a-dependent, information is not transmitted from a to b because the condition is *not* a-dependent *given* [a = 9].

Formally define

Definition A-5 ρ is A-independent given ϕ

$$(\forall\sigma1, \sigma2)(\sigma1 \frac{\phi}{A} \sigma2 \supset \rho(\sigma1) = \rho(\sigma2))$$

This definition is much like definition 3-8, except only those states are considered which satisfy the entry assertion ϕ.

Next consider the program

P: *if* a = 0 *then* b ← b + m *fi*

with the entry assertion

ϕ: m = 0

Even though an assignment is made to b, the value of b does not change and as a result, again no information can be transmitted from a to b. Formally, we require that S does not change b given ϕ(the negation of definition A-2).

We can now state the theorem for conditionals as

Theorem A-6

If P is *if* t *then* S' *fi*

and $\phi \wedge t \supset \phi'$ then

(t is A-independent given ϕ

S' does not change b given ϕ') $\supset$

$$(\neg (A \overset{S'}{\underset{\phi'}{\triangleright}} b) \supset \neg (A \overset{P}{\underset{\phi}{\triangleright}} b))$$

This theorem can be easily extended to handle conditionals with two branches by simple noting that the "else" part is executed only for states satisfying both ϕ and $\neg$t. Formally

Theorem A-7

If P is *if* t *then* S1 *else* S2 *fi*

and $\phi \wedge t \supset \phi1$

and $\phi \wedge \neg t \supset \phi2$ then

(t is A-independent given ϕ

     (S1 does not change b given $\phi1 \vee$

       S2 does not change b given $\phi2$)) $\supset$

$$(\neg (A \overset{S1}{\underset{\phi1}{\triangleright}} b \vee A \overset{S2}{\underset{\phi2}{\triangleright}} b) \supset \neg (A \overset{P}{\underset{\phi}{\triangleright}} b))$$

This proof rule cannot be guaranteed to demonstrate absence of information transmission. For example, consider the program

    P: *if* a > 0 *then* b ← 8 *else* b ← m *fi*

with the entry assertion

    ϕ: m = 8

b is assigned the value 8 regardless of the value of a and it can be shown directly (by Theorem A-1) that

$\neg (A \overset{P}{\underset{\phi}{\triangleright}} b)$. Yet Theorem A-7 cannot be usefully applied because [a > 0] is not a-independent given ϕ and both assignments change b.

As other researchers have noted [Denning & Denning 77, Jones & Lipton 75], there is no way to generally resolve this difficulty without transforming the program to an equivalent one - in this case, the program

    P: b ← 8

D.   *Loops*

Information transmission in the program

    P: *while* t *do* S *od*

is analyzed by considering the equivalent program (in the sense of Section 2), the infinite sequence of statements of the form

S*: *if* t *then* S *fi*

Let A = M_0 and define

$$M_{i+1} = M_i \cup (M_i \triangleright^{S*} *)$$

In effect, M_i is the set of variables to which information

initially in A could be transmitted after i or fewer iterations of the loop. If the loop terminates after k iterations, then $M_k = M_{k+1} = M_{k+2} = \cdots$. Thus, the M_i's converge to some M''

with the property that

$$M* = M* \cup (M* \triangleright^{S*} *)$$

from which we can see that

$$(M* \triangleright^{S*} *) \subseteq M*$$

In fact, M* is the smallest set that satisfies that formula having the property (since M_0 = A) that

A $\subseteq$ M*

Now, to demonstrate that information cannot be transmitted to b over execution of P, we need only show that b $\notin$ M*. Formally,

Theorem A-8

If P is *while* t *do* S *od*
and S* is *if* t *then* S *fi* then

$$(\exists M*)(A \subseteq M* \wedge (M* \triangleright^{S*} *) \subseteq M* \wedge b \,/\, M*)$$

$$\supset \neg(A \triangleright^{P} b)$$

If an entry assertion ϕ holds, then there is some (perhaps weaker) inductive assertion $\phi*$ which holds at the beginning of each iteration of the loop – that is – on entry to S*. Naturally, this may restrict the growth of M*. Formally, we extend the theorem to show

Theorem A-9

If P is *while* t *do* S *od*

and S* is *if* t *then* S *fi*

and $\phi \supset \phi*$

and $\phi* \supset \phi* \circ S$ then

$$(\exists M*)(\; A \subseteq M* \wedge (M* \; \triangleright_{\phi*}^{S*} \; *) \subseteq M* \wedge b \notin M* \;)$$

$$\supset \neg (A \; \triangleright_{\phi}^{P} \; b)$$

As an example, consider the program P

```
P:   i ← 0;

     b ← 1;

     mult ← a1;

     while i ≤ a2 do

           b ← b* mult;

           mult ← mult + a* a3;

           i ← i + 1

     od
```

with entry assertion

$\phi 1$:   a2 = 0

Now, we will prove $\neg (a \; \triangleright_{\phi 1}^{P} \; b)$.   First, represent P as

```
P:   S1; S2
S1:   i ← 0; b ← 1; mult ← a1
S2:   while   i ≤ a2 do S3 od
S3:   b ← b*mult; mult ← mult + a* a3; i ← i + 1
```

and

> S2*:   *if* i $\leq$ a2 *then* S3 *fi*

First, take $\phi 2$, where $\phi 1 \supset \phi 2 \circ$ S1, as [a2 = 0 $\wedge$ i $\leq$ 0 $\wedge$

(i = 0 $\supset$ (mult = a1 $\wedge$ b = 1))].   Now, (a $\triangleright^{S1}_{\phi 1}$ *) = a.   So

by theorem A-5, we only need to show that $\neg$ (a $\triangleright^{S2}_{\phi 2}$ b).

Pick $\phi 2$* = $\phi 2$, noting that $\phi 2$* $\supset \phi 2$* $\circ$ S2*.   By theorem A-9, we need to find an M* such that

a ϵ M* $\wedge$ (M* $\triangleright^{S2*}_{\phi 2*}$ *) $\subseteq$ M* $\wedge$ b $\notin$ M*

Such an M* is {a, mult}.   Syntactically, it appears that (M* $\triangleright^{S2*}_{\phi 2*}$ *) might be {a, mult, b}.   We need to show that (M* $\triangleright^{S2*}_{\phi 2*}$ b).

Take $\phi 3$ as [mult = a1 $\wedge$ b = 1], noting that $\phi 2$* $\wedge$

[i $\leq$ a2] $\supset \phi 3$, and that [i $\leq$ a2] is M*-independent.   By theorem A-6, we need only show that $\neg$ M* $\triangleright^{S3}_{\phi 3}$ b.

Well, by direct substitution of $\phi 3$ in S3, it's easy to see that $\phi 3(\sigma) \supset$ S3(σ).b = .a1.   So, for any $\sigma 1$ and $\sigma 2$ such that $\sigma 1 \frac{\phi 3}{M*} \phi 2$, S3($\sigma 1$).b = S3($\sigma 2$).b.   Thus, directly by the definition of strong dependency, $\neg$ M* $\triangleright^{S3}_{\phi 3}$ b.

It is just as easy (sic) to show that $\neg$ a $\triangleright^{P}_{\phi 1}$ b when φ1:   a3 = 0

For this proof, we can pick φ3 = φ2* = φ2 = φ1 and M* = {a}.
And, we have to prove that ¬ a $\triangleright\genfrac{}{}{0pt}{}{S2*}{\phi2*}$ mult.   This follows

directly from theorem A-2, since

φ3(σ) ⊃ σ.mult = S3(σ).mult

MONOTONIC PROTECTION SYSTEMS*

M. A. Harrison†
W. L. Ruzzo†

Computer Science Division
University of California, Berkeley

I. INTRODUCTION

In recent years, it has become widely accepted that many of
the important issues concerning protection in operating systems
can best be viewed abstractly. A variety of different models
have been proposed for abstracting the essential features under
study. Cf. [Har 75, HRU 76, LiS 77, LiS 78, and Sny 77]. We
shall concentrate in this paper on the model introduced in
[HRU 76] because this model is very general and contains a
number of the other models as special cases. It is also true
that this model over-simplifies a number of important practical
considerations which are very hard to abstract mathematically.
Nonetheless, the theorems which will be proven here will also be
true in more elaborate models as the constructions that we shall
give will still work.

* *This research was sponsored by the National Science Foundation
Grant GJ-43332 and MCS74-07636-A01.*
† *Present address: Department of Computer Science, University
of Washington, Seattle, WA 98195.*

Our main concern in the present paper is the comparative
power of the operations which form part of the basic model of
[HRU 76].   Crudely speaking, a protection system is a set of
simple procedures for modifying an access matrix which records
who can get what access to which objects.   The basic operations
are as follows:

enter r into (X_s, X_o)

create subject X_s

create object X_o

delete r from (X_s, X_o)

destroy subject X_s

destroy object X_o

One might surmise that the last three operations are very
important and powerful.   For example, destroying a subject means
that an entire row and column are lost from a protection matrix.
As the matrix can grow without limit, an unbounded amount of
information can be lost.   In fact, we shall show that no loss of
computational power occurs if we have protection systems in
which these last three commands do not occur.

In preparation for the results to come, we recall the formal
definition of a protection system.

Definition.   A *protection system* consists of the following
parts:
(1)   a finite set of *generic rights* R,
(2)   a finite set C of *commands* of the form:

command $\alpha(X_1, X_2, \ldots, X_k)$

   if r_1 in (X_{s_1}, X_{o_1}), r_2 in (X_{s_2}, X_{o_2}), ..., and

   r_m in (X_{s_m}, X_{o_m})

  then

    op_1
    ...
    op_n

end

or if m is zero, simply

    command $\alpha(X_1, \ldots, X_k)$

        op_1

        ...

        op_n

    end

In our definition, α is a name and $X_1, \ldots, X_k$ are formal parameters. Each op_i is one of the primitive operations mentioned earlier. By convention $r, r_1, r_2, \ldots, r_k$ denote generic rights and $s, s_1, s_2, \ldots, s_m$ and $o, o_1, o_2, \ldots, o_m$ are integers between 1 and k. The expression "r_1 in (X_{s_1}, X_{o_1}), r_2 in ..." will be referred to as the command's *conditions*, and "$op_1 \cdots op_n$" as the command's *body*. The number of conditions is m. We also need to discuss the "configurations" of a protection system.

Definition. A *configuration* of a protection system is a triple (S, O, P), where S is the set of *current subjects*, O is the set of *current objects*, $S \subseteq O$, and P is an *access matrix*, which has a row for each subject in S and a column for each object in O. $P[s,o]$ is a subset of R, the set of generic rights, and gives the rights that s enjoys with respect to o. A number of examples may be found in [HRU 76] which indicate the use of protection systems. It is our contention that this type of formal system is conceptually simple and natural. It can be used to describe protection policies in real operating systems.†

Next, we need the rules for changing configurations in a protection system.

---

† *See the UNIX example in [HRU 76] or the work on MULTICS in [ScA 77].*

Definition. Let (S,O,P) and (S',O',P') be configurations of a protection system, and let op be one of the six primitive operations. We shall say that:

$$(S,O,P) =>_{op} (S',O'P')$$

(which is read (S,O,P) yields (S',O',P') under op) if either:

(1) op = enter r into (s,o) and $S = S'$, $O = O'$, $s \in S$, $o \in O$, $P'[s_1,o_1] = P[s_1,o_1]$ if $(s_1,o_1) \neq (s,o)$ and $P'[s,o] = P[s,o] \cup \{r\}$,

   or

(2) op = delete r from (s,o) and $S = S'$, $O = O'$, $s \in S$, $o \in O$, $P'[s_1,o_1]=P[s_1,o_1]$ if $(s_1,o_1) \neq (s,o)$ and $P'[s,o]=P[s,o]-\{r\}$, or

(3) op = create subject s', where s' is a new symbol not in O, $S'=S \cup \{s'\}$, $O'=O \cup \{s'\}$, $P'[s,o]=P[s,o]$ for all (s,o) in $S \times O$, $P'[s',o]=\emptyset$ for all $o \in O'$, and $P[s,s']=\emptyset$ for all $s \in S'$, or

(4) op = create object o', where o' is a new symbol not in O, $S'=S$, $O'=O \cup \{o'\}$, $P'[s,o]=P[s,o]$ for all $(s,o) \in S \times O$ and $P'[s,o'] = \emptyset$ for all $s \in S$, or

(5) op = destroy subject s', where $s \in S$, $S'=S-\{s'\}$, $O'=O-\{s'\}$, and $P'[s,o]=P[s,o]$ for all $(s,o) \in S' \times O'$, or

(6) op=destroy object o', where $o' \in O-S$, $S'=S, O'=O-\{o'\}$, and $P'[s,o] = P[s,o]$ for all $(s,o) \in S' \times O'$.

Next, we need to recall how protection systems execute commands.

Definition. Let $Q = (S,O,P)$ be a configuration of a protection system containing:

$\underset{\sim\sim\sim\sim\sim\sim}{\text{command}}\ \alpha(X_1,\ldots,X_k)$

   $\underset{\sim\sim}{\text{if}}\ r_1\ \text{in}\ (X_{s_1},X_{o_1})\ \text{and}$

     . . .

    $r_m\ \text{in}\ (X_{s_m},X_{o_m})$

   $\underset{\sim\sim\sim\sim}{\text{then}}$

     op_1

     . . .

     op_n

   $\underset{\sim\sim\sim}{\text{end}}$

Then we say that

$$Q \ \vdash_{\alpha(x_1,\ldots,x_k)} Q'$$

where Q' is the configuration defined as follows:

    (1) If α's conditions are not satisfied, i.e., if there is some i, $1 \leq i \leq m$ such that r_i is not $P[x_{s_i},x_{o_i}]$, then $Q = Q'$.

    (2) Otherwise, i.e., if for all i between 1 and m,

$r_i \ \varepsilon \ P[x_{s_i},x_{o_i}]$, then if there exist configurations $Q_0,Q_1,\ldots,Q_n$

such that

$$Q = Q_0 \underset{op_1^*}{=>} Q_1 \underset{op_2^*}{=>} \ldots \underset{op_n^*}{=>} Q_n$$

where op_i^* denotes the primitive operation op_i with the actual parameters $x_1,\ldots,x_k$ replacing all occurences of the formal parameters $X_1,\ldots,X_k$, respectively, then $Q' = Q_n$.

    We simplify the notation by writing $Q \vdash_{\alpha} Q'$ if there exist parameters $x_1,\ldots,x_k$ such that

$$Q \vdash_{\alpha(x_1,\ldots,x_k)} Q'$$

Also, we write $Q \vdash Q'$ when there exists a command α such that $Q \vdash_{\alpha} Q'$.

It is also useful to write $Q \vdash^{*} Q'$, where $\vdash^{*}$ is the reflexive-transitive closure of $\vdash$. That is $\vdash^{*}$ represents some finite number of occurrences of $\vdash$, possibly none at all.

In [HRU 76], we devoted a great deal of our attention to trying to find algorithms for deciding if a protection system is "safe" or not in the following sense.

Definition. Given a protection system, we say command $\alpha(X_1,\ldots,X_k)$ *leaks generic right* r *from configuration* $Q = (S,O,P)$ if α, when run on Q, can execute a primitive operation which enters r into a cell of the access matrix which did not previously contain r. More formally, there is some assignment of actual parameters $x_1,\ldots,x_k$ such that $\alpha(x_1,\ldots,x_k)$

(1)   has its conditions satisfied in Q, i.e., for each clause "r in (X_i,X_j)" in α's conditions we have $r \in P[x_i,x_j]$, and

(2)   if α's body is $op_1,\ldots,op_n$, then there exists an m, $1 \le m \le n$, and configurations $Q=Q_0,Q_1,\ldots,Q_{m-1}=(S',O',P')$, and $Q_m = (S'',O'',P'')$, such that

$$Q_0 \underset{op_1^{*}}{=>} Q_1 \underset{op_2^{*}}{=>} \cdots \underset{op_{m-1}^{*}}{=>} Q_{m-1} \underset{op_m^{*}}{=>} Q_m$$

where op_i^{*} denotes op_i after substitution of $x_1,\ldots,x_k$ for $X_1,\ldots,X_k$, and moreover, there exist some s and o such that

$$r \notin P'[s,o] \text{ but } r \in P''[s,o]$$

(Of course, op_m must be enter r into (s,o)).

The term "leak" sounds pejorative. However, leaks are in fact the way in which sharing takes place. The term assumes its usual negative significance only when applied to some configuration, most likely modified to eliminate "reliable" subjects, and to some right which we hope cannot be passed around.

Definition. Given a particular protection system and generic right r, we say that the initial configuration Q_0 is *unsafe* for r (or *leaks* r) if there is a configuration Q and a command α such that

(1) $Q_0 \overset{*}{\vdash} Q$, and

(2) α leaks r from Q.

We say Q_0 is *safe* for r if Q_0 is not unsafe for r.

In [HRU 76], we investigated the decidability of the safety question. In the special case of "mono-operational systems", there is an algorithm to solve the safety problem. First, we need the definition of such a system.

Definition. A protection system is *mono-operational* if each command's body is a single primitive operation.

Theorem 1. There is an algorithm which decides whether or not a given mono-operational protection system and initial configuration is unsafe for a given generic right r.

If, on the other hand, there are no restrictions placed on a protection system, we get the following result.

Theorem 2 (from [HRU 76]). It is undecidable whether a given configuration of a given protection system is safe for a given generic right.

Straightforward techniques show that this situation is "robust" and the class of theorems one gets would not change under different variations in the definition of safety.

Theorems 1 and 2 indicate that the power of these systems is not completely clear. What other special cases are there which are interesting? Exactly where is the line between decidability and undecidability of the safety question?

One natural restriction would be to make certain that the systems do not grow. In that case, a result of [HRU 76] tells us that the safety problem is decidable but is not something we would like to compute.

Theorem 3 (from [HRU 76]). The question of safety for protection systems without create commands is complete in polynomial space.

The proof techniques that were employed in [HRU 76] all make
use of the diagonal of the access matrix in an essential way.
What would happen if there were only a finite number of subjects?
Would the safety problem then become "tractable"? Lipton and
Snyder [LiS 78] have provided an answer.

Theorem 4 (from [LiS 78]). The safety problem for protection
systems with a finite number of subjects is decidable.

Moreover, it is shown that such protection systems are
recursively equivalent to vector addition systems and a connection
between the safety question for the former and the covering
problem for the latter is obtained. Although the safety question
is decidable, it is again not something one would care to compute.

These results have implications to proving systems to be safe
as well. Cf. [DDGHR 77].

II.   MONOTONIC SYSTEMS

In an attempt to better understand wherein lies the
computational power of protection systems, we shall now consider
systems which can only increase in both size and in the entries
in the matrix.

Definition. A protection system is *monotonic* if no command
contains a primitive operation of the form

$$\text{destroy subject s}$$
$$\text{destroy object o}$$
$$\text{delete r from (s,o)}$$

A number of our colleagues who are familiar with operating
systems conjectured that monotonicity would reduce the computing
power of protection systems. We shall show that it does not do
so. It merely requires a different kind of proof which is more
intricate and hence more interesting.

Theorem 5. It is undecidable whether a given configuration
of a given monotonic protection system is safe for a given
generic right.

Proof. The idea of the proof would be to encode an instance
of the Post Correspondence Problem [Pos 46] on the main diagonal
of the access matrix. We would like to be able to grow an x-list
and a y-list and at a suitable point in time, to compare them.
Because of the monotonic restriction, the x and y lists must be
"interlaced" and the check for equality is done by "pointer-

chasing."

Formally, suppose we have an instance of the Post Correspondence Problem given by

$$\underset{\sim}{x} = (x_1, \ldots, x_n) \text{ and } \underset{\sim}{y} = (y_1, \ldots, y_n)$$

where x_i, $y_i \in \{0,1\}^+$. It is convenient to define

$$x_i = x_{i1}, \ldots, x_{i\ell_i} \text{ and } y_i = y_{i1}, \ldots, y_{im_i}$$

where x_{ij}, $y_{ik} \in \{0,1\}$ for all i, j, k such that $1 \leq i \leq n$, $1 \leq j \leq \ell_i$, and $1 \leq k \leq m_i$.

We shall construct a protection system which has the following set of generic rights

$$R = \{0,1,\text{link},\text{start},\text{match},\text{yx-end},\text{leak}\}$$

and the following commands: For each i, $1 \leq i \leq n$, we have a procedure

    command START$_i (X_1, \ldots, X_{\ell_i}, Y_1, \ldots, Y_{m_i})$
        for $j:=1$ to ℓ_i do create subject X_j [†]
        for $j:=1$ to ℓ_i do enter x_{1j} into (X_j,X_j)
        for $j:=1$ to ℓ_i-1 do enter link into (X_j,X_{j+1})
        for $j:=1$ to m_i do create subject Y_j
        for $j:=1$ to m_i do enter y_{ij} into (Y_j,Y_j)
        for $j:=1$ to m_i-1 do enter link into (Y_j,Y_{j+1})
        enter yx-end into (Y_{m_i},X_{ℓ_i})
        enter match into (Y_{m_i},X_{ℓ_i}) if $y_{m_i} = x_{\ell_i}$ [††]
        enter start into (Y_1,X_1)
    end

[†] *This notation is a shorthand for* create subject X_1

$$\vdots$$

create subject X_{ℓ_i}

[††] *The notation means that this primitive operation is included in the command if* $y_{m_i} = x_{\ell_i}$.

For each i, $1 \leq i \leq n$, we have a procedure

<u>command</u> $\text{GROW}_i (\text{YEND}, \text{XEND}, X_1, \ldots, X_{\ell_i}, Y_1, \ldots, Y_{m_i})$

    <u>if</u> yx-end ε (YEND, XEND)

    <u>then</u>

        <u>for</u> j:=1 <u>to</u> ℓ_i <u>do</u> <u>create</u> <u>subject</u> X_j

        <u>for</u> j:=1 <u>to</u> ℓ_i <u>do</u> <u>enter</u> x_{ij} <u>into</u> (X_j, X_j)

        <u>for</u> j:=1 <u>to</u> ℓ_i-1 <u>do</u> <u>enter</u> <u>link</u> <u>into</u> (X_j, X_{j+1})

        <u>for</u> j:=1 <u>to</u> m_i <u>do</u> <u>create</u> <u>subject</u> Y_j

        <u>for</u> j:=1 <u>to</u> m_i <u>do</u> <u>enter</u> y_{ij} <u>into</u> (Y_j, Y_j)

        <u>for</u> j:=1 <u>to</u> m_i-1 <u>do</u> <u>enter</u> <u>link</u> <u>into</u> (Y_j, Y_{j+1})

        <u>enter</u> <u>yx-end</u> <u>into</u> (Y_{m_i}, X_{ℓ_i})

        <u>enter</u> <u>match</u> <u>into</u> (Y_{m_i}, X_{ℓ_i}) <u>if</u> $y_{m_i} = x_{\ell_i}$

        <u>enter</u> <u>link</u> <u>into</u> (XEND, X_1)

        <u>enter</u> <u>link</u> <u>into</u> (YEND, Y_1)

    <u>end</u>

For each $b \in \{0,1\}$, we have a procedure

    command MATCH$_b$(Y,X,AY,AX)

       if

          match $\in$ (Y,X) and

          link $\in$ (AY,Y) and

          link $\in$ (AX,X) and

          $b \in$ (AX,AX) and

          $b \in$ (AY,AY)

       then

          enter match into (AY,AX)

     end

Lastly,

    command LEAK(Y,X)

       if

          start $\in$ (Y,X) and

          match $\in$ (Y,X)

       then

          enter leak into (Y,X)

     end

Intuitively, this protection system "computes", starting with an empty configuration, as follows: Each command START$_i$ encodes strings of x_i and y_i into the protection matrix. The location of the first pair of symbols, (x_{i1}, y_{i1}), is marked by start while the last pair, $(x_{i\ell_i}, y_{im_i})$, is marked by yx-end.

Each command GROW$_i$ adds x_i and y_i to the end of some sequence of x's and y's which have been previously entered into the matrix. The locations of the ends of such a sequence are indicated by the yx-end right. Similarly, GROW$_i$ marks the end of the new sequence with yx-end.

Notice that $GROW_i$ is conditional only upon some yx-end, which is never deleted. Thus, several different $GROW_i$ commands may be applied to the same yx-end. Each $GROW_i$ may then be thought of as growing a new branch on each of two trees -- one in which paths from the root represent sequences of x's, the other representing corresponding sequences of y's. The start right associates the roots of the two trees while the link rights associate ancestors and descendents, and finally the yx-end rights indicate ends of corresponding paths. Moreover, the $START_i$ commands are unconditional so that we may actually get a forest of these pairs of trees.

Before starting the formal proof, an intuitive example will be worked. Suppose

$$\underset{\sim}{x} = (01,1) \text{ and } \underset{\sim}{y} = (0,11)$$

Imagine that the following sequence of commands is executed.

$$START_1(X_1,X_2,Y_1)$$
$$GROW_1(Y_1,X_2,X_3,X_4,Y_2)$$
$$GROW_2(Y_1,X_2,X_5,Y_3,Y_4)$$
$$MATCH_1(Y_4,X_5,Y_3,X_2)$$
$$MATCH_0(Y_3,X_2,Y_1,X_1)$$
$$LEAK(Y_1,X_1)$$

Figure 1 displays the matrix after this sequence has been executed.

We attempt to match corresponding x and y sequences by working from the bottom of the tree to the top. This seems easier than working down from the root, since there is a unique chain of links to follow from any node to the root in each tree, whereas working down from the root, it is not clear how to arrange to follow corresponding paths through the two trees. The $START_i$ and $GROW_i$ commands start matching two corresponding sequences by matching their last symbols. The $MATCH_b$ commands then compare the two prececessors (i.e., ancestors in the tree) of any pair of matched nodes.

	X_1	X_2	Y_1	X_3	X_4	Y_2	X_5	Y_3	Y_4
X_1	0	link							
X_2		1		link			link		
Y_1	start match leak	yx-end	0			link		link	
X_3				0	link				
X_4					1				
Y_2					yx-end	0			
X_5							1		
Y_3		match						1	link
Y_4							yx-end		1

Figure 1

The leak right can be entered if and only if matching proceeds all the way up to the root nodes. Next, we show that this can happen if and only if the Post Correspondence Problem has a solution; this is known to be a recursively unsolvable problem [Pos 46]. Thus, we will have shown that it is recursively unsolvable whether or not this protection system is safe for the right leak and the empty initial configuration.

Notation. Let Φ be the empty configuration $(\emptyset,\emptyset,\emptyset)$. For any configuration (S,O,P), and any $X \in S$, let $A(X) = \{Y \in S \mid \text{link} \in P[Y,X]\}$. (In our tree interpretation, $A(x)$ is the parent of node (X,X).) We may extend this notation by defining $A^{i+1}(X) = A(A^i(X))$. Let $C(X)$ be the contents of $P[X,X]$.

Lemma 1.   If $\Phi \vdash^* Q = (S,O,P)$, then for all $X \in S$ we have

(1) $P[X,X] = \{0\}$ or $\{1\}$

(2) $|A(X)| \leq 1$

(3) $A(X) = \emptyset$ if and only if there is a Y such that start $\in P(X,Y)$ or start $\in P(Y,X)$. Furthermore, any such Y is unique.

(4)   For each $Y \in S$, if yx-end $\in P(Y,X)$ then there exist $m \geq 1$, $i_1,\ldots,i_m$ each between 1 and n such that $x = x_{i_1} \cdots x_{i_m} = C(A^{\lg(x)-1}(X))\cdots C(A(X))C(X)$,[†] $y = y_{i_1}\cdots y_{i_m} = C(A^{\lg(y)-1}(Y))\cdots C(A(Y))C(Y)$, and start $\in P(A^{\lg(y)-1}(Y), A^{\lg(x)-1}(X))$.

(5)   For each $Y \in S$, if match $\in P(Y,X)$ then there exist $m \geq 1$, X', $Y' \in S$ such that yx-end $\in (Y',X')$, $Y = A^{m-1}(Y')$, $X = A^{m-1}(X')$, and for each j, $0 \leq j < m$, we have $C(A^j(X')) = C(A^j(Y'))$.

[†] *There is a natural identification taking place here. If we concatenate the contents of the appropriate cells of the matrix, this line becomes something like $x = x_1 x_2 = 011 = $ "0""1""1".*

This claim formalizes the discussion above. In (1), it is shown how strings are encoded on the diagonal. In parts (2) and (3) every node has a unique parent, except the root. In part (3), the root and only the root of every tree is paired with some other tree, and that tree is uniquely determined. $\underset{\sim\sim\sim\sim\sim}{yx\text{-}end}$ joins the ends of corresponding sequences in paired trees according to part (1). Finally, in (5), matching proceeds along corresponding sequences.

We are now ready to do the proof.

The argument is an induction on the length of the computation of $\Phi \overset{*}{\vdash} Q$.

Basis: The argument is trivial for

$$\Phi \overset{0}{\vdash} \Phi$$

Induction Step: Assume that $Q = (S,O,P)$ satisfies the conditions. We will show that

$$Q \underset{\alpha}{\vdash} Q'$$

where $Q' = (S',O',P')$ implies that Q' does also.

If $\alpha = \text{START}_i$, it is clear that all the rights entered are placed into created entries so that the[†] "old portion" of P' is unchanged. Moreover, the "new portion" of P' satisfies conditions (1) through (5) by construction. There is no possible connection between the old and new portions of P' because

$$P'[X,X'] = P'[X',X] = \emptyset$$

with $X \in S$, $X' \in S' - S$. Thus $\underset{\alpha}{\vdash}$ where $\alpha = \text{START}_i$ preserves (1) through (5).

[†] *We prefer to say "old portion" of P' rather than $P' \cap (S \times O \times 2^R)$ and "new portion" of P' instead of $P' \cap (S'-S) \times (O'-O) \times 2^R$.*

If $\alpha = \text{GROW}_i$, it is clear that one of $\underset{\sim}{0}$ and $\underset{\sim}{1}$ is entered in each new diagonal element, and all other entries are made off the diagonal, so condition (1), $P[X,X] = \{0\}$ or $\{1\}$, will still hold. The link right is never entered in an old object, and only entered once in each new object, so condition (2) $(|A(X)| \leq 1)$ still holds. The start right is not entered so (3) still holds. If $yx\text{-end} \ \varepsilon \ P'[Y,X]$ with Y, $X \ \varepsilon \ S$ (not $S'-S$), then (4) holds in P' since (1)-(3) hold in P' and (4) held in P. If $yx\text{-end} \ \varepsilon$ $P'[Y,X]$ with[†] Y, $X \ \varepsilon \ S' - S$, then it is easy to see that (4) holds with x_i and y_i continuing the sequence ending at (YEND,XEND). That is, we have $yx\text{-end} \ \varepsilon$ (YEND, XEND) and there exist $m \geq 1$, $i_1,\ldots,i_m$ such that

$$(i) \quad x = x_{i_1} \ \ldots \ x_{i_m} = C(A^{\lg(x)-1}(\text{XEND}))\cdots C(\text{XEND})$$

$$(ii) \quad y = y_{i_1} \ \ldots \ y_{i_m} = C(A^{\lg(y)-1}(\text{YEND}))\cdots C(\text{YEND}) \quad \text{and}$$

$$(iii) \quad \text{start} \ \varepsilon \ (A^{\lg(y)-1}(\text{YEND}), \ A^{\lg(x)-1}(\text{XEND})).$$

Finally, (5) is not affected at all in the old portion of P' and moreover it holds vacuously in the new portion of P' except possibly for (Y_{m_i},X_{ℓ_i}) in the case where $y_{m_i} = x_{\ell_i}$. In that case it holds with $m = 1$. Thus, $\vdash_\alpha$ where $\alpha = \text{GROW}_i$ preserves properties (1) through (5).

If α is MATCH_b, we see that the link right is not entered anywhere so conditions (2) through (4) are not affected. The other rights are entered by this command off the main diagonal so property (1) is also unaffected. If   is

$$\text{MATCH}_b(Y,X,AY,AX)$$

then we must have had match in $P[Y,X]$. Then, by property (5), there must have been $m \geq 1$, X', $Y' \ \varepsilon \ S$ such that

$$yx\text{-end} \ \varepsilon \ P[Y',X']$$

$$Y = A^{m-1}(Y'), \quad X = A^{m-1}(X')$$

[†] *Assume that the command GROW_i is called with actual parameters (YEND,XEND); the Y and X here are formal parameters.*

and

$$C(A^j(X')) = C(A^j(Y')),$$

for each j, $0 \le j < m$. It is clear that after the $MATCH_b$ command is executed, similar conditions hold in P', since

$$AY = A(Y), \quad AX = A(X),$$
$$C(AY) = C(AX),$$

and the other entries are unchanged, so (5) is satisfied by $m+1$, X', and Y'.

If α is LEAK, then no rights are entered on the diagonal so property (1) still holds and link, start and match are not entered, so properties (2)-(5) are unaffected.

Thus, the induction is extended, and we see that Lemma 1 is true.

We are now ready to prove Theorem 5. Suppose the Post Correspondence Problem has a solution, say $(i_1, i_2, \ldots, i_m)$. Then commands $START_{i_1}$, $GROW_{i_2}, \ldots, GROW_{i_m}$ could be executed with appropriate parameters so that the indicated solution is constructed. Since a solution ends with i_m, we certainly must have the "enter match ..." command in "$GROW_{i_m}$", so execution of several "$MATCH_b$" commands with appropriate parameters would result in placing the match right in the same position as the start right, thus allowing the LEAK command to enter the leak right. Conversely, if leak is ever entered, it must be because start and match appear in the same position of the matrix. By property (5) of Lemma 1, we see that there must be some Y', X' such that yx-end ε $P[Y', X']$, and their predecessors match. But then by property (4) for Y', X', we see that their predecessors must be corresponding sequences of x_i's and y_i's, i.e., the Post Correspondence Problem must have a solution. Thus, the protection system is safe for the right leak and the initial configuration

Φ if and only if the Post Correspondence Problem has no solution, and hence safety is recursively unsolvable. Q.E.D.

It is possible to improve this result somewhat.

Theorem 7. The safety question for monotonic protection systems is undecidable even when each command has at most two conditions.

Proof. The construction is similar to the one used in the proof of the preceding theorem, except that a more complex sequence of commands must be used for the matching. The set of generic rights is

$$R = \{0,1,\text{link},\text{start},\text{match},\text{yx-end},\text{leak},\text{my},\text{myx},\text{myx0},\text{myx1}\}$$

The set of commands includes the START_i, GROW_i, and LEAK commands of the previous proof. Note that these commands all have only one or two conditions. The MATCH_b commands, which had five conditions, are replaced by the following six commands having two conditions each.

    command FOLLOWY(Y,X,AY)
        if match ε (Y,X) and link ε (AY,Y)
        then
            enter my into (AY,X)
    end

    command FOLLOWX(AY,X,AX)
        if my ε (AY,X) and link ε (AX,X)
        then
            enter myx into (AY,AX)
    end

For each b ε {0,1}, we have

    command GETY_b(AY,AX)
        if myx ε (AY,AX) and b ε (AY,AY)
        then
            enter myxb into (AY,AX)†
    end

---

† *If b = 0 then myx0 is to be entered.*

For each b ε {0,1}, we have

    command MATCHX$_b$ (AY,AX)

        if myxb ε (AY,AX) and b ε (AX,AX)

        then

            enter match into (AY,AX)

    end

Next, we need a result which characterizes computation in the new system.

Lemma 2. If $\Phi \models^* Q = (S,O,P)$, then for each X ε S, we have (1)-(5) of Lemma 1 as well as the following conditions.

(6) If my εP(Y,X) then there exists Y' ε S such that Y = A(Y') and match εP(Y',X).

(7) If myx εP(Y,X) then there exists X' ε S such that X = A(X') and my εP(Y,X').

(8) If myxb εP(Y,X) with b = 0, 1 then myx εP(Y,X) and b εP(Y,Y).

Proof. Since (1) through (4) of Lemma 1 were unaffected by the MATCH$_b$ command in the previous construction, the absence of that command does not matter. Similarly, the six new commands don't enter the start, link, or yx-end rights so (2)-(4) are not affected. Since these commands don't enter rights on the diagonal, they preserve property (1) also. Since the original commands do not use any of the rights my, myx, myx0 or myx1, they will not effect (6)-(8). Thus (6)-(8) just reflect the conditions and actions of the commands FOLLOWY, FOLLOWX, and GETY$_b$ respectively, so they will hold. Finally, looking at the MATCHX$_b$ commands, and combining its conditions with properties (8), (7) and (6) we see that MATCHX$_b$ enters the match right in (Y,X) just in case there exist Y', X' ε S such that Y = A(Y'), X = A(X'), C(Y) = C(X), and match ε (Y',X'). These are precisely the conditions which allow us to inductively extend property (5). Hence the claim is proven.

Now to complete the proof of Theorem 6.

Proof of the Theorem. The argument parallels the proof of Theorem 5 but uses Lemma 2 instead of Lemma 1.

III. MONOCONDITIONAL MONOTONIC SYSTEMS

Theorem 7 shows that the safety question for monotonic protection systems is undecidable, even if each command has at most two conditions. However, in many important practical situations, commands need only one condition. For example, a procedure for updating a file may only need to check that the user has the "update" right to the file. Similarly, to execute some program, the user may only need to have the "call" right to the program. Other examples abound. In contrast to the undecidability of the cases discussed in the preceding section, the safety question is decidable if each command of a monotonic protection system has at most one condition. This result will now be established.

Definition. A *monoconditional* protection system is one in which each command has at most one condition.

Monoconditional protection systems are much more complicated than one might anticipate. It is still not known whether or not the safety problem is solvable for such systems.

Before stating our next result, there are some useful observations which can be made.

In any protection system, if a command can execute in some configuration Q, then it can execute similarly in any "super" configuration Q' obtained from Q by adding rights and/or objects. Also, objects in Q' may be renamed, so long as the pattern of rights in the access matrix is not disturbed.

Definition. Let $Q = (S,O,P)$ and $Q' = (S',O',P')$ be configurations of an arbitrary protection system. We say that Q' *covers* Q (symbolically $Q \subseteq Q'$) if there exists a one-to-one mapping ρ from O into O' which preserves subjects and objects (i.e., $\rho: S \rightarrow S'$ and $\rho: (O-S) \rightarrow (O'-S')$) such that

$$P[s,o] \subseteq P'[\rho s, \rho o]$$

for each $s \in S$, $o \in O$.

Now we prove a simple lemma about covers.

Lemma 3. Let Q_1, Q_1', and Q_2 be configurations of an arbitrary protection system such that $Q_1 \subseteq Q_1'$. If $Q_1 \overset{*}{\vdash} Q_2$ then there exists Q_2' such that

$$\text{(i)} \quad Q_2 \subseteq Q_2'$$

and   (ii) $Q_1' \overset{*}{\vdash} Q_2'$.

In addition, if command α leaks right $\hat{r}$ from Q_2 then α leaks $\hat{r}$ from Q_2'.

Proof.   A command sequence which demonstrates (ii) may be easily obtained from one for

$$Q_1 \overset{*}{\vdash} Q_2 \tag{*}$$

by systematically renaming all actual parameters occurring in (*) in accordance with the covering map ρ. The details are omitted.

In a *monotonic* protection system, a similar result may be proven for a weaker notion of covering. Here Q' may be formed from Q as before, and/or by merging the rows and columns corresponding to two or more objects (including subjects). More precisely, we say $Q' = (S', O', P')$ *weakly covers* $Q = (S,O,P)$ ($Q \subseteq_w Q'$) if there is a many-to-one map ρ from O to O' which preserves subjects (i.e., $\rho: S \to S'$; although ρ may take $o \in O-S$ into S') such that $P[s,o] \subseteq P'[\rho s, \rho o]$ for all $s \in S$, $o \in O$.

Lemma 4. Let Q_1, Q_1', and Q_2 be configurations of a *monotonic* protection system such that $Q_1 \subseteq_w Q_2$. If $Q_1 \overset{*}{\vdash} Q_2$ then there exists Q_2' such that $Q_2 \subseteq_w Q_2'$ and $Q_1' \overset{*}{\vdash} Q_2'$. In addition, if α leaks $\hat{r}$ from Q_2, then α leaks $\hat{r}$ from Q_2'.

Proof.   The argument is quite similar to the proof of Lemma 3 and is omitted.

It will sharpen the reader's intuition if we explain why Lemma 4 does not hold for general protection systems. Suppose at some point in the computation sequence $Q_1 \overset{*}{\vdash} Q_2$ a state is reached where the right r occurs in two places in the access matrix. Further, suppose a subsequent destroy or delete operation removes one copy of r and that a still later command uses the remaining r to help satisfy its condition. If Q_1' covers Q_1 then of course a similar sequence of actions can take place in some computation $Q_1' \overset{*}{\vdash} Q_2'$. However, suppose Q_1' only *weakly* covers Q_1. In particular, suppose Q_1' is formed from Q_1 by merging rows/columns so that both r's will end up in the same cell. Then the delete or destroy operation will remove "both" r's, and the subsequent command may not find any other r to satisfy its condition. Thus the computation sequence starting from Q_1' may "block" before reaching any configuration $Q_2' \overset{\supseteq}{_w} Q_2$.

We are now ready to begin the argument that monoconditional monotonic protection systems have a decidable safety problem.

Theorem 8. The safety question is decidable for monotonic monoconditional protection systems.

Proof. Suppose we have a monoconditional monotonic protection system. A computation[†]

$$Q_0 \underset{\alpha_1}{\vdash} Q_1 \vdash \cdots \underset{\alpha_k}{\vdash} Q_k \underset{\alpha_{k+1}}{\vdash} \hat{r} \tag{1}$$

is called a *chain from* $r \in (x,y)$ if α_1's condition is $\underset{\sim\sim}{if}$[††] $r \in (x,y)$ then ...., and for each $i \geq 1$, every command α_{i+1} has its conditions satisfied by some right which was entered by α_i. That is, if $Q_i = (S_i, O_i, P_i)$ and α_{i+1} has the condition "$\underset{\sim\sim}{if}$[††] $r_{i+1} \in (x_{i+1}, y_{i+1})$" then $r_{i+1} \in P_i[x_{i+1}, y_{i+1}]$ but

$r_{i+1} \notin P_{i-1}[x_{i+1}, y_{i+1}]$.

[†] *By convention, we denote the statement "α leaks $\hat{r}$ from Q" by $Q \underset{\alpha}{\vdash} \hat{r}$. By the definition of a leak, this is not equivalent to "there exists Q' such that $Q \underset{\alpha}{\vdash} Q'$ and $\hat{r}$ is in Q".*

[††]*Here x,y (respectively x_{i+1}, y_{i+1}) represent the actual parameters passed to α_1 (respectively α_{i+1}) in the call which gives $Q_0 \underset{\alpha_1}{\vdash} Q_1$ (respectively $Q_i \underset{\alpha_{i+1}}{\vdash} Q_{i+1}$).*

Claim 1. If we have a chain of the form (1) and if Q_0' is any configuration with $r \in P_0'$ [x,y] there is a similar chain starting from Q_0'.

Proof. This is trivial since $r \in P_0'[x,y]$ implies that α_1's condition is satisfied and hence α_1 enters the right which satisfies α_2's condition, etc. An obvious induction proof is omitted.

Now, define for any configuration $Q = (S,0,P)$ and any $s \in S$, $o \in 0$ and generic right r a new configuration Q^{rso} as follows.

Note, for future reference, that there are only three possible configurations Q^{rso} per generic right r. If g is the number of generic rights, there is a total of $3g$ such configurations.

Claim 2. For each chain from $r \in (x,y)$ of the form (1), there is a similar chain starting from Q_0^{rxy} .

Proof. From Q_0' form Q_0 by deleting all rights except $r \in P[x,y]$. By Claim 1, there is a similar chain from Q_0', and $Q_0' \subseteq_w Q_0^{rxy}$, so by Lemma 4 there is also a similar chain starting from Q_0^{rxy} .

We are now ready for the main claim.

Claim 3. Suppose that in our protection system, all commands have one condition, and that $Q_0 = (S_0, O_0, P_0)$ with $|S_0| \geq 1$.

Further, suppose that

$$Q_0 \vdash_{\alpha_1} Q_1 \vdash_{\alpha_2} Q_2 \vdash \cdots \vdash_{\alpha_n} Q_n \vdash_{\alpha_{n+1}} \hat{r} \qquad (2)$$

is a computation of minimal length among all computations which leak $\hat{r}$ from Q_0. Let $Q_i = (S_i, O_i, P_i)$ and suppose that α_i's condition is "$\underset{\sim}{if}\ r_i\ \varepsilon\ (x_i, y_i)\ \underset{\sim\sim\sim}{then}\ \ldots$". Then

(1) Sequence (2) is a chain from $r_1\ \varepsilon\ (x_1, y_1)$.

(2) For all i, $1 \leq i \leq n+1$,

   (a) $Q_{i-1} \overset{r_i x_i y_i}{\underset{w}{\subseteq}} Q_{i-1}$,

   (b) but for each $j < i-1$, $Q_{i-1} \overset{r_i x_i y_i}{\underset{w}{\not\subseteq}} Q_j$

(3) We have $n \leq 3g$ where g is the number of generic rights in the system.

Proof. Clearly sequence (2) must be a chain because of the minimality condition. If not, let i be the greatest integer $\leq n+1$ such that α_i is conditional upon the presence of a right entered into Q_j with $j < i-1$. Thus, $Q_{i-1} \vdash_{\alpha_i} Q_i \vdash \cdots \vdash_{\alpha_{n+1}} \hat{r}$

is a chain, so by Claim 1 we would have a shorter computation equivalent to sequence (2) in which $Q_j \vdash \cdots \vdash Q_{i-1}$ were omitted, contradicting the minimality condition. This proves part (1).

Next we consider (2a). Note that

$$Q_{i-1} \vdash_{\alpha_i} Q_i$$

(or $Q_n \vdash_{\alpha_{n+1}} \hat{r}$), where α_i's condition is $\underset{\sim}{if}\ r_i\ \varepsilon\ (x_i, y_i)$, so that $r_i\ \varepsilon\ P_{i-1}[x_i, y_i]$. Clearly then $Q_{i-1} \overset{r_i x_i y_i}{\underset{w}{\subseteq}} Q_{i-1}$ for we may merge all of Q_{i-1}'s objects (other than y_i) into x_i. Then (2a) holds.

Assume, for the sake of contradiction, that (2b) does not hold. Let i, $1 < i \leq n+1$ be the largest integer for which the statement is false and let j be some integer $< i-1$ such that

$$Q_{i-1}^{r_i x_i y_i} \subseteq_w Q_j$$

We have that

$$Q_{i-1} \vdash_{\alpha_i} Q_i \vdash \cdots \vdash_{\alpha_n} Q_n \vdash_{\alpha_{n+1}} \hat{r} \qquad (3)$$

is a chain from $r_i \in (x_i, y_i)$ by our assumption about sequence (2) and part (1) of this claim. Moreover

$$Q_{i-1}^{r_i x_i y_i} \subseteq_w Q_j$$

from above so by Claim 2 and Lemma 4 there is a similar computation

$$Q_j \vdash_{\alpha_i} Q_i' \vdash \cdots \vdash_{\alpha_n} Q_n' \vdash_{\alpha_{n+1}} \hat{r} \qquad (4)$$

Thus

$$Q_0 \vdash_{\alpha_1} Q_1 \vdash \cdots \vdash_{\alpha_j} Q_j \vdash_{\alpha_i} Q_i' \vdash \cdots \vdash_{\alpha_n} Q_n' \vdash_{\alpha_{n+1}} \hat{r} \qquad (5)$$

By assumption $j < i-1$, so (5) contradicts the minimality of (2) which establishes all of part (2) of the claim.

Now (3) is easily obtained. From (2), each Q_i, $1 \leq i \leq n$, covers some configuration Q^{rso} which isn't covered by any of $Q_0, \ldots, Q_{i-1}$. Since there are only 3g distinct configurations Q^{rso}, n must be $\leq 3g$. This completes the proof of Claim 4.

We will complete the proof of the theorem by arguing that there was no loss of generality in Claim 3 by (a) assuming that all commands had conditions or (b) that Q_0 has one subject. For (a) we note that we can make sure that all commands have conditions by adding a new right r_0 to the system, entering it at some position in the initial configuration, and giving all unconditional commands two new parameters X and Y and a condition "$\underset{\sim\sim}{if}$ r_0 ε (X,Y) ...". There is an obvious one-to-one correspondence between computations in the modified and unmodified systems. For (b), when Q_0 has no subjects, simply test whether there is any α such that $Q_0 \underset{\alpha}{\vdash} \hat{r}$ or whether there is any Q_0' having at least one subject such that $Q_0 \underset{\alpha}{\vdash} Q_0'$ where Q_0' is unsafe for r (which is decidable by Claim 3). Q.E.D.

We should remark that the decision procedure given in the above theorem is[†] in *NP*, but it's not hard to see that a polynomial time procedure is possible. Construct a (3g × 3g) relation "→" where $Q_1^{rso} \to Q_2^{r's'o'}$ if $Q_1^{rso} \vdash Q_2$ where $Q_2^{r's'o'} \subseteq Q_2$ (note: not $\underset{w}{\subseteq}$). The transitive closure of the → relation gives all necessary information about which rights may be entered by some chain of commands. This will give a decision procedure whose running time is $O(p + q_0 + g^{2.81})$ where p is the size of the protection system, q_0 is the size of the initial configuration, and g is the number of generic rights.

This result can also be generalized to prove the following.

Theorem 9. Safety of monoconditional systems with $\underset{\sim\sim\sim\sim\sim}{create}$, $\underset{\sim\sim\sim\sim}{enter}$, and $\underset{\sim\sim\sim\sim\sim}{delete}$ (but without $\underset{\sim\sim\sim\sim\sim\sim}{destroy}$) commands is decidable.

The proof is beyond the scope of this paper.

The decidability of safety for arbitrary monoconditional systems (i.e., with destroy commands) is still open.

[†] *Details about basic concepts of modern complexity theory may be found in [AHU 74].*

REFERENCES

[AHU 74]   Aho, A. V., Hopcroft, J. E., and Ullman, J. D., "The Design and Analysis of Computer Algorithms," Addison-Wesley Publishing Co., Reading, Mass., 1974.

[DDGHR 77]   Denning, D. E., Denning, P. J., Garland, S. J., Harrison, M. A., and Ruzzo, W. L., "Proving Protection Systems Safe," submitted for publication.

[Har 75]   Harrison, M. A., "On Models of Protection in Operating Systems," in *Mathematical Foundations of Computer Science 1975* (J. Becvář, editor), pp. 46-60, Springer-Verlag, Berlin, 1975.

[HRU 76]   Harrison, M. A., Ruzzo, W. L., and Ullman, J. D., "Protection in Operating Systems," *Communications of the Association for Computing Machinery, 19,* (Aug 1976), pp. 461-471.

[LiS 77]   Lipton, R. J. and Snyder, L., "A Linear Time Algorithm for Deciding Subject Security," *Journal of the Association for Computing Machinery, 24,* (1977), pp. 455, 464.

[LiS 78]   Lipton, R. J. and Snyder, L., "On Synchronization and Security,"

[Pos 46]   Post, E. L., "A Variant of a Recursively Unsolvable Problem," *Bulletin of the American Mathematical Society, 52,* (1946), pp. 264-268.

[ScA 77]   Schneider, F. B. and Akkoyunln, E. A., "Use of a Formalism for Modeling the Protection Aspects of Operating Systems," Technical Report 74, Department of Computer Science, State University of New York, Stony Brook, July 1977.

[Sny 77]   Snyder, L., "On the Synthesis and Analysis of Protection Systems," *Proceedings of the 1977 SIGOPS Conference,* pp. 141-150, 1977.

DISCUSSION

Minsky: In the context of you model, the principle of attenuation of privileges means that rights can move only along the subject rows. My question is how would you model this discipline in your scheme?

Harrison: Let me comment on that. There are things in our model which are not completely obvious. One of these things is the parameter mechanism. Although types were considered in some detail in Anita's thesis, it was our intention to omit them from our model. Much to our surprise, we found out that we had some type conventions and even a form of type checker built into the model. The type checker appears in the formal description of the "move relation". If you have a command which expects a certain kind of parameter and a different type is provided, the command does not execute. For example, the command

delete subject s

cannot execute if s is not a subject name. The principle of attenuation could be implemented by augmenting the model to have additional checking which controlled where rights were entered.

Cohen: A way of doing what Naftaly Minsky suggested is putting some restrictions on the form of the commands themselves. For example, the name of an object could not appear on one side of the statement unless one of your conditions specified it. In other words, you could not add something to a column unless you checked to see that that right should be in the column, but in a different row in that column. You could just switch rows in the column.

Harrison: The present formalism is not set up for that sort of condition but would be easy to modify. In my talk, I didn't really discuss the use of the formalism to model protection in real operating systems. In our original paper [1], we described most (but not all) of the aspects of the protection mechansims in UNIX. In [2], Schneider and Akkoyunlu indicate modifications to the model which make it more useful for dealing with real operating systems.

1. Harrison, M. A., Ruzzo, Walter L. and Ullman, J. D., "Protection in Operating Systems", *Communications of the ACM*, Vol. 19, pp. 461-471, 1976.
2. Schneider, F. B. and Akkoyunlu, E. A., "Use of a Formalism for Modeling the Protection Aspects of Operating Systems", Technical Report 74, Dept. of Comp. Sci., State Univ. of New York at Stony Brook, July 1977.

ON SYNCHRONIZATION AND SECURITY*

Richard J. Lipton
Lawrence Snyder

Department of Computer Science
Yale Universuty
New Haven, Connecticut

I. INTRODUCTION

In this paper, we will demonstrate that the synchronization structure of systems of parallel processes, as represented by Karp and Miller's vector addition systems [1], and the capability maintenance structure of security systems, as represented by a restricted form of the Harrison, Ruzzo and Ullman protection system [2], are recursively equivalent. Our interest in this unexpected similarity flows from several sources.

At the highest level, the discovery of a common structure among a wide variety of problem areas usually suggests the presence of a "fundamental" phenomenon. For example, the recursively enumerable sets and the NP-complete problems are phenomena that occur in a wide variety of circumstances and it is this fact that accounts in large measure for the intensity of our interest in them. Vector addition systems have previously been shown to be equivalent to Petri nets [4], matrix grammars [5] and other computational models, so our result can be seen as further evidence of the importance of these elegant systems.

* *This research was funded in part by the Office of Naval Research under Grant N00014-75-C-0752.*

Viewed at a different level, the equivalence provides insight into the Harrison, Ruzzo, Ullman (HRU) security model. In their original paper, the safety problem, i.e., the problem of deciding whether a particular system leaked information, was shown to be undecidable. In an effort to establish more positive results, we have restricted their system in such a way that the safety problem is recursively equivalent to the "covering" problem for vector addition systems. The decidability of this problem, then resolves the question and solves an open problem for subject restricted HRU systems. However, complexity results indicate that even for this restricted protection system, safety is an intractable problem (see section 5).

On yet another level, we note that theoretical analysis of protection systems is in its infancy and the Harrison, Ruzzo and Ullman model is one of the first attempts at formalizing the problem. We anticipate that other efforts will refine or supplant their model. Our success at embedding vector addition systems in the model suggests a paradigm for analyzing the complexity of alternatives. Systems capable of simulating vector addition systems are likely to have a complex safety problem. Models incapable of such simulation might hold more promise.

The remainder of this paper is organized as follows: section 2 gives definitions and preliminaries. In section 3, we show how the protection system simulates vector addition systems. Section 4 shows the opposite. In section 5 we combine these two results with known facts from the literature to establish our main results. The complexity issues are also discussed in section 5.

II. DEFINITIONS

In this section we introduce the formal models for protection [2] and vector additions systems [1]. The reader who is not familiar with these models is encouraged to consult the references for motivation, and examples. The reader already familiar with these models may skip this section.

A *protection system* $P = (R,C)$ consists of finite set R of *generic rights* and a finite set C of *commands*. Commands have the form

$$command \ D(X_1, \ldots, X_p):$$

$$when \ r_1 \ \varepsilon \ (X_{s_1}, X_{o_1}) \ \wedge \ldots \wedge \ r_q \ \varepsilon \ (X_{s_q}, X_{o_q})$$

$$do \ b_1; \ldots ; b_t$$

where D is the command *name*, X_1, ... , X_p are its *formal para-meters*, the (X_{s_i}, X_{o_i}) are *subject-object pairs* (see below) and b_1, ... , b_t are *operations* chosen from the following set of *primitive operations*:

> enter r into (X_s, X_o)
>
> delete r from (X_s, X_o)
>
> create subject X_s
>
> create object X_o
>
> destroy subject X_s
>
> destroy object X_o

and $r, r_1, \ldots, r_q \in R$; $1 \leq s, s_1, \ldots, s_q, o, o_1, \ldots, o_q \leq p$.

A *configuration* of $P = (R, C)$ is a triple (S, O, P) where S is the set of *current subjects,* O is the set of *current objects,* $S \subseteq O$ and P is an *access matrix* with a row for every subject in S and a column for every object in O. For $s \in S$ and $o \in O$, $P[s, o] \subseteq R$ and defines the rights to object o possessed by subject s.

Let (S, O, P) and (S', O', P') be configurations and b be a primitive operation, then

$$(S, O, P) \underset{b}{=>} (S', O', P')$$

provided one of the following holds for actual parameters s and o:

(i) b is *enter r into* (s, o) and

  $s \in S$, $o \in O$, $S = S'$, $O = O'$,

  $P'[s, o] = P[s, o] \cup \{r\}$,

  $P'[s', o'] = P[s', o']$ for $(s', o') \neq (s, o)$

(ii) b is *delete r from* (s, o) and

  $s \in S$, $o \in O$, $S = S'$, $O = O'$,

  $P'[s, o] = P[s, o] - \{r\}$,

  $P'[s', o'] = P[s', o']$ for $(s', o') \neq (s, o)$

(iii) b is *create subject* s, and

$s \notin 0$, $S' = S \cup \{s\}$, $0' = 0 \cup \{s\}$

$P'[s,o'] = \phi$ for all $o' \in 0'$

$P'[s',s] = \phi$ for all $s' \in S'$

$P'[s',o'] = P[s',o']$ for all $(s',o') \in S \times 0$

(iv) b is *create object* o, and

$o \notin 0$, $S = S'$, $0' = 0 \cup \{o\}$

$P'[s',o] = \phi$ for all $s' \in S$

$P'[s',o'] = P[s',o']$ for all $(s',o') \in S \times 0$

(v) b is *destroy subject* s, and

$s \in S$, $S' = S - \{s\}$, $0' = 0 - \{s\}$

$P'[s',o'] = P[s',o']$ for all $(s',o') \in S' \times 0'$

(vi) b is *destroy object* o, and

$o \in 0 - S$, $S' = S$, $0' = 0 - \{o\}$

$P'[s',o'] = P[s',o']$ for all $(s,o) \in S' \times 0'$

Let $P = (R,C)$, $Q = (S,0,P)$ be a configuration and

command $D(X_1,\ldots,X_p)$:

  when $r_1 \in (X_{s_1},X_{o_1}) \wedge \ldots \wedge r_q \in (X_{s_q},X_{o_q})$

  do $b_1;\ldots;b_t$

be a command in C, then

$$Q \; |\text{------------} \; Q'$$
$$D(x_1,\ldots,x_p)$$

where Q' is a configuration provided for $1 \leq i \leq p$, $X_i = x_i$ and either

(i) $r_1 \in (X_{s_1},X_{o_1}) \wedge \ldots \wedge r_q \in (X_{s_q},X_{o_q})$ is false and $Q'=Q$

or

(ii) $r_1 \varepsilon (X_{s_1}, X_{o_1}) \wedge \ldots \wedge r_q \varepsilon (X_{s_q}, X_{o_q})$ is true or $q = 0$

and there exist configurations $Q_0, \ldots, Q_t$ such that

$$Q = Q_0 \underset{b_1}{=>} Q_1 \underset{b_2}{=>} \ldots \underset{b_t}{=>} Q_t = Q'.$$

We write $\left|\overset{*}{-}\right.$ for the reflexive transitive closure for $\left|-\right.$.

Given a protection system, we say that a command $D(x_1, \ldots, x_k)$ *leaks generic right r from configuration* $Q = (S,O,P)$ if D when run on Q can execute a primitive operation which enters r into a cell of the access matrix which did not previously contain r. Further, we say that an initial configuration Q_0 is *unsafe* for r if there is a configuration Q with $Q_0 \left|\overset{*}{-}\right. Q$ and some command leaks r from Q. Configuration Q_0 is said to be *safe* if it is not unsafe.

The model just defined is essentially that of Harrison, Ruzzo and Ullman [2]. In [2] the safety problem (i.e., deciding for a particular right r whether or not the system is safe for r) is shown to be undecidable. The proof of this result involves encoding the tape of a Turing Machine along the diagonal of the matrix. Thus, the creation of subjects is essential to the result. But what if subjects cannot be created? The resulting system is not finite since the objects can grow. We will study protection systems with this restriction throughout the remainder of this paper.

A protection system $P = (R,C)$ is said to be *subject-restricted* (S-R protection system) if for no command $D \varepsilon C$ is it the case that b_i is *create subject* x_s, $1 \le i \le t$. (For simplicity and without loss we assume that there are no *destroy subject* x_s operations either.)

A v-dimensional *vector addition system* $V = (I,W)$ consists of an *initial vector* $I \varepsilon N^v$ and a finite set of *transition* vectors $W = V^1, \ldots, V^m$ where $V^i \varepsilon Z^v$, $1 \le i \le m$.† A *computation* is a set of indices $i_1, \ldots, i_k$ defining the *state* $S \varepsilon N^v$ where

---

† *N is the set of nonnegative integers, Z is the set of integers. Superscripts index vectors, subscripts refer to coordinate positions.*

$$S = I + \sum_{j=1}^{k} v^i_j$$

provided for all $t \le k$,

$$0 \le I + \sum_{j=1}^{t} v^i_j \ .$$

A vector addition system $V = (I,W)$ is called a *binary vector addition system* provided for all i, $1 \le i \le |W|$, $-1 \le v^i \le 1$. Hence, each coordinate position is either 0 or ± 1.

III.   VECTOR ADDITION SYSTEMS REDUCE TO PROTECTION SYSTEMS

Our objective in this section is to show first that V.A. systems can be simulated by S-R protection systems. Then we demonstrate that the simulation has the property that the coverability problem reduces to the safety problem. These two lemmas will then be used later (section 5) to prove our main results.

The problem at hand is to show how an S-R protection system is to be interpreted as a vector addition system. The easiest way to do this would be to dedicate one right per coordinate position. Then the value of a coordinate of the state of the VAS would be given by the number of occurences of the corresponding right in the access matrix. This method solves the problem, but we seek a more efficient encoding. Therefore, instead of using single rights, we use sets of rights to correspond to a coordinate position. The sets will be chosen to be incomparable so that no collision will result.

A configuration $Q = (S,O,P)$ of a S-R protection system $P = (R,C)$ is said to *correspond to a vector* $V \in N^\nu$ provided there exists an injective function* f: $\{1,2,\ldots,\nu\} \to 2^R$ such that for $1 \le j \le \nu$

$$V_j = |\{(s,o) \ \varepsilon \ S{\times}O \ | \ P[s,o]=f(j)\}|$$

---

* 2^R *denotes the set of all subsets of* R.

Therefore, a configuration corresponds to a state vector V, when the number of access matrix entries equal to f(j) equals the value of the *jth* coordinate of V. If Q corresponds to V, by f, we write $Q >_f V$.

A S-R protection system $P = (R,C)$ and configuration Q_0 *simulates* a vector addition system $V = (I,W)$ provided there exists an f such that

(i) $Q_0 >_f I$

and

(ii) $i_1, \ldots, i_n$ is a computation for $T^n \in R(V)^\dagger$ if and only if

$$Q_0 \Big|_{\substack{- \\ D_{i_1}}} Q_1 \Big|_{\substack{- \\ D_{i_2}}} \cdots \Big|_{\substack{- \\ D_{i_n}}} Q_n \text{ and for all } j, \ 1 \le j \le n,$$

$$Q_j >_f T^j.$$

We can now define f. For any position integer v let k be the least integer such that $v \le \binom{k}{k/2}$. Let R_k be a finite set of k generic rights. Define

$$f: \ \{1, \ldots, v\} \to 2^{R_k}$$

such that $1 \le i, \ j \le v$ and $i \ne j$ implies $f(i) \not\subseteq f(j)$. This fact is referred to as "the incomparability of f."

$\dagger$ *R(V) is the reachability set of the VAS V and is the set of all states definable by V.*

$$T^{i+1} = T^i + v^j \ \varepsilon \ R(V) \ \text{implies} \ Q_i \mid_{\overline{D}_j} Q_{i+1} \ \text{and} \ Q_{i+1} >_f T^{i+1} \qquad (3.1)$$

in steps (i) - (iv) and

$$Q_i \mid_{\overline{D}_j} Q \ \text{implies} \ T^{i+1} = T^i + v^j \ \varepsilon \ R(V) \ \text{and} \ Q_{i+1} >_f T^{i+1} \qquad (3.2)$$

in steps (v) - (vii).

By hypothesis, $T^i \ \varepsilon \ R(V)$, $Q_0 \mid^{\underline{*}} Q_i$, $Q_i >_f T^i$ and is $Q_i = (S,0,P)$

then $r \ \varepsilon \ P[s_1,s_1]$ where $\{s_1\} = S$. Let $v^j \ \varepsilon \ W$ be such that

$T^i + v^j = T^{i+1} \ \varepsilon \ R(V)$.

(i) The *when* condition of D_j is satisfied. Suppose not,
     then because $r \ \varepsilon \ P[s_1,s_1]$ the failure is due to the
     falsity of E_u for some u. But E_u false implies
     $f(b_u) \not\subseteq P[s_1,o]$ for all o ε 0. By construction then,

     $T^i_{b_u} = 0$ contradicting $T^i + v^j \ \varepsilon \ R(V)$. Hence the *when*

     condition of D_j is satisfied.

(ii) $Q_i \mid_{\overline{D}_j} Q_{i+1}$ by (i) and the construction since no

      operations are *delete*, none fails to apply. Let

$$Q_i \underset{B_1}{\Rightarrow} Q_B \underset{B_2}{\Rightarrow} \ldots \underset{B_n}{\Rightarrow} Q_{B_n} \underset{A_1}{\Rightarrow} Q_{A_1} \underset{A_2}{\Rightarrow} \ldots \underset{A_\ell}{\Rightarrow} = Q_{A_\ell} = Q_{i+1}$$

      and $Q_{i+1} = (S',0',P')$. Clearly S = S'.

(iii) Suppose it is not the case that $Q_{i+1} >_f T^{i+1}$, and let z

be such that

$$T^{i+1} \neq |\{P'[s_1,o] = f(z) | o \in O'\}|. \tag{3.3}$$

If $v_u^j = 0$, then either not $Q_{B_u} >_f T^i$ or not $Q_{A_w} >_f T^i$

for any u or w contradicting the incomparability of f.

If $v_z^j = -1$ then not $Q_{B_u} >_f T^i$ for $b_u < z$ or not

$Q_{B_u} >_f T^{i+1}$ for $b_u > z$ or not $Q_{A_w} >_f T^{i+1}$ contradicting

the incomparability of f. If $v_z^j = 1$ then not $Q_{B_u} >_f T^i$

for any u or not $Q_{A_w} >_f T^i$ for $a_w > z$ or not $Q_{A_w} >_f T^{i+1}$

for $a_w > z$ contradicting the incomparability of f.

Hence (3.3) is false and $Q_{i+1} >_f T^{i+1}$

(iv) It is immediate that $P[s_1,s_1]$ is not changed and thus

$P'[s_1,s_1] = r$.

Thus, (3.1) is established.

By hypothesis, $T^i \in R(V)$, $Q_0 \mid^{\overset{*}{}} Q_i, Q_i > T^i$ and if $Q_i = (S,O,P)$

then $r \in P[s_1,s_1]$ where $\{s_1\} = S$. Let $D_j \in C$ and $Q_i \mid_{\overline{D_j}} Q_{i+1}$.

(v) $T^{i+1} = T^i + V^j \in R(V)$. Suppose not and let z be such that

$V^j_z = -1$ and $T^i_z = 0$. Since $Q_i \mid_{\overline{D}_j} Q_{i+1}$ the *when* condition

is satisfied and this implies by construction that for

some u, $b_u = z$ and E_u is true. But this means $f(b_u) =$

$P[s_1, o]$ for some $o \in O$ contradicting $Q_i >_f T^i$.

(vi) $Q_{i+1} >_f T^{i+1}$ by an argument similar to (iii).

(vii) It is immediate that if $Q_{i+1} = (S, O', P')$ then

$P'[s_1, s_1] = r$.

Thus (3.2) is established and the lemma follows.   □

IV. ENCODING PROTECTION SYSTEMS INTO VAS

In this section we accomplish the encoding of protection
systems into VAS. First, we show that k-subject-restricted
protection systems can be encoded into 1-subject restricted.
Next, we show that 1-subject restricted protection systems can
be encoded in vector addition systems.

The following development is simplified considerably if we
observe that a bound of $k \geq 1$ on the number of subjects is
recursively equivalent to a bound of 1 on the number of subjects.
Specifically, there are only finitely many different entries in
any array position and there are only k positions in a column,
so by expanding the alphabet and modifying the instructions, a
one subject system can be found that is equivalent to the k
subject system.

Intuitively, the commands will be changed so that the S×S
portion of P can be represented by a single position and the
S×(O-S) portion will have its columns represented by single calls:

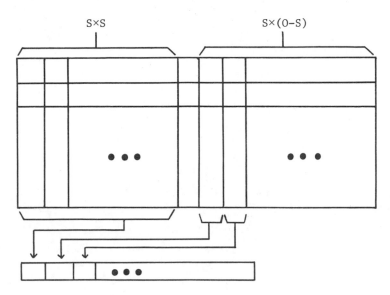

The alphabet will use triples, (row, column, right), as "expanded" rights for describing the S×S portion of P while pairs, (rows, rights), will be used to specify the information in a column of S×(O−S).

Lemma 4.1: Let $P = (R,C)$ be a k-subject protection system, then there exists a 1-subject protection $P' = (R',C')$ and a function $f: Q_k \rightarrow Q_1$ mapping k-subject configurations to 1-subject configurations such that $Q_o \mid_{\overline{P}}^* Q_n$ implies $f(Q_o) \mid_{\overline{P'}}^* f(Q_n)$.

Proof. To construct P' from P, follow the steps:

1. Define $R' = \{(i,j,r_\ell) \mid 1 \le i, j \le k, r_\ell \in R\} \cup$

   $\{(i,r_\ell) \mid 1 \le i \le k, r_\ell \in R\} \cup \{(0,0)\}$

2. Find for each command $D \in C$ with formal parameters $X_1, \ldots, X_p$, the subset of formal parameters $X'_1, \ldots, X'_x$ that must be subjects, i.e., those parameters that occur as the first term in a subject-object pair in the definition. Denote the remaining parameters $X'_{x+1}, \ldots, X'_p$.

Remark: The must-be-subject parameters $X'_1, \ldots, X'_x$ may be assigned subjects from $s_1, \ldots, s_k$ in any manner while the may-be-

subjects-or-objects parameters $X'_{x+1}, \ldots, X'_p$ may be assigned
subjects or objects in any manner. From the viewpoint of the
construction all objects o ε O-S behave the same. Note that in
all but the most trivial systems, $x \neq 0$.

3.   For each D define $D_1, \ldots, D_n$ to be $n = k^x(k+1)^{p-x}$ copies
     of D such that each one corresponds to a different
     assignment of the formal parameters $X_1, \ldots, X_p$:   the
     must-be-subject elements $X'_1, \ldots, X'_x$ are assigned from
     $\{s_1, \ldots, s_k\}$ while $X'_{x+1}, \ldots, X'_p$ are chosen from
     $\{s_1, \ldots, s_k, o\}$, where o represents an arbitrary non-subject
     object.

4.   For each D_ℓ $(1 \leq \ell \leq k^x(k+1)^{p-x})$ add, if $p \neq x$, the predicate
     $(0,0)$ ε (X'_1, X'_i) to the *when* clause for $x+1 \leq i \leq p$.
     In addition, effect the following replacements.

replace	*by*
$r_a \varepsilon (X'_b, X'_c)$	$(i,j,r_a) \varepsilon (X'_b, X'_b)$
	if X'_b corresponds to s_i
	and X'_c corresponds to s_j.
enter r into (X'_b, X'_c)	*enter* (i,j,r) *into* (X'_b, X'_b)
delete r from (X'_b, X'_c)	*delete* (i,j,r) *from* (X'_b, X'_b)
$r_a \varepsilon (X'_b, X'_c)$	$(i,r_a) \varepsilon (X'_b, X'_c)$
	if X'_b corresponds to s_i
	and X'_c corresponds to o

enter r into (X'_b, X'_c) *enter* (i,r) *into* (X'_b, X'_c)

delete r from (X'_b, X'_c) *delete* (i,r) *from* (X'_b, X'_c)

create object X'_o *create object* X'_o

                              enter $(0,0)$ *into* (X'_1, X_o)

Remark: The role of $(0,0)$ is to mark all non-subject objects. The proper definition of f is now clear. It maps configurations from $(\{s_1, \ldots, s_k\}, \{s_1, \ldots, s_k\} \cup O, P)$ into $(\{s\}, \{s\} \cup O, P')$ such that

$$P'[s,s] = \bigcup_{1 \le i,j \le k} \{(i,j,r_\ell) \,|\, r_\ell \varepsilon P[s_i, s_j]\}$$

$$P'[s,o_j] = \bigcup_{1 \le i \le k} \{(i,r_\ell) \,|\, r_\ell \varepsilon P[s_i, o_j]\}.$$

The result now follows by a laborious induction which is left to the reader.   □

We will now show how to use a VAS to simulate a k-subject protection system. By the previous result, it is sufficient to consider the case when k = 1. Now, intuitively, the VAS V will do this simulation by using its counters to keep track of the contents of each cell. If R is the set of generic rights, then there are $m = 2^{|R|}$ possible cells. V will therefore have m counters which will keep track of the number of each type of cell.

Let $P = (R, C)$ be a 1-subject protection system. We will now describe a VAS $V_p = (I, W)$ by the following construction. (As in [3] we will view V_p as having a set of counters that it can increment and decrement but cannot test for zero.)

Let V_p have counters (in the sense just described) $v_1, \ldots, v_m$ where $m = 2^{|R|}$. Also let $S_1, \ldots, S_m$ be the subsets of R in some order. Initially, v_i is set to the number of cells with contents exactly equal to S_i $(i = 1, \ldots, m)$. Now V operates as follows:

(1) First it guesses a command D from C nondeterministically.

(2) It then simulates this command, say (s = only subject)

$$command \ D \ (x_1, \ldots, x_n):$$

$$when \ E_1 \quad \ldots \quad E_t$$

$$do \ A_1; \ldots; A_\ell$$

as follows. First let us assume that $x_1, \ldots, x_n$ are all objects. For each cell x_i we can collect into T_i those rights that must lie in x_i in order for D to execute. Now we nondeterministically guess a S_{j_i} $(i = 1, \ldots, n)$ such that $T_i \subseteq S_{j_i} \subseteq R$. Then V_p executes the instructions

$$v_{j_i} \leftarrow v_{j_i} - 1 \qquad (i = 1, \ldots, n)$$

and then

$$v_{j_i} \leftarrow v_{j_i} + 1$$

By induction, these will be successful if and only if there are cells which contain $S_{j_1}, \ldots, S_{j_n}$. Now V_p is ready to update the cell contents. It does this in a similar manner. There are several cases.

(i) *enter r into* (s, X_i).

This is done by $v_{j_i} \leftarrow v_{j_i} - 1$ and

$$v_{j_k} \leftarrow v_{j_k} + 1$$

where $S_{j_i} \cup \{r\} = S_{j_k}$

(ii) *delete r from* (s, X_i).

This is done by $v_{j_i} \leftarrow v_{j_i} - 1$ and

$$v_{j_k} \leftarrow v_{j_k} + 1$$

where $S_{j_i} - \{r\} = S_{j_k}$

(iii) *destroy object* X_i.

This is done by $v_{j_i} \leftarrow v_{j_i} - 1$.

(iv) *create object* X_i.

This is done by $v_{j_i} \leftarrow v_{j_i} - 1$

where $S_{j_i} = \phi$.

It only remains to consider the case where some of the cells $X_1, \ldots, X_n$ are subjects. Since, however, there is only one subject, we can handle this by having V_p encode into its finite state control the contents of the cell (s, s), i.e. which of the $2^{|R|}$ values it has at any one time.

It follows that

Lemma 4.2: Let $P = (R,C)$ be a 1-subject protection system and let $V_p = (I,W)$ be the VAS that corresponds to the above construction. Then there is a recursive function f from vectors of V_p to configurations of P such that

$$\{Q \,|\, Q_o \,|\overset{*}{\overline{P}}\, Q\} = f(R(V_p))$$

where Q_o is the initial configuration used in the construction of V_p.

Proof: This follows by an easy induction and is omitted.   □

V.   MAIN RESULTS

In section 3 it was established that S-R protection systems can simulate binary vector addition systems, and from the result of Karp and Miller [1], that an arbitrary VAS can be "simulated" by a binary VAS, we conclude,

Theorem 5.1: Every vector addition system can be simulated by a binary vector addition system.

Corollary 5.3: Vector addition systems and subject-restricted protection systems are recursively equivalent.

The primary consequence of these results can now be indicated. For any vector $T \in N^V$ and VAS V, the *covering predicate* $C(T,V)$ is true iff there exists $T' \in R(V)$ such that $T \leq T'$.

The task of determining whether or not the covering predicate is true for given T and V is called the *covering problem*. Another useful result from [1] is

Lemma 5.4: [1] The covering problem is decidable.

We are now able to prove

Theorem 5.5: The safety problem for k-subject restricted protection systems is decidable.

Proof: Let V be the v-dimensional vector addition system (constructed in section 4) that simulates $P = (R,C)$, the k-subject restricted protection system for which safety is to be tested. Let r be the right for which safety is to be tested, and let co-ordinate i be the "counter" in V that keeps track of the instances of r in any protection array. For every vector v of V that was constructed to increment coordinate i to effect an *enter r into* (s,X_o) instruction (when r wasn't already in (s,X_o)), add an additional + 1 to a new coordinate v+1. All other vectors of V should have 0 in coordinate v+1 and the result will be V'. For any initial configuration Q_o, then the predicate $C(0^v1, V')$ is true iff Q_o is unsafe for r with respect to P.

REFERENCES

[1] R. M. Karp and R. E. Miller, *Parallel Program Schemata,* JCSS, Vol. 3(2): pp. 147–195.

[2] M. A. Harrison, W. L. Ruzzo and J. D. Ullman, *Protection in Operating Systems,* CACM, 19:8 (1976).

[3] R. J. Lipton, *Vector Addition Systems are Exponential-Space Hard,* Yale Computer Science Dept., Technical Report (1975).

[4] M. Hack, "Decision Problems for Petri Nets and Vector Addition Systems", *Computation Structures Note,* No. 10, Project NAC, MIT, May 1973.

[5] S. Abraham, "On Matrix Grammars", TR3, Computer Science, Technion, Haifa, Israel, 1970.

CONVERSATIONS ON SECURE COMPUTATION

On Tuesday afternoon, October 4, the authors of the papers in this volume met for three hours to discuss issues that had crystalized during the previous formal presentations and the informal discussions.

The editors prepared the agenda of leading questions. The conversations were taped and edited and appear on the following pages in excerpted form.

Lipton: In protection, we've looked at a lot of different problems and a lot of complicated mechanisms. Many interesting, practical and mathematical problems have arisen. One question that I would like to ask both the practitioners and theoreticians is what is the utility of these problems? Do they correspond at all to the kinds of things that people like to do? If I had a UNIX system today that handled very complicated kinds of access controls, would it be easier at all on the mini-UNIX system? Or, is read/write protection sufficient for most real computation? What kind of computing requires very complicated and sophisticated protection mechanisms?

Gaines: I'll start by remarking that simple read/write conventions are just not sufficient. In using them now, we're already up against certain kinds of limits. Just how far in the other direction you should go, I just don't know.

Jones: I would like to comment. If you look at evolution in programming languages, you will find that programming languages are being designed so that a programmer builds his program by defining objects, then defining the operations that are applicable to those kinds of objects. The two together are what Fabry was referring to as a type manager. One can make the argument that in languages we use basically the same kinds of techniques that we're using for the capability-based access-control systems. The languages can do most of the checking statically. I think that the issue is broader than just the dynamic protection mechanisms that we spent most of our time on here. So, I think that these protection mechanisms are going to have a fairly large pay-off. But, I believe most of the pay-off comes not from securing yourself against the malicious acts of an adversary, but from building programs in which one program doesn't do something that is inconsistent with respect to another program. You are, in some sense, defending yourself against yourself.

Cohen: I'd like to second that. I like to think in terms of what you might call the paranoia model versus what you might call the reliability model. For example, a system like Hydra guarantees that a particular capability cannot be passed out of a certain domain, and that seems to be useful pragmatically. But, in terms of a programming language, it is certainly important to guarantee that the particular capabilities will stay within certain types of objects. That's starting to become a widely applicable principle in programming languages. And, I perceive that it's going to be even more useful later, just for reliability.

Gaines: I'm not sure that either of these remarks answered Lipton's question. The question was, "What is the need?" Not, "How nice are they?" In other words, can we use them at all?

Jones: I was giving you an answer to that, I thought. I was making a point that I thought that the protection mechanisms were extremely useful for complementing the programming methodology for building modular programs. And, in fact, that's just how Hydra is being used at CMU right now. The way that people tend to program is that they define a new type manager. Using protection mechanisms, they ensure the integrity of the service one program provides to another. This use of the protection mechanism was not one of the motivations for the Hydra design. During the design, we mainly thought about the ability to protect data from malicious users. But, in fact, this other serendipidous use of it has been tremendously productive. Can I give you an example of the read/write kind of protection and why it doesn't always work? I'd like to build an object containing data, and I want to share that data with you. If what I do is to build a type manager and the way that we share the object is by always calling this type manager who in fact is the only one that can read and write implementations, we have much more a controlled and disciplined system. And we will also have a lot more protection.

Gaines: I think we're still avoiding the question. Are there substantial cases where something of the complexity of the bibliographic system in Hydra is actually needed?

Harrison: There is a computer application that nobody has talked about so far. One estimate has suggested that its value could exceed all other applications combined. This is the area of office automation. One of the vital aspects of such systems is protection and security. I'd like to give an example of this type of application, but first, let me remind you that digital computers do one operation absolutely perfectly. When they copy a discrete object, it is a perfect copy down to the last bit. For example, consider an automated office in which requests for travel funds are processed. There must be sophisticated mechanisms built into such a system so that an employee's request is processed by a superior with the proper authority. Moreover, his "signature" should not be forgeable. In the absence of any protection mechanisms, signatures could be copied perfectly, employees can authorize their own travel, etc. The omission of such protection features in current systems is quite striking.

Shapiro: Granted that the issue is "does that kind of application require the complex kinds of methodologies"?, are there much simpler strategies to accomplish the same task?

Harrison: There are certainly some simple and ingenious solutions that go part of the way, but not all of the way. If an inappropriate individual attempts to authorize a request for which he does not have the proper authority, a "form" can destroy itself or send an alarm, etc.

Fabry: Ultimately, I foresee a network of systems having the complexity of all of society. The proper implementation of such a network will require us to understand access-control much better than we do today. If we had such a network in which the protection were almost trivial, we could automate much of what we do manually today. If each user had some information which was private and if there were some way to make information public, people could make information available to each other. Selectivity could be achieved by encryption. Access-control decisions could be made by applications programs at the nodes.

****

Dobkin: The next thing we might consider is whether we should pursue more database results than, say, that compromise is easy. In general, what types of problems should we be working on? What directions should we be going in terms of databases and security in general?

Shapiro: There are two directives that contradict each other. One is that privacy be protected database information. This is a directive that has come down to us from institutions. Another directive is that society has been managed in such a way that databases will be maintained and accessed. The results that we've seen about database compromise address themselves to relatively simple extractions from the databases, such as means or medians. These may be questions of the kind that are not socially necessary to be able to ask. Asking very general policy-type questions of a database doesn't necessarily involve making available means or medians or any other type of summaries or statistical information about the database. It means making available far-higher order statistics. So that brings into question what happens to results about database compromise when the interrogations involved are not nearly as direct and as simple.

Minsky: In addition to the question of how do we restrict what one can get from the database, there is the problem of how does one ensure the correctness of the contents of a database, and by implication, the correctness of responses to user's queries. Errors in data may be introduced either inadvertantly or maliciously and it is the responsibility of the system to protect itself against such errors. Failure to do this would have grave consequences both to the privacy of individuals about whom misinformation is distributed, and to the society at large, if wrong information serves as a basis for social decisions.

Gaines: The issue of databases of credit information and the passing of that information around people who you don't want to see it or who you haven't authorized to see it, seems to be indicative of the larger social question. There just is information that people can use to their own benefit and you may want to keep that information away from them for that reason.

Minsky: But, there still is the question of how one ensures the correctness of large masses of information for long periods of time.

Gaines: But if somebody doesn't gain anything by modifying it, they just won't bother. We know of more cases where somebody gained just by learning the information.

Minsky: Then there's also the problem of people sneaking into the system and deliberately making mistakes.

DeMillo: These are all public policy issues.   They're not necessarily security issues.

Dobkin: Yes, these things seem to be issues that do not have so much to do with computers as with, let's say, collection agencies.

Kline: I think that the issues are not going to be whether information can be kept private, but whether or not it is kept private.   Will someone enforce the personnel policies in order to secure the information?   Since it takes statutes to do that, I agree these are public policy issues and not technical issues.

Budd: Getting back to the original question about whether or not we need any more papers on database security, it seems theoretical computer scientists are always running up against these situations.   The problem cannot be modelled in it's full generality, and so we abstract certain pieces of it and study restricted kinds of database cracking.   I think we are at the point now where we should go back and look at these results we have concerning these restricted classes and ask whether or not they carry over into the real world.   That is, can I go out and obtain information about an individual from the Census Bureau just using the Reiss median strategy?   To cite an example of when I think we are not being realistic, most models that are studied only allow queries of fixed sign.   There are other assumptions made that I think cannot be justified in practice.   I think there is a need now for more empirical study, in which people look at databases in the real world rather than at mathematical database models.

Lipton: There are also questions that DeMillo, Dobkin and I have called inference questions.   There may be some very interesting interplay between them and database questions.   If I use some of Ron Rivest's ideas for encrypting a file and give the user only certain restricted operations, it may be quite difficult to see whether the user can put together restricted predicates to determine what he would really like to know.   So, I'm very positive that there are some directions that we should go. It may not be exactly a database model, but it is related I think.

Gaines: First of all, I'd like to comment about this terminology, "crack a database".   It implies a binary choice and that is one of the difficulties here.   We're not just concerned that you get or don't get one bit of information, but whether or not useful information is transmitted; and if so, how much?   A secondary question is to study how information flows out of it. The goal is to get far less than what you want up to certain special circumstances.

Dobkin: You're saying that if I get some piece of information, say the salary of some person that I don't know then that is not a piece of useful information and who should care? But, what about the person whose salary I got? He'll care. Even if I can't use it today, I may be able to use it some day, and that is certainly an issue.

Cohen: Yes, I am concerned about the kind of work that's been done in compromising databases. It seems to me to be concerned with the selling of security, and I think that that's probably a dangerous thing to do -- both for technical reasons and for realistic reasons. In terms of the kinds of things that has happened technically, I think one thing that we have not taken into account technically with any of these models is the extent of a priori information. That's going to be very hard to model. Realistically, it's clear that the most dangerous thing about databases is not the security mechanism, but that there are other ways of getting into the system. If we keep on doing this kind of work, then we just have to be very clear that it's just a game. We're really not protecting anything. What's happening is that large databases still get built and it is exceedingly dangerous for people to perceive these results as saying that we can protect your database and that it's okay if you stick that piece of sensitive information in it, because nobody is going to be able to get it out with a certain probability. I think that what is important to consider is not the techniques for guaranteeing that a compromise can't occur, but to build systems that involve the dismantling of databases instead.

DeMillo: I would tend to agree with you if the results that we're talking about went that way, but they go the other way. They say you *can* compromise; therefore, you should *not* assume that something is secure. This might limit the kinds of things that you try to do.

Cohen: Sure. I think that negative results are useful. But keep in mind that it's always just a game. All of these results have nothing to do with the security of information. My discussion about the dismantling of databases is irrelevant to the discussion of whether or not we should de research in the area. In fact, what I'm saying is that the realities of databases are totally distinct from the issues of mathematics basis.

DeMillo: Does anybody know of any human information processing results that say that an expert who knows a good strategy does well in actually getting information out of the databases?

Fabry: I can't answer that question. But, I think that what I'm going to say is relevant. I came to this conference not having looked at the question of whether or not you can get sensitive information out of the databases by asking tricky questions. I naively assumed that there were simple strategies that would be fairly effective in keeping people from figuring out specific information. I suspect that is a common misconception. I think that it is going to fall to us over the next few years to call the attention of the public to the fact that no simple strategy works. This is particularly true, as Ellis Cohen mentioned, when you cannot know what kinds of information a penetrator may have obtained outside the system. Over the next few years, databases will become increasingly important. They will be pushed by institutions for whom they will be extremely cost-effective. Companies producing such systems will be under pressure to make assurances to the public about the non-penetrability of their systems. We may have quite a job on our hands trying to keep making sure that the appropriate agencies and the public are aware of the limitations on such assurances. The conclusion that I would draw is that there must be legal responsibility and human judgement invoked on a fine-grained basis wherever these systems are employed. And, that's not an obvious conclusion. Many who install database systems will be hoping to reduce such factors.

Minsky: I would like to try to correct what seems to me a misconception about the nature of database systems and of the interaction with them. People seem to consider a database system as a mechanism which answers mostly statistical types of questions. The fact of the matter is that an information system, which is based on a database, contains large numbers of programs which have to navigate through the database, and update parts of it. An important security problem is how to control the interaction of these programs with the database interaction that is not "statistical".

Dobkin: It seems to me that what you are saying is that there is first the issue of running a database then there is the issue of security. I've been more interested in the security. Assuming that the database is totally correct and totally perfect and did what it was told in every way possible, then is it secure?

Minsky: But there is no sharp distinction between the programs that are part of the database, and the "application programs" that interact with it. I contend that for the sake of security, we must control the interaction of every subject with the database, be it a human user, one of his programs, or a program built into the system itself.

Cohen: I have a general question. Even though we know that it is going to be enormously difficult to protect the databases against compromise, there are those of us here who still advocate the building of large databases. How do we guarantee individuals that databases are not going to be misused?

Gaines: A sobering thought for all of us might be there's a whole legal question of who is liable when things are stolen. (nervous laughter) It is entirely possible that those computer scientists who have said that the system is secure may be liable when the code is broken, even those of us who say here's the probability .000002 that the system is secure. I was recently at a meeting on computer security and was amazed because over half of the people in the audience were lawyers. They were getting their feet wet in this whole question of liability. And, I think that it was brought up in that meeting that billions of dollars are being transferred electronically all around the country. And if that's stolen, who's responsible?

Kline: There aren't big incentives to crack a database for the personal reason of reading somebody's file. There may be institutions that would want to do that, but I think the average person is not going to have that in mind. But the electronic funds transfer is going to bring us into a whole new game. In that case, there's going to be a big pay-off for being undetected.

Dobkin: One of the things about electronic funds transfer is that someone can go into the system and see who bought an electric lawnmower from Sears, so that he can knock on their door to sell them grass seed. Presumably, Sears is going to protect people from that. Suppose that I can go in and ask what was the average purchase of people who spent over a hundred dollars at Sears last month? What is the average address? (laughter) Now maybe we can't compromise the census data, but maybe we can compromise the electronic funds data. And that will start being a nuisance to people.

Kline: I think that what you're talking about is at a very different level. Most large corporations would rather go out and buy your medical history than try to crack it in a large database. I think the damage that's likely to occur in that way is relatively small.

Fabry: I think that we're really underestimating the problem. Information is power. The need for computer databases is tremendous. It is too easy to underestimate the potential for abuse, the potential for economic exploitation, and the potential for invading people's privacy.

Kline: I just have to reemphasize that I do not think that the statistical access is the way databases will be compromised. I do not think that that's the place right now where we should be spending alot of our resources.

Rivest: It seems that the models we have available for authorization and access-control are still very simple in comparison to what we might need. You can imagine in a large corporation the complexity of the patterns of not just accessing information, but who is authorized to authorize someone else to access the information, etc. I'm thinking back to the comments such as those made by Rabin this morning about different kinds of authorization. These patterns can become very complex, and I suggest that we need to study more complicated ways of sharing information and sharing authorization, particularly in passing the ability to authorize an access. I would also like to suggest that the objectives of creating systems that are decidable and modelling what really happens in a typical information system may be contradictory.

****

Harrison: Just a question to the technologists among us. Some years ago, all I heard about was the information utility. Now with hardware costs dropping, the utility system's much less interesting. Since we can now give people an 11/70 on a chip in their own home, maybe we'll have safer computations because we won't share. Does anybody have any comments on what this new technology is likely to bring?

Rabin: Maybe I'll start with the last question first. I
think you will have computers within the home. But, at the same
time, you will also have very large data banks because there are
some things which you don't want to store in your home. Now,
since Ron Rivest has generalized the discussion to future
directions of research, I would just like to very briefly raise
one point. Namely, that all of the considerations here are
almost exclusively centered around software. We talked about
operating systems with certain take/grant features which make
them secure according to some definition. However, the consideration of hardware has to enter somewhere. Suppose you were using
various keys, there arises the question as to where these keys
are stored. Unless you want to have some sort of circular
argument, you won't be able to solve it unless you stipulate that
the system will contain some hardware security features which are
going to be secure places in which you can construct everything
else. Let's consider other questions. We are talking about an
operating system being constructed so that you can't gain access
to certain places. But, who's going to secure the cop? Nothing
was said about the possibility of just starting to introduce a
portion of the operating system which is different and alien and
which does what the interloper would like it to do. Who is going
to protect his operating system from that type of intrusion?
These questions of security are important because so much will
depend on computers. So if you have computers controlling some
critical systems, then even though the probability of some
malicious or stupid act will be small, the penalty would be so
enormous that the expectation of damage would still be large.
Thus, it is incumbent upon us to make provisions for secure
operation. We should not disregard the question of certain types
of secure hardware which in certain senses cannot be tampered
with. How can we minimize the danger of tampering with the
hardware? The answer lies in a strategy of duplication. These
components are small and inexpensive. By extensive duplication,
you can ensure that tampering with the system will require an
enormous amount of work, literally getting into remote corners,
and so on. So, there is really a potential for safety which
emenates from secure hardware. If we intend to explore this
direction, then our thinking should involve a merger of secure
hardware with secure software. For example, to create models
where you are talking not only about procedures and restrictions
on various operations, but along the way you postulate certain
hardware guards that are unalterable.

Jones: I don't think that the distinction is between hardware and software. I think that there are a number of security
procedures and then there is implementation. Someone will see
that these are quite appropriately implemented in hardware or in
software. In some cases, software running on a stand-along
machine achieves the same effects as a hardware implementation.

Rabin: Can I add something to that? I think that the point that I made was diametrically opposed to the point that you just made. Namely, if you talk about safeguards which are implemented in software, then we have to realize that computers operate with enormous speed. One approximately placed instruction may change things in a very radical way. You can wipe out, for instance, a whole memory. What I was talking about was the design of hardware which has certain built-in features rendering it immutable. So it is not some program which behaves like hardware, but certain pieces of machinery which are there and which cannot be altered. We even consider components having the property that any attempt to fool with them will result in some sort of self-destruct wipeout. The idea is that hardware is hard and cannot be changed, while programs are soft and can be easily altered.

Jones: I think there is still a spectrum and we can build software with some of the properties that you outlined.

Snyder: Let me just add a point to what Michael Rabin said. We still much grapple with problems like machines going down from time to time. The operator can put up a program that is not one that you wrote and he can do what he wants to do regardless of how clever you have been in your program. In Rabin's view, you would have had the machine operating with some kind of hard-wired protection to avoid that. We still have the problem that one has a very direct route to the machine simply by bribing the operator.

Dobkin: Well, I still think that he would have the same problem in hardware. What about the guy who interchanges boards? What kind of system are you going to have to monitor the guy who has his hands on the hardwware?

Snyder: Sure, you're pushing the problem a little further along. There you get into the situation that we were talking about earlier today. How long an interval do you have to observe the system? That is perhaps a different time frame.

Furtek: I do agree that these hardware traps are extremely desirable, and I agree that hardware is essentially different than software, but there's one regard in which hardware is very similar to software. And that is that it needs to be verified for security properties in the same way that software has to be verified. As far as I can tell, at least at this conference, nobody is addressing that problem.

DeMillo: I think that the case can be made that neither hardware nor software should or could be verified. If you are thinking of processes like verification and security together then there is something inconsistent. If you have a verified piece of software and you are certain that it is correct and secure, then you are going to abandon all of those safeguards that you would have built in if you had not been quite so sure that it wasn't going to fail. There is a tongue and cheek phenomenon called the *Titantic Effect* which says simply that the severity with which a system fails is directly proportional to the degree of confidence with which you believe the system won't fail. So, I think there is by no means any concensus in this group that verification is desirable.

Furtek: I thought that that's what you did in order to gain some confidence that your system is secure. What is the process that you go through to make your systems secure?

DeMillo: It's not verification.

Davida: Yes, DeMillo was getting into what I wanted to get into later. I noticed that there is a distinct lack of work in what I call testing rather than verification. If you go back to look at what hardware people do, they don't bother proving that their chips work, they just test them. And what they do is run diagnostic routines which tend to run in the background. And, they report any errors that they find so that someone can go in later and fix them. By the same token, I don't think we should be running some kind of background diagnostics continuously challenging and testing the systems and perhaps reporting the compromise whenever it does occur. Just because the finite access-matrix is decidable doesn't mean that security can be proven in practice. It may just be too complex and you might have to resort to adhoc methods.

DeMillo: I think all too often we apologize for adhoc techniques. Often times, adhoc techniques are the only ones that we know work.

Davida: I don't mean that adhoc means necessarily badly chosen. We can have very carefully chosen heuristics.

Kline: I think that there's some chip designs that are proven by verification.

Lipton: What chip design?

Kline: Certain kinds of gates, but most chips done by testing. In many cases, they completely exhaustively test. You get a thorough verification by exhaustion. That is a form of verification. There are alot of cases in chips where you can get it by induction of some sort. But, I'm not convinced that adhoc testing methods are adequate.

****

Jones: I'd like to get back to the issues of what kinds of research we should see in the areas of secure computation. If you look back five years, the action was in designing protection mechanisms for operating systems. Looking ahead, what I see is an "information revolution". And I don't see ways of building mechanisms that guarantee privacy. I suspect that what we will see are what might be called "threshold mechanisms". They are the same kinds of checks that we build into society: different semi-autonomous entities that check each other. The reason that a guard happens to be a very good protection mechanism is that he has all kinds of threshold tests that he's constantly per- forming, because he's a human being. He will notice that certain things are out of the ordinary. There is no absolute mechanism that prevents failure - in our case the leakage of information. Instead, you have all these scattered mechanisms that raise warnings. That is, what we do in society. We do not have any guarantees that information doesn't leak; we just have a lot of mechanisms that check thresholds.

Millen: I think that there is an assumption there that you can put your fingers on something like the granting of a certain capability which would be the only time a compromise could occur. That idea is based on using a model that may or may not apply. There are questions about whether or not access control models really address all of the questions about software channels for compromising information.

Ruzzo: I'd like to make a comment about that approach to systems security. That was used in an earlier version of OS360 and when the operating system itself violated those security constraints, the system crashed.

Kline: Every security system I know of that's been built
has reasonable checks to see whether or not what we are doing is
something that should be done. And, you could prove a priori
that nothing bad will ever be done or you can do the run-time
check, if there is a reasonably short definition of security.
Now, the issue therefore becomes how complex are your safety
criteria?

Fabry: There is some implication in the way that we got
started on this conversation that because of the HRU[†] results,
we should be scared away from our present protection systems.
I have unsuccessfully tried to find any practical implication of
the HRU results. I think it would be premature for people to
be scared away from conventional approaches to systems security,
or to feel that such systems were in some way inadequate, based
on the HRU results. One avenue for future research is to
understand the relationship of those results to real systems.
I am convinced that all interesting safety questions are decidable for the protection systems which I use and design.

Cohen: One of the things that I said earlier was that undecidability is only a relative issue. Theoretical results
assume a particular arbitrary configuration. The problem is to
determine whether or not a particular security violation can
occur. No real problem I've seen has had that flavor to it.
I'd be interested if anybody could generate one. Real problems
generally have the flavor of writing a specification for the set
of safety configurations to guarantee that you could never have
a security violation. Does anybody have any ideas when you have
arbitrary configuration?

Lipton: I didn't understand your question. It seems that if
you have an ongoing system in which people are being added and
deleted in arbitrarily complicated mechanisms, then it would
seem that you are coming in the middle of something very complicated.

Cohen: I do not think that I buy that completely. It seems
to me what happens is that you initiate some request for service
with another user. What is really going on is that you set up
the initial configuration. You set up communication, and all
you have to do is to guarantee that communication is set up
properly. Then, you guarantee that if your system has perfect
mechanisms, you'll never get into the situation where the
policy you want to enforce will ever be violated. There are

---

† *i.e., the Harrison-Ruzzo-Ullman decidability theorem (eds.)*

alot of instances where that happens. For example, if you want
to guarantee that confinement is enforced, you begin by calling
the program in a certain way. Then you have to guarantee that
no matter what happens afterwards, e.g., the program that's
supposed to be confined goes off and calls another program, that
transitivity holds and the other program is going to be confined
also. So, the point is that as long as you set up the initial
configuration properly, you guarantee that the program that you
are calling cannot act maliciously. So, it seems to me that to
ask that given an arbitrary configuration, whether or not it can
be violated is really a moot issue. What you are really asking
is can you set up an initial configuration or is there a class
of initial configurations that guarantee that confinement will
be enforced? And, the answer to that is our mechanisms are
exactly an embodiment of that idea. It would be surprising if
these mechanisms would allow violation in that way. So, the
undecidability results are really unrelated.

   Lipton: I think there are really two questions. One is
that you can set up a policy and then check to see whether or
not that policy is ever violated. Another is to have lots of
commands that have to ask "may I" at many places. In the latter
case, I'll prove a little theorem to myself to see if the
sequence of "may I"'s will ever get me in trouble. There is
probably a whole spectrum of tradeoffs in which you could prove
smaller and simpler theorems, and those would be tractible.
I'm just suggesting that there must be a very wide spectrum
and that we not lock ourselves in.

   Ruzzo: Let me make another point about the relevance of
the initial configuration. Given a particular system such as
Hydra, it may or may not be trivial to decide whether there is
some configuration from which confinement can be guaranteed.
But, given an *arbitrary* protection system - that's undecidable.
I think that this is an example of a kind of tradeoff we have
between our general results and results about any particular
operating system.

   Snyder: Let me try to just reiterate in a different
language Larry Ruzzo's results. When you look at results
referring to any formal model, you must be very careful about
the quantifiers. That is, you must be very careful about what
is allowed to vary and what remains fixed. In particular, what
things are you allowed to choose a priori and what things once
chosen are allowed to be modified over time? I think that the
controversy we are having here over the undecidability results
is a matter of quantification. You're saying that for Hydra, a
particular choice was made, including a particular choice of
initial states. And the Harrison-Ruzzo-Ullman result is
quantified differently. There is no inconsistency here. The

Take/Grant system, for example, is restrictive, it has a particular set of commands, too.

Jones: I have just been told, in effect, that the HRU results are irrelevant.

Lipton: You've misquantified the statement (laughter).

Jones: Not at all. We produce ten operating systems a year in the world. Therefore, it is uninteresting to me to quantify across all possible operating system protection mechanisms. There are only ten new ones of interest every year, so I'll just go out and check those ten.

****

DeMillo: I have a final question. What shall we tell the reader of this book who wants to know what's happened in security in the last five years and what is likely to happen next year?

Kline: There are approaches to network security. Encryption chips are being developed, as are public key systems and signature systems. These all have happened in the last five years and are going to have significant impact.

Fabry: Be careful not to equate encryption chips, public key systems and signature systems to security. These are merely tools which are available for implementing desired security policies. At best, their existence allows us to focus on the remaining issues more clearly.

Lipton: It's interesting that Kline said "secure" and not usable and secure.

Cohen: I'd like Bob Fabry to relate some things that he thinks will result in open problems in operating systems.

Fabry: Security, at the operating level, with a realistic definition of security. We ignored confinement at this workshop; the hard part of confinement is the treatment of covert channels.

Lipton: Secure will presumably mean that you will have reasonable confidence that your operating system will do certain things and won't do others. But, it will simply be an information processing tool. It will be used with a lot of applications on top of it and that are subject to mistakes and errors. I think that calling it "secure" is very misleading. Really, what we're saying is that we'll have some very nice property, though it is not even clear that it will. You can't legislate that people don't use a general purpose operating system incorrectly. As long as you call it secure, it sounds very dangerous.

Kline: But the point is that the security mechanisms that you enforce will, in fact, work.

Lipton: So, in some sense, you have passed the buck. In another ten years, we will have things built called security applications kernels and then we'll say, let's pass the buck to x.

Kline: That's right. And at each point, we'll hopefully have gained something.

Lipton: The point is now that you cannot write an application program that's safe. Why should we believe that it is any easier in principle using take/grant, when before we had to do it in machine language? You are doing everything at a higher level, but you are more ambitious today than you were five years ago, anyway. People are going to become increasingly ambitious and you will probably be lagging just that far behind all the time.

Kline: You are saying you can never achieve security.

Lipton: I think that what's happening in the secure kernel area and related areas, is that you're looking at systems as they were many years ago. So that by looking at the same system many, many times and resolving the same problem over and over again, you will be able to say something. What you get may have a much higher chance of being correct. But I'm still skeptical about whether or not it will be right. But, that's not what we want. What we want is, as Mike Harrison points out, office information systems and other systems of very complicated types that weren't being built ten years ago. And, those systems are so much more ambitious than compared to the very simple kinds of services that you're going to apply, that it's not clear that you really will help. And, indeed, it may mean that we will have to go to other techniques.

Jones: Let me make an analogy. You're saying that if the office automation system is the moon and the operating system is the tree, then climbing it is not going to help. But, both of those things are software products. And, if you understand one, you will hopefully glean a few things that will help you understand the other.

Harrison: I'm optimistic. Systems are getting better and theoretical techniques have exposed some fundamental concepts and limitations. It concerns me that some of the more theoretical results such as our undecidability theorems appear to be misunderstood and misinterpreted. It would be very unfortunate if such results inhibited a designer from making some improvements in a future system. Such theorems should rather be a guide to which problems can be realistically attempted.

Cohen: I'd like to raise an issue that we haven't looked at at all. And, that is that as we allow people more freedom with these systems, they are going to want to build their own policies and their own ways of using the system securely. They're going to be inevitable conflicts between users. We don't know how to deal with that. I suspect that within the next five years, as larger systems with multiple policies get built, that there will be more and more work on this.

Fabry: You are getting to the root of my discomfort with Charlie Kline's point of view. The definition of the security policies we will be called upon to implement, will ultimately derive from our social and legal systems. We cannot choose policies. We know how to implement, and then equate those policies with security. Not only will security policies evolve over time, in response to our increasing ability to process information, but the ground rules for expressing security policies will change as our society and our legal system become more attuned to the increasing potential for abuse. From this prespective, what we know how to do today is surely very crude.

DeMillo: I think that's a challenging note on which to close the discussion. Thank you, all.